C++ and
Object-Oriented Programming

Kip R. Irvine
Miami-Dade Community College—Kendall

Prentice Hall, Upper Saddle River, New Jersey 07458

Library of Congress Cataloging-in-Publication Data

Irvine, Kip R.,
      C++ and object-oriented programming / Kip R. Irvine.
          p. cm.
      Includes bibliographical references and index.
      ISBN 0-02-359852-2 (pbk.)
      1. C++ (Computer programming language) 2. Object-oriented programming
  (Computer science)   I. Title.
QA76.73.C153I78   1997
005.13′3-dc20   96-27476
                                        CIP

Publisher: **ALAN APT**
Editorial production supervisor: **KATHLEEN M. CAREN**
Editor-in-chief: **MARCIA HORTON**
Production manager: **BAYANI MENDOZA de LEON**
Managing editor: **LAURA STEELE**
Director of production and manufacturing: **DAVID W. RICCARDI**
Copyeditor: **CAMIE GOFFI**
Manufacturing buyer: **DONNA SULLIVAN**
Cover designer: **BRUCE KENSELAAR**
Editorial assistant: **SHIRLEY McGUIRE**

 ©1997 by Prentice-Hall, Inc.
Simon & Schuster / A Viacom Company
Upper Saddle River, NJ 07458

The author and publisher of this book have used their best efforts in preparing this book. These efforts include the development, research, and testing of the theories and programs to determine their effectiveness. The author and publisher make no warranty of any kind, expressed or implied, with regard to these programs or the documentation contained in this book. The author and publisher shall not be liable in any event for incidental or consequential damages in connection with, or arising out of, the furnishing, performance, or use of these programs.

Printed in the United States of America

10 9 8 7 6 5 4 3

ISBN 0-02-359852-2

Prentice-Hall International (UK) Limited, *London*
Prentice-Hall of Australia Pty. Limited, *Sydney*
Prentice-Hall Canada Inc., *Toronto*
Prentice-Hall Hispanoamericana, S.A., *Mexico*
Prentice-Hall of India Private Limited, *New Delhi*
Prentice-Hall of Japan, Inc., *Tokyo*
Simon & Schuster Asia Pte. Ltd., *Singapore*
Editora Prentice-Hall do Brasil, Ltda., *Rio de Janeiro*

This book is dedicated to
Raymond Vaught
of the University of Hawaii Music Department:
a teacher, scholar, and friend.

TABLE OF CONTENTS

Contents

Preface

No doubt, C++ is a challenging language to master. Yet much of its difficulty arises from its strengths: It is a rich and flexible language that embodies all of the important principles of object-oriented programming. C++ sits on the shoulders of C, one of the most important and widely used programming languages ever for both systems programming and applications. These factors have contributed greatly to its acceptance in the professional world. Fortunately, C++ programmers command high salaries and are given challenging, performance-intensive projects.

Effective use of C++ requires one to internalize object-oriented design principles. C++ programmers do not just write code according to rigid specifications as might have been done in earlier times. As object-oriented practitioners, they must understand the broader implications of how classes are designed, implemented, tested, and maintained. Also, C++ programmers are often cast in the role of introducing object-oriented programming to others in their domain.

I believe that C++ syntax and semantics should be introduced alongside object-oriented design and programming principles. A student's knowledge of C++ techniques should be paced so that it is consistent with an understanding of how the techniques can be applied to the writing of better programs.

This book has been designed to meet the following needs of my own C++ students, and hopefully, students elsewhere:

- Concise, clear discussions of C++ syntax, with accompanying short examples.
- Text adheres to the current draft of the C++ standard.
- Early introduction of objects and classes, with their immediate application to real-world problems.

- Basic concepts of objects, classes, and inheritance, with motivational discussions showing how they improve the lives of programmers.
- Examples of object-oriented diagrams that show object dependencies and relationships.
- A discussion of the differences between C and C++, to help C programmers make the transition to C++.
- Five case studies, showing separate steps for the specifications, analysis, design, and implementation of programs.
- The introduction of stream I/O at multiple levels of understanding, at different points in the learning curve.
- Complete program listings, in print and on disk.
- Chapter exercises that suggest ways that the case studies can be extended and improved, recognizing that there is no single "right" way. Such exercises can lead to interesting discussions among students.
- A chapter sequence that matches the gradual accumulation of skills and knowledge, rather than one based purely on language syntax.
- Construction and applications of dynamic data structures.
- Integration of exception handling into classes and applications.
- Portable utility classes such as lists, strings, and dynamic arrays that transfer well to new applications.

Target Audience

This book is designed for students and programmers who know at least one structured high-level language, such as Pascal, C, Structured BASIC, Ada, or Java. Students who already know C will find the transition to C++ easiest, of course, because C++ is very nearly a superset of C.

The manuscript version of this book has been used by the following types of students:

- First- and second-year computer science and engineering students, who usually complete one or two semesters of C before using this book. In schools that use C++ as the language for CS-1, students could begin using classes immediately in Chapter 2.
- We have good news for those teaching both C++ and Java: The programs in the first six chapters of this book do not use pointers, and can easily be adapted for use with Java. You can download translations of all sample programs from these chapters into Java, by accessing one of the following Web sites:

  http://www.pobox.com/~irvinek or
  http://www.prenhall.com/002/u34910/u3491-0.html
- Professional programmers, who are often looking for a way to jump-start their transition to C++ and plan to program in Microsoft Windows. Because of their

skills and experience, they do not always need to take a course in C before using this book. I encourage such persons to first learn generic C++ from a book such as this one, and then to tackle the Windows 95 application interface later.

The Computer and Information Systems Department at Miami-Dade Community College has offered C++ for several years as a follow-up to one or two semesters of C programming. We are challenged to accommodate all of the aforementioned types of students in the same class, with the same textbook.

The first challenge we face when teaching C++ is getting students to think in terms of classes and objects. Before bringing up the C++ syntax for creating classes, it helps to spend some time talking about classes, objects, attributes, and behaviors. I introduce several short problem specifications and try to engage the class in a lively discussion of alternate solutions. This helps to motivate them to approach program design and implementation in an object-oriented way.

If nothing else, I hope that this book is easy to read. Many computer science students speak English as a second language, so any book we use must be straightforward and concise. Unfortunately, C++ terminology varies from one source to another. While it is important to be flexible in the use of terminology, I try as much as possible to use the same term consistently for each concept or technique.

Above all, because knowledge of C++ is a marketable skill, one should keep in mind the practical aspects of the language. Users of the book should at least be able to design and implement short application programs that use interrelated classes and deal effectively with dynamic memory allocation. I also believe that students should be able to transfer skills learned here to other object-oriented languages such as SmallTalk, Java, and Ada.

Throughout the book, I emphasize through examples the importance of carefully analyzing and designing a program before coding. Because of the iterative nature of object-oriented design, the text often presents alternative approaches to a program design, emphasizing that there is no single *right* way. The book presents applications that involve the active interaction between classes, with diagrams that show class dependencies.

Organization of the Book

Chapter 1, *C++ Basics*, contains an overview of the language basics, showing syntax that overlaps with ANSI (standard) C. C++ features are also discussed.

Chapter 2, *Introducing Classes*, forms the foundation of all other chapters in the book because it introduces classes, member access, constructors, destructors, and member functions. It concludes with a short case study that demonstrates a range of skills introduced in this chapter.

Chapter 3, *Functions*, explores reference parameters, friend functions, and overloaded functions. It also has an improved version of the case study begun in the previous chapter. The chapter contains a detailed discussion of stream I/O formatting, and introduces two optional topics: recursion and reading a program's command line.

Chapter 4, *Class Features*, introduces enumerated constants, composite classes, member initialization lists, static class members, and a fixed-length string class. The chapter concludes with an object-oriented simulation program called *Robot Wars*.

Chapter 5, *Designing Classes*, is all about object-oriented design, providing the theoretical foundation for classes, objects, and components. It briefly describes and demonstrates the object-oriented analysis and design process, and concludes with a case study dealing with appointment scheduling in a doctor's office.

Chapter 6, *Derived Classes*, introduces single inheritance, multiple inheritance, and constructor-initializers. It includes a program that deals with graphics shapes, as well as an application called the Vehicle Management System. We carefully analyze and design this application, weighing design alternatives where necessary.

Chapter 7, *Pointers and Dynamic Memory Allocation*, represents a major step in the thinking of students, as they learn a more flexible approach to memory management. They are able to overcome limitations that were pointed out in earlier chapters. We discuss some of the finer points of conversions between pointers to objects of related classes. This chapter shows why copy constructors are needed, and it gives examples of their use. The chapter concludes with a dynamic array class.

Chapter 8, *Polymorphism and Exceptions*, introduces virtual functions, polymorphism, abstract classes, and exception handling. This chapter contains a case study for a package shipping program that may be expanded in many interesting ways.

Chapter 9, *Operator Overloading*, is devoted to one of the trickiest topics in C++. We show examples of arithmetic, relational, conversion, assignment, and subscript operators. After briefly reviewing bit manipulation operations, we introduce the BitArray class, which uses a bit-mapped array to implement set operations.

Chapter 10, *Templates*, covers both function and class templates. The implementation has an array template, a fixed string template, and a Dictionary class template.

Chapter 11, *Object-Oriented Containers*, introduces the linked list data structure, with examples of singly and doubly linked lists, graph searching, and iterators.

Stream I/O is a recurring topic in several chapters. Basic iostream operations are introduced in Chapter 1. In Chapter 2, we show how to use text file streams. In Chapter 3, we present refinements such as manipulators, option flags, string streams, and overloaded stream operators.

Key Pedagogical Features/Devices

- A list of new terms begins each chapter.
- Programming tips are located at the ends of chapters and in boxed text.

- Each chapter begins with an introductory paragraph summarizing what will be covered in the chapter, and why the topics are important.
- Each chapter ends with a summary.
- The programming exercises at the end of each chapter are varied in difficulty and scope. Many exercises build on exercises from previous chapters, so the student can refine the programs as more knowledge of C++ is gained. Other exercises extend and improve program examples from the same chapter.
- Important computer science concepts, such as graph structures, stacks, queues, lists, and dynamic memory allocation are introduced throughout.
- Several chapters contain a complete case study, with a program design and source code.
- Complete source code listings of all programs are located in Appendix A.

Acknowledgments

I would like to warmly thank Laura Steele, supervising editor at Prentice Hall, for her continued support and encouragement through a long project. Also, Betsy Jones was the acquisition editor at Macmillan, and helped obtain many of the early reviews of the book.

I thank the many reviewers who contributed their time and talents to the early development of this book, including Dr. Dilip Sarkar of the University of Miami, Dr. Nagaraja Prabhakaran of Florida International University, Mike Jones, Manuel Bermudez of the University of Florida, Robin Rowe, Jeff Naughton of the University of Wisconsin, and Thomas Bytner of the University of Maine.

Most of all, I greatly appreciate the in-depth criticism and advice given by the following persons:

- Dr. Jan Plane of the University of Maryland, who freely contributed teaching strategies and general C++ advice.
- Rex Jaeschke, author, professional C and C++ trainer/consultant, Chair of the ANSI C Committee (X3J11), and a veritable encyclopedia of C++ knowledge.
- George Kamenz, professional C++ programmer and Internet consultant; a programmer who always tests his code.

Production editing was handled by Kathleen M. Caren; illustrations were done by Emilcomp/Preparé Inc.; copyediting was by Camie Goffi; the cover designer was Bruce Kenselaar.

I would also like to thank my family for their enduring patience, and to tell them, "Yes, the book is finally finished" (until the second edition, that is...).

CHAPTER *1*

C++ Basics

This chapter introduces you to some of the basic terminology in object-oriented programming, such as classes and objects. Two essential features of C++ are demonstrated: stream I/O and reference parameters. There is also a brief discussion of the differences between C and C++ for those switching over from C.

Terms Introduced in this Chapter:

abstract data type
application domain
attribute
automatic
base class
class
const-qualified
declaration
definition
derived class
dynamic binding
encapsulate
function argument
function parameter
inheritance
instance
is-a relationship

name mangling
object
object-oriented
operation (behavior)
passing messages
polymorphism
procedural
process-oriented
reference parameter
static binding
storage class
storage duration
stream
stream manipulator
strongly typed language
type-safe linkage

1.1 INTRODUCING C++

Welcome to the C++ programming language, a widely recognized tool for object-oriented programming. C++ is well-known for combining the power and efficiency of the C language with extensions that permit object-oriented programming. C++ combines strong type checking and software engineering features with the speed and flexibility required for high-performance applications.

Another reason why C++ is so useful is because you can easily combine traditional C programming with object-oriented programming in C++. Existing libraries written in C may be used by C++ programs. In general, C++ compilers compile Standard C programs with only minor modifications. C++ is sometimes called "a better C" because it has stronger type checking and better protection against run-time errors. It is possible to use C++ to write better C programs, but one would be missing out on the advantages of object-oriented programming. C++ has also been called a "hybrid language" because it allows one to mix object-oriented programming with traditional procedural programming.

A *strongly typed* language is one in which the compiler performs strict type checking on variables and expressions, helping to catch some errors that would otherwise go unnoticed and wind up being execution errors. This was a major goal in the design of C++—for the language to help programmers create robust, reliable programs.

Prior to the introduction of object-oriented languages, programmers wanting to write object-oriented programs had to make heroic efforts to impose an artificial structure on their programs. In response to this problem, experimental object-oriented languages were created for use by a small group of researchers and programmers, but few were adopted by industry. C++ has the advantage of being standardized by both American and international organizations (ANSI and ISO), leading to its widespread acceptance.

An *object-oriented* approach focuses on the physical entities that make up an application problem. In a student registration program, for example, some of the entities might be: student, registrar, college course, and transcript. In a programming context, we call these entities *objects*. The program's structure would be based on the relationships between its objects. Associated with each object are certain operations that manipulate the data inside the objects and pass information to other objects.

In contrast, a *process-oriented* approach means that a program is organized around a hierarchy of tasks. Each main task is divided into subtasks, all the way down to detailed operations. Data are passed into and out of subroutines, but the data do not dictate the program's structure. Languages such as Pascal and C, which are categorized as *procedural* programming languages, support this approach.

C++ is an ideal language for creating user interface libraries or mathematical libraries, where new data types and related operations must be transported from one program to another. Libraries for Microsoft Windows programming, for example, are usually written in C++. Using a technique called *inheritance,* you can customize and expand existing libraries for your own programs.

1.1.1 Standardization of C++

The C++ language has been undergoing a worldwide standardization process since 1990, creating what we will call Standard C++.[1] As the committee has released working papers of the draft standards, C++ compiler vendors have implemented many of the recommendations. The *Annotated C++ Reference Manual*, 1991, (called the *ARM*) served as the C++ committee's first base document. Because many compiler vendors base their implementations on this book, we will refer to it throughout our discussions of C++.

The most recent description of C++ (as of this writing) is the April 1995 draft standard[2], which contains many new keywords and features that are not yet available in most C++ compilers. Further, the draft has not yet been approved and will no doubt undergo some changes. Still, the document makes interesting and informative reading. Those interested in learning more about the personalities and processes involved in the evolution of C++ are encouraged to read Bjarne Stroustrup's book, *The Design and Evolution of C++* [Stroustrup94].

1.2 OOP = OBJECTS + INHERITANCE + POLYMORPHISM

1.2.1 Objects

From an object-oriented point of view, the individual entities that comprise an application are called *objects*. We model objects according to the real-world problem that our program is supposed to solve. For example, a college student transcript program might be made up of objects such as:

Student: A college student
Course: A single course taken by a student

Each object has characteristics that describe both what it contains and what it does. A Student object would contain information such as: ID number, last name, and first name, all of which we call *attributes*. A Student object should also have the ability to perform certain *operations,* such as stream I/O, CalculateGrade, GetName, SetName, and so on. A Course object might have operations such as GetTitle, SetCredits, and GetGrade.

An *operation* (or *behavior*) is some functionality given to an object. It might be a response to a query, such as CalculateGrade, which asks for the student's grade average, or, it might be an action such as Display, which displays the student record on the screen.

---

[1] The standardization efforts have been through the joint effort of the American National Standards Institute (ANSI) Committee X3J16 and the International Standards Organization (ISO) SC22/WG21.

[2] Publication ISO/IEC JTC1/SC22, available through the American National Standards Institute.

An object *encapsulates* both attributes and operations, meaning that the attributes and behaviors are inseparably bound to the object. Good programming style dictates that when a program creates and uses an object, it must communicate with the object via the object's operations. In fact, we often speak of objects *passing messages* to each other. A `Student` object, for example, might contain a `Course` object, which represents a course that the student has completed. The `Student` could send a message to the `Course`, asking it to display itself.

It might be helpful to think of objects in terms of *abstract data types* (ADTs), which have been a standard topic in computer science for many years. In fact, *classes* are the way C++ implements abstract data types. Classes go much further than ADTs, implementing inheritance, polymorphism, and operator overloading. These topics are discussed at length in Chapters 6, 8, and 9, respectively.

1.2.2 Classes

A *class* is a description of the characteristics shared by all objects of the same type. In a student transcript program, we might define a class called `Student` that describes the characteristics of students in general. When an instance of the `Student` class is created, we call that a *Student object.* All such objects contain the same data members and support the same operations.

In C++, we use a class definition to identify the class name and the names and attributes of its attributes and operations. The `Student` class, for example, might be described as follows:

```
class Student {
   long id;
   char lastName[30];
   char firstName[30];
   int totCredits;
   .

   .
   void Input();
   void Print();
   float CalculateGrade();
};
```

Without being concerned with C++ syntax for the moment, we should be able to recognize which names refer to attributes (id, lastName, firstName, totCredits), and which refer to operations (Input, Print, CalculateGrade). Attributes are implemented as variables inside the class, and operations are implemented as functions, also inside the class.

On the other hand, each `Student` object has a different identification number, name, and other information. We can also call this object an *instance* of the

`Student` class. The following diagram shows the difference between the `Student` class and two `Student` objects:

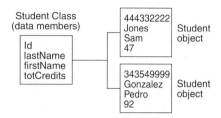

1.2.3 Inheritance

Objects of different types can be related to each other by common attributes and behaviors, permitting an *inheritance* or *is-a* relationship to be expressed. A *base class* contains characteristics that are shared by a *derived class*; the derived class, a superset of the base class, contains additional attributes and behaviors not found in the base class. We sometimes refer to such a group of related classes as a *component*.

For example, packages and letters are both sent by a postal carrier from one location to another; each has a mailing address, a return address, a postage amount, and so on. But, we might want to give packages additional attributes, identifying their weight and insured value, for example. We could create a base class called `MailItem`, which contains attributes common to both packages and letters. From this, we could derive the `Package` and `Letter` classes, each containing additional (unique) characteristics. This family of classes would be expressed graphically as

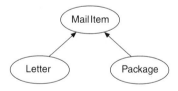

Object-oriented programming uses object relationships from the application domain (the problem being solved) as the basis for a program's design. This direct relationship makes it much easier, with practice, to go directly from an initial problem to the solution program.

1.2.4 Polymorphism

Polymorphism means that a single name can denote objects of different types. In C++, objects that are polymorphic must be instances of classes that are related by inheritance. Polymorphism is valuable in situations where you want to initiate an operation by an object that belongs to a family of classes, but you don't know at compile time exactly what type of object it is.

Using our `MailItem-Letter-Package` family, for example, we could assume that all objects in this family are able to respond to a *send* message. This message would send the letter or package to its mailing address. The internal workings of the `Send` function could be different in each of these classes, but the program calling `Send` should be unconcerned with those details.

Polymorphism is a great idea, but most programming languages do not support it. Instead, they require the exact type of each variable to be stated at compile time, this is called *static binding,* or *early binding*. Object-oriented languages offer an alternative called *dynamic binding*[3], where the exact type of object referenced by a pointer does not have to be known at compile time.

1.3 SOME BASIC TERMINOLOGY

1.3.1 Declarations and Definitions

The terms declaration and definition have an unfortunate tendency to be used interchangeably by programmers. We would like to differentiate between the two, using the terminology in the C++ standard. A *declaration* introduces an identifier into a program and states its attributes. A *definition* does everything a declaration does, and more. A variable defintion or function definition allocates program storage.

For example, the following definitions of variables and functions take up storage space in a program:

```
int n;

int sum( int a, int b )
{
    return a + b;
}

extern const long count = 0;
```

But, the following are declarations, which use no storage at all. These are uninitialized identifiers using the `extern` specifier and function prototypes:

```
extern int n;
int sum( int a, int b );
extern const long count;
```

Definitions of structures, enumerated constants, and classes do *not* allocate storage.

---

[3] Some non-OOP languages, such as BASIC, Prolog, and Lisp, also support dynamic binding.

For example,

```
struct Z {
  float r;
};

enum { up, down };

class Student {
  long id;
  char lastName[30];
};
```

1.3.2 Storage Duration

Any named object in C++ has a certain lifetime, the time period in which the object exists within a program's execution. The *storage duration,* or *storage class* of an object determines its lifetime. There are three storage durations defined in Standard C++: automatic, static, and dynamic.

Objects with *automatic storage duration* are declared inside a block (or nested block) and are destroyed when execution leaves the block. As C and C++ are implemented, automatic variables tend to be created on the runtime stack, a specialized memory buffer that also holds function parameters and function return values. The keyword `auto` can be used in a variable declaration to document the automatic duration of an object that is already automatic, but it has no effect. For example, both n and m have automatic storage duration:

```
void sub()
{
  int n;
  auto int m;
}
```

Objects with *static storage duration* can exist as long as the program. Objects declared outside of any block, having file scope, are static. Also, an automatic object can be made static by inserting the `static` specifier before the object's declaration. The object is initialized by the first time its enclosing block is entered, and retains its value when execution leaves the block. In the following program example, myArray implicitly has static duration. The local variable sCount is explicitly declared static; it retains its previous value each time ShowStatic is called, but aCount is recreated and initialized:

```
#include <iostream.h>

void ShowStatic()
{
  static unsigned sCount = 0;
  auto unsigned aCount = 0;
```

```
        cout << "aCount = " << aCount++ << ", "
             << "sCount = " << sCount++ << '\n';
    }

    int myArray[10];

    int main()
    {
      ShowStatic();
      ShowStatic();
      ShowStatic();
      ShowStatic();
      return 0;
    }
```

The variable aCount is automatic by default, so the auto keyword is unnecessary. The program's output shows the difference between static and auto local variables:

```
            aCount = 0, sCount = 0
            aCount = 0, sCount = 1
            aCount = 0, sCount = 2
            aCount = 0, sCount = 3
```

An object with *dynamic storage duration* is created by program statements during program execution, using the C++ new operator. Such objects can also be destroyed or deallocated by program statements. Chapter 7 covers dynamic objects in detail.

1.3.3 Function Parameters and Arguments

The terms *function parameter* and *function argument* vary somewhat in their usage among writers. To avoid confusion, throughout this book we refer to a *function parameter* as a member of the list of identifiers and types that appears in a function declaration. A *function argument*, on the other hand, is a member of the list of names passed to a function when the function is called. In the next example, x is a function parameter, and m is a function argument:

```
    void f( int x ) { //...   }
              .

              .
    f( m );
```

1.4 MOVING FROM C TO C++

By having programmed in C, you already know a major part of the C++ language. Because C++ was designed as a logical extension of C, close compatibility was an important goal. In this section, we will outline the basic differences between Standard C and C++. In most cases, the changes to C++ should make writing programs easier. You may find it relatively easy to convert existing programs from C to C++, although the greatest benefits from programming in C++ appear when programs are designed with object-oriented principles in mind.

1.4.1 C/C++ Differences

Most of the differences between C and C++ are caused by Standard C's need to be downward-compatible with earlier versions of C. We would like to summarize the more basic differences.

1.4.1.1 New Keywords. The following words are keywords in C++ but not in C, and will conflict with existing C programs using them as identifiers:

```
asm                  operator
bool                 private
catch                protected
class                public
const_cast           reinterpret_cast
delete               static_cast
dynamic_cast         template
explicit             this
false                throw
friend               true
inline               try
mutable              typeid
namespace            typename
new                  using
                     virtual
                     wchar_t
```

In addition, the following should not be used as identifiers because they are reserved for use as alternates to certain operators and punctuators:

```
bitand, and, bitor, or, xor, compl, and_eq, or_eq,
xor_eq, not, not_eq
```

Do not create any identifiers beginning with two underscores (__) or an underscore followed by a capital letter. These are reserved for use by C++ implementations.

C++ compilers are supposed to be case-sensitive. The ARM specifies that upper- and lower-case letters are different, but concedes that some implementations exist that are case-insensitive in external names (names exported to the linker, such as global variable names and public function names).

In C, program comments are delimited by /* ... */. C++ supports this, as well as single-line comments that begin with a double slash (//). Any characters to the right of this delimiter are ignored by the compiler, up to the end of the line.

In C++, all characters in an identifier are significant. However, practically speaking, individual compilers may set limits on the number of significant characters.

The type of a character constant is char in C++; in C, it is int. However, C++ still allows implicit conversion of a character constant into an integer:

```
int n += 'A';
```

The C language requires variables to be defined at the beginning of their enclosing block, whereas C++ allows variables to be declared anywhere in the block prior to their first use. In the next example, sum and k are declared just before being used and remain active until the end of the block:

```
float arraySum( float * array, int count )
{
  printf( "Summing an array" );

  float sum = 0.0;
  int k;

  for(k = 0; k < count; k++)
    sum += array[k];

  return sum;
}
```

In C++, a global data object can be defined only once, whereas in C, the redefinition of a global object leads to undefined behavior. This type of checking may also extend across module boundaries, depending on the linker being used. In the next example, the name tableSize is defined in module1 and module2. The linker we use issues an error message saying that tableSize has been redefined:

```
module1.cpp contains:       int tableSize = 20;
module2.cpp contains:       int tableSize;
```

1.4.1.2 Cast Operator.   In C++, a cast operator may be written in two different ways: either as a C-style cast or as a function notation cast. The following are equivalent:

```
float g = (float) i / 2;   // C-style
float g = float(i) / 2;    // function notation
```

Unlike C, C++ does not allow a *void* pointer to be automatically assigned to any other pointer. C++ requires a cast into the target type. For example,

```
void * v;
float * f;
.

.

f = v;                 // error: cast required
f = (float *) v;       // ok
```

1.4.1.3 Functions. In Standard C, the function declaration `int f()` means that the number and type of arguments is unknown. In C++, the same declaration means that f takes *no* arguments.

In C, a function can be called without a declaration for it being in scope. In C++, the compiler must encounter a function's prototype (declaration) before trying to compile a call to the function. This prevents the programmer from inadvertently passing the wrong types of arguments to the function. The following is an example of a function prototype:

```
long int calcSum( int * array, int count );
```

A call to `calcSum` with incorrect arguments would be flagged as an error. In the next example, `rainFall` is an array of `float`, which conflicts with `calcSum`'s first parameter type:

```
float sum;
float rainfall[100];
.

.
sum = calcSum( rainFall, 100 );
```

1.4.1.4 Type-Safe Linkage. When a function call and a function definition are in different compilation units, the linker checks for consistency between the function call and function definition. This checking across module boundaries is called *type-safe linkage*. We will spend more time on this topic in Chapter 3.

1.4.1.5 Linking to C Functions. When linking a library of C functions to a C++ program, function prototypes must begin with the `extern` "C" qualifier. Here, for example, is a prototype of the standard `strcpy` function defined in the `string.h` header:

```
extern "C" char * strcpy(char *__dest, const char *__src);
```

This prevents the name of the function from being mangled by the C++ compiler. *Name mangling* refers to the automatic extending of a function name to distinguish between two functions having the same name.

In C, a structure, union, or enumeration type, or an enumerator declared in a structure are all exported to the scope enclosing the structure. In C++, on the other hand, structures, unions, and enumeration tag names share the same name space. In C++, the same identifier should not be used as both a structure tag and as the name of a different type. The following declarations of `address`, for example, would be incorrect in C++:

```
enum address { local, permanent };

struct address {
  char street[30];
  char city[30];
  char state[3];
  char zip[10];
};
```

1.5 C++ FEATURES

Now we're going to introduce some of the new features in C++ that make it different from C. The first of these, the `const` qualifier, is available in C, but its use is more widespread in C++. The second feature, reference parameters, is not part of the C language.

1.5.1 Named Constants

The `const` qualifier is used in C++ to define a named constant. The constant may appear anywhere that a compile-time integer constant expression is required. For example, `ArraySize` specifies the number of components in the `scores` array. We also say that `ArraySize` is *const-qualified:*

```
const int ArraySize = 100;
  .
  .
float scores[ArraySize];
```

In C, this would have to be done with #define:

```
#define ArraySize 100;
  .
  .
float scores[ArraySize];
```

In general, it's best to use `const` rather than #define in C++. For one thing, you can limit the scope of a const-qualified object, which would not be possible with #define:

```
void makeList()
{
  const int count = 10;  // local scope

  int list[count];

  int i;
  for(i = 0; i < count; i++)
    list[i] = i;
  //...
}
```

C++ compilers usually avoid allocating storage for a const-qualified object by substituting its value into the compiled program wherever it is referenced. C++ cannot do this when the address of the constant is taken, or when the object in question has global scope.

Qualifying an object's declaration with const is a promise that its value will not be altered during the program's execution. This encourages the compiler to use a storage format well-suited to constants. On some systems, that might mean that the object is located in a read-only area of memory.

1.5.1.1 C/C++ Differences.

In C, a global constant defaults to external linkage. In C++, the default linkage is internal. To clarify the ambiguity, it is best to explicitly declare a global constant as either *static* or *extern*:

```
extern const int count = 5;        // external linkage
static const float average = 0.0;  // internal linkage
```

Unlike C, in C++, constants must be initialized at the same time they are declared, unless they are declared *external.* For example,

```
const float f;          // invalid: not initialized
extern const float f;   // ok: external constant

const int count = 100;  // ok: internal, initialized
```

1.5.2 Enumerated Constants

Enumerated constants are used widely in C++ because they provide straightforward documentation and implicit range checking on constants. They can be declared without a tag, requiring the programmer to consistently use the constant names:

```
enum { red, yellow, blue };

int wincolor = red;
```

They can also be declared with a tag name, creating an enumerated type. This enforces the use of the appropriate constants, because in C++, an integer cannot be directly assigned to an enumerated type:

```
enum PrimaryColor { red, yellow, blue };

PrimaryColor wincolor;
wincolor = red;    // ok
wincolor = 0;      // error
```

The only way to assign an out-of-range value to `wincolor` would be to cast it to `int`, which would rarely be a good idea.

1.5.3 Reference Parameters

A *reference parameter* is a function parameter that is an alias (substitute name) for the corresponding argument passed to the function. If a statement within the function assigns a new value to a reference parameter, the object aliased by the parameter is immediately assigned the same value. For example, the following function exchanges the values of its parameters x and y:

```
void swap( int & x, int & y )
{
  int temp = x;
  x = y;
  y = temp;
}
```

If we pass the arguments A and B to the function, their values will be exchanged. We say that A and B are passed *by reference:*

```
int A = 10;
int B = 20;
swap( A, B );
cout << A << ',' << B;   // output: "20,10"
```

Reference parameters help to simplify source code because they eliminate the need to pass variables by address. If we were to write the `swap` function in C, for example, we would have to use pointer parameters and dereference the pointers within the function body:

```
void swap( int * x, int * y ) // C version
{
  int temp = *x;
  *x = *y;
  *y = temp;
}
```

In C, we would also have to preface the arguments with the address operator:

```
int A = 10;
int B = 20;
swap( &A, &B );   // C version
```

The spacing between a parameter and the reference operator is arbitrary. For better program readability, it helps to use a consistent format. All of the following formats are widely used by C++ programmers:

```
void swap( int& x, int& y );
void swap( int &x, int &y );
void swap( int & x, int & y );
```

A reference parameter can be const-qualifed, indicating that the parameter will not be modified inside the enclosing function. For example,

```
void Test( const int & x );
```

1.6 STREAM I/O

C++ programs use streams for character-based input/output. The term *stream I/O* refers to input/output based on streams. A *stream* is a sequence of bytes that may be either input to a program or output from a program. Input can be from a keyboard, file, or some other input device. Output can be to the programmer's screen, or to a file, printer, or some other output device.

There are three standard stream I/O objects: `cin`, `cout`, and `cerr`. The first, `cin` (pronounced "see-in"), refers to the standard input device, `cout` (pronounced "see-out") refers to the standard output device, and `cerr` (pronounced "see-err") is the standard error output device. By default, the latter two are tied to the programmer's screen. In other words, `cin`, `cout`, and `cerr` correspond to the predefined FILE pointers in C, `stdin`, `stdout`, and `stderr`.

In order to use stream I/O, C++ programs require, at a minimum, the `iostream.h` header file. Some systems use a suffix of `.hxx` or `.hpp` instead of `.h`, but we will use `.h` throughout.

`cin` generally buffers its input, so that each request by the program for an input character will not require a physical access to the input device. The same is true in reverse, for `cout`. This buffering of input-output improves system efficiency by reducing the amount of time each program requires access to physical I/O devices such as disk drives and printers. This also means that characters in the output buffer might not appear on the screen until the buffer has been *flushed* (its contents written to the output device). The error output stream, `cerr`, is unbuffered.

1.6.1 Stream Output

The stream output operator (<<) appends an expression to an output stream. This operator is also the left-shift operator, but C++ allows the operator to have multiple meanings (called operator overloading). In its simplest usage, the << operator is placed between a stream variable and the expression whose value is to be written. The following statement writes the value of n to the standard output stream:

```
int n = 26;
cout << n;        // "26"
```

The cout stream will choose the most appropriate form of output for n, based on its data type. When cout writes a float expression, only the minimum number of digits appear:

```
float f = 5.0 / 2.0;
cout << f;            // "2.5"
```

You can write multiple expressions to a stream in the same statement. For example, we write an int and a float, separated by a comma, and followed by a newline character:

```
cout << 5 << ',' << 26.5 << '\n';
```

Error messages are usually written to cerr. Here we use it to report an out-of-range subscript:

```
if( i >= arraySize )
    cerr << "Subscript out of range: " << i;
```

When writing an expression to cout, use parentheses to force the expression to be evaluated before being written to the stream. For example,

```
cout << 2 + 3;    // ambiguous: parentheses needed
cout << (2 + 3); // ok: outputs "5"
```

We use endl, called a *stream manipulator*, to output a newline character and flush the output buffer. Some computer systems wait for the output buffer to fill or wait for the buffer to be flushed before writing the buffer to the output device. The following writes each number on a separate line:

```
cout << 2 << endl << 3 << endl;
```

Flushing the output buffer after every line is not efficient for multi-user computer systems. The best approach is to consider which output should be displayed as a group, and use the `endl` manipulator only at the end of the group. Within the group, use the newline (`'\n'`) character. For example, each integer is written to a separate line, but the buffer is flushed only at the end of the loop:

```
for(int j = 0; j < 20; j++)
   cout << j << '\n';

cout << endl;
```

1.6.1.1 *Character Output.* When writing a character to a stream, the output defaults to a character, not an integer. For example,

```
char ch = 'A';
cout << ch;    // "A"
```

In order to display the numeric representation, such as the ASCII code, of a character, the cast operator may be used. The ASCII representation of `'A'` is 65, so the following output would be 65:

```
char ch = 'A';
cout << int(ch);  // "65" on an ASCII-based system
```

Conversely, an integer may be cast into a character. Using the ASCII character set, the following would output the letter A:

```
int n = 65;
cout << char(n); // "A" on an ASCII-based system
```

1.6.2 Stream Input

The >> operator extracts data from an input stream. In this example, we read an integer from the standard input stream and place the result in n:

```
int n;
cin >> n;      // read from input stream
```

By default, the stream input operator skips leading whitespace, which makes it useful for reading data delimited by spaces, tabs, or newlines. Given the following input, where \t is a single tab character and \n is a newline,

```
" 26 \t 34 \n 5.4 A\n"
```

the following statements would store 26, 34, 5.4, and 'A' into separate variables:

```
int a, b;
float r;
char ch;
cin >> a >> b >> r >> ch;  // a=26, b=34, r=5.4, ch='A'
```

In this case, the stream's input pointer would be left pointing at the newline (\n) character following the letter A.

1.6.2.1 *Using cin.get() For Character Input.*   Strings are most effectively input from streams by using the `cin.get` function. It has one optional argument, a variable of type `char`, and it does not skip leading whitespace. The following statements prompt for a name, input each character, and stop when a newline character is entered:

```
#include <iostream.h>

char name[80];
char ch = '\0';
int i = 0;

cout << "Enter your name: ";
while(1)
{
  cin.get(ch);
  if( ch == '\n') break;
  name[i++] = ch;
}
name[i] = '\0';
```

An alternate form of `get()` in the sample program could omit the argument and save the return value in a variable:

```
char ch;
ch = cin.get();
```

If, for example, the user entered the name "Fred" and pressed the Enter key, the `cin` stream input pointer would point immediately after the newline. The name array would contain a null byte after the letter d:

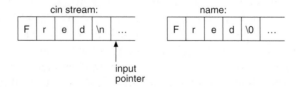

Of course, the user might immediately enter a newline, making the name blank. It is also important to avoid storing a newline character in the last position of the name.

We're not quite ready to explain why you need the period (.) when calling the `cin.get` function, but we can give you a hint: in our discussion about objects and classes, we said that every class has a set of operations associated with it, and operations are implemented as functions. So, the `get` function belongs to a class called `iostream`, and `cin` is an object of type `iostream`.

Most C++ implementations store input characters in a temporary buffer and flush the buffer when a newline character is read. The following loop looks as if it should write each character to the output stream immediately after it is entered, but on our system, the name is echoed only after the loop finishes:

```
while(1)
{
  cin.get(ch);
  if( ch == '\n') break;
  cout << ch;
  name[i++] = ch;
}
name[i] = '\0';
```

1.7 CHAPTER SUMMARY

C++ is what might be called an *industrial-strength* language. It combines the power and efficiency of C with object-oriented features such as classes, inheritance, and polymorphism. C++ is particularly well-suited to writing large, complex software systems that involve teams of programmers. It is also an ideal language for developing libraries that can be easily installed and modified in application programs. C++ is what we call a *strongly typed* language, meaning that the compiler helps to prevent the use of incorrect expressions involving incompatible data types. Also, function calls across module boundaries are checked against function prototypes to make sure the number and types of the passed arguments agree with the function parameters.

C++ is called a hybrid language because it allows you to mix procedural code and object-oriented code in the same program. This has helped win it acceptance in the C programming community.

Objects represent the real-world entities that play an active part in an application. Designers try to model object-oriented programs around these real-world entities. An object encapsulates (contains) both attributes and operations (also called behaviors). The attributes represent the state of the object, the values of which change at run time. The operations represent the way the object communicates with other objects. A class object is an instance of some class.

A class is a description of the common characteristics shared by all objects of the same type. It is in fact a user-defined data type, with all the rights and privileges (from a language point of view) given to standard data types such as int, float, or double. As we learn to use the tools of C++, we will find that the classes we define can incorporate the same types of operators and implicit conversions available to standard data types.

Inheritance is a powerful tool in object-oriented programming that lets us derive new classes by refining and adding to the attributes and behaviors of existing classes. With inheritance, we can begin with an existing class library and customize it for a particular application.

Polymorphism allows the same name to denote objects of different types. In C++, these types must be classes that are related by inheritance.

We described some of the differences between C and C++, for programmers with a background in C who are moving to C++.

We introduced stream I/O, showing how to write to the standard cout stream object, and how to read from the standard cin stream object. Although the keyboard is the default input device and the screen is the default output device, both input and output can be redirected to other devices.

We briefly introduced reference parameters, a topic that we will cover thoroughly in Chapter 3.

1.8 EXERCISES

1 Stream Output.   Write a program that creates variables of the following standard types, initializes the variables to the largest and smallest values allowed in your C++ implementation, and writes them to an output stream:

```
signed char, unsigned char, int, unsigned int
long int, unsigned long, float, double, long double
```

The standard header files float.h and limits.h contain the specific ranges of numeric types for your C++ compiler.

2 Stream Input.   Write a program that uses an input stream to read the following information from the user:

```
unsigned idNumber;
char firstName[30];
char lastName[40];
int hoursWorked;
float hourlyPayRate;
```

Assuming that the user does not type first or last name with embedded spaces, you can use the >> operator for stream input.

Next, write all of this information to an output stream, adding labels before each variable. For example,

```
ID Number:     12343434
First Name:    John
Last Name:     Smith
Hours Worked:  45
Pay Rate:      22.5
```

3 Strings with Embedded Blanks. Write a short program that reads a sentence. Use the `cin.get` function to read the characters, including the blanks between words. Redisplay the sentence to verify that it was read and stored correctly.

4 Reference Parameters. Write a function that has at least three reference parameters of differing types such as `int`, `char`, `float`, and `long`. Modify the parameters inside the function and verify that the variables passed as arguments were also modified.

5 Object-Based and Object-Oriented Languages. Compile a list of hybrid computer languages you know of that incorporate object-oriented features. Find out if these languages support classes (each containing attributes and operations), inheritance, and polymorphism. Find one or more articles that discuss these languages, and for each language, determine the types of applications that best suit the language.

6 Verify Level of C++ Support. Read your C++ compiler's manual and find out what version of C++ it supports. The compiler used for this book, for example, is a full implementation of AT&T's C++ Release 3.0 language definition. Does your compiler support templates and exception handling? We cover templates in Chapter 10 and exception handling in Chapter 11. These are now considered essential parts of the C++ language.

7 Screen Manipulation. Some of the programs presented later in this book can be enhanced by manipulating the text screen display. In anticipation of this, find out if there are any control codes or escape sequences that may be used to manipulate the video display in your C++ implementation. Find out if your system is capable of performing the following video tasks in text mode:

clear screen, home cursor, clear to end of line, locate cursor at row/column, scroll video display, display reverse video, display colors, blink, and beep (sound bell)

CHAPTER 2

Introducing Classes

In this chapter we introduce the most fundamental component of object-oriented programming, the *class*. Our goal is to give the reader enough information to make it possible to create simple classes and begin using them in applications. Along those lines, we show how class objects are created and destroyed, and how to encapsulate data members and member functions inside classes. We introduce file streams so that future programs will be able to easily read and write data for program testing. Finally, we develop a case study dealing with a student registration report program, showing the specifications, analysis, design, and implementation phases.

Terms Introduced in this Chapter:

access specifier	inline
alternate constructor	interface
class	intrinsic type
composition (has-a) relationship	iterator
composition class	link (uses-a) relationship
const member function	member access operator (.)
constructor	member function
copy constructor	model
data member	modifier
declaration	object, instance
default constructor	overloaded constructor
definition	public, private, protected access
destructor	scope resolution operator

encapsulation
header file
implementation file
information hiding

selector
selector, modifier, iterator
state, behavior, identity

2.1 OBJECTS AND CLASSES

2.1.1 What Are Objects?

In the real world, people identify objects as things that can be perceived by the five senses. Objects have recognizable properties, such as location, size, color, shape, texture, and so on. Objects also have certain behaviors that make them different from other objects. From this concept, it is interesting to imagine the effectiveness of using objects in computer programs.

[Booch] defines an *object* as something that "has state, behavior, and identity." Let's explore this idea for a moment, using a machine in a factory. The *state* of the machine might consist of its on/off state, its horsepower, maximum speed, current speed, temperature, and so on. Its *behavior* might include actions to start and stop the machine, obtain its temperature, activate or deactivate other machines, signal error conditions, or change speed. Its *identity* is based on the fact that every instance of a machine is unique, perhaps identified by a serial number. The characteristics we choose to emphasize in the machine's state and behavior would be based on how a machine object would be used in an application. In an object-oriented program design, we would create an abstraction (a simplified model) of the machine based on the properties and behaviors that are useful to us at the time.

[Martin/Odell] say that an object is "any thing, real, or abstract, about which we store data and those methods (operations) that manipulate the data." To this, we add that each class object contains its own data and is associated with member functions belonging to the class.

The user of an object communicates with the object via its *interface*, a set of operations defined by the object's class so as to be visible to all of a program. You might think of an interface as a simplified view of an object. For example, electronic devices generally have well-designed user interfaces. The user of a fax machine, for example, uses an abstract interface that includes the paper feed, dialing buttons, receiver, and the "send" button. The user does not have to know anything about the construction of the machine's circuit board, communications protocol, or other details. In fact, opening the machine may even void the manufacturer's warranty. Similarly, a class has the same implicit contract with its users: use its interface as much as you want, but if you tinker with the insides, all promises as to the reliability of the class are void.

Consistent with the idea of an abstract interface, the internal integrity of a class must be preserved. An important function of the class interface is to perform various types of validation on data passed by the class user. This includes, but is not limited to, range checking, reasonableness checking, sequence checking, and consistency checking. For example, the abstract interface for the can dispenser in a soft drink vending machine would have to perform the following validations before a can could be dispensed:

- A minimum amount of money must have been deposited in the machine.
- At least one can of this flavor must exist.

Similarly, a student transcript object would not allow a college course to be added to the transcript unless it had a reasonable number of credits, a course name, and a semester identifier that was consistent with the college's numbering system.

2.1.1.1 Modeling.
Object-oriented programs attempt to model or emulate real-world problems and applications. Because of this, objects in a program usually have a close correlation to the real-world objects in the problem domain. Not only do objects model tangible entities defined by the current application, but they also model processes and events. A process might only be implied by the application, or a process might be purely invented by the programmer to enable the software to solve the problem at hand.

Let's use a television factory as an example. The components being assembled would be objects, as would the workers performing the assembly. If we were to program a simulation of the factory, we would create a number of process objects that do the following: move parts down the assembly line, check the quality of parts and construction, queue assembled parts for packing, and so on. We also might define event objects that are created when a machine breaks down, a bad component is detected, and so on.

2.1.2 What Are Classes?

In practical terms, a *class* is a user-defined type. A class can be given the same rich set of behaviors that characterize standard data types. Classes are the fundamental building blocks of object-oriented programs. Entire application programs are designed around clusters of related classes that have relationships with each other. To use an analogy, a baseball team is made up of players, each of whom has specific responsibilities and attributes based on the position being played, as well as the personal characteristics of the player.

[Booch] calls a *class* "a set of objects that share a common structure and common behavior." That is not to say that every class actually contains a set of objects; rather, that the class implies a general set. When an object is created, it has the general attributes that belong to other objects of the same class. At the same time, the *state* of those attributes varies from object to object. All `Point` objects, for example, have x and y coordinates, but the states of x and y in each object can be different.

The term *encapsulation* refers to the ability to combine both operations and data inside a class. Because of encapsulation, a class can frequently be copied from one program to another. All member data and functions belonging to the class are contained within the class.

2.1.2.1 Classes in C++.
C and C++ have standard data types such as `int`, `float`, and `double`, each with their own semantics for assignment, conversion, and use in expressions. We call these *intrinsic* types. But what is new about C++ is that it gives the same status to user-defined types as intrinsic types. We can define how our classes will respond to assignment, conversion, and expressions. Both data and functions are encapsulated within classes, resulting in sophisticated responses by class objects to their environment. In fact, one often speaks of class objects sending "messages" to one another in (almost) human terms.

2.1.2.2 Relationships Between Classes.
Classes are rarely isolated from each other in an application design; instead, classes collaborate with each other, sending messages and returning replies. In our television factory simulation, for example, a testing device would send messages to each assembled television set to verify the condition of the latter's components.

The two most common types of interaction between classes are *links* (or *uses-a*) and *composition* (or *has-a*). A *link* relationship exists between two classes that need to communicate. An instance of one class sends a message to an instance of another class. In our television factory simulation, for example, a testing object might send a predefined signal to an electronic component. Or, a control process object might send a message that includes the location of an assembled television to the packing department (another object).

A *composition* relationship exists when a class contains data members that are also class objects. This makes it possible to create new classes from combinations of existing ones. In general, it is possible to navigate from a composite class to each of the objects it contains. For example, a television set knows about its component parts; but a component, such as a resistor, need not be aware that it is inside a television set. A resistor functions the same, whether it is inside a television, radio, or any other electronic device.

In some cases, an object might not be physically contained in a composite object. For example, a student transcript contains references to various college courses that the student has completed, but the complete information about each course is stored elsewhere. The transcript does, however, provide a path to the course information, and may still be considered a composite.

2.2 CREATING CLASSES

2.2.1 Class Definition

Here is the basic form of a class definition:

```
class class-name {
  member-list
};
```

Class-name is a user-defined name that identifies the class, and *member-list* is comprised primarily of data members and member functions. Unless a class definition has been nested inside another class or inside a function, the class name has file scope and external linkage.

For example, let's define a class called `Point` that holds the *x* and *y* coordinates of a point on a two-dimensional cartesian graph:

```
class Point {
public:
  int GetX();
  // Returns the value of x.

  void SetX();
  // Sets the value of x.

private:
  int x;    // x-coordinate
  int y;    // y-coordinate
};
```

No storage is allocated by the members of a class definition. Instead, storage is allocated when a class object (or class *instance*) is created.

Referring to the foregoing example, the keywords `public` and `private` are called *access-specifiers*; they control the degree to which programs using the `Point` class can directly access class members. `x` and `y` are *data members* and `GetX` and `SetX` are *member functions*. The `GetX` member function returns the current value of `x` belonging to a `Point` object, and the `SetX` function allows a program to set the value of `x` belonging to a `Point`.

A class *declaration* consists of just the keyword `class` and the class name. A class declaration is used when we simply need to let the compiler know that a certain class is fully defined somewhere else in the program. For example,

```
class Point;  // defined somewhere else
```

2.2.2 Class Objects

Once a class has been defined, a program can contain an *instance* of the class, called a *class object*. The following is the general form for declaring a class object, followed by a definition of a `Point` object:

```
class-name identifier;

Point P;
```

The *member access* operator (`.`) selects an individual member of a class object. The following statements, for example, create a `Point` P, set its x coordinate, and display its x coordinate:

```
Point P;
P.SetX( 300 );
cout << "x-coordinate is " << P.GetX();
```

We can assign one class object to another; by default, C++ performs a bitwise copy of all data members. In other words, all memory physically contained in the data area of the source object is copied into the receiving object. For example, the following creates a `Point` called P2 and initializes it with the contents of P:

```
Point P;
//...
Point P2;
P2 = P;
```

2.2.3 Controlling Member Access

A key principle in object-oriented programming is *information hiding,* which disallows class users from accessing the internal details of a class. A class user should only see the class interface, based on the operations the class supports, plus any public data members. This helps to protect an object's data from being corrupted, and it also means that modifications can be made to a class implementation without requiring modifications to programs that use the class. Communication with a class object should be handled exclusively through its public members. Data members are usually private, while member functions are usually public.

We use three different *access specifiers* to control access to class members. They are `public`, `private`, and `protected`. We use the following general format in class definitions, placing the public members first, followed by protected and private members:

```
class class-name {
public:
    // public members
```

```
protected:
  // protected members

private:
  // private members
};
```

Members following the `public` specifier can be accessed by any function. Members following the `private` specifier can only be accessed by member functions in the same class, or by friend classes or functions.[1] Members following the `protected` specifier can be accessed by member functions either of the same class or in classes derived from it, as well as friends. The `public`, `protected`, and `private` keywords can appear in any order. In the following table, each "X" indicates that access is permitted to the type of class member listed in the left column:

Type of Member	Member of the Same Class	Friend	Member of a Derived Class	Non-Member Function
Private	X	X		
Protected	X	X	X	
Public	X	X	X	X

If the access specifier is omitted, the default access is private. In the following `Student` class, for example, all the data members are private, while the member functions are public:

```
class Student {
    long idNum;
    char name[40];
    int age;

public:
    long GetIdNum();
    char * GetName();
    int GetAge();
};
```

The same access specifier can appear more than once in a class definition, but this is not particularly easy to read:

```
class Student {
private:
    long idNum;
```

---

[1] Friend functions and friend classes are discussed in Section 3.3.

```
      public:
        long GetIdNum();

      private:
        char name[40];
        int age;

      public:
        char * GetName();
        int GetAge();
      };
```

2.2.4 Example: The Point Class

Let's create a more complete definition of the `Point` class we introduced earlier.
For each data member, we provide a member function that returns its value, and
one that sets its value:

```
      class Point {
      public:
        int GetX() { return x; }
        int GetY() { return y; }
        void SetX( int xval ) { x = xval; }
        void SetY( int yval ) { y = yval; }

      private:
        int x;
        int y;
      };
```

The function declarations in this example are also definitions because we have
included the body of each function. If a function body consists of only a single statement, many programmers place the function body on the same line as the function
name. On the other hand, if a function contains multiple statements, each should go
on a separate line. For example,

```
      class Point {
      public:
        void SetX( int xval )
        {
          if(( xval >= -100) && ( xval <= 100 ))
            x = xval;
          else
            cerr << "Error: SetX() argument out of range.";
        }
        //...
      };
```

2.2.4.1 Types of Member Functions.   A few basic types of member functions are based on the type of operation they support:

- *Constructors* and *destructors*, which are member functions that are automatically called when an object is created or destroyed, respectively.
- *Selectors* that return the values of data members.
- *Modifiers* or *mutators* that let a client program change the contents of data members.
- *Operators* that let you define standard C++ operators for class objects.
- *Iterators* that process collections of objects, such as arrays and lists.

2.2.5 Inline and Out-Of-Line Definitions

Until now, all of our member functions have been defined within the body of the class definition. These are called *inline* function definitions. For longer functions, we prefer to code only the function prototype within the class block, and to code the function implementation outside. This allows the creator of a class to hide the function implementation from the class user by supplying source code only for the header file, along with a precompiled class implementation file.

In the next example, `SetX` in the `Point` class is declared but not defined in the class definition:

```
class Point {
public:
  void SetX( int xval );

private:
  int x;
  int y;
};
```

The implementation of `SetX` appears outside the class definition, making it an *out-of-line* function definition. Its name must be preceded by the name of the class and the : : punctuator:

```
void Point::SetX( int xval )
{
  x = xval;
}
```

The : : punctuator lets the compiler know that `SetX` belongs to the `Point` class and is therefore different from a global function that happens to have the same name, or from a function by that name that might exist in another class. The following global function, for example, could coexist within the same scope as `Point::SetX`:

```
void SetX( int xval )
{
  //...
}
```

The symbol : : is also known as a *scope resolution operator* when used in run-time statements that access class members. For example, the expression `Point::x` refers to the x data member of the `Point` class.

2.2.5.1 *The* `inline` *Keyword.*   There is a runtime efficiency issue when de-ciding between using inline versus out-of-line functions. An inline function usually runs faster because, if at all possible, the compiler inserts a fresh copy of the func-tion into a program at every point that the function is called. Defining a member function inline does not guarantee that the compiler will actually make it inline; it is a decision made by the compiler, based on the types of statements within the func-tion, and each C++ compiler makes this decision differently.

If a function is compiled inline, CPU time is saved by not having to execute a *call* instruction to branch to the function, and by not having to execute a *return* in-struction to return to the calling program. If a function is short and is called thou-sands of times, the increase in efficiency of an inline function can be noticeable.

A function located outside the class definition block can still benefit from the advantages of inline functions if it is prefaced by the `inline` keyword:

```
inline void Point::SetX( int xval )
{
  x = xval;
}
```

Depending on your compiler implementation, functions using the `inline` keyword might have to be placed in the same header file as the class definition. Functions not using `inline` are placed in the same program module, but not in the header file. They are placed in a `.cpp` file (`.cc`, `.cxx`, `.c`, etc.).

2.2.5.2 *Member Function Parameter Names.*   As is true with global func-tion prototypes, you can omit the parameter names from a member function decla-ration and identify the parameter types only. For example,

```
class Point {
public:
  void SetX( int );
  //...
};
```

However, this is not always desirable. Because the class definition is also the class interface, a member function such as the following would not give the class user enough information about how to call the function:

```
class MyClass {
public:
  void DoSomething( int, float, int, char *, int );
  //...
};
```

**PROGRAMMING TIP: USING COMMENTS
AFTER FUNCTION DECLARATIONS**

As a general recommendation, one or more lines of comments should
follow a function declaration that explain what the function does and
what the function's input/output values should be. It can also be argued
that certain functions are so self-explanatory that comments are
redundant. A function such as `Point::SetX`, for example, obviously sets
the value of the x data member. When in doubt, err on the side of
redundant comments to be sure that the class user knows what each
function does and what input/output values are required for the function.

If parameter names appear in both the function declaration and function implementation, the names do not have to be the same. Their order and type, on the
other hand, must be identical. For example,

```
class Point {
public:
  void MoveTo( int xval, int yval );
  //...
};

void Point::MoveTo( int XV, int YV )
{
  //...
}
```

2.2.6 Constructors

A *constructor* is a special-purpose member function that is automatically executed
when a class object is created. The constructor always has the same name as its class,
with no return type. A constructor with no parameters is called a *default constructor*. In the `Point` class, for example, we could create a default constructor that initializes both x and y to 0:

```
class Point {
public:
  Point()
  {
    x = 0;
    y = 0;
  }
private:
  int x;
  int y;
};
```

Now that we have a constructor for `Point`, when a `Point` object is declared, its x and y data members are initialized to 0. This is a convenience for the class user and is a good programming practice:

```
Point Z;    // Z.x == 0,  Z.y == 0
```

If a `Point` is declared inside a function, its constructor is called as soon as the program's execution reaches the `Point`'s declaration:

```
void subroutine()
{
  Point W;  // constructor called here
  //...
}
```

If a `Point` is declared outside any function, giving it file scope, its constructor is executed before `main()` begins.

C++ automatically creates a default constructor when no other constructors exist. But such a constructor does not initialize the class data members to any predictable values. So, it's almost always better to create your own default constructor, thus giving you the option of initializing data members with predictable values.

2.2.6.1 Alternate Constructors.

We might also want to pass arguments to a constructor, to assign specific values to each class object's data members. A constructor with parameters is called an *alternate constructor*. In the case of `Point` objects, we can set the x and y coordinates:

```
Point P( 100, 200 );  // define and intialize P
```

A constructor can be called directly, creating a temporary object. For example, the following constructs a `Point` and assigns it to Z:

```
Point Z = Point( 100, 200 );
```

The following is an alternate constructor for the `Point` class:

```
Point::Point( int xval, int yval )
{
    SetX( xval );
    SetY( yval );
    cout << "Point constructor called.\n";
}
```

Notice also that we added a statement to the constructor that displays a message when a `Point` is constructed. This can be a useful debugging tool.

In the `Point` constructor, we could have assigned the `xval` and `yval` parameters directly to the data members x and y. Instead, by calling `SetX` and `SetY`, we reserve the right to later implement validity checks on x and y. Also, if we should ever change the names of x and y, we would have to modify all functions that make direct references to the data member names. It is to our advantage to minimize the number of functions that do this.

2.2.6.2 Overloaded Constructors.   A class can have more than one constructor, as long as each has a different parameter list. If so, we say that the constructor is *overloaded*. One and only one constructor is ever executed when an object is created, regardless of how many constructors have been defined. Rather than go into the details of overloaded functions here, we devote Section 3.4 to the topic.

In the `Point` class, we can declare both a default constructor and an alternate constructor:

```
class Point {
public:
    Point();
    Point( int xval, int yval );
    //...

private:
    int x;
    int y;
};
```

When a `Point` object is declared, we have the option of calling either constructor. For example,

```
Point P;            // call default constructor
Point Q( 10, 20 );  // call alternate constructor
```

PROGRAMMING TIP: DEFAULT CONSTRUCTOR

Beware of writing the following, which appears to be a call to the default constructor. Instead, it declares a function named P that has no parameters and returns a result of type Point:

```
Point P();
```

If an alternate constructor exists, C++ will not generate a default constructor. To prevent class users from creating an object with no parameters, you can either omit the default constructor or make it private. For example,

```
class Point {
public:
  Point( int xval, int yval );

private:
  Point();
  //...
};
.
.
.
Point P;  // error: constructor not accessible
```

2.2.6.3 Copy Constructors. There is a specialized type of constructor called a *copy constructor*, which is created automatically by the compiler. The copy constructor is automatically called when an object is passed by value: a local copy of the object is constructed. The copy constructor is also called when an object is declared and initialized with another object of the same type. For example, the declarations of Q and Z both result in calls to a copy constructor:

```
Point P;
Point Q(P);
Point Z = P;
```

By default, C++ makes a bitwise copy of an object. However, we can also implement our own copy constructor and use it to notify the user that a copy has been made, perhaps as a debugging aid:

```
Point::Point( const Point & p2 )
{
    cerr << "Point class copy constructor called.\n";
    x = p2.x;
    y = p2.y;
    return *this;
};
```

The parameter p2 is *const-qualified*, meaning that p2 cannot be modified by the function. Also, a copy constructor always returns a reference to the current object, which is denoted by the expression *this. We will discuss copy constructors at some length in Section 7.5 when demonstrating classes containing pointer data members.

2.2.7 Array of Class Objects

An array of class objects is useful in applications that require multiple instances of the same class. If, for example, we define an array of Point objects called figure, the default Point constructor is called for each array member:

```
Point figure[3];
```

Optionally, an alternate constructor can be invoked for each object, particularly when the constructor has only one parameter. For example, we initialize an array of Student objects with student identification numbers:

```
class Student {
public:
    Student( long n )
    {
        SetId( n );
    }
    void SetId( long );
    //...
};

Student AIseminar[4] = { 11234, 23457, 30101, 44321 };
```

2.2.8 Destructors

A *destructor* is a special member function that is automatically called when a class object is logically deleted. The name of a destructor is the name of the class, preceded by the ~ (tilde) character. In the Point class, for example, a destructor would be called ~Point. If a destructor is not explicitly declared, C++ creates an empty one automatically.

If an object has local scope, its destructor is called when control passes out of its defining block. If an object has file scope, the destructor is called when the main program ends. If an object was dynamically allocated (using `new` and `delete`), the destructor is called when the delete operator is invoked. For example, input/output stream objects such as `cin` and `cout` are automatically constructed by the C++ run-time system. When a program ends, these streams are closed and their buffers flushed by a destructor.

A destructor has no parameters, not even `void`, and has no return type. A class can have only one destructor. Take, for example, the `Point` class, with a destructor that notifies us when a `Point` has been destroyed. Displaying such a message can useful when debugging programs:

```
class Point {
public:
  ~Point()
  {
    cout << "Point destructor called\n";
  }
  //...
};
```

2.2.9 Composite Classes

When a class contains data members that are themselves class objects, we call it a *composite* class. Before the body of a composite class constructor executes, the individual data members must be constructed, in their order of declaration.

The following `Student` class contains data members of type `Transcript` and `Address`. The default constructors for these objects will be called before `id` and `gradeAverage` are initialized:

```
class Transcript { //... };

class Address { //... };

class Student {
public:
  Student()
  {
    SetId( 0 );
    SetGradeAverage( 0.0 );
  }
  void SetId( long );
  void SetGradeAverage( float );
```

```
private:
    long id;
    Transcript tr;
    Address addr;
    float gradeAverage;
};
```

It should be emphasized here that although a `Student` contains a `Transcript` and `Address`, the `Student` constructor does not have access to the private or protected members of `Transcript` or `Address`.

When a `Student` object goes out of scope, its destructor is called. The body of `~Student` executes before the destructors for the `Transcript` and `Address` members. In other words, the order of destructor calls for composite classes is exactly the opposite of the order of constructor calls.

2.3 EXAMPLE: SPRINGBOARD DIVING SCORES

Most of us have watched the Olympic springboard diving competition at one time or another, perhaps because of the pure drama and grace of the sport. Understandably, the total points awarded for dives are highest for dives with a high judge score and high degree of difficulty. Judge scores range from 0 to 10, in increments of .5, and the degree of difficulty ranges from 1.0 to about 4.0. In the following example, we're going to create a class called `Dive` that holds and calculates diving statistics.

2.3.1 Design

Our program creates and tests a class called `Dive` whose data members are the average judge score and the degree of difficulty. A `Dive` object is able to calculate its total number of points and display itself. The program is divided into three source code files, as is typical of any class: the header contains the `Dive` class definition and inline member functions; the implementation file contains the `Dive` class implementation and the test program contains `main()`. The following table summarizes the files used in this program:

File Usage	Sample Filename
Dive class definition	dive.h
Dive class implementation	dive.cpp
Test program	main.cpp

The class definition is stored in the header. The constructor has two parameters, both of which are assigned to data members: `judgeScore` and `difficulty`. `CalcTotalPoints` calculates the total score for the dive, and the `Display` function displays the dive on the screen:

```
class Dive {
public:
  Dive( float avg, float diff );

  float CalcTotalPoints() const;

  void Display() const;

  void SetDifficulty( float diff );

  void SetJudgeScore( float score );

private:
  float judgeScore;    // average judges score
  float difficulty;    // degree of difficulty
};
```

Two of the functions are const-qualified, meaning that they never modify the current `Dive` object. We explain this type of function in greater detail in Chapter 3.

When designing classes, we always try to keep the interface simple, including only the essential operations. In general, if a class is already implemented in a program, it is much easier to add new member functions than it is to remove functions. Assuming that class users have designed their code around a certain class interface, removing a member function or changing its parameters has a drastic effect on the users' code.

2.3.2 Dive Class Implementation

The complete `Dive` class implementation appears in Example 2-1. Notice that it begins with an *include* directive to insert the header containing the `Dive` class definition. We keep the definition and implementation separate so the header could be `#included` by other program modules, depending on where `Dive` objects are declared. The `Dive` class implementation, on the other hand, is compiled only once, and there can be only one copy of it in a single program.

Another important reason for keeping the header and implementation separate is that class users should not see the source code of the implementation file. If they were to see the source code, they might make programming decisions based on the class implementation. This would be a mistake because a class implementation is always subject to internal changes. An important principle in object-oriented programming is that user code should be unaffected by changes in class implementations. (If the same person happens to be both the creator and user of a class, he/she must pretend not to know about the class implementation when writing user code.)

The constructor receives two arguments that set the averaged judge score and degree of difficulty. Notice that we do not directly reference the data members `judgeScore` and `difficulty`; instead, we call the `SetJudgeScore` and

Example 2-1. The Dive Class Implementation

```
#include "dive.h"

Dive::Dive( float avg, float diff )
{
  SetJudgeScore( avg );
  SetDifficulty( diff );
}

void Dive::Display() const
{
  cout << "[Dive]: "
    << judgeScore << ','
    << difficulty << ','
    << CalcTotalPoints()
    << endl;
}

void Dive::SetDifficulty( float diff )
{
  difficulty = diff;
}

void Dive::SetJudgeScore( float score )
{
  judgeScore = score;
}

float Dive::CalcTotalPoints() const
{
  return judgeScore * difficulty;
}
```

SetDifficulty member functions. This permits validation to be implemented for these data members at a later time:

```
Dive::Dive( float avg, float diff )
{
  SetJudgeScore( avg );
  SetDifficulty( diff );
}
```

The Display member function automatically recalculates the total points for the dive. This relieves the class user from the burden of having to explicitly calculate the total points and ensures that the latest version of the total is always displayed.

2.3.3 Test Program

The main test program creates and initialzes three dives: D1, D2, and D3. It displays each dive, modifies D2, and redisplays the dives:

```cpp
#include "dive.h"

int main()
{
  // Create three Dive objects.
  Dive D1( 8.5, 3.0 );
  Dive D2( 9.0, 2.5 );
  Dive D3( 8.0, 3.3 );


  // Display the Dives.
  D1.Display();
  D2.Display();
  D3.Display();


  D2.SetDifficulty( 3.0 );


  // Display the Dives again.
  cout << "\nChanging Dive 2\n";
  D1.Display();
  D2.Display();
  D3.Display();

  return 0;
}
```

Here is the output from the program, showing the original three dives before and after modifying D2. We can see, for example, that a dive having an average judge's score of 8 with a 3.3 degree of difficulty produces 26.4 points:

```
[Dive]: 8.5,3,25.5
[Dive]: 9,2.5,22.5
[Dive]: 8,3.3,26.4


Changing Dive 2
[Dive]: 8.5,3,25.5
[Dive]: 9,3,27
[Dive]: 8,3.3,26.4
```

Notice also that changing D2 had no effect on the other Dive objects. The data members in each Dive object are separate from those in the other objects.

**PROGRAMMING TIP: VALIDATING CHANGES
TO DATA MEMBERS**

To preserve the internal integrity of an object, it is a good idea to perform range checking before allowing class users to modify data members. Here is a better version of the Dive::SetDifficulty function that permits difficulty levels between 1.0 and 5.0 only:

```
void Dive::SetDifficulty( float diff )
{
  if((diff >= 1.0) && (diff <= 5.0))
    difficulty = diff;
  else
    cerr << "Range error in Dive::SetDifficulty()"
         << " value: " << diff << endl;
}
```

How error conditions are handled is a difficult issue that we will not try to resolve just now. Upon discovering an error, the approach we have taken is to display a message and refuse to modify the data member in question. There is an advanced technique, called *exception handling* (discussed in Chapter 8), that deals with such situations more effectively.

2.4 CLASS MEMBERS

2.4.1 Class Objects

A class object contains a copy of the data members[1] defined in the class, so the data are distinct from all other instances of the same class. Most important, changes made to one instance will not affect other instances. Member functions, on the other hand, are shared by all instances, because it would not be efficient to create duplicate copies of the same functions.

---

[1] The nonstatic data members, which are the only ones we have created so far.

For example, let's create three instances of the `Point` class called P, Q, and R. Each might have different values for x and y, but there would be only one copy of the member functions:

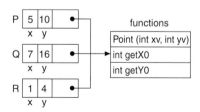

As the diagram shows, the class member functions are accessed through a class object.

2.4.2 Constant Member Functions

A *constant member function* is one that is guaranteed not to modify the state of the current class object. This is very useful, because the class interface clearly indicates which member functions can modify an object, and it allows us to declare const-qualified objects that can be protected against changes. In the `Point` class, for example, the `GetX` member function is declared `const`:

```
class Point {
public:
    Point( int xval, int yval );

    int GetX() const;

    void SetX( int xval );
    //...
};
```

Notice that the `const` keyword must also appear in the function implementation; otherwise, it would not be considered the same function:

```
int Point::GetX() const
{
    return x;
}
```

Constant member functions can be applied to both const-qualified and non-const-qualified objects, as the following example demonstrates:

```
const Point P1(10, 20); // const-qualified
Point P2( 30, 50 );     // non-const-qualified

P1.GetX();
P2.GetX();
```

On the other hand, a non-constant function cannot be applied to a const-qualified object. SetX cannot be called for Point P1, for example, but it can be called for P2, a non-constant object:

```
P1.SetX( 100 );  // error
P2.SetX( 100 );  // ok
```

Constructors and destructors cannot be declared with const. On the other hand, they can be invoked for both non-constant and const-qualified objects.

2.5 TEXT FILE STREAMS

2.5.1 Reading from an Input File Stream

If a program requires more than a minimal amount of input, it is often easier to store the input data in a text file and let the program get its input from there. To that end, let's look at some basic techniques for reading input file streams.

An input stream can easily be read from a text file by declaring an ifstream object and passing a filename to its constructor. This should be followed by a statement that checks the stream variable for a non-zero value indicating that the file was opened successfully. Once a file stream has been opened, it behaves exactly the same as cin, the standard input stream. Both iostream.h and fstream.h must be included when declaring a file stream.

In the following example, infile is an object of type ifstream. We declare the variable and pass a filename to its constructor. The constructor attempts to open the file for input, as follows:

```
ifstream infile("payroll.dat");
```

The following example opens an input file containing an employee ID, number of hours worked, and pay rate:

```
#include <iostream.h>
#include <fstream.h>

int main()
{
  long employeeId;
  int hoursWorked;
  float payRate;
```

```
ifstream infile("payroll.dat");

if( !infile )
  cerr << "Error: cannot open input file.\n";
else
{
  infile >> employeeId
       >> hoursWorked
       >> payRate;
  //...
}
return 0;
}
```

The expression `!infile` calls a function in `infile`'s class that returns 1 if the file is not open. We use the return value from this expression to display an error message and avoid trying to read from the file.

When `infile` is destroyed, the `ifstream` destructor closes the input file. In our example, that happens when `main()` ends. You can explicitly close a file stream by calling the `close` member function:

```
infile.close();
```

A stream can also be opened for input by calling the `open` function and passing the `ios::in` flag as an argument:

```
infile.open("payroll.dat", ios::in );
```

It is necessary to check for end of file using the `eof` function when reading multiple records from a file stream. Assuming that `infile` has already been opened, the following loop reads all of the records:

```
while( !infile.eof() )
{
  infile >> employeeId >> hoursWorked >> payRate;
  //...
}
```

2.5.1.1 Moving the Input File Position.   Every file stream keeps track of its current position within the file. When a file is opened for input, the current position (by default) is at the beginning of the file. You can use the `seekg` stream function to manipulate the input position. This would be useful for reading a specific record in a file with fixed-length records. Suppose we created the following file, where each record was exactly ten bytes long (including the two-byte end of line sequence used by our computer system):

```
10101010
20202020
30303300
44040404
50550505
```

To move to the third record, we would call `seekg` to set the file position at 20 bytes from the beginning of the file, calculated as follows:

```
recordLen = 10;
recNum = 3;
offset = (recNum - 1) * recordLen;


infile.seekg( offset, ios::beg );


char buf[10];
infile.get( buf, 10 );
cout << buf << endl;
```

A word of caution: Random access with text files poses a problem because computer systems vary in the way they implement *newline*. Some use a single character, others use two.

The `offset` argument passed to the `seekg` function can be an offset from the beginning of the input stream, the end of the stream, or from the current position. These options are specified by the following:

```
ios::beg   Offset is from the beginning of the stream
ios::end   Offset is from the end of the stream
ios::cur   Offset is from the current position
```

The offset can be either positive or negative. For example, the following moves the pointer ten bytes prior to the end of the file:

```
infile.seekg( -10, ios::end );
```

The following moves the position backward one byte from the current position:

```
infile.seekg( -1, ios::cur );
```

The `tellg` function returns the current file position. Its return value is of type `streampos`, which is usually a long integer:

```
streampos p = infile.tellg();
```

2.5.2 Writing to an Output File Stream

An output file stream is created in much the same way as an input file stream. To create an output file stream, we must define an ofstream variable and pass it a filename. For example, ofile is opened for output:

```
ofstream ofile( "payroll.dat", ios::out );

if( !ofile )
  cerr << "Error: cannot create output file.\n";
```

The expression !ofile returns 1 if the output stream could not be created. Always test this before writing to the stream.

The following example creates a file called payroll.dat and writes three numbers to it, separated by spaces:

```
#include <iostream.h>
#include <fstream.h>

long employeeId;
float hoursWorked;
float payRate;
ofstream ofile( "payroll.dat", ios::out );

if( !ofile )
  cerr << "Error: cannot create output file.\n";
else
{
  ofile << employeeId  << ' '
        << hoursWorked << ' '
        << payRate << endl;

  //...
}
```

As with input file streams, the output file is automatically closed when the stream variable ofile is destroyed. An output file stream can be explicitly opened with the following statement:

```
ofile.open( "payroll.dat", ios::out );
```

By default, a file stream opened for output destroys any existing file by the same name. Instead, you can open a file in the append mode by using the app flag. If the file exists, your program will append to the file:

```
ofile.open( "payroll.dat", ios::app );
```

No error will be generated if the file does not exist.

2.6 CASE STUDY: STUDENT REGISTRATION

2.6.1 Specifications

We would like to write a program that prints a report showing students registering for college courses. A course is identified by its name, section letter, and the number of credits. The program gets its input from a text file and writes a formatted report to a text file. The first line of the input file contains a student ID number, a semester number, and the number of courses in the file. The semester number is represented by the year (two digits), followed by the semester number (1-3). Here are some sample data with explanations:

```
102234          student ID
962             semester (96/2)
CHM_1020 C 3    section C, 3 credits
MUS_1100 H 1    section H, 1 credit
BIO_1040 D 4    section D, 4 credits
MTH_2400 A 3    section A, 3 credits
```

2.6.2 Analysis

We create a class called `Registration` that encompasses all of the input data, from the student ID and semester number, to the individual courses. We place the individual course information in a second class called `Course`. Both classes are responsible for their own stream I/O. Input and output file streams are used.

2.6.3 Design

The `Registration` class contains an array of `Course` objects, so that all courses taken by one student can be kept together. This creates a composite relationship between `Registration` and `Course`, as shown by the following diagram (the solid circle designates ownership):[1]

---

[1] This diagramming method is loosely based on the "Booch Lite" method [Booch]. We will use it consistently in the case study designs.

The `Course` class contains a default constructor, an `Input` member function to read a `Course` from an input file stream, and an `Output` member function to write a `Course` to a file stream:

```
const unsigned CnameSize = 10;

class Course {
public:
  Course();
  void Input( ifstream & infile );
  void Output( ofstream & ofile ) const;

private:
  char name[CnameSize+1];  // course name
  char section;            // section (letter)
  unsigned credits;        // number of credits
};
```

The `Registration` class contains a default constructor, an `Input` member function to read a `Registration` object from an input file stream, and an `Output` member function to write a `Registration` object to a file stream:

```
const unsigned MaxCourses = 10;

class Registration {
public:
  Registration();
  void Input( ifstream & infile );
  void Output( ofstream & ofile ) const;

private:
  long studentId;        // student ID number
  unsigned semester;     // semester year, number
  unsigned count;        // number of courses
  Course courses[MaxCourses]; // array of courses
};
```

A `Registration` object can contain up to `MaxCourses` courses. The `count` data member indicates the number of courses in the array.

2.6.4 Main Program

The main program, shown in Example 2-2, is the easiest part of the program to write because all of the hard work is done inside the two classes. In `main()` we just

Example 2-2. Main Registration Program

```
#include <iostream.h>
#include <fstream.h>
#include "course.h"

int main()
{
    // Read some Registration objects from one
    // file and append them to another file.

    ifstream infile("rinput.txt");
    if( !infile ) return -1;

    Registration R;
    R.Input( infile );

    ofstream ofile("routput.txt", ios::app );
    if( !ofile ) return -1;

    R.Output( ofile );

    return 0;
}
```

create an input file stream called infile, and a Registration object called R. We also read R from the file stream. Then, we create an output file stream and write R to the file.

To test the program, we create the following input file containing four courses for a single student:

```
102234 962 4
CHM_1020 C 3
MUS_1100 H 1
BIO_1040 D 4
MTH_2400 A 3
```

Here is the output produced by the program:

```
Student ID: 102234
Semester:   962
  Course:   CHM_1020
  Section: C
  Credits: 3
```

```
Course:   MUS_1100
Section:  H
Credits:  1


Course:   BIO_1040
Section:  D
Credits:  4


Course:   MTH_2400
Section:  A
Credits:  3
```

2.6.4.1 Class Implementations.

A complete listing of the `Course` class implementation is found in Example 2-3. The `Input` function in the `Course` class uses the stream input operator to read three data members. To keep this simple, no range checking is performed on the course name. The `Output` function displays the same data, with text labels.

The `Registration::Input` function reads the student ID number, semester numbers and a count of the number of courses. It then uses the count to control a loop that inputs each of the courses taken by the student:

```cpp
void Registration::Input( ifstream & infile )
{
  infile >> studentId >> semester >> count;

  for(unsigned i = 0; i < count; i++)
    courses[i].Input( infile );
}
```

The expression `courses[i].Input(infile)` selects a single `Course` object (element `i` in the `courses` array) and uses it to call the `Course::Input` member function.

Similarly, the `Output` member function displays all data members, including `courses`:

```cpp
void Registration::Output( ofstream & ofile ) const
{
  ofile << "Student ID: " << studentId << '\n'
        << "Semester:   " << semester << endl;

  for(unsigned i = 0; i < count; i++)
    courses[i].Output( ofile );
}
```

Example 2-3. The Course and Registration Class Implementations

```
#include "course.h"

Course::Course()
{
  name[0] = '\0';
}

void Course::Input( ifstream & infile )
{
  infile >> name >> section >> credits;
}

void Course::Output( ofstream & ofile ) const
{
  ofile << "  Course:  " << name << '\n'
        << "  Section: " << section << '\n'
        << "  Credits: " << credits << '\n' << endl;
}

Registration::Registration()
{
  count = 0;
}

void Registration::Input( ifstream & infile )
{
  infile >> studentId >> semester >> count;

  for(unsigned i = 0; i < count; i++)
    courses[i].Input( infile );
}

void Registration::Output( ofstream & ofile ) const
{
  ofile << "Student ID: " << studentId << '\n'
        << "Semester:   " << semester << endl;

  for(unsigned i = 0; i < count; i++)
    courses[i].Output( ofile );
}
```

2.7 CHAPTER SUMMARY

This chapter introduced the fundamentals of defining and using classes. The emphasis was on creating simple, useful classes in this chapter, so that in future chapters we can deal with the more subtle aspects of class design.

An object has three properties: its state, consisting of the current values of its data members; its behavior, implemented as member functions; and, its identity, which makes it distinct from all other instances of the same class.

Object-oriented programs attempt to model real-world problems and applications. Because of this, objects in a program usually have a close correlation to the real-world objects in a certain problem domain.

A *link* relationship exists when a class member function sends messages to an object of another class. A *composition* relationship exists when a class contains data members that are class objects themselves.

Objects in programs hide their details, presenting only an outside view, called an *interface.* An interface is an abstracted or simplified view of an object that is presented to the object's user.

Classes can be given the same rich set of behaviors that characterize C/C++ built-in data types.

A class name whose definition is not nested inside a function or another class has file scope and external linkage. For such a class, the class name defines a type, and objects of that type can be declared anywhere in the same program.

By default, class members are private, meaning that they have class scope and can only be accessed by functions in the same class or by friends of the class. On the other hand, class members that are declared public are accessible from outside the class. Each class member name must be unique within the class scope.

Member functions are categorized as constructors, destructors, operators, selectors, modifiers, and iterators. A *constructor* is a member function that runs automatically whenever a class variable is defined. The compiler automatically generates a default constructor if and only if you have not defined any constructor for the class. A *destructor* is a member function that executes when a class variable is logically deleted. A destructor has no parameters or return type. A class can have only one destructor.

Rarely should a class contain public data members, as this makes it impossible for the class to regulate changes to its own data. Member functions that will only be called from other member functions and friend functions in the same class should be made private.

While a program is in its development and testing phases, some programmers believe that inline functions should be avoided. Runtime efficiency is rarely important until after a program has been thoroughly debugged and tested, at which point, critical areas of code can be optimized to improve runtime efficiency.

2.7.1 Coding Style Suggestions

Most professional programmers adopt a coding style that is consistent and readable to aid themselves and others who must read their code. Here are some suggested style guidelines which you may choose to follow. The following are strong suggestions, which are widely followed:

- Avoid using numeric literals in program code. Instead, use named constants such as

```
const int MaxPoints = 10;
const float HighRange = 3.5;
```

Use `Get` and `Set` prefixes on member functions that get and set the values of data members, e.g. `GetX` and `SetX`.

- Choose function names that clearly express what they do, such as `GetLast-Name`, `SetLastName`, or `CalcGrossPay`. Avoid ambiguous names such as `LastName`, `Calculate`, or `GrossPay`.
- Place constructors and destructors first in the list of class member functions.
- Place comments below member functions in class definitions if they help the reader to understand what the functions do.

The following are suggestions that we *generally* follow:

- Place members in the following order: public first, then protected, then private. If possible, avoid switching back and forth between private and public members, as it makes a class definition harder to read.
- Avoid implementing functions inside a class definition block because it unnecessarily reveals class implementation details in what should be the class interface. In addition, function implementations inside a class definition make the class hard to read.
- Either use underscores to separate words in function names or don't use them. Don't mix styles.
- Either capitalize member function names or don't captialize them. Don't mix styles.
- Place the opening brace for the list of class members on the same line as the class name (some programmers place the brace on a line by itself).

2.8 EXERCISES

2.8.1 Miscellaneous

1 Playing Cards.   Create a class called `Card` that represents a playing card (such as the Ace of Spades). A card value is represented by the integers 2-10, plus

Jack = 11, Queen = 12, and King = 13, and Ace = 14. The suit is represented by an integer (0-3). You may want to declare the following enumerated constants in the class:

```
enum { club, diamond, heart, spade };
enum { Jack=11,Queen=12,King=13,Ace=14 }
```

Include a constructor that initializes a card's data members, a function that displays a card on the screen, a function that inputs a card from the user, and a default constructor. Write a short test program that creates several `Card` objects and calls each of the class member functions. Store the class definition in a header and the class implementation in a module (`.cxx`, `.cpp`, etc.). *Extra:* Display the card name and suit as strings (e.g., "King of Hearts") rather than integers.

2 Integer Stack.   Implement a stack data structure using a class. A stack is called a LIFO (last-in, first out) structure because the last value placed in a stack is the first one to be taken out. Similar to a stack of plates, one always removes the plate at the top of the stack rather than one from the middle or bottom (which could be risky!). Stacks are used in a great many computer applications and are discussed in nearly every intermediate-level programming textbook.

Write a complete implementation of the `Stack` class and write a test program that demonstrates pushing and popping several values onto and from the stack. Do not `Pop()` when the stack is empty, or `Push()` when the stack is full. It is always good practice to implement error-trapping statements in these functions. The `top` data member should be initialized to 0; it is incremented whenever a value is pushed onto the stack, and decremented when a value is popped from the stack. Here is the class definition:

```
class Stack {
public:
  Stack();
  // Default constructor.

  int Empty() const;
  // Return 1 if the stack is empty, 0 if not.

  int Full() const;
  // Return 1 if the stack is full, 0 if not.

  void Push( int item );
  // Push a new value onto the stack.

  int Pop();
  // Pop a value from the stack.
```

```
private:
  enum { StackSize = 40 };
  int top;
  int data[StackSize];
};
```

2.8.2 Student Registration

1 Student Class.   When a college student registers for classes, we must keep track (among other things) of the student's ID number, credits taken, and expected tuition fee. Using the following class definition, create the full implementation and write a short test program that initializes and displays several students on the screen:

```
class Student {
public:
  Student();
  // Default constructor

  Student( long idVal, unsigned nCredits );
  // Construct Student from id, credits.

  long GetId() const;
  // Return the ID number.

  unsigned Credits() const;
  // Return the credits.

  float Tuition() const;
  // Return the tuition amount.

private:
  long  id;          // student ID
  unsigned credits;  // registered credits
  float tuition;     // tuition due
};

const float TuitionRate = 60.0;
```

The tuition must be recalculated whenever the `credits` data member changes, i.e., multiply the `TuitionRate` constant by the number of credits.

2 Student Class Modifications.   Using the `Student` class from the previous exercise, add a `Display` member function that displays a `Student` on the screen with appropriate labels, such as

```
Id:      200021
Credits: 15
Tuition: 900
```

Add an `Input` member function that lets the user enter a student ID and number of credits from the screen. Write a short test program that demonstrates the `Input` and `Display` functions.

2.8.3 Office Supply Store

All of the exercises in this section relate to a program that manages a simple inventory for an office supply store. The program is designed to be built in stages. You may choose to complete only some of the following exercises, but be aware that some depend upon the completion of others. Exercise 2, for example, depends upon the completion of Exercise 1. The dependencies (using exercise numbers) are as follows:

```
1 <- 2
3 <- 4
5 <- 6 -> 7 -> 8 -> 9
```

1 The Product Class. Create a class called `Product` that represents a single product sold by an office supply store. It should contain the following data members:

```
long id;        // 5-digit product ID number
long manufId;   // 4-digit manufacturer's ID
float price;    // wholesale price
float markup;   // markup from wholesale, .nn
```

The class should contain a default constructor, a constructor that initializes all data members, const-qualified functions that return the values of data members, a function that displays a `Product` on the screen, and a function called `RetailPrice` that returns the `Product`'s price increased by the markup percentage. Write a short test program that creates and displays several `Product` objects.

2 Reading Products from a File. Add a member function to the `Product` class (from the previous exercise) that reads a product from an input file stream. Let the function parameter be a reference to a file stream. Write a test program that reads the following data from a file and uses it to initialize Product objects. The latter are displayed on the screen:

(id, manuf, price, markup)

```
10001 5001  15.00 .20
10002 5020   5.00 .25
10003 5005  35.50 .15
10004 5001   2.00 .22
10005 5001   7.00 .23
```

```
10006 5020   22.75 .18
10007 5030   75.00 .19
10008 5005  120.00 .15
10009 5030    4.50 .30
10010 5030     .40 .50
```

3 The Manufacturer Class.   Create a class for the office supply application called Manufacturer, which represents the company that makes a product sold by the store. It should contain the following data members:

```
long id;          // 4-digit ID number, unique
char name[30];    // name of manufacturer
char phone[15];   // manufacturer phone number
```

The class should contain a default constructor, a constructor that initializes all data members, const-qualified functions that return the values of data members, and a function that displays a manufacturer on the screen. Write a short test program that creates and displays several manufacturers.

4 Reading Manufacturers from a File.   Add a member function to the Manufacturer class (from the previous exercise) that reads a manufacturer from an input file stream. Let the function parameter be a reference to an ifstream object. Write a test program that reads the following records from a file and displays them on the screen:

(id, name, phone)

```
5001 Shawm_Office_Products 301-232-4099
5005 ABC_Enterprises       204-353-2110
5010 Zemco_Products        901-200-4021
5020 Balboa_Manufacturing  907-421-2020
5030 Ziekel_Millston       808-721-8033
```

Notice that we have connected the names with underscores between words. This is just a convenience to make it possible for you to read them from a file with the stream input (>>) operator.

5 The Inventory Class.   Create a class for the office supply application called Inventory, which represents the stock of products currently on hand. Each Product contains the following data members:

```
long productID;        // ID number of product
unsigned quantity;     // quantity on hand
```

The class should contain a default constructor, a constructor that initializes all data members, constant member functions that return the values of data members, and a function that displays an `Inventory` object on the screen. Write a short test program that creates and displays several `Inventory` objects.

6 Reading Inventory from a File.   Add a member function to the `Inventory` class (from the previous exercise) that reads an `Inventory` object from an input file stream. Write a test program that reads the following records from a file and displays them on the screen:

(id, quantity)

```
10001 150
10002 200
10003  18
10004  80
10005  42
10006 120
10007  22
10008  10
10009 100
10010 500
```

7 Displaying Product Information.   Enhance the previous exercise by writing a program that displays the quantity, manufacturer's ID, and price for each product in the store's inventory. As you probably noticed, each `productID` in the Inventory File (Exercise 6) matches one of the `productID` values from the Product File (Exercise 2). Produce an attractively formatted report with headings. As each `productID` is read from the Inventory File, you may want to reopen the Product File and scan the records sequentially until a matching `productID` is found.

8 Displaying Manufacturer Information.   Enhance the previous exercise by writing a program that also displays the manufacturer's name and phone number next to the `productID`, `quantity`, and `price`. Produce an attractively formatted report with headings.

9 Using Arrays to Look Up Information.   Re-implement the previous two exercises by loading the Product File and Manufacturer File into two separate arrays. Then, read each record from the Inventory File and use the arrays to look up related information for each product.

CHAPTER *3*

Functions

In this chapter, we focus on the process of defining and calling functions, with special emphasis on the features that make C++ different from C. Function overloading and argument conversions help to build a foundation for more sophisticated use of classes in future chapters. We show how to define stream I/O operators for classes and how to format numeric data for streams. Finally, we improve the Student Registration application from the previous chapter by adding new C++ features.

Terms Introduced in this Chapter:

compilation unit

default argument initializers

default arguments

delimiter

function name encoding

function overloading

internal linkage

modifiable lvalue

module

name mangling

parameterized manipulator

postcondition

precondition

recursion

reference parameter

signature

streammable class

string stream

this

type-safe linkage

3.1 GENERAL COMMENTS

When the return type of a function is not specified, it defaults to `int`. It is considered poor style, however, to omit the return type. The following are equivalent:

```
f( void );
int f( void );
```

The `void` keyword indicates that a function has no parameters, as does a declaration containing no parameters. The following declarations, in other words, are equivalent:

```
int f();
int f(void);
```

Leaving out the return type and omitting `void` changes the meaning of a function declaration to a function call:

```
f();
```

A function *signature* consists of a function's name along with the types of its parameters. It does not include the function's return type. C++ uses function signatures to differentiate functions with the same name but different parameter lists.

3.1.1 Internal and External Linkage

A program can be thought of as a collection of separate modules, or *compilation units* linked together. A *module* consists of one or more source files that are compiled together. When a function in one module is called from another module, the function must have *external linkage.* By default, names of functions and variables are external. The calling module must be given information about the function name and parameter types. This is usually accomplished by including a header containing the function's prototype:

In module1:

```
int sum( int a, int b )
{
   return a+b;
}
```

In module2:

```
int sum( int, int );  // function prototype
//...
int n = sum( 5, 2 );
```

The `static` keyword assigns *internal linkage* to a name, thus making it hidden inside a module. A function with internal linkage cannot be called directly by name from another module. In the following example, we hide the `sum` function inside `module1` and declare a variable by the same name in `module2`:

In module1:

```
// function definition
static int sum( int a, int b ) { return a+b; }
```

In module2:

```
// variable definition
float sum = 0.0;
```

3.1.2 Function Name Encoding

The C++ compiler creates unique names out of functions that have identical names but different parameters. This technique is called *function name encoding* (or *name mangling)*, whereby the C++ compiler alters the name of each instance of the function by encoding the function's signature as a string and attaching it to the function name. Hypothetically, two global functions called `sum` might be encoded as follows:

Function prototypes:

```
int sum( int x, int y );
int sum( float g, float h );
```

Encoded as:

```
sum__Fii
sum__Fff
```

The main reason for having function name encoding is to provide *type-safe linkage*, a method of checking all function calls against their corresponding function signatures. This prevents one from inadvertently calling a function with the wrong arguments.

A function encoding method suggested in [ARM] is used here: A function name is followed by two underscores, followed by the encoded information. A global function is identified by `'F'`, an integer parameter is encoded as `'i'`, and a float parameter is encoded with `'f'`. The actual encoding scheme varies from one implementation to another, so this is just a sample.

Notice that the function's return type, not being part of the signature, is not encoded. This makes it possible for two functions in different modules with identical signatures to have different return types, an error which the linker cannot catch:

In module1:

```
extern int fred();
```

In module2:

```
float fred() { return 1.0; }
```

3.2 FUNCTION PARAMETERS

3.2.1 Preconditions and Postconditions

An important tool for creating reliable programs is to clearly state input requirements for function arguments. We can predict what a function will do if and only if all function *preconditions* are satisfied. Conversely, a *postcondition* is a statement about what the function does, given that all preconditions are satisfied.

For example, we might state that a function called `drawRectangle` works properly only when it is passed valid arguments for `row` and `col`. Assuming that we have declared constants for the minimum and maximum argument values, we can state the following preconditions:

```
void drawRectangle( int row, int col );

// Requires: row is between MinRow and MaxRow
//           col is between MinCol and MaxCol
```

But, it is not clear how these requirements will be enforced. Source code comments can easily be ignored, and can become obsolete due to changes in the program.

An easy way to enforce the stated requirements is to use the standard assert macro that tests function arguments for correct values. This macro, defined in `assert.h`, evaluates its argument and halts the program if the result equals zero:

```
#include <assert.h>

enum { MinRow = 0, MaxRow = 24,
       MinCol = 0, MaxCol = 79 };
```

```
void drawRectangle( int row, int col )
{
  assert( row >= MinRow && row <= MaxRow );
  assert( col >= MinCol && col <= MaxCol );
  //...
}
```

If `assert` halts a program, it displays the current source file name, line number, and the expression that failed. This is particularly helpful during program development and testing to identify and correct the conditions that led to the failure. When the program is ready to be fine-tuned for performance, the code generated by `assert` can be removed from the compiled program. To do this, place the following definition in the source file just before the line that includes `assert.h`:

```
#define NDEBUG
```

A frequent use of `assert` is to check the range of array subscripts. For example,

```
assert( index >= 0 && index < ArrayMax );
array[index] = 0;
```

A serious drawback to using `assert` is that it aborts a program without providing a graceful exit. Files may be left open, memory allocated, database transactions incomplete, and so on. To some extent, the host operating system will take care of memory cleanup, but data may still be lost, particularly when output file buffering is in effect.

In Chapter 8 we will introduce exception handling, a recent addition to the C++ language that is a major improvement over `assert`. In the meantime, `assert` is the best tool we have for validating function arguments, array subscripts, and other values that would cause programs to corrupt data or behave in undefined ways.

3.2.2 Reference Parameters

By default, arguments are passed to functions by *value*. In general, this protects passed arguments from undesirable side effects. It is important for us to know that after a function returns, variables that were passed as arguments are unchanged.

If a parameter is going to be modified, it should be a *reference parameter*, identified by an ampersand (&) preceding the parameter's name. For example, we pass a `Student` reference to `UserInput`, allowing new values to be stored in its data members:

```
void UserInput( Student & S )
{
  cout << "Student ID? ";
  long n;
```

```
                              cin >> n;
                              S.SetID( n );
                              //...
                          }

                          Student temp;
                          UserInput( temp );
```

A function argument passed by reference must be what we call a *modifiable lvalue*, which is an object that is updatable and could appear on the left-hand side of an assignment statement (as in $x = y + z$;). For example, the following call to `locate` is invalid because the expression arguments are not modifiable lvalues:

```
        void locate( int & row, int & col );  // prototype
        //...

        locate( x+2, y-4 );  // error
```

The following call to `UserInput` is invalid because the temporary `Student` object being passed to the function is automatically const-qualified:

```
                    UserInput( Student(temp) );
```

If a class object is passed by value, the parameter becomes a temporary copy of the passed argument. This causes the class's default constructor to execute. When the function ends, the temporary object's destructor is executed. All of this uses up valuable time and storage. Therefore, class objects are usually passed by reference.

3.2.3 Constant Parameters

Reference and pointer parameters should be const-qualified whenever possible to prevent their being inadvertently modified by a called function. For example, the `Student` reference passed to `CalcTuition` is guaranteed not to be modified:

```
            void CalcTuition( const Student & S );
```

Similarly, the pointer to `Student` parameter in `CalcGradeAverage` guarantees that the `Student` object addressed by the pointer will not be modified:

```
        float CalcGradeAverage( const Student * sp );
```

The `const` qualifier can also be valuable when the argument passed to a function might be either a variable or an expression. For example, the following `Display` function has a non-constant reference parameter; this prevents the expression $5 + x$ from being passed to the function:

```
void Display( int & n );
void Display2( const int & n );


//...
Display( 5 + x );    // error
Display2( 5 + x );   // ok
```

On the other hand, if a parameter is const-qualified, the argument can be an expression.

For parameters already passed by value, using `const` is redundant and should be avoided, as in the following example:

```
void Display( const int n );
```

3.2.3.1 Argument Conversions.
There is no standard implicit conversion in C++ from a constant to a non-constant. A function having a non-constant reference parameter, for example, cannot accept a constant argument. The following call to `UpdateCredits` is invalid:

```
void UpdateCredits( Student & aStudent );
//...
const Student S(111111);
UpdateCredits( S );               // invalid
```

Never cast away the constant property of an object, because this defeats the purpose of using `const`. The object might also be stored in read-only memory, and attempting to modify it could cause a runtime error. The following is an example of what not to do:

```
const Student S(111111);
UpdateCredits( (Student &)S );  // poor style!
```

On the other hand, we often pass a non-constant object to a function having a constant reference parameter. In the following example, this simply assures us that the function will not modify the `Student` object:

```
void ProcessEnrollment( const Student & aStudent );
//...
Student S(111111);
ProcessEnrollment( S );
```

3.2.4 Default Arguments

Default arguments (or *default argument initializers*) can be supplied for all or some of the parameters in a function declaration. Here, for example, the `Point` constructor has default arguments:

```
class Point {
public:
  Point( int xval = 0, int yval = 0 );
  //...
};

Point::Point( int xval, int yval )
{
  x = xval;
  y = yval;
}
```

When a function is called and one or more arguments are missing, the compiler inserts default values for those arguments. For example, if we call the `Point` constructor with no arguments, the x and y data members are automatically set to 0:

```
Point P;
```

Or, if we supply only the first argument, the second will default to 0:

```
Point P(10);   // P.x == 10, P.y == 0
```

One thing we cannot do is omit the first argument and try to pass the second:

```
Point P( ,10);  // invalid
```

Also, any parameters following one with a default argument must also have default arguments. That is why the following declaration of the `Point` constructor would be invalid:

```
Point( int xval = 0, int yval );
```

3.2.4.1 Window Class Example.

Many programs and user interface libraries contain a `Window` class that assists a program in drawing a text or graphical window. The following constructor contains parameters to set the x and y coordinates of the window:

```
class Window {
public:
  Window( int x, int y );
  // (etc.)
```

At some point, we might decide to improve the class interface by adding two new parameters for setting the window frame and color. We would prefer not to force all programs already using the class to modify their calls to the constructor, so

we could supply default arguments for the new parameters. This would provide a
smooth way to integrate the new function parameters into the class interface:

```
enum { white, blue, red, green };

class Window {
public:
  Window( int x, int y,
               int color = blue,
               int frame = white );
private:
  int xPos;
  int yPos;
  int insideColor;
  int frameColor;
};
```

If the function declaration and implementation are separate, the default arguments
do not appear in the implementation:

```
Window::Window( int x, int y,
                  int color, int frame )
{
  xPos = x;
  yPos = y;
  insideColor = color;
  frameColor = frame;
}
```

The `Window` constructor can now be called with varying numbers of arguments:

```
int main()
{
  Window W1( 10, 20 );
  Window W2( 10, 20, green );
  Window W3( 10, 20, green, red );
  return 0;
}
```

Once an argument is skipped, all remaining arguments must be skipped. The following, for example, would be invalid:

```
Window W3( 10, 20, , red );
```

3.2.5 Functions That Return References

C++ functions can return references to either intrinsic types or class objects. Member functions, for example, often return constant references to class data members.

The use of the `const` keyword prevents the caller from indirectly modifying the data member. For example, a user of the `Student` class may need to access the `transcr` data member. `GetTranscript` returns a constant reference to `transcr`, which is then used to call `Transcript::Print`:

```
class Transcript {
public:
  void Erase();
  void Print() const;
  //...
};

class Student {
public:
  const Transcript & GetTranscript();
  //...
private:
  Transcript transcr;
  //...
};

Student S;
S.GetTranscript().Print();
```

`Print` is a constant function, which guarantees that it will not alter the state of a `Transcript` object. Because of this, it can be called for either a constant or non-constant object.

Never return a non-constant reference to a private data member. That would allow the caller to write directly to the member, effectively piercing the layer of data protection that is so fundamental to object-oriented programming. For example, if `GetTranscript` were to return a non-constant reference,

```
class Student {
public:
  Transcript & GetTranscript();
  //...
};
```

a caller could use `T` (the `Transcript` reference) to erase the student's transcript. Note that `Erase` is a non-constant function, which cannot be called for a constant object:

```
Student aStudent;
//...
Transcript & T = aStudent.GetTranscript();
//...
T.Erase();  // erase aStudent's transcript
```

If it really were necessary to erase a student's transcript, a member function such as EraseTranscript could be added to the Student class.

A word of warning: Never return a reference to an automatic object, because after the object is destroyed, any references to it will be invalid. The following example shows this:

```
int & BadExample()
{
   int n = 20;
   //...
   return n;
}

int & Z = BadExample();
Z = 10;                 // int doesn't exist
```

3.2.5.1 *Self-Referencing with* This.   Within a member function, the keyword this is the name of an implicit pointer to the current object. The latter is the object through which the function was invoked. If, for example, we declare a point P and call Point::Set, P is the object associated with the function:

```
Point P;
P.Set( 100, 200 );
```

Internally, a member function locates the data for the current object through the this pointer. It is sometimes useful to dereference this in order to return a reference to the current object. For example, if Point::Set returns a reference to a Point, we can use the reference to call the Draw function:

```
P.Set(100,200).Draw();
```

This is how Point::Set would be implemented:

```
Point & Point::Set( int xVal, int yVal )
{
   x = xVal;
   y = yVal;
   return *this;
}
```

The Set function cannot return the value of this because the latter is a pointer. Instead, we must dereference the pointer to get a reference to the current object.

3.3 FRIENDS

3.3.1 Friend Functions

Sometimes a function not belonging to a certain class requires access to the class's private and protected members. The function might be a global function or it might be a member of some other class. Usually the function requiring private access is a helper function of some sort, providing additional functionality to the class. Using `friend`, a class grants member access to a specific function. But, a function cannot declare itself a friend of another class; the class must declare who its friends are. This is necessary because the function prototype becomes part of the class's interface and other users of the class can see who has direct access to the class.

For example, we present two classes, `Student` and `Employee`. A global function called `HireStudent` sets the employment status of a `Student`, and at the same time, updates pay rate information in a separate `Employee` object. For this example, we will assume that we do not want `HireStudent` to be a `Student` member function:

```
void HireStudent( Student & S, Employee & E, float rate )
{
  S.employed = 1;
  E.payRate = rate;
}
```

The `Student` class contains a student ID number and a flag indicating whether the student is employed. The `Employee` class contains an ID number and an hourly pay rate:

```
class Student;   // forward declaration

class Employee {
public:
  Employee( long idVal );
  friend void HireStudent( Student & S,
          Employee & E, float rate );

private:
  long id;          // ID number
  float payRate;    // pay rate
};

class Student {
public:
  Student( long idVal );
  friend void HireStudent( Student & S,
          Employee & E, float rate );
```

```
private:
   long id;            // ID number
   int employed;       // 1 = true, 0 = false
};
```

Notice that we had to forward-declare the `Student` class so that the `HireStudent` declaration in the `Employee` class would be accepted by the compiler.

Why not provide public member functions such as `SetEmployed` and `SetPayRate` to allow `HireStudent` to modify each class's private data members? We might not want to provide these member functions, because they would become part of the class interfaces. Any user of these classes would be able to call the functions.

Finally, it should be mentioned that friend functions are rarely necessary and are not allowed in some OOP languages. While friend functions appear to be a convenience, they circumvent the protection provided by the `private` and `protected` specifiers. A friend should be used only when it is not practical to use a class member function.

3.3.2 Friend Classes

A *friend class* is a class in which all member functions have been granted full access to the private and protected members of another class. The friend class is declared inside the class granting friendship:

```
class class-1 {
   friend class-2;
   //...
};

class class-2 {
   friend class-3;
   //...
};
```

Friend status among classes is not transitive. That is why `class-3` is not automatically a friend of `class-1`. Of course, `class-1` could explicitly grant friendship to `class-3`, but we haven't done that here.

Declaring a friend class creates a close coupling between two classes. Ordinarily, we prefer loosely coupled classes so that internal modifications to a class do not have a cascading effect on the implementations of other classes. But there are occasions when programmers require more direct access to class members, possibly for reasons of runtime efficiency. It would be possible, of course, to select only certain functions from a class to be friend functions, but that would force the class granting friendship to know the name and parameter types of every function in the class that requires friend status.

3.4 FUNCTION OVERLOADING

3.4.1 Definition

Function overloading makes it possible for multiple functions to have the same name. A major advantage of this feature is that we don't have to invent unique names for different functions that essentially do the same thing. In sorting applications, for example, we often use a function to exchange the values of two objects. The following `swap` function is overloaded to work with different argument types:

```
void swap( unsigned long &, unsigned long & );
void swap( double &, double & );
void swap( char *, char * );
void swap( Point &, Point & );
```

Function overloading allows the same function name to be re-used, as long as each function has a different signature. Recall that a *signature* consists of a function's name, as well as the order and type of its parameters. It does not, however, include the function's return type. Therefore, two overloaded functions with the same signature cannot vary *only* in their return types.

A poor use of function overloading occurs when multiple functions have the same name but perform different operations. For example, using the same function name to both set and return the value of a data member is an all-too-common, poor practice:

```
class Student {
public:
   unsigned credits();
   // Get the number of credits.

   void credits( unsigned n );
   // Set the number of credits.

   //...
};
```

A much better way to do this is to use different names for different operations:

```
unsigned GetCredits();
// Get the number of credits.

void SetCredits( unsigned n );
// Set the number of credits.
```

3.4.1.1 Overloading Constructors. The most common use of function overloading is for class constructors, to provide alternate ways of constructing ob-

jects. The `Figure` class contains a default constructor, a constructor taking a single `Point`, and a constructor taking an array of `Point` objects and a counter:

```
class Point {
public:
  Point( int x = 0, int y = 0 );
  //...
};

class Figure {
public:
  Figure();
  Figure( const Point & center );
  Figure( const Point vertices[], int count );
  //...
};
```

These constructors allow one to create an array of Figures, a `Figure` specified by its center point, and a `Figure` specified by an array of vertices:

```
Figure fig1[50];
Point center( 25, 50 );
Figure fig2( center );

const int VCount = 5;
Point verts[VCount];
Figure fig3( verts, VCount );
```

Note that the `Point` class does not require an overloaded constructor; it simply uses default arguments to optionally receive the x and y coordinates. But, default arguments could not have helped us in the `Figure` class constructor, where objects were passed by reference.

3.4.1.2 istream Example.
Another way that a member function might be overloaded is when two functions provide the same basic operation, with variations in the parameter lists. For example, in the standard `istream` class, the `get` member function provides four different versions of single-character input:

```
istream & get( char &);
istream & get( signed char & );
istream & get( unsigned char & );
int get();
```

This gives the class user some flexibility in how the `get` function may be called. The following function calls demonstrate the different versions of `get`:

```
char ch;
signed char sch;
unsigned char uch;

cin.get( ch );
cin.get( sch );
cin.get( uch );
ch = cin.get();
```

3.4.2 Argument Conversion

Sometimes a function will be called with argument types that are different from its parameter types. As long as the types are assignment-compatible, arguments can be converted. For example, an `int` passed to a function containing a `long` parameter will be promoted to a `long`. Conversely, a `long` passed to a function expecting an `int` will be converted to `int`, possibly losing significant digits.

In the next example, the `calculate` function is passed a `long`, `int`, `double`, and a `float`. The second argument is converted to a `long`, and the fourth argument is converted to a `double`:

```
void calculate( long p1, long p2, double p3, double p4 );
//...

long a1 = 12345678L;
int a2 = 1;
double a3 = 2.5234323441;
float a4 = 3.1;

calculate( a1, a2, a3, a4 );
```

If no function exists with assignment-compatible parameters, the compiler reports an error. This would be the case for the following call to `calculate`, where a `Student` cannot be converted to a `long`:

```
Student S;
//...
calculate( S, 10, 5.5, 6 );
```

3.4.3 Overloading Resolution

In general, the C++ compiler is able to differentiate between overloaded functions by their parameter types. It will try to find a function whose parameter list best matches the actual arguments. This is informally called the *best-matching function* principle: For each actual argument, the compiler finds the set of all functions that best match the parameter. If the intersection of these sets yields a single function, it is selected for the call. If more than one function results from the intersection, an error results. As the ARM says, "The function thus selected must be a strictly better match for at least one argument than every other possible function (but not necessarily the same argument for each function)."[ARM]

In the next example, the first two calls to the display function easily resolve to a single choice for each call because the arguments match exactly. But the third call does not match and requires an implicit conversion from either double to int or double to float; it is ambiguous and will not compile:

```
void display( int x );     // version 1
void display( float f );   // version 2
.
.
.
int i;
float f;
double d;

display( i );  // version 1
display( f );  // version 2
display( d );  // error: ambiguous
```

The situation is tricky when two or more arguments are involved. The compiler creates a list of all functions matching the first argument, another list of all functions matching the second argument, and so on. The intersection of these lists must be a single function, or a syntax error will result. Consider, for example, the following overloaded print functions, labeled Version 1 and Version 2:

Version 1:

```
void print( float a, float b )
{
  cout << "version 1" << endl;
}
```

Version 2:

```
void print( float a, int b )
{
  cout << "version 2" << endl;
}
```

If we pass two integers to print, the first argument matches both Versions and 2; but the second argument forms a best match with Version 2. Similarly, calling print with arguments of type (int, float) results in an exact match for the second argument, and Version 1 of print is called:

```
int i, j;
float f;
double d;

print( i, j );  // int, int - version 2
print( i, f );  // int, float - version 1
print( d, f );  // double, float - version 1
```

Calling `print` with arguments (`double`, `float`) matches Version 1 of `print`; the first argument is ambiguous, but the second is an exact match.

Problems occur, however, when all arguments require conversion. The following calls to `print` are ambiguous and will not compile:

```
int i;
float f;
double d;

print( i, 10L ); // int, long
print( f, 10L ); // float, long
print( d, 3.0 ); // double, double
print( i, d );   // int, double
```

These errors can be corrected by simply casting one or more of the actual arguments into an exact match. For example,

```
print( i, int(10L) );    // int, int
print( f, float(10L) );  // float, float
print( d, float(3.0) );  // double, float
print( i, int(d) );      // int, int
```

3.5 BETTER STREAM I/O

3.5.1 String Input

3.5.1.1 The istream::get() and getline() Functions. There is a problem when using the stream input operator (>>) to input a string: If too many characters are read before the first whitespace is found, memory following the string can be corrupted. To avoid this problem, we introduced the `get` function in Chapter 1, showing how it reads a single input character:

```
char ch = cin.get();
cin.get( ch );          // alternate format
```

The `get` function is overloaded, and one of its forms is set up to read a block of characters and stop when a chosen delimiter character is encountered. The format is

```
istream & get( char * buf, int len, char delim = '\n' );
```

The get function extracts characters from an input stream and copies them to buf. It does not skip whitespace. Characters are extracted until (len - 1) characters have been read, or until the chosen delimiter character has been read. Any remaining characters (including the delimiter) are left in the input stream, and will be picked up by subsequent calls to get. The first parameter, buf, can also be a signed char * or an unsigned char * type. The input stream is returned as the function result. For example, we can read user input into a variable called name, stopping when a newline character is found or when 29 characters have been read:

```
char name[30];
cin.get( name, sizeof(name));
```

In our example, the get function will automatically append \0 to name and leave \n in the input stream. This causes a problem if we don't remove the \n before the next attempt to read a name; in that case, we would simply read an empty string. A simple way to remove the \n is to call the ignore function:

```
char name[30];
char address[50];

cin.get( name, sizeof(name));
cin.ignore( 255, '\n' );

cin.get( address, sizeof(address));
cin.ignore( 255, '\n' );
```

The first argument passed to ignore can be any unsigned integer, as long as it is greater than the number of excess characters you think the user might enter.

Programs generally need to handle excess input gracefully. One way to do this is to input a string, get the next character, and if it is not \n, notify the user that an error has occurred, clear the input buffer, and ask for more input. This is what happens in the next example if the user enters a name that is too long:

```
char name[30];

while(1)
{
  cout << "Enter a name: ";
  cin.get( buf, 30, '\n' );

  if( cin.get() == '\n' )
    break;
  else
  {
```

```
          cout << "excess input!" << endl;
          cin.ignore( 1000, '\n' );
      }
   }
```

The getline function is similar to get, except that it removes the trailing \n from the input stream. The next call to getline will begin reading characters on the following line.

Be careful when mixing the >> operator with the get or getline functions. The >> operator leaves the trailing \n character typed by the user in the input stream. This is a problem if we follow it with a call to getline, because the latter does *not* skip leading whitespace and will think that the input has already been completed. For example, the program will not wait for the user to enter a name because of the \n left over from the first input:

```
          cout << "Enter your age: ";
          cin >> age;
          cout << "Enter your name: ";
          cin.getline( name, 30 );
```

Many events can occur between any two stream input statements, making it particularly difficult to debug this type of error. We suggest placing responsibility for cleaning up the input buffer with the statement that messed it up in the first place. Here, we call ignore right after the first input, which ignores as many as ten excess characters and removes \n from the input stream:

```
          cout << "Enter your age: ";
          cin >> age;
          cin.ignore(10,'\n');
```

3.5.1.2 Example: The getYN() Function.

The following function, called getYN, displays a prompt string on the console, waits for the user to press Y or N (upper-case or lower-case), and returns true when Y is pressed, or false otherwise.

```
          #include <ctype.h>
          #include <iostream.h>

          enum bool { false, true };

          bool getYN( const char * st )
          {
            char ch;
            cout << st << " [Y/n]: ";
            cin >> ch;
            cin.ignore( 80,'\n' );
```

```
if( toupper(ch) == 'Y' )
    return true;
return false;
}
```

The `ctype.h` header is required because we call the standard `toupper` function that converts a character to upper-case. The following is a sample function call:

```
if( getYN("Do you want to continue?"))
{
  //...
}
```

3.5.1.3 Improving Stream Input Error Detection.
An input stream enters an error state when the input does not conform to the data type being input. The stream becomes corrupted so that further input is nearly impossible. It is a good idea to check the state of an input stream by calling `ios::good`, which returns 1 if no errors have occurred[1]. For example, the following program fragment fails if the user types in characters rather than numbers. A runtime error may occur (such as *invalid floating point*), or some of the variables may contain zeros:

```
#include <iostream.h>

int i;
float r;
long n;

// Try entering invalid input
// and watch the program fail.

cin >> i >> r >> n;
cout << "i = " << i << '\n'
     << "r = " << r << '\n'
     << "n = " << n << '\n'
     << "cin.good() = " << cin.good() << endl;
```

In any case, if the user mistypes the data, the final call to `cin.good` returns 0. Because of the likelihood of such errors, many programmers prefer to read each line into a character buffer, and then process the buffer manually. In the next section, we show you how to use a string stream to accomplish this.

3.5.1.4 String Streams.
A *string stream* is a stream that is tied to a character buffer rather than an input-output device. We can still use formatting func-

---

[1] In the 1995 draft, `ios::good ()` returns the new keyword `true`, of the new `bool` type.

tions and overloaded operators with string streams. For input, we declare an `istrstream` object, and for output, an `ostrstream` object. Both require inclusion of the `strstream.h` header. In the following example, the input string stream called `inp` will take its input from `buf` rather than the console. After the final statement, i = 10, j = 35, and k = 40:

```
int i,j,k;
char buf[80] = "10 35 40";
istrstream inp( buf, 80 );

inp >> i >> j >> k;
```

The following program fragment prompts the user for three numbers, copies the input to a character buffer, creates a string stream, extracts the numbers, checks for errors, reports the stream status, and displays the variables holding the numbers. If the user makes mistakes, the program identifies the bad input without leaving `cin` in a corrupted state:

```
#include <iostream.h>
#include <strstream.h>  2

int i;
float r;
long n;
char buf[80];

int k;
for(k = 0; k < 3; k++)
{
    cout << "Enter an integer, float, and long: ";
    cin.getline( buf, 80 );
    istrstream inp( buf, 80 );

    inp >> i;
    if(!inp.good()) cout << "Error in first item\n";

    inp >> r;
    if(!inp.good()) cout << "Error in second item\n";

    inp >> n;
    if(!inp.good()) cout << "Error in third item\n";

    cout << i << ',' << r << ',' << n << endl;
}
```

[2] DOS systems only allow filenames of 1-8 characters, so the extra character in the first part of the filename is ignored.

An `ostrstream` object is useful for creating a formatted string, because it takes advantage of the built-in number formatting capabilities of ouptut streams. The following statements create an output stream called `out`, consisting of strings and numbers. The output is written to a character array, including `ends`, a standard identifier for the `'\0'` character:

```
int k = 10;
float r = 2.5;
long n = 30303;
char buf[80];      // character array

ostrstream out( buf, 80 );
out << "k = " << k << ", r = " << r
    << ", n = " << n << '\n' << ends;

cout << buf;   // display the buffer
```

3.5.1.5 *Reading a Delimited String.*   Text files often contain records with a special character between the individual fields. The character, called a *delimiter*, can be a comma, semicolon, slash (/), or any other character that is not found in the fields themselves. Here, for example, is a comma-delimited record (from a file) containing an ID number, last name, and first name:

```
10221,Smith,John
```

An effective way to separate delimited records is to call `istream::get`. By passing it a string variable, a length count, and a delimiter character, we can tell it to input characters until the delimiter is found in the input stream. For example, the following statements open a file stream and read the ID number and a comma. The second argument passed to the `get` function limits the maximum characters that can be read:

```
char ch;
char id[10];
char lastName[30];
char firstName[20];

ifstream input("sample.txt");  // open a file
input.get( id, 10, ',' );      // get id
input.get( ch );               // skip the comma
```

We can do the same for the last and first names, remembering that the first name has no trailing comma:

```
input.get( lastName, 30, ',' );   // get last name
input.get(ch);
input.get( firstName, 20, '\n' ); // get first name
input.get( ch );
```

3.5.2 Stream Manipulators

Stream manipulators are stream member functions that affect the format of data read from and printed to streams. Stream manipulators recognize the << and >> operators, so they can be placed in stream input and output expressions.

The dec, hex, and oct manipulators affect the format of integer stream I/O. The name of the manipulator is inserted in the stream using the << operator for an output stream, and >> for an input stream. The manipulators are *persistent*, meaning that they remain in effect until changed by the program.

3.5.2.1 Stream Input. By default, the leading digit determines the format of an integer input from a stream. A leading digit of 1-9 causes a number to have a decimal radix; a leading 0 implies an octal radix; and, a leading "0x" implies a hexadecimal radix. For example, if we execute the following statements and enter "8", the same number is echoed.

```
int n;
cin >> n;
cout << n;
```

But if we entered "08", the output would be 0; 8 is not a valid octal digit, so the input stream would stop reading after the 0.

If we inserted a dec mainpulator in the stream and tried again, the number would be recognized as decimal 8:

```
int n;
cin >> dec >> n;   // enter "08"
cout << n;         // displays "8"
```

For hexadecimal input, use the hex manipulator. For example,

```
unsigned n;
cin >> hex >> n;   // enter "FFFF"
cout << n;         // displays "65535"
```

3.5.2.2 Stream Output. Radix manipulators also affect the display format of integers. In the next example, the variable A displays in decimal, octal, and hexadecimal; the variable B displays in hexadecimal and decimal:

```
int A = 65;
int B = 42;
cout << A    << ','
     << oct << A << ','
     << hex << A << ','
     << B << ','
     << dec << B << endl;
```

Output:

```
65,101,41,2a,42
```

Persistent `iostream` flags must be used with care. Unless you save and re-store the flags, other stream I/O statements using the same stream will not be aware that the radix has changed. The following example shows the proper way to save and restore the flags, using the `ios::flags` function:

```
int x;

long currflags = cout.flags();
cout << hex << x << '\n';
cout.flags( currflags );
```

3.5.2.3 Parameterized Manipulators.

Certain stream manipulators re-quire arguments. This is the case with `setw`, which controls the width of an out-put field. It is called a *parameterized manipulator,* of which there are several. To use parameterized manipulators, include the `iomanip.h` header along with `iostream.h`.

The `setw` manipulator has one parameter, the minimum width of the field. The manipulator is not persistent, so the width will return to its default state of 0. In the next example, `'1'` displays right-justified with a width of five positions. Imme-diately after that, the output stream reverts to a width of 0 and displays `'2'`. Last, we set the width to 6 and display `'3'`:

```
cout << ".........." << '\n'
     << setw(5) << 1    << '\n'
     << 2          << '\n'
     << setw(6) << 3    << endl;
```

Output:

```
..........

         1

2

       3
```

To write a number with a particular leading character, use the `setfill` function. The effect is persistent, so all subsequent output on the stream uses the same leading character. For example,

```
int j = 200;
cout << setfill('*')
     << setw(10) << j++  << '\n'
     << setw(6)  << j    << endl;
```

Output:

```
*******200

***201
```

3.5.3 Stream Output Formatting

Internally, stream output classes use flags to control the formatting of output data. Conceptually, a flag always has a value of on or off, and typically, flags are implemented as individual binary bits. The trick is to turn on the right combination of flags in the stream class to produce the desired output format. Several member functions in the `ios` class control the formatting of output data. They are:

```
long flags();
// return the current flag values

long flags( long newflags );
// replace all of the current flag values,
// and return a copy of the old flags.

long setf( long setbits );
// set one or more flags,
// and return a copy of the old flags.

long setf( long setbits, long field );
// set flags in a particular field,
// and return a copy of the old flags.

long unsetf( long clearbits );
// clear one or more flags,
// and return a copy of the old flags.
```

3.5.3.1 Types of Flags.   There are several types of flags. The first type, which we call *on/off* flags, are turned on or off by calling `setf` and `unsetf` with the name of the flag. These may be used in any combination. Each defaults to *off* except `skipws`:

Flag Value	Description
`ios::stdio`	Synchronize stream with `stdio`.
`ios::skipws`	Skip whitespace on input (the default is on).
`ios::unitbuf`	Flush the stream after each output.
`ios::showbase`	Show the base of the number being displayed as octal, decimal, or hexadecimal.
`ios::showpoint`	Force a decimal point to be displayed in floating-point numbers.
`ios::uppercase`	Use upper-case letters for hexadecimal digits (A-F) and exponents (E).
`ios::showpos`	Show a plus sign for positive numbers.

These constants are represented as different bits in a single long integer, stored as a data member in the stream object.

For example, we can use `setf` to force a trailing decimal point to display in all subsequent use of `cout`:

```
cout.setf( ios::showpoint );
```

Two values can be set at the same time by using the bitwise | operator. This performs an arithmetic OR operation between the `showbase` and `uppercase` constants:

```
cout.setf( ios::showbase | ios::uppercase );
```

A group of flags called the *basefield* affect the default format of integers:

Flag Value	Description
`ios::dec`	Display or input in decimal format (default).
`ios::hex`	Display or input in hexadecimal format.
`ios::oct`	Display or input in octal format.

A group of flags called the *floatfield* affect the display format of floating-point numbers. The output is also affected by the `ios::precision` function:

Flag Value	Description
`ios::automatic`	Automatically choose the shortest display format.
`ios::fixed`	Fixed-point format, as in 1234.56.
`ios::scientific`	Scientific format, as in 1.23456E+02.

The *adjustfield* group of flags affect the alignment of output data:

Flag Value	Description
ios::left	Left-justify the output, pad with the current fill character.
ios::right	Right-justify the output, pad with the current fill character.
ios::internal	Add fill characters, a leading sign, or base indicator.

Functions relating to the fill character, input/output width, and numeric precision are listed next:

Function	Description
int ios::fill	Returns the current fill character.
int ios::fill(int ch)	Sets the new fill character and returns the previous fill character.
int ios::precision	Returns the current floating-point precision.
int ios::precision(int n)	Sets the floating-point precision and returns the previous precision.
int ios::width	Returns the current width. May be used with both input and output.
int ios::width(int w)	Sets the width and returns the previous width. Only affects the output of the next numeric expression.

One popular C++ compiler, for example, uses the space as the default fill character, a precision of 6, and width of 0.

It is often important to preserve the existing fill character or precision when setting a new one, so the original can be restored. For example,

```
float g = 1.23456;
cout << g << '\n';              // output: "1.23456"

// Save and set the fill character and precision:
char oldfill = cout.fill( '0' );
int oldprecis = cout.precision( 4 );
cout << setw(8)
     << g << '\n';              // output: "0001.235"

// Restore default values:
cout.fill( oldfill );
cout.precision( oldprecis );
cout << g << '\n';              // output: "1.23456"
```

3.5.3.2 Examples. In the next example, f is printed out with four digits precision, right-justified for a width of ten characters. All options are persistent ex-

cept the width, so g is left-justified. The `ios::fixed` and `ios::showpoint` flags
are required if we want trailing zeros to appear after the decimal point:

```
double f = 1.2345;
float g = 2.1;
cout.setf( ios::fixed | ios::showpoint );

cout << setfill('*') << setprecision(4)
     << setw(10) << f << '\n'
     << g << endl;
```

Output:

```
****1.2345

2.1000
```

3.5.3.3 Using setw() for Stream Input.

You can use the `setw` manipulator to prevent buffer overflow when reading a string variable from an input stream.
The argument passed to `setw` is the maximum number of characters (plus 1) that
can be transferred to the input variable. For example, we can declare `lastName`
and input a name from the console. If the user types more than 30 characters, the
extra characters remain in the input stream, but `lastName` does not overflow:

```
char lastName[31];
cin >> setw(31) >> lastName;
```

It is very important to remember that without the `setw` manipulator, the user's input could overflow the `lastName` storage area.

We may also want to purge any excess characters from the rest of the user's input by calling `cin.ignore`. The following ignores as many as 1000 excess characters typed on the input line up to the end-of-line marker:

```
char lastName[31];
cin >> setw(31) >> lastName;
cin.ignore( 1000, '\n' );
```

A slightly more refined way to pass the size argument to `setw` is to use the *sizeof*
operator. This only works for arrays of characters having a fixed allocation size:

```
char lastName[31];
cin >> setw( sizeof(lastName) ) >> lastName;
```

3.5.4 Overloading Stream I/O Operators

In all the examples shown so far, we have displayed a class object on the console by
calling a member function such as `Show` or `Display`. But we can tap into more of

the elegance and power of C++ by overloading the stream output operator (<<) for each of our classes. We use the term *streammable class* to mean a class that can be automatically written to or read from a stream.

To use the nonmember stream operators with class objects, the operator functions need to be friend functions. This is demonstrated in the following `Point` class:

```
class Point {
public:
  Point( int xVal, int yVal );
  friend ostream & operator << (ostream & os, const Point & p);
  friend istream & operator >> (istream & is, Point & p);

private:
  int x;
  int y;
};
```

The << and >> operators are binary operators written as nonmember functions, in which the left-hand operand corresponds to the first function parameter, and the right-hand operand is the second parameter. For example, the expression `cout << P` implies the function call `operator <<(cout, P)`:

```
Point P;
cout << P;                // expression
operator <<( cout, P ); // function call
```

The reason that operator << is a friend instead of a `Point` class member has to do with the order of the operands in the expression `cout << P`. Its first operand is not of this class's type; it is an `ostream` object.

3.5.4.1 Stream Output.

Let's implement the stream output operator for the `Point` class. We separate the x and y data members by a single space:

```
ostream & operator << ( ostream & os, const Point & p );
{
  os << p.x << ' ' << p.y << endl;
  return os;
}
```

When the operator << function is called, the stream argument can be `cout`, `clog`, `cerr`, or a file stream. The function returns a reference to the stream as the function result, making it possible to chain together several objects in a single statement:

```
Point P1( 10, 20 );
Point P2( 15, 12 );
cout << P1 << P2;
```

3.5.4.2 Stream Input.   The stream input function takes a reference to an input stream as the first argument, and a reference to a class object as the second. It
returns a reference to the stream object. We assume that the input stream contains
two integers separated by whitespace:

```
istream & operator >> ( istream & is, Point & p )
{
  is >> p.x >> p.y;
  return is;
}
```

This is the same format used for stream output in the `Point` class, so if we created a
file containing data for `Point` objects, we could easily read the objects from the
file.

The following loop reads all the points stored in an input file and displays each
on the screen. We place a second stream input statement at the end of the loop so
when the end of the input file is found, the loop will stop:

```
Point P;
ifstream ifs( "points.dta" );

ifs >> P;
while( ifs )
{
  cout << P << endl;
  ifs >> P;
}
```

Chapter 9 is devoted to the details of operator overloading, particularly the
cases where operator functions are class members. We will defer the details of the
process until then. In the meantime, any class can have friend operator functions for
stream I/O, so long as it follows the format used in the `Point` class.

3.6 CASE STUDY: STUDENT REGISTRATION

3.6.1 Specifications and Analysis

We would like to enhance the Student Registration program that was introduced in
Chapter 2, with the following additional requirements:

- The program will count the number of courses read from the file and calculate
  the total credits taken by the student.
- We will also add a number of programming features that were introduced in
  this chapter, including stream operator functions, constant member functions,
  constant parameters, and overloaded member functions.

None of the classes or class relationships have changed since the first version of this program. The classes will support some new operations, however. The `Course` class will allow both retrieving and modifying the credits. The `Registration` class now supports operations to retrieve both the number of courses and the total number of credits taken by one student.

3.6.2 Design

In keeping with our preference for simple class designs, we will introduce only a minimal number of member functions to support the program specifications. Additional functions could be added later, as needed.

The `Course` class has two constructors, including one that allows a course to be created from a name, section, and number of credits. Two friend functions provide for convenient stream I/O. In this program and all future ones, we make frequent use of the `const` qualifier:

```cpp
#include <iostream.h>

const unsigned CourseNameSize = 10;

class Course {
public:
  Course();
  Course( const char * nam, char sect, unsigned cred );
  // Construct from name, section, credits.

  unsigned GetCredits() const;
  // Return the number of credits.

  void SetCredits( unsigned cred );
  // Set the number of credits.

  friend ostream & operator <<( ostream & os,
        const Course & C );

  friend istream & operator >>( istream & input,
        Course & C );

private:
  char name[CourseNameSize];  // course name
  char section;   // section (letter)
  int  credits;   // number of credits
};
```

The `Registration` class returns the total number of credits taken by a student, plus a count of the number of courses. We also include stream I/O operator functions:

```
#include <iostream.h>
#include "course.h"

const unsigned MaxCourses = 10;

class Registration {
public:
  Registration();
  // Default constructor.

  unsigned GetTotalCredits() const;
  // Return the total credits taken by student.

  unsigned GetCount() const;
  // Return the number of courses.

  friend ostream & operator <<( ostream & os,
       const Registration & R);

  friend istream & operator >>( istream & input,
       Registration & R );

private:
  long studentId;            // student ID number
  unsigned semester;         // semester year, number
  unsigned count;            // number of courses
  Course courses[MaxCourses]; // array of courses
};
```

3.6.3 Main Program

The main program opens and reads an input file stream into a `Registration` object. Notice that we use the overloaded stream input operator for the `Registration` object. We write the same object to an output file stream, along with the number of courses and total credits:

```
#include <iostream.h>
#include <fstream.h>
#include "course.h"  // Course class
#include "regist.h"  // Registration class

int main()
{
  ifstream infile("rinput.txt");
  if( !infile ) return -1;
```

```
Registration R;
infile >> R;

ofstream ofile("routput.txt");

ofile << R
   << "Number of courses = " << R.GetCount() << '\n'
   << "Total credits    = " << R.GetTotalCredits() << endl;
```

To test the `Course` class constructor, we first initialize a course with a name, section, and credits. Then, we call `Course::SetCredits` to modify the credits:

```
Course aCourse( "MTH_3020", 'B', 2 );
aCourse.SetCredits( 5 );
cout << aCourse << endl;
```

3.6.4 Class Implementations

We plan to show the highlights of the Student Registration program here, but shorten the code somewhat. A complete listing of the Student Registration program may be found in Appendix A.

3.6.4.1 Course Class. The constructor for the `Course` class uses the standard function `strncpy`, declared in `string.h`, to copy a string into the `name` data member:

```
Course::Course( const char * nam, char sect,
                unsigned cred )
{
  strncpy( name, nam, CourseNameSize );
  section = sect;
  credits = cred;
}
```

`GetCredits` and `SetCredits` get and set the credits for an individual Course object, respectively. Both are declared inline and placed in the same source file as the `Course` class definition:

```
inline unsigned Course::GetCredits() const
{
  return credits;
}

inline void Course::SetCredits( unsigned cred )
{
  credits = cred;
}
```

Stream operator functions for the Course class replace the Input and Output functions used in the previous version of this program shown in Chapter 2. Notice that each data member must be qualified by C, the name of the Course parameter. The functions both return references to streams:

```
istream & operator >>( istream & input, Course & C )
{
  input >> C.name >> C.section >> C.credits;
  return input;
}


ostream & operator <<( ostream & os, const Course & C )
{
  os << "  Course:   " << C.name << '\n'
     << "  Section: " << C.section << '\n'
     << "  Credits: " << C.credits << '\n' << endl;
  return os;
}
```

In the operator >> function, we're assuming that a course name contains no embedded spaces; if that were not the case, we would call input.get to read the course name. We also assume that the length of the course name is less than CourseNameSize, the named constant.

There is a subtle argument conversion performed by C++ when stream operator functions are called. Their arguments are supposed to be references to istream and ostream, yet we pass ifstream and ofstream arguments from main. This is possible only because ifstream and istream are related types that allow implicit type conversion. The same is possible for ofstream and ostream types.

3.6.4.2 Registration Class. GetTotalCredits is implemented by looping through the array of Course objects and obtaining each of their credits. These are added to a student's total credits:

```
unsigned Registration::GetTotalCredits() const
{
  unsigned sum = 0;
  for(unsigned i = 0; i < count; i++)
    sum += courses[i].GetCredits();

  return sum;
}
```

The Registration class also implements stream I/O functions similar to those in the Course class:

```
istream & operator >>( istream & input, Registration & R )
{
  input >> R.studentId >> R.semester >> R.count;

  for(unsigned i = 0; i < R.count; i++)
    input >> R.courses[i];

  return input;
}

ostream & operator <<( ostream & os, const Registration & R )
{
  os << "Student ID: " << R.studentId << '\n'
     << "Semester:   " << R.semester << endl;

  for(unsigned i = 0; i < R.count; i++)
    os << R.courses[i];

  return os;
}
```

3.6.5 Overall Program Structure

The best way to build the Student Registration program is to create a separate source file for each of the following parts of the program. We have also listed suggested filenames:

Part of Program	Suggested Filename
1. Course class definition	`course.h`
2. Course class implementation	`course.cpp`
3. Registration class definition	`regist.h`
4. Registration class implementation	`regist.cpp`
5. Main program	`main.cpp`

Files 2, 3, and 5 each contain an `#include` directive naming `course.h`. Files 4 and 5 each contain an `#include` directive naming `regist.h`. File 5 contains the `main` function.

The C++ compiler must be run on files 2, 4, and 5 to produce three object modules. Then, the C++ linker must link the object modules together, producing a single executable program. Most C++ compilers are furnished with a utility called MAKE that automates this process. Consult your compiler manuals to find out how to use this utility. Alternatively, some compilers (such as Borland C++ and Microsoft C++) have an integrated development environment that simplifies the compiling and linking of multiple program modules.

3.6.5.1 Preprocessor Directives. In any module that refers to a class name, a header containing the class definition must be included. In a multimodule program, it is likely that the same header will be included more than once. But C++ does not allow a class to be redefined, because that would leave open the possibility that two definitions for the same class might be different. In our sample program, including the `course.h` header twice would generate a syntax error.

We can avoid the problem of redefinition by using preprocessor directives. The preprocessor is a program that scans a program's source code before the program is compiled. Comments are removed from the code and all preprocessor directives are examined and interpreted.

We will insert the following directives at the beginning of `course.h`. The first one checks to see if the symbol `COURSE_H` has already been defined. If it has, all remaining source lines in the file are skipped up to the `#endif` directive. If `COURSE_H` has not been defined yet, the lines following the `#ifndef` directive are compiled up to the `#endif`:

```
#ifndef COURSE_H
#define COURSE_H
    .
    .
    .
#endif
```

The `#define` directive defines the symbol `COURSE_H` so that it will be recognized by subsequent `#ifndef` directives. The symbol we define (`COURSE_H`) is based on the name of the header file or class.

3.7 RECURSION (OPTIONAL)

Recursion is a programming technique by which a function directly or indirectly calls itself. Without any way of terminating the function calls, this would result in endless recursion, as in the following function. This, by itself, is not very interesting:

```
void recursive()
{
  cout << "Executing recursive()" << endl;
  recursive();
}
```

Here is an example of indirect recursion:

```
void recur1()
{
  //...
  recur2();
}
```

```
void recur2()
{
    //...
    recur1();
}
```

Recursion, when used properly, can provide elegant solutions to many programming problems. A simple, often-used example is the definition of *N!*, called *N factorial*. For example, 5! is equal to 5 * 4 * 3 * 2 * 1. But we can also express N! as follows:

```
N!   =   1 if N = 0
     =   N * (N-1)! if N > 0
```

Using this recursive definition, starting with 5!, we eventually arrive at the terminating case, 0!:

```
5! = 5 * (5-1)!
4! = 4 * (4-1)!
3! = 3 * (3-1)!
2! = 2 * (2-1)!
1! = 1 * (1-1)!
0! = 1
```

This sequence of operations can be neatly expressed by a recursive factorial function that repeatedly calls itself until n equals 0. As each successive call backs up and returns a value, it is multiplied by the next largest value of n:

```
int factorial( int n )
{
    if( n == 0 )
        return 1;
    else
        return n * factorial(n - 1);
}
```

The use of recursion has two distinct disadvantages: first, it exacts a toll on runtime performance because of the overhead involved with calling and returning the same functions repeatedly; second, recursive calls tend to use up valuable stack space, because the program saves the return address of each function call along with arguments and local variables. But these disadvantages are often outweighed by a clear advantage to the programmer: a recursive solution to a problem may be the simplest one, and therefore easier to debug and understand. This will be demonstrated in Chapter 11, when we process linked lists.

3.8 READING THE COMMAND LINE (OPTIONAL)

When you run a program from the operating system command line, additional information can be passed as command-line arguments. Suppose we wrote a program
named `process` that read its data from `infile` and sent its output to `outfile`.
Our command line might be

```
process infile outfile
```

Within a C++ program, the command line is represented as an array of strings,
subscripted from 0 to `argc` - 1, where `argc` is the number of command-line arguments. In our example, the three parameters would be represented as `argv[0]`,
`argv[1]`, and `argv[2]`, respectively; `argv[0]` is the program name, which may
or may not include the complete directory path.

We access the `argv[]` array by declaring it in the definition of `main`:

```
int main( int argc, char * argv[] )
{
   //etc.
```

The first parameter in `main` is a count of the number of passed command-line
arguments. A simple program to retrieve and display all command-line arguments is
shown here:

```
#include <iostream.h>

int main( int argc, char * argv[] )
{
   for(int i = 0; i < argc; i++)
     cout << argv[i] << '\n';

   return 0;
}
```

Note that `argv[argc]` is guaranteed to be 0, so `argc` is not really necessary for
processing the array.

3.9 CHAPTER SUMMARY

A *function signature* consists of a function name and the order and types of its parameters, but not its return type.

We use the term *linkage* to describe the visibility of names between program
modules. When a function in one module is called from another module, for example, the function must have *external* linkage. By default, names of functions and

variables are external. The opposite of external linkage is *internal linkage*, meaning that a name is visible only in its declared module.

Function name encoding is the process whereby the C++ compiler creates unique identifiers out of functions that have identical names but different parameter lists.

Preconditions are used when we want to state input requirements for function arguments. *Postconditions* explain what a function will do, given that the preconditions were satisfied. The `assert` macro can be used to enforce preconditions.

If a class object is passed to a function, it should be passed by reference to prevent the inefficient construction of a temporary object. Whenever possible, pass an object by constant reference to ensure that it cannot be modified.

A function with a non-constant reference parameter cannot receive a constant argument. But a function with a constant reference parameter can receive a non-constant argument.

Although it may be tempting to do so, never cast a constant object into a non-constant. The reason the object was declared `const` in the first place was to prevent it from being modified.

A function can be declared (with a function prototype) but not implemented, as long as the function is never called, and its address is never taken. Because of this, whenever you test a new class, be sure to call every member function to verify that the function was implemented.

Default function arguments are useful as a way to make functions more flexible, thus allowing them to be called with varying numbers of arguments. They can, for example, reduce the number of constructors in a class.

Never return a non-constant reference to a private class member; it would improperly allow a class client to have direct write access to the member.

A *friend* function is a global function that has been granted privileged access to the private members of a specific class. Friend functions are often used to overload stream I/O operators.

Function overloading allows multiple functions with the same signature to exist in the same scope. Overloading is particularly useful for different functions that perform similar actions but have different parameter lists.

We discussed *implicit conversions* of function arguments. In general, when an argument of one type is passed to a function whose parameter list contains a similar type, the argument is converted to the parameter's type.

We demonstrated a way of preventing an input stream from entering an error state, by using an input string stream. This makes it much easier to recover from bad user input.

We demonstrated the stream manipulators `setw`, `setfill`, `setprecision`, `oct`, `dec`, and `hex` to control the formatting of numeric and string output.

We designed and implemented a Student Registration case study, demonstrating the specifications, analysis, design, and implementation steps. We plan to use this format for presenting case studies throughout the book.

We discussed recursion and showed an example of a recursive function that calculates the factorial of an integer. We also showed how a program can retrieve its command-line arguments.

3.10 EXERCISES

3.10.1 Miscellaneous

1 Non-Constant Parameter.   Write an example of a function in which you would not want the function parameter to be constant.

2 Name Mangling.   If name mangling were not used by the C++ preprocessor, how might the compiler distinguish between different versions of a function name? Discuss the advantages and disadvantages of your approach.

3 Inline Function Call.   If you have access to an assembly level debugger, trace through a function call that passes an integer argument by value. You will probably see the calling program push the function argument on the stack before calling the function. In the first few lines of the function, try to find the statements that access the argument. Next, declare the parameter as a reference, and make the function inline. Recompile the program and trace it again. Take note of the number of machine instructions that have been eliminated.

4 Standard Header Files.   Inspect several headers used by your C++ programs, such as `stdio.h`, `stdlib.h`, and `string.h` (these libraries are imported from C compilers). Find the declarations that prevent name mangling and make it possible for C++ programs to link to these functions. *Hint:* the "C" qualifier may be hidden inside a macro created with the `#define` directive.

5 Overloading a Constructor.   We presented a `Window` class definition when introducing default arguments, showing how constructor calls could omit one or more arguments from the end of the list. An alternative approach would be to overload the constructor as follows:

```
class Window {
public:
  Window( int x, int y );
  Window( int x, int y, int color );
  Window( int x, int y,
          int color, int frame );
  //...
```

What reasons would you give in favor of using default constructor arguments rather than overloading the constructor?

6 Student Class Stream I/O.   Using the `Student` class created in Chapter 2, create a stream input operator function that allows a `Student` object to be read from keyboard input or from a text file. Create a stream output operator function that writes a `Student` to the screen or to a text file in exactly the same format as the input file. For example, you might want to separate the fields by a single space:

```
1234567 50 175
```

Write a test program that reads a list of ten or more Student objects from a disk file, displays them on the screen, and writes the same records to an output file.

7 Default Arguments. It has been suggested in this chapter that default arguments can simplify program maintenance by allowing new parameters to be added to existing functions. Statements that called these functions would not require modification, but new calls to the functions could take advantage of the extra parameters. Create an example that demonstrates this. Write a short program in two stages: in Stage I, do not use default arguments; in Stage II, introduce the default arguments to two or more functions. One possible function might be a console input function called `get_num` that checks for invalid characters:

```
float get_num( int x, int y, char * charSet,
        int foreColor, int backColor );
```

The following shows sample calls to `get_num` with varying numbers of arguments:

```
salary = get_num( 10, 15, "0123456789.", BLACK, GRAY );
age = get_num( 10, 17, "0123456789" );
```

Other possible arguments might be the minimum and maximum values that check the range of the input number. An argument might contain a pointer to a function that checks the input value for correctness.

8 String Encryption with the SecureString Class. Data encryption has always been a popular subject in computer science because it has a great many practical applications. In this exercise, we would like you to use the power of C++ to encapsulate the encryption process inside a class called `SecureString`. One should be able to create a `SecureString` object by passing it a plaintext string and an encryption key. Use the encryption key to alter the plaintext string, producing an encrypted string. Provide operations to encode and decode the string and output it to a stream. Here is a sample class definition:

```
class SecureString {
public:
  SecureString(){ key[0] = '\0'; }
  // Default constructor.
```

```
    SecureString( const char * plain, char * keyV );
    // Construct a secure string from an existing
    // string and an encryption key.

    void Decode( char * plain );
    // Create the decoded string.

    void Encode( const char * plain, const char * keyV );
    // Initialize key and encode a string.

    friend ostream & operator <<( ostream & os,
                    const SecureString & S );
    // Stream output operator.

private:
    enum { keyMax = 50, stringMax = 1000 };
    char key[keyMax+1];       // encryption key
    char data[stringMax+1]; // encrypted string
    unsigned length;          // length of string

    void translate( const char * inputStr,
                         char * outStr );
    // Translate a plaintext input string into an encoded output
    // string, or translate an encoded input string into
    // plaintext.
};
```

Here is a sample program that tests the class. Create a similar one of your own:

```
char temp[500];
SecureString S;
S.Encode("BBBBBBBBBBBBBBBBBBBBB", "xy4r921" );
cout << "Encoded: " << S << '\n';
S.Decode(temp);
cout << "Decoded: " << temp << "\n\n";

SecureString st("AAAAAAAAAAAAAAAAAAAAAAAAAAAAAAAAAA", "645195" );
cout << "Encoded: " << st << '\n';
st.Decode( temp );
cout << "Decoded: " << temp << endl;
```

3.10.2 Card-Playing Application

1 Playing Cards.   Using the Card class created in the Chapter 2 exercises, make the following changes:

Pass a Card object by reference to a global function called maxCard that returns the larger of two Card objects. A possible declaration of maxCard is:

```
        Card & maxCard( Card & C1, Card & C2 );
```

Create member functions called `GetId` and `GetSuit` in the `Card` class that return the values of appropriate data members.

Create the `SetId` and `SetSuit` functions, which let a class user change the values of the data members. Provide error checking in both functions.

Call all of the new member functions from a short test program.

3.10.3 Payroll Application

The exercises in this section relate to an Employee Payroll Processing application. We use the employee's pay rate and hours worked to calculate weekly pay. The exercises are cumulative, and must be finished in sequential order.

1 Employee Class.   Create a class called `Employee`, representing information in an employee payroll database. The operations performed on employees should include ways to set and retrieve individual fields, to construct and destroy an employee object, and to calculate an employee's pay. The following should be public member functions:

`Employee`	Constructor
`GetId`	Return the Employee's ID number
`GetLastName`	Return the Employee's last name
`GetPayRate`	Return the Employee's pay rate
`GetHours`	Return the Employee's hours worked
`CalcGrossPay`	Calculate and return gross pay
`SetHours`	Set the hours worked
`SetPayRate`	Set the pay rate

The following should be friend functions:

`operator <<`	Write an Employee to a stream
`operator >>`	Read an Employee from a stream

Include the following private data members:

```
long  id;              // identification number
char  lastName[30];    // last name
float payRate;         // hourly pay rate
float hours;           // hours worked per pay period
```

Allow `Employee` objects to be initialized in two different ways, using default arguments in the constructor. For example,

```
Employee E1( 10000 );
Employee E2( 10000, "Johnson", 30.5, 55.0 );
```

Write a short program that tests the `Employee` class by constructing, initializing, and displaying objects. Calculate and display the weekly gross pay for a single employee. Use stream manipulators and option flags to format the pay rate and gross pay with two digits after the decimal point.

2 Creating a Multimodule Project.   In this chapter we showed how to compile and link multimodule programs, and how to use the #ifndef and #define directives to prevent the multiple inclusion of header files. If you have not already done so, place the Employee class declaration in a header file, the class implementation in a source module (.cpp, or .cc, or .cxx), and place main in a separate source module. Compile and link the program.

3 Validating the Input Data.   In this chapter we showed how to use string streams to better recover from input stream errors. Implement these techniques in the operator >> function for the Employee class.

Create a data file containing at least ten Employee records, and intentionally insert a few errors. Write a program that reads the employees from the input file and flags all input errors by identifying the erroneous field and displaying the complete input record. For example,

```
Invalid Employee ID:  A1422 Jones 12.5 50
Missing last name: 21400 14.5 42
Invalid hours worked: 12345 Johnson 15.5 4X
Invalid pay rate: 20112 Matheson 12Z.2 45
```

Make a copy of the original data file, correct the errors, and run the program again. Read all records and display each employee record, along with its weekly gross pay. After all employees have been read, display the average hours worked and the average gross pay for all employees.

4 Further Input Validation.   In the Employee class, limit the ranges of the pay rate and hours worked when setting the values of those data members. For any out-of-range value, display an error message. Declare the following constants in the same header as the Employee class definition:

```
const float PAYRATE_MIN = 0.0;
const float PAYRATE_MAX = 50.0;
const float HOURS_MIN =   0.0;
const float HOURS_MAX =   60.0;
```

Modify some of the field values in the input data file and test the program to make sure that it flags range errors when setting the pay rate and hours worked.

3.10.4 Pharmacy Application

The following group of exercises relate to a database of customer and drug prescription information for a pharmacy.

1 Prescription Class.   Create a class called `Prescription` that describes data for a single prescription in a pharamacy database. Include the following data members, all strings:

```
char id[10];          // Unique ID for every prescription
char lastDate[10];    // Last refill date
char lastName[30];    // Customer last name
char firstName[20];   // Customer first name
char drug[30];        // Name of drug
char dosage[40];      // Description of dosage
```

Create a constructor that lets the calling program initialize each of the data members (use the `strncpy` function to copy the constructor parameters into the data members). Create a stream output operator function for the class that displays each data member with a descriptive label. Write a test program that creates and displays a prescription. For example,

```
Prescription ID:   20164
Last refill date: 960831
Patient name:     Jones, Bob
Drug [dosage]:    Xylocane [200cc/3x daily]
.................................................
```

2 Reading a Prescription File.   Use the `Prescription` class from the previous exercise. Create a text file containing at least fifteen prescription records, or use the file on the diskette available to instructors. Use commas to separate the fields within each record. Here are a few sample records:

```
20164,960831,Jones,Bob,Xylocane,200cc/3x daily
21746,961231,Gomez,Jose,Fiorinal,100cc/1x daily
30122,970101,Chong,Daniel,Avocet,150cc/4x daily
```

Write a test program that reads each record from the input file, separates it into individual fields, and redisplays the record. Earlier in this chapter, we explained how to use the `istream::get` function to read characters from a stream up to a delimiter character.

CHAPTER 4

Class Features

In this chapter we cover a number of class features that lend themselves to writing applications in C++. For example, we demonstrate composite classes, which are classes that contain class objects as data members. We show how constructor-initializer lists initialize data members, reference members, and const-qualified members. Static data members and static member functions are introduced, and it is shown how they apply to all instances of a class. Enumerated constants in our programs improve readability and reliability. At the end of the chapter, we present a short simulation program called Robot Wars that ties together techniques learned in the previous three chapters.

Terms Introduced in this Chapter:

automaton	enumerated type
composite class	static class member
composition relationship	static data member
const-qualified	static member function
constructor-initializer	tag name
enumerated constant	

4.1 ENUMERATED CONSTANTS

4.1.1 Declaring

An enumerated constant associates one or more symbols with corresponding integer constants. The format for declaring such a list follows. *Tag-name* is optional, and *enum-list* is a list of identifiers separated by commas:

```
enum tag-name { enum-list };
```

The compiler automatically assigns values to enumerated constants, if none are explicitly given, in the order 0, 1, 2, 3, and so on. For example, we enumerate several constants having to do with a machine's current status:

```
enum { running, standby, offline, inoperative };
```

On the other hand, we could assign specific values to each constant:

```
enum { running = 0, standby = 99, offline = 50,
       inoperative = 10 };
```

A useful application of enumerated constants is for defining symbolic names. Good programming style dictates that we use symbolic names for constants. For example, in the following Student class, we define idSize and nameSize. This eases program maintenance if we should ever decide to change the sizes of these fields, because the names would often be used in many different places within the class:

```
const int idSize = 7:
const int nameSize = 30:

class Student {
//...
private:
  char id[idSize+1];
  char name[nameSize+1];
};
```

A drawback to this approach is that idSize and nameSize are defined outside the class, and will clash with other global identifiers having the same names. Alternatively, we can declare idSize and nameSize as enumerated constants inside the class, making them private if we wish:

```
class Student {
//...
private:
  enum { idSize = 7, nameSize = 30 };
  char id[idSize+1];
  char name[nameSize+1];
};
```

4.1.2 Tag Names

We can assign a *tag name* to an enumerated list, turning it into an *enumerated type*. Variables can then be declared using the type. In the next example, status is of type TStatus:

```
enum TStatus { running, standby, offline, inoperative };

TStatus currentStatus;
```

C++ performs type-checking on enumerated types, so only TStatus constants can be assigned to currentStatus. An integer may not be assigned directly to an enumerated type, even when the integer happens to match the ordinal value of an enumerated constant:

```
currentStatus = running;      // ok
currentStatus = 1;            // error
```

We can, however, assign a TStatus value to any standard numeric type:

```
int n = currentStatus;
unsigned x = standby;
float f = inoperative;
```

The TStatus declaration could be hidden inside the Machine class, in which case we would provide access to it through member functions such as SetStatus and GetStatus:

```
class Machine {
public:
  enum TStatus { running, standby, offline, inoperative };

  TStatus GetStatus();
  // Get the machine status.

  void SetStatus( TStatus S );
  // Set the machine status.
```

```
private:
  TStatus currentStatus;
};
```

If we now declare a `Machine` object and set the status, we must qualify
`running` with `Machine::`, the name of the class where `running` was declared:

```
Machine M;
M.SetStatus( Machine::running );
```

The same technique is used when setting flags in the standard C++ stream classes.
For example, the `ios` class contains an enumerated constant called `showpoint`
that sets a flag inside a `cout` stream object. This flag forces floating-point numbers
to contain a decimal point when written to `cout`:

```
float f = 3.0;
cout.setf( ios::showpoint );
cout << f;
```

4.2 COMPOSITE CLASSES

When a class contains instances, references, or pointers to other classes, we call it a
composite class, and say that a *composition* relationship exists. This can be very useful when the relationship matches the application domain. A geometric figure, for
example, can be represented as a collection of vertices. An automobile may be a
collection of parts. A student transcript may be a collection of course records, student biographical data, and course catalog information.

In the next example, we create a composite class called `Figure` that contains
an array of points (vertices of a geometric figure). The figure's center is also a
`Point`. The `Point` class contains a constructor that initializes its x and y coordinates. The `Figure` class includes functions to set the center, color, and individual
vertices of a `Figure`:

```
class Point {
public:
  Point( int xv = 0, int yv = 0 );

private:
  int x;
  int y;
};

const unsigned MaxVertices = 10;
enum Colors { white, blue, green };
```

```
class Figure {
public:
  Figure();

  void SetCenter( const Point & p );

  void SetColor( Colors c );

  void SetVertex( unsigned vnum, const Point & p);
  // Set vertex vnum to value of Point p.

private:
  Point vertex[MaxVertices]; // array of vertices
  unsigned vcount;           // number of vertices
  Point center;              // center of rotation
  Colors color;              // color of figure
};
```

Now we declare a `Figure` object F and initialize its rotational center and four vertices:

```
Figure F;
F.SetVertex( 0, Point( 1, 1 ));
F.SetVertex( 1, Point( 10, 2 ));
F.SetVertex( 2, Point( 8, 10 ));
F.SetVertex( 3, Point( -2, 2 ));
F.SetCenter( Point( 6, 5 ));
```

The following statements create an array of figures and set their color to green:

```
const unsigned FigCount = 5;

Figure figList[FigCount];        // array of Figures

for(unsigned j = 0; j < FigCount; j++)
  figList[j].SetColor( green );
```

When a class contains other class objects, C++ has a pre-defined order for calling constructors and destructors:

- The constructors for all member objects are executed in the order in which they appear in the class definition. All member constructors execute before the body of the enclosing class constructor executes.
- Destructors are called in the reverse order of constructors. Therefore, the body of the enclosing class destructor is executed before the destructors of its member objects.

In the `Figure` class, for example, the default constructor for each of the vertices is called first, then the constructor for the center, followed by the body of the `Figure` constructor. To demonstrate this order, we have created simplified versions of the `Point` and `Figure` classes that show when the constructors and destructors execute. The `Figure` class has only three vertices:

```
#include <iostream.h>

class Point {
public:
  Point() { cout << "Point constructor\n"; }
  ~Point() { cout << "Point destructor\n"; }
};

const int MaxVertices = 3;

class Figure {
public:
  Figure() { cout << "Figure constructor\n"; }
  ~Figure() { cout << "Figure destructor\n"; }

private:
  Point vertex[MaxVertices]; // array of vertices
  Point center;
};
//...
Figure F;
```

The output from the program shows four `Point` constructors executing before the `Figure` constructor. The `Figure` destructor executes before the destructors for each of the `Point` objects:

```
Point constructor
Point constructor
Point constructor
Point constructor
Figure constructor
Figure destructor
Point destructor
Point destructor
Point destructor
Point destructor
```

4.2.1 Passing Messages Directly to Data Members

It often happens that a class is simply a container for other class objects, and users of the class need to send messages directly to the members. We have steadfastly refused to make any data members public, because that would violate the principle of encapsulation and prevent the class designer from making future changes to the names or types of data members.

To illustrate, let's create a `Chart` class that graphs the revenue earned for each product sold by a company. A `Chart` contains two `Axis` objects and a `ChartData` object:

```
class Axis {
public:
  void SetTitle( const char * st );
  void SetRange( int min, int max );
  //...
};

class ChartData {
public:
  void Read( istream & inp );
  //...
};

class Chart {
public:
  void Draw();          // draw the chart

private:
  Axis hAxis;           // horizontal axis
  Axis vAxis;           // vertical axis
  ChartData dataset;    // array of numbers
  //...
};
```

We could return const-qualified references to each of the data members, but that would not permit calling functions in the `Axis` and `ChartData` classes that modify those objects:

```
class Chart {
public:
  const Axis & HorizontalAxis()  { return hAxis;   }
  const Axis & VerticalAxis()    { return vAxis;   }
  const ChartData & DataSet()    { return dataset; }
  //...
};
```

On the other hand, for every public function in the `Axis` and `ChartData` classes, we could create a similar function in the `Chart` class that would simply pass the message on to the member object:

```
class Chart {
public:
  void SetHorizontalTitle( const char * st );
  void SetHorizontalRange( int min, int max );
  void SetVerticalTitle( const char * st );
  void SetVerticalRange( int min, int max );
  void ReadDataSet( istream & inp );
  etc., etc., etc...
};
```

This, however, would bloat the `Chart` class interface and prove to be a maintenance nightmare when new operations were added to the `Axis` and `ChartData` classes.

A compromise solution is to add `Chart` member functions that return non-constant references to the data members. Normally, we would forbid non-constant references, but this approach makes it possible to send messages to data members:

```
class Chart {
public:
  Axis & HorizontalAxis()  { return hAxis;   }
  Axis & VerticalAxis()    { return vAxis;   }
  ChartData & DataSet()    { return dataset; }
  void Draw();

private:
  Axis horizAxis;
  Axis verticalAxis;
  ChartData dataset;
};

Chart sales;
sales.HorizontalAxis().SetTitle( "Revenue" );
sales.HorizontalAxis().SetRange( 0, 5000 );
sales.VerticalAxis().SetTitle( "Products" );
(etc.)
```

Suppose the class designer later decided to make `dataset` a pointer to a `ChartData` object. Then, the `DataSet` function could dereference `dataset` without affecting the class interface:

```
class Chart {
public:
  //...
  ChartData & DataSet() { return *dataset; }
```

```
private:
  //...
  ChartData * dataset;
};
```

Finally, it must be said that returning non-constant references as we have done here is only valid for member objects with their own class interfaces. In the `Chart` class, for example, `hAxis`, `vAxis`, and `dataset` were all class objects. We would be far less likely to return a non-constant reference to a member that was not a class object.

Many C++ programmers support the idea that classes should be composed entirely of class objects, each with their own interfaces and encapsulation. For example, [Eckel], in his programming guidelines, says, "Avoid C's built-in types. They are supported in C++ for backward compatibility, but they are much less robust than C++ classes, so your bug-hunting time will increase."

4.2.2 Initializing Class Members

When a class contains other class objects, its constructor has the job of passing arguments to the constructors of its members. The member constructors are executed before control returns to the body of the enclosing class constructor. The argument passing is accomplished by using a *constructor-initializer*. A colon follows the enclosing class constructor's parameter list, followed by a list of member names and arguments passed to their constructors:

```
class-name( argument-list )
: member1( ctor-arglist1 ), member2( ctor-arglist2 ), ...
{
  //...
}
```

In the following example, the `Point` class contains a copy constructor, which is a constructor that allows a new `Point` to be constructed as a copy of an existing one. The `Figure` class contains a `Point` data member called `center`, and a constructor with parameters that initialize the `Figure`'s center of rotation and its color:

```
enum Colors { white, blue, green };

class Point {
public:
  Point( const Point & P );
  //...
};

class Figure {
public:
  Figure( const Point & ctr, Colors aColor );
  //...

private:
  Point center;      // center of rotation
  Colors color;      // color
};
```

The constructor-initializer passes the two constructor parameters to their matching data members. This causes the `Point` class constructor to be called, initializing the center of the figure:

```
Figure::Figure( const Point & ctr, Colors aColor )
        :color(aColor), center(ctr)
{
  //...
}
```

When multiple class data members are initialized, the order of their assignment is based on the order of member declaration, not on their order in the constructor-initializer list. In the `Figure` class, for example, `center` is constructed before `color` is initialized.

4.2.3 Reference and Const-Qualified Data Members

Sometimes it is better to let a class data member be a reference to a class object rather than an instance of an object. Suppose a `Student` object was already in existence and we decided to initialize a `Grade` object with a reference to the `Student`, as in the following:

```
void ProcessTest( Student & S )
{
  int score;
  //...
  Grade G( S, score );
  //...
}
```

```
Student S;
ProcessTest( S );
```

Rather than make a separate copy of the `Student` object and store it inside a `Grade` object, it might make more sense to let the `Grade` contain a reference to the `Student`. To initialize a reference data member, we must use a constructor-initializer. For example, this is how the `Grade` class constructor initializes the `student` data member:

```
class Student { /*...*/ };

class Grade {
public:
  Grade::Grade( Student & S, float aScore )
       :student(S)
  {
     score = aScore;
  }

private:
  Student & student;  // reference
  float score;
};
```

Similarly, const-qualified data members require a constructor-initializer. The `GradeReport` class initializes the student data member as a const-qualified reference:

```
class GradeReport {
public:
  GradeReport::GradeReport( const Student & S )
              : student(S) {   }
  //...
private:
  const Student & student;
};
```

4.3 STATIC CLASS MEMBERS

A *static class member* is declared with the keyword `static`. Both data members and functions may be declared static. Regardless of how many instances of a class might exist at any time, there can be only one copy of a static member. The member is not part of any single class object.

In some ways, a *static data member* is similar to a global variable: only a single copy exists, and if it is a member of a global class, it has external linkage. Unlike a global variable, however, access to a static data member is controlled by its enclosing class.

A static member is affected by the private, public, and protected access specifiers just as any other class member. Any member function can access its own class's static members. Since the latter do not exist inside instances of that class, member functions operating on a const-qualified object can still modify static data members.

A *static member function* may only access the static members and enumerated constants of a class. We ordinarily use a static member function as a public interface to static data members, which are usually private.

4.3.1 Student Class Example

The following Student class contains a static member called count that keeps track of the number of existing Student objects:

```
typedef unsigned long ulong;

class Student {
public:
  Student( ulong id );
  // Construct Student from an id number.

  Student( const Student & S );
  // Construct from another Student.

  ~Student();

  static ulong GetCount();
  // Return the static instance count.

private:
  static ulong count;  // instance count
  ulong idNum;         // identification number
};
```

Notice that the class contains two constructors, the second of which is a copy constructor.

The count static data member must also have a storage-allocating definition, usually within the same program module as the class definition:

```
ulong Student::count = 0;   // define, initialize
```

We increment count in each constructor and decrement it in the destructor. Only one constructor is ever executed when a Student object is constructed:

```
Student::Student( ulong id )
{
  idNum = id;
  count++;
}

Student::Student( const Student & S )
{
  idNum = S.idNum;
  count++;
}

Student::~Student()
{
  count--;
}
```

In the following, the static member function GetCount does not use the static keyword in its implementation:

```
ulong Student::GetCount()
{
  return count;
}
```

Static member functions can be called in one of two ways: either by being qualified by a class name and ' : : '; or, by being qualified by a class object using the '.' operator. Of the two options, we prefer the first because GetCount has nothing to do with S, a specific Student object.

```
cout << Student::GetCount();
Student S;
cout << S.GetCount();
```

Using the same Student class definition, let's write a short program that creates several Student objects and displays the class instance count:

```
#include <iostream.h>

void MakeStudent()
{
  Student C( 200001L );
  cout << Student::GetCount() << endl;     // displays "3"
}

int main()
{
  Student A( 100001L );
  cout << Student::GetCount() << endl;     // displays "1"
```

```
    Student B( A );
    cout << Student::GetCount() << endl;     // displays "2"
    MakeStudent();
    cout << Student::GetCount() << endl;     // displays "2"

    return 0;
}
```

The program calls a function containing a local `Student` object, in which `count` is incremented. On returning from the function, the `Student` is destroyed and `count` is decremented. The output from the program is as follows:

```
1
2
3
2
```

4.3.2 Rectangle Class Example

Static class data can be used effectively when initializing data members to default values. Let's use a `Rectangle` class as an example. We might have a static data member called `defaultColor` that is used by the constructor to set the rectangle's default drawing color:

```
enum Colors { white, red, green, blue };

class Rectangle {
public:
  Rectangle( int xv, int yv,
             int ht, int wd );

  static Colors GetDefaultColor();
  static Colors SetDefaultColor( Colors );

private:
  static Colors defaultColor;
  int x;
  int y;
  unsigned height;
  unsigned width;
  Colors color;
};

Colors Rectangle::defaultColor = white;

Rectangle::Rectangle( int xv, int yv,
           int ht, int wd )
```

```
{
  x = xv;
  y = yv;
  height = ht;
  width = wd;
  Color = defaultColor;
}


inline Colors Rectangle::GetDefaultColor()
{
  return defaultColor;
}


inline Colors Rectangle::SetDefaultColor( Colors newColor )
{
  Colors oldColor = defaultColor;
  defaultColor = newColor;
  return oldColor;
}
```

`SetDefaultColor` not only sets the new color, but it returns the old color so that a calling program can choose to restore the previous color. Assigning a new color to `defaultColor` does not change the color of existing rectangles, but it affects the color of any new rectangles. For example,

```
Rectangle::SetDefaultColor( red );
Rectangle r1( 10, 15, 200, 400 );  // red rectangle
Rectangle::SetDefaultColor( blue );
Rectangle r2( 30, 100, 200, 400 ); // blue rectangle
```

The `static` keyword does not appear in the out-of-line function definition of `SetDefaultColor`:

```
Colors Rectangle::SetDefaultColor( Colors newColor )
{
  //...
}
```

4.4 EXAMPLE: FSTRING CLASS

4.4.1 Specifications

A common source of bugs in C and C++ programs occurs when dealing with C-style strings. No bounds checking is performed on subscripts, making it easy to inadvertently overrun the end of a string. A common solution to this problem is to create a string class that encapsulates everyday string operations and provides built-in error checking. Standard C++ includes a string class specification, but at present, many differences exist between available string class implementations.

We're going to create a simple string class called FString, which uses a fixed memory allocation. This class will prove useful in many of the programs presented in this book. In this early version of the FString class, we want to support the following operations:

- Construction: Construct an FString object from a C-style string, or from another FString.

- Assignment: Use the assignment operator to assign one string to another.

- Conversion: Convert a C-style string to an FString.

- Comparison: Compare two FString objects using the character collating sequence of the current implementation.

- Stream output: Overload the stream output operator (<<) to write an FString to a stream.

- Stream input: Overload the stream input operator (>>) to read an FString from a stream, and provide a function to input an entire text line.

Because FString uses a fixed allocation, we must limit the lengths of strings to some reasonable number, which we will set at 256. This also means that every FString object will occupy 256 bytes, whether the storage is needed or not. This limitation can be overcome, but it will require dynamic memory allocation, which is covered in Chapter 7.

4.4.2 Class Interface

Here is the FString class definition:

```
#include <iostream.h>
#include <iomanip.h>
#include <string.h>

class FString {
public:
  // Construction and assignment functions:

  FString();
  FString( const char * s );
  // Construct from a C-style string.

  FString( const FString & s );
  // Construct from another FString.
```

```
FString & Append( const FString & s );
// Append another FString to current object.

FString & Assign( const char * s );
// Assign a C-style string to current object.

FString & Assign( const FString & s );
// Assign an FString to current object.

// Constant functions:

const char * CString() const;
// Convert current object to a C-style string.

int Compare( const FString & s ) const;
// Implement the standard strcmp() function.
// Case-sensitive.

int IsLess( const FString & s ) const;
// Return 1 if current object is less than s.

int IsGreater( const FString & s ) const;
// Return 1 if current object is greater than s.

int IsEqual( const FString & s ) const;
// Return 1 if current object is equal to s.

// Input-output functions:

FString & GetLine( istream & inp );
// Get a line of input from a stream.

friend istream & operator >>( istream & inp,
        FString & s );

friend ostream & operator <<( ostream & inp,
        const FString & s );

enum { MaxSize = 256 };   // Maximum allowable string size

private:
  char str[MaxSize+1];  // String characters
};
```

The Compare function works the same as the standard strcmp function in string.h. We have also included the IsLess, IsGreater, and IsEqual functions to provide a more intuitive way of comparing strings.

4.4.2.1 Using the FString Functions. Here are a few examples showing how `FString` objects are used. The `Assign` function assigns a new string to the current one. `Assign` is overloaded, which lets us pass either a C-style string or an `FString` argument:

```
#include "fstring.h"

FString name1;
FString name2;
name1.Assign( "Fred" );
name2.Assign( name1 );
```

`Append` concatenates another `FString` to the current one:

```
name1.Assign( "Fred " );
name2.Assign( "Smith" );
name1.Append( name2 );    // "Fred Smith"
```

`CString` converts an `FString` into a const-qualified C-style string:

```
const char * vp = name1.CString();
```

`Compare` compares the current `FString` to another `FString` by calling the standard `strcmp` function in `string.h`. Let n be the return value of `strcmp`; if `str < S2.str`, $n < 0$; if `str == S2.str`, $n == 0$; if `str > S2.str`, $n > 0$. The following statements input two strings, compare them, and display the results:

```
cout << "Enter two names:\n";
name1.GetLine( cin );
name2.GetLine( cin );
int n = name1.Compare( name2 );
if( n < 0 )
  cout << "The first name is less\n";
else if( n == 0 )
  cout << "The names are equal\n";
else
  cout << "The second name is less\n";
```

Or, we can simply call the `IsLess` function when comparing two strings:

```
if( name1.IsLess( name2 ))
  cout << "The first name is less\n";
```

Because the `Assign` and `Append` functions return references to the current `FString` object, the return value from one call can be used to call another function. Here, we first assign "`Fred`" to `name1`, and then concatenate a trailing space:

```
name1.Assign( "Fred" ).Append( " " );
```

The following multiple calls to Concat are not recursive because each function call returns before the next call takes place:

```
name1.Concat( "Fred" ).Concat( " " ).Concat( "Smith" );
```

The >> operator implements the same operation as the >> operator in the istream class. Leading whitespace is skipped, a string is read, and input stops at the next whitespace. operator >> writes to an output stream:

```
FString name;
cout << "Enter name: ";
cin >> name;
ostream ofile("sample");
ofile << name;
```

GetLine implements istream::getline, so it is suited to input streams containing embedded blanks and tabs:

```
FString name;
cout << "Enter full name [first last]: ";
  name.GetLine( cin );
```

4.4.3 Class Implementation

We have chosen the easy way out when dealing with errors in the FString class. For example, if the user concatenates two strings that produce an oversized string, or if the user tries to assign too large a string, we truncate the resulting string to MaxSize (currently set at 256). To provide more sophisticated error handling would require one of the following approaches:

- Add error-checking statements to each function that would report the nature of the error and let the calling program decide how to handle the error.
- Use assert to abort the program without releasing memory and closing files.
- Implement *exception handling,* a relatively sophisticated C++ feature, which is able to report errors and perform cleanup. Chapter 8 discusses exception handling.

We will keep this class simple for now and live with its limitations. But it is always nice to know that better implementations exist, given a more in-depth knowledge of C++.

Let's take a look at the member function implementations. The following two constructors either initialize the first position of an empty string or copy an existing C-style string:

```
FString::FString()
{
   str[0] = '\0';
}

FString::FString( const char * S )
{
   strncpy( str, S, MaxSize );
   str[MaxSize] = '\0';
}
```

Append implements the standard strncat function, which stops copying characters when MaxSize is reached. This will prevent memory overrun:

```
FString & FString::Append( const FString & S )
{
  strncat( str, S, MaxSize );
  return *this;
}
```

The overloaded Assign function takes either a C-style string argument or an
FString argument. It returns a reference to the current FString object (called
*this):

```
FString & FString::Assign( const char * S )
{
  strncpy( str, S, MaxSize );
  return *this;
}

FString & FString::Assign( const FString & S2 )
{
  strncpy( str, S2.str, MaxSize );
  return *this;
}
```

GetLine implements istream::getline, reading up to MaxSize characters
from a stream, stopping at the \n character:

```
FString & FString::GetLine( istream & inp )
{
  inp.getline( str, MaxSize+1 );
  return *this;
}
```

CString returns the str data member as a constant. Compare implements the
standard strcmp function:

```
const char * FString:: CString() const
{
   return str;
}

int FString::Compare( const FString & S2 ) const
{
   return strcmp( str, S2.str );
}
```

The stream input operator uses the `setw` manipulator to prevent overflowing the string's memory space. The stream output operator simply outputs the string data member:

```
istream & operator >>( istream & inp, FString & S )
{
   inp >> setw( S.MaxSize+1 ) >> S.str;
   return inp;
}

ostream & operator <<( ostream & os, const FString & S )
{
   os << S.str;
   return os;
}
```

4.4.3.1 Using an FString as a Class Member. The `FString` class is ideal for creating string data members in classes. The strings can be manipulated just as easily as any other data type, without having to work with low-level functions such as `strcpy` and `strcmp`. For example, let's create a `Name` class containing a first name and a last name, both `FStrings`:

```
class Name {
public:
   Name( const char * lname, const char * fname );
   friend ostream & operator <<(ostream & os, const Name & N);

private:
   FString lastName;
   FString firstName;
};
```

The constructor uses a constructor-initializer to set the values of `lastName` and `firstName`.These, in turn, call the `FString` constructor:

```
Name::Name( const char * lname, const char * fname )
   :lastName(lname), firstName(fname) {   }
```

The stream output operator invokes the << operator in the FString class:

```
ostream & operator <<( ostream & os, const Name & N )
{
  os << N.firstName << ' ' << N.lastName;
  return os;
}
```

4.5 THE SCREEN CLASS

In a few programs presented in this book, we will exert some control over screen I/O that goes beyond stream I/O. We might need to clear the screen, position the cursor on a particular line and column, or wait for a single key to be pressed. Because of the variety of C++ environments, functions dealing with console I/O are not very portable.

A class is an ideal place to encapsulate implementation-specific features, because programs using the features need only communicate with the class interface. How the particular features are implemented will vary from one C++ implementation to another. The class implementation is written for the target computer system. For example, here is a declaration of a class called Screen. It supports a few basic screen functions that we need:

```
class Screen {
public:
  void SetCursorPosition( int x, int y );
  void ClearScreen();
  void ClearToEol();
  int KbHit();
};
```

ClearToEol clears the current line, from the cursor position to the end of the line. KbHit returns 1 if a key was pressed by the user. On systems using asynchronous terminals, this function is rarely implemented.

For each target C++ implementation, we use a #define directive that enables statements that implement Screen class functions. The following example shows the section for the Borland C++ compiler. This particular compiler has a library called conio.h, which must be included. The library contains functions that implement each of our Screen operations:

```
#ifdef __BCPLUSPLUS__   // Borland C++ implementation

#include <conio.h>
```

```
inline void Screen::SetCursorPosition( int x, int y )
{
  gotoxy( x, y );
}

inline void Screen::ClearScreen()
{
  clrscr();
}

inline void Screen::ClearToEol()
{
  clreol();
}

inline int Screen::KbHit()
{
  return kbhit();
}

#endif  // end of BORLAND definitions
```

Of course, various C++ compilers will either implement these functions differently or not at all. For example, a system using VT-100 terminals would use stream I/O to send escape sequences to the terminal to clear the screen, locate the cursor, and so on. If a system absolutely cannot support a function such as KbHit, the function implementation can just be left empty, or it can return 0. For example,

```
inline int Screen::KbHit()  // not implemented
{
  return 0;
}
```

4.6 ROBOT SIMULATION

4.6.1 Specifications

We're going to demonstrate a simple object-oriented simulation, using the tools we have developed in the last two chapters. It is whimsically called "Robot Wars" because it consists of a large number of *automatons* (small robots) that move within a grid. Each robot acts independently, moving where it wants to, and attacking any robot it encounters.

Each position in the grid is called a *cell,* and a single cell can contain any number of robots. When a robot moves into an empty cell, it claims the cell for itself. If another robot enters the cell, a battle ensues and the newcomer is weakened. When a robot's energy level reaches zero, it dies. The program displays the grid as the battle is in progress, showing the number of active robots in each cell.

One of the enjoyable aspects to writing a simulation is that we can change the arguments and sit back and watch the simulation unfold. In the robot simulation, we allow the user to set the number of robots, the starting energy level of the robots, and the population level to be reached before stopping the simulation. In general, the lower the population, the fewer the encounters, and the longer it takes for any of the robots to die. It's interesting to start with several thousand robots and note how quickly they disappear.

The program's output is a representation of the grid that is updated after each cycle in the battle. On the status line at the top, we show the number of remaining robots and the number of battle cylces completed. In each remaining screen position, we show the number of robots in each cell. Ordinarily, a '1', '2', or '3' is displayed in each cell. In one simulation test, we began with 1000 robots each having a starting energy level of 10. After 42 cycles, the following display showed the positions of the remaining 499 robots:

```
Active: 499    Time: 42

. . . . . . . . . . . . . . . . . . . . . . . . . . . . . . . . . . . . . . . . . . . . . . . . . . . . . . .
   111 22    2    1 113 12  1 11  1     1 11        12 121    1  1 1 1  212
   1     1 111  2    11   1 11  3 1  1  1 11     1 1 1 2    1111  1111  1    1 11 1
 1         111        2    1 1 11  1 111  11    11  1       1                   1
 1 1         1 1  1        1     1 1   1         1     1 11          11    1
       1           11  1  1  2   1 111     3        1 1    1            1    11
 1 21         1  1   1 1     2    11      1 1 1   21    21 1   11   1 11
 1 1      11       1  11 12   1     12     1 3    2      11 1  11 11
     1 31 12  2           11   111 1  11   1 1 1  1     211 11  21  11 21      112
 1  11 1 1           1     21 2 1   11 1       1      11  3     1 1  1
 2       1    11  11  12 2          1 11111111  1 11 211     1
 1  11     1       1 111   1      11 1   111     2 11   1         1 1111
 1  1     111     2 1  1 21 1   1 1 1   1 1              21
 12     111 1           1     11   1 11     1 11    1      1 1         1
  1 31     2111 11 1 2       1   1    111   11  1      1 1          1 1
 1 1       1     1     1       11    1 1      1 11 1  1  2    1 1 11
 1 1  1 2   1 1 1     11   1          1      1  1 1     11  1 1        1
 1  2   1     2     1  11    1  1     1    21  1 1  1  1 1       11 1
       1  1   1        1     121         2    1 1 1 1  1    1    1
       11   1 111      1       1  1 2     1       1         1    1
  112       11 1 1    1     1  11  1   1  1 11    1       1
  1   21                 1 1    1 1        1     1 1       1    1
                       1  11   1   1 1            1        1
```

4.6.2 Design

Four classes are used in the simulation: Position, which keeps track of an object's position in a two-dimensional plane; Robot, which has a position on the grid, a direction of movement, and an energy level; Grid, a two-dimensional array of cells (Grid also contains a one-dimensional array of robots); and Screen, a screen utility class presented earlier in this chapter. The following is a diagram of the class dependencies, showing a one-to-many relationship between Grid and Robot, and a one-to-one relationship between Robot and Position:

4.6.2.1 Position Class.   The Position class contains two data members, x and y, which identify an object's coordinates on a grid. In our simulation, the upper-left corner of the grid will be position 0,0, and the lower right corner will be 79, 21. Here is the class interface:

```
#include <stdlib.h>

enum Direction { up, down, left, right, none };

class Position {
public:
  enum { xMax = 80, yMax = 22 };
  Position();
  unsigned GetX() const;
  unsigned GetY() const;
  void SetX( unsigned newX );
  void SetY( unsigned newY );
  void Move( Direction dir, unsigned xMax, unsigned yMax );

  static Direction ChooseRandomDirection();

private:
  unsigned x;       // x-position
  unsigned y;       // y-position
};
```

We also include two constants, xMax and yMax, to limit the range of positions so they will fit onto a standard computer screen.

The following statements create a Position object and move it down one square in the grid; the range parameters limit the new position to x < 80 and y < 22:

```
Position P( 10, 20 );
P.Move( down, 80, 22 );
```

4.6.2.2 Robot Class.   The Robot class defines a single robot, or *automaton* in the simulation:

```
#include "position.h"

class Robot {
public:
  Robot();
  Position & Move();
  unsigned IsActive() const;
  void Fight();
  unsigned GetX() const;
  unsigned GetY() const;
  static void SetEnergyStart( unsigned n );

private:
  Position  where;              // shield x,y position
  Direction direction;          // 0,1,2,3
  unsigned  energy;             // energy level
  static unsigned energyStart;  // starting energy level
};
```

We also include inline functions that are placed in the same header file:

```
inline unsigned Robot::GetX() const
{
  return where.GetX();
}


inline unsigned Robot::GetY() const
{
  return where.GetY();
}
```

The `Robot` class has a static data member called `energyStart`, which is the starting energy level for all robots when they are created. Each `Robot` object contains the following data members:

where   A `Position` object indicating the robot's location in the grid.

direction   The robot's current direction of movement.

energy   The robot's current energy level.

4.6.2.3 Grid Class.   A grid contains a two-dimensional array of cells that represents the battlefield. It also manages an array of robots and assorted other information for the simulation. It is the grid's job to instigate the movement of each robot, and to deduct each robot's energy level when the robot enters a cell occupied by another robot:

```
#include <iostream.h>
#include <assert.h>
#include "screen.h"    // for clearScreen()
#include "robot.h"      // the Robot class

class Grid {
public:
  Grid( Robot * robotArray, unsigned numRobots );
  void Battle();
  unsigned CountActive() const;
  void Draw() const;

private:
  Robot * robots;          // array of robots
  unsigned cells[Position::xMax][Position::yMax];
  unsigned robotCount;         // starting num of robots
  unsigned activeCount;        // num of active robots
  unsigned timeCount;          // elapsed seconds
  void clearCells();    // clear all cells
};
```

A `Grid` contains an array of robots so we can keep track of each robot's position and energy level. In the two-dimensional array `cells`, each element holds an integer representing the number of robots currently in the cell. Other variables keep track of the grid during the simulation: `robotCount` holds the starting number of robots when the grid is created; `activeCount` contains the current number of active robots as the simulation progresses; and, `timeCount` is increased by 1 during each simulation loop.

4.6.3 Main Driver Program

The source code for the Robot Wars program is rather long, so we have omitted many details here. The complete source code listing can be found in Appendix A.

The main program has a `configure` function that displays the program title and asks the user to input the starting energy level of each robot and the final number of robots when the simulation is to be halted:

```
#include "grid.h"
#include "robot.h"

Screen theScreen;  // global Screen object

void configure( unsigned & startE, unsigned & stopC )
{
  theScreen.ClearScreen();
  cout << "ROBOT WARS (battle simulation)\n\n"
```

```
                << "Starting energy level of each robot? ";
  cin >> startE;
  cout << "Stop when population reaches which number? ";
  cin >> stopC;
}
```

We declare a global array of robots. Ordinarily, it would be a local variable, but the array would use up a great deal of stack space in some C++ implementations.

```
// NumRobots can be any integer 1 - 5000.
const unsigned NumRobots = 2000;
Robot robots[NumRobots];  // array of robots
```

From `main` we call `configure`, verify that the `stopCount` is less than the number of robots, and set the starting energy level of the robots:

```
#include <assert.h>

int main()
{
  unsigned startEnergy, numRobots, stopCount;

  configure( startEnergy, stopCount );
  assert( stopCount < NumRobots );

  Robot::SetEnergyStart( startEnergy );
```

`stopCount` is necessary because as the number of robots dwindles, there is so little contact between robots that robots almost never die. The starting energy value is passed to the `Robot` class so that every robot created by the simulation will have the same starting energy value.

Next, we declare and construct a `Grid` object, passing it the array of robots and number of robots:

```
Grid G( robots, numRobots );
```

The simulation is now ready to begin. A *do..while* loop repeats until the number of robots dwindles to the level specified by the user. Each iteration of the loop calls `Grid::battle` and redraws the grid on the console:

```
do {
  G.Battle();            // carry out one battle cycle
  G.Draw();              // draw the grid
} while ( G.CountActive() > stopCount );
```

4.6.3.1 File Structure.   The following table lists the contents of each of the source files that belong to the Robot Wars program:

Filename	Contents
screen.h	Screen class definition
position.h	Position class definition
position.cpp	Position class implementation
robot.h	Robot class definition
robot.cpp	Robot class implementation
grid.h	Grid class definition
grid.cpp	Grid class implementation
battle.cpp	Main driver program

4.6.4 Class Implementations

4.6.4.1 Position Class.   The Move function checks the direction of movement and calculates the new x and y positions; it also performs range checking to prevent the current position from going out of bounds:

```
void Position::Move( Direction dir, unsigned xMax, unsigned yMax )
{
  if( (dir == up) && ( y > 0) )
    y--;
  else if( dir == down )
    y++;
  else if( (dir == left) && (x > 0) )
    x--;
  else if( dir == right )
    x++;
  x = x % xMax;
  y = y % yMax;
}
```

The static ChooseRandomDirection function returns a randomly chosen direction. The ordering of constants in the Dir[] array here must match those in the Direction enumerated type. The rand function is defined in stdlib.h:

```
Direction Position::ChooseRandomDirection()
{
  const unsigned dcount = 4;
  Direction Dir[dcount] = {up, down, left, right};
  unsigned n = rand() % dcount;
  return Dir[n];
}
```

4.6.4.2 Robot Class.   The `Robot` constructor chooses random x, y coordinates for the robot, sets its position accordingly, chooses a random direction, and initializes the robot's energy level:

```
Robot::Robot()
{
  energy = energyStart;
  unsigned x = rand() % Position::xMax;
  unsigned y = rand() % Position::yMax;
  where.SetX( x );
  where.SetY( y );
  direction = Position::ChooseRandomDirection();
}
```

The `Move` function selects a random direction and updates the `where` data member, a `Position` object, by calling its `Move` function:

```
Position & Robot::Move()
{
  direction = Position::ChooseRandomDirection();
  where.Move( direction, Position::xMax, Position::yMax );
  return where;
}
```

The `Active`, `EnergyStart`, and `Fight` functions are straightforward. Fighting decreases a robot's energy level by 1:

```
unsigned Robot::IsActive() const
{
  return energy > 0;
}

void Robot::SetEnergyStart( unsigned n )
{
  energyStart = n;
}

void Robot::Fight()
{
  if (energy > 0) energy--;
}
```

4.6.4.3 Grid Implementation.   The `Grid` class constructor makes a copy of the pointer to the array of robots and initializes both the robot counter and the time counter:

```
Grid::Grid( Robot * robotArray, unsigned numRobots )
{
   robots = robotArray;
   activeCount = robotCount = numRobots;
   timeCount = 0;
}
```

CountActive iterates through the robot array and checks each robot's status. We increment a counter for each active robot:

```
unsigned Grid::CountActive() const
{
   unsigned sum = 0;
   unsigned i;
   for(i = 0; i < robotCount; i++)
      if( robots[i].IsActive() )
         sum++;
   return sum;
}
```

The Grid::Battle function also iterates through the array of robots. If a robot is still active, it moves one unit in a random direction. Using the robot's new position, we add to the count of robots in the robot's new cell. If the cell is already occupied, we subtract 1 from the current robot's energy level:

```
void Grid::Battle()
{
   Position p;
   unsigned x, y;
   clearCells();

   unsigned j;
   for(j = 0; j < robotCount; j++)
   {
      if( robots[j].IsActive() )   // is the robot alive?
      {
         p = robots[j].Move();
         x = p.GetX();              // get its position
         y = p.GetY();
         (cells[x][y])++;           // increment cell count

         if( cells[x][y] > 1 )      // cell occupied?
            robots[j].Fight();      // robots fight!
      }
   }
   timeCount++;
}
```

4.6.5 Conclusion

The Robot Wars simulation provides a simple demonstration of a number of techniques. It contains three classes working as a group, where each `Robot` object contains a `Position` object, and a `Grid` contains an array of `Robot` objects. We made the robots somewhat independent, allowing each to move randomly around the grid. We used static data members and functions, showing how these values would apply to all instances of the `Robot` class.

On the other hand, one of the greatest weaknesses of the simulation is that each robot has no idea as to the contents of the grid around itself. Another problem is that the sequential processing of the robot array is biased in favor of robots occurring earlier in the array, since they are moved into cells first. Robots arriving later are penalized by losing one energy point. The chapter exercises suggest possible solutions to these problems, which you may find to be an interesting incentive to create your variation of this program.

4.7 CHAPTER SUMMARY

Enumerated constants help to document the use of constants in a class and should be used whenever possible. Enumerated types are usually given public access, and when used outside of the class scope, must be qualified by the class name.

Classes often contain other class objects. We express this as a *composition* relationship and recongnize that it allows us to build powerful and complex data structures. Most applications are comprised of groups of related objects, many containing other objects.

A *constructor-initializer list* is used by a constructor to initialize class data members, particularly ones that are class objects. We presented the `Point` and `Figure` classes as examples of this.

Classes can contain *reference* and *const-qualified* data members. These must be initialized by the enclosing class constructor, using a *constructor-initializer list*. References are useful for forming a connection to an object that already exists.

Static data members are variables that belong to all instances of the same class. We showed an example of a `Student` class that kept a reference count of the number of instances of students created by the program. We showed how a static data member can be effectively used by a class constructor.

Static member functions provide access to static data members. They are useful for operations that involve an entire class, such as initializing static data members. We showed an example of a `Rectangle` class that used a static member function to set the default drawing color of all `Rectangle` objects.

We introduced the `FString` class, which implements operations on fixed-length strings. This class makes it easier to assign, initialize, copy, compare, and display strings, without having to deal directly with character arrays. We will use the FString class throughout the book.

The Robot Wars simulation program was an example of a larger program involving several interacting classes. We followed the same program development steps introduced in Chapter 2, including specifications, analysis, design, and implementation. Recognizing that no useful program is ever completely finished, we discussed ways in which the program could be improved.

4.8 EXERCISES

4.8.1 Miscellaneous

1 Inline Function Call. If you have access to an assembly-level debugger, trace through a call to a function that has an integer argument passed by value. You will probably see the calling program push the function argument on the stack before calling the function. In the first few lines of the function, try to find the statements that access the parameter. Next, declare the function as *inline,* recompile the program, and trace it again. Take note of the number of machine-level statements that have been eliminated.

2 Student Registration Application. Write a program that reads an input file containing student data and a list of courses taken by the student. Create a report that shows the students, courses, and tuition owed by each.

The input file should contain a student ID, last name, and a list of courses taken by the student. Each course consists of a course name followed by the number of credits. The first number in the line containing the courses is a counter of the number of courses to follow. For example,

```
10001 Baker
4 COP_1170 4 CGS_1060 4 ENC_1101 3 MAT_1033 3
20002 Chong
3 ENC_1101 3 GEO_2011 4 PHY_1001 3
30001 Gonzalez
0
```

The output report should show each student ID and name, followed by a formatted list of courses taken by the student. For each student, the tuition should be calculated and the total number of credits shown. For example,

```
.............. Student Registration Report ..............

10001: Baker
COP_1170-4,CGS_1060-4,ENC_1101-3,MAT_1033-3,
   Tuition equals $700.00 for 14 credits.

20002: Chong
ENC_1101-3,GEO_2011-4,PHY_1001-3,
   Tuition equals $500.00 for 10 credits.

30001: Gonzalez
   Tuition equals $0.00 for 0 credits.
```

Create a `Course` class that holds the name and number of credits for a single course. Create a `Student` class that contains an ID number, name, and an array of `Course` objects. Use the `FString` class (from this chapter) for any data members holding character strings.

3 Student Record Example.   In a student registration file, each student's data begins with a *header record,* containing the student ID, last name, and first name. The header record is followed by zero or more *course records* indicating the course name and credits taken. The first field in each record is a *tag* that identifies the type of record (H = header, C = course). A blank line identifies the end of each student's data:

```
H,10000,Jones,Sam
C,CGS 1060,4
C,ENC 1101,3
C,MAT 1033,3

H,20000,Baker,Ann
C,ENC 2301,3
C,COP 2400,4
(etc.)
```

Read several records from the console (or a file) and write a display function that displays the records with their appropriate fields. *Extra:* For each student, tally and print the total number of credits taken. Print a formatted report with each student's name, course names, and credits taken. Include a total of credits taken by all students.

4 Table Lookup, Single Result.   Write a function called `lookup` that searches an array of long integers for a matching value. There are several ways to implement this function. For example, you might want to return the array position of the found value as the function result, using −1 to indicate that the value was not found:

```
    n = lookup( table, tableSize, val );
    if( n != -1 )
        cout << "found in position" << n;
```

Or, you could have the function return 1 when the search was successful, and 0 otherwise:

```
    if( lookup( table, tableSize, val, index )
        cout << "found in position" << index;
```

Implement the function both ways (using overloading) and write a short program that tests both functions and displays the results.

5 Table Lookup, Multiple Results.   Write a function called `multiSearch` that searches an array of integers for a single value and returns a list of all the indices where matching entries were found. Use the standard `rand` function to generate a large array of random integers within a limited range, say 1 to 100. Write and test the search function and print out the resulting list of matching indices. You might want to use a special value (such as −1) to terminate the result list. The `multiSearch` function will have to allocate its own array of results, possibly as big as the table being searched.
Extra: Once all matching indices have been found inside `multiSearch`, if their number is substantially lower than the size of the table, copy them to a smaller array and release the original results array.

6 Playing Cards.   Using the `Card` class created in the exercises of Chapters 2 and 3, provide the following enhancements:

1. Declare the constructor parameters `const`.
2. Change the display member function to a friend operator << function for stream output. Its declaration is

```
    friend ostream & operator <<( ostream & os, const Card & C );
```

3. Let the operator << function display the name and suit of a card, such as "Ace of Spades". You may want to declare arrays of strings containing the suit names and card names. Here, for example, is an array of suit names that exactly matches the enumerated constants already declared in the class:

```
    char * sNames[] = { "None","Clubs","Diamonds",
                        "Hearts","Spades" };
```

4. In the test program, create an array of `Card` objects that represents the entire deck. Shuffle the deck and deal a round of hands to four players. Display each hand on the console.

The `rand` function in `stdlib.h` generates a pseudorandom number between 0 and RAND_MAX (also defined in stdlib.h). You can scale this down to a specific range by using the modulus (%) operator. The following, for example, generates an integer between 0 and 12:

```
unsigned n = rand() % 13;
```

7 EncryptedFile Class.   In the Chapter 3 exercises, we introduced the `SecureString` class and showed several ways to encrypt a string. In this exercise, we would like you to create an `EncryptedFile` class, that makes it convenient for a program to to read an encrypted file. The class constructor could take the filename and encryption key as parameters:

```
class EncryptedFile {
public:
  EncryptedFile( const FString & fileName,
                 const FString & key );

  friend ostream & operator <<( ostream & os,
        const EncryptedFile & f );

private:
  ifstream efile;
  SecureString str;
};
```

The `efile` data member is an `ifstream` object corresponding to the file, and `str` is a `SecureString` object that holds the last block of data read from the file.

8 Date Class.   Create a class called `Date` that stores a calendar date. Use a private static data member to keep track of the desired display format. Some formats you may want to include are shown with a sample date:

```
dd/mm/yy     22/10/96
mm/dd/yy     10/22/96
dd-Mmm-yyyy  22-Oct-1996
```

Use an enumerated type in the `Date` class to identify the formats. For example,

```
enum DateFormat { ddmmyy, mmddyy, ddmmmyyyy };
```

Supply `GetFormat` and `SetFormat` static member functions to let the class user retrieve and modify the date format. Overload the << operator for stream output, and use a switch statement to display the date according to the current format. Create additional date formats as you deem necessary.

4.8.2 Payroll Application

The following exercises are a continuation of the Payroll application that was introduced in the Chapter 3 exercises.

   1 The Employee and Payroll Classes.   In Chapter 3, each `Employee` object contained an ID number, last name, pay rate, and hours worked. Now, we would like to give each employee a first name and identify the pay period ending date. The problem is, some of these data remain relatively permanent, while some (such as the hours worked and period ending date), change every week. It makes more sense to divide up the data into two objects: an `Employee` object, containing the ID, name, and pay rate; and a `Payroll` object, containing the hours worked and the period ending date. Here are the new data members of the `Employee` class:

```
long id;                // identification number
FString lastName;       // last name
FString firstName;      // first name
float payRate;          // hourly pay rate
```

(We have switched from C-style strings to `FString` objects because the latter is much easier to use.) The `Payroll` class contains the following data members:

```
long empId;             // employee ID number
float hours;            // hours worked this week
float grossPay;         // pay before taxes for the week
float tax;              // taxes paid for the week
float netPay;           // pay after subtracting taxes
long endingDate;        // payroll period ending date
```

Both objects contain an ID field, which forms the connection between `Payroll` and `Employee` objects: Each instance of `Payroll` has an `empID` that matches the ID of some `Employee` object.

   In addition, the `Payroll` class should contain a static data member called `taxRate` to be used when calculating the amount of withholding. Provide a static member function in this class to let the main program initialize `taxRate`.

   Write a short test program that creates instances of `Employee` and `Payroll` objects, and displays the following formatted information:

```
Period ending date:  09/31/96
Employee name:       Johnson, Eugene
Hours worked:        40.00
Hourly pay rate:     10.50
Gross pay:           420.00
Tax (.15 rate):      -63.00
Net pay:             357.00
```

2 Reading Employee and Payroll Files.   Create an employee file containing five records. Create a payroll file containing five records for one ending date, and five more records with a different ending date. Make sure that each ID in the payroll file matches some ID in the employee file (the order of records is unimportant).

Write a main program that lets the user enter a period ending date. The program should then scan the payroll file, and for each record having the same ending date, locate its matching record in the employee file. Display each `Payroll` record in the same format as for the previous exercise.

3 Payroll Records for a Single Employee.   Using the classes and data files from the previous exercise, choose one employee ID and add at least six more records to the payroll file containing consecutive period ending dates. Write a program that lets the user enter an employee ID. Then, display all payroll records, in chronological order by period ending date, for the employee. Display the average number of hours worked per week and the total gross pay earned for the current year.

4 Employee Pension Accounts.   Let's assume that one or more pension accounts are established for each employee. Some might be paid for by the employer, and some might involve regular deductions from the employee's weekly paycheck (before taxes). We need to create a `Pension` class that represents this information with the following data members:

Pass by Reference   *Use bitwise copy.*

```
Employee & emp;         // reference to an employee
Payroll & payRoll;      // reference to payroll data
unsigned pType;         // type of pension (enumerated)
float amount;           // amount deposited in account
```

The type of pension can be represented by enumerated constants that indicate whether the contribution is made by the company or employee:

```
enum { companyPays, employeePays };
```

hard code

Write a program that lets the user enter an employee ID, pension type, and amount to be contributed. The program should construct a `Pension` object and display the following information: employee last and first names, contribution amount, and whether or not the contribution is made by the employee.

5 Deducting Pensions from the Payroll.   Using all of the classes and data files created in the previous employee payroll exercises, create another file containing employee pension information: employee ID, pension type, and pension amount. Write a program that lets the user enter an employee ID and payroll period ending date. Locate the following information in the data files: employee last and first names, gross pay, pension type, and pension amount. For employees that pay into their own pension fund, deduct that amount from the gross pay and recalculate the taxes and net pay. Display the recalculated pay, using the following sample as a guide:

```
┌─────────────────────────────────────────────────────┐
│  Period ending date:   09/31/96                      │
│  Employee name:        Johnson, Eugene               │
│  Gross pay:            420.00                         │
│  Pension deduction:     50.00                         │
│  Adjusted gross:       370.00                         │
│  Tax (.15 rate):       -55.50                         │
│  Net pay:              314.50                         │
└─────────────────────────────────────────────────────┘
```

4.8.3 Wind Velocities

The exercises in this section deal with a weather station that records wind velocities at regular intervals. We will assume that velocities are expressed as real numbers, in kilometers per hour (kph).

1 The WindArray Class.   Create a class called `WindArray` that contains an array of wind velocity readings from a weather station; each wind reading (kph) is type float, with one decimal digit of precision. We assume that the readings are ten minutes apart, beginning at 0000 hours and continuing up to 2350.

Calculate the average wind velocity every hour, using a 30-minute *moving average*. The moving average calculated at 0810, for example, would be the average of the readings taken at 0800, 0810, and 0820. Then at 0820, the moving average would be calculated from the readings at 0810, 0820, and 0830. The moving average, in other words, has a "smoothening" effect on the minor changes in wind velocities that occur throughout the given time period.

2 Graphical Representation of Moving Averages.   (Graphics display required.) Using the moving averages from the previous exercise, draw a two-dimensional plot of the actual wind velocity readings, overlayed by a plot of the 30-minute moving average.

3 Wind Velocity Search.   Using the `WindArray` class from the previous exercises, provide a member function called `Search` that lets the user search for a range of values. Let the function display the times (24-hour clock) of all wind readings that fall within the requested range. For example:

```
function call:
    Search( windTable, 40.0, 50.0 );

output:
    Range [40.0 - 50.0]: 1030, 1040, 1050, 1320, 1330, 1800, 1810
```

4.8.4 Robot Wars

The following exercises are based on the Robot Wars simulation program that was presented earlier in this chapter. The exercises are mutually independent.

1 Sequencing the Playing Grids.   As mentioned in our discussion of the Robot Wars program, there is a bias in favor of robots that occur in the earlier part of the robot array. The array is processed in sequential order, resulting in a penalty against robots entering cells already occupied by other robots. One solution to this problem would be to create two Grid objects, representing the positions of the robots before and after each move. For example, robots R3 and R4 would arrive in the same cell simultaneously, fight, and according to a random choice, one of them would lose. But this places both robots on an equal basis. Here is just a small section of a grid, before and after:

(R3 and R4 battle)

2 Varying the Robot Types.   A nice improvement to the Robot Wars program would be to create robots that could be either hunter robots or defensive robots (use a data member to determine this). The hunters would scan surrounding cells and try to trap another robot; defensive robots would seek to avoid other robots. To implement this idea, you need to find a way for each robot to access its neighboring grid cells. The current version of the program doesn't allow this because the array of robots is contained in the Grid class. Instead, you might consider having each Robot object contain a pointer to the grid. Explore this design modification and re-implement the Grid and Robot classes. Implement and test the program with the new types of robots.

4.8.5 Go-Moku Game

1 Go-Moku Playing Board. Create a program that displays a playing board from the ancient Japanese game of Go-Moku. The game is played on a board of 19 by 19 squares, with one player using disk-shaped black stones and the other using white. The stones are placed in the intersections of the lines. For convenience, number the rows and columns from 0 to 18:

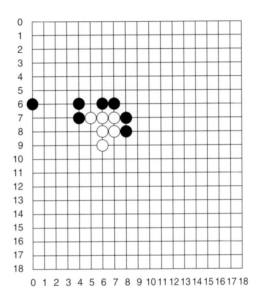

The winner of the game is the first player to place five consecutive stones of the same color on the board, so that they form a continuous horizontal, vertical, or diagonal line. The two players take turns placing individual stones on the board, with black going first. A stone cannot be moved once it has been placed. In the diagram above, for example, both players have completed five turns and white is about to add another stone to the board.

Your program should take each input move from the user as a pair of integers containing the row and column where a stone is to be placed on the board. The user enters moves for both white and black, and the program redraws the board after each move.

Create a class that encapsulates operations and data for the game board. Enumerated constants MaxRow and MaxCol define the board size; the constants empty, black, and white indentify the contents of each square on the board; finished and `playing` identify the current status of the game. For example, we could call the class `GoBoard`:

```
class GoBoard {
public:
  enum { MaxRow = 19, MaxCol = 19 };
  enum { empty, black, white };
  enum { finished, playing };

  GoBoard();
  // Constructor

  void Draw() const;
  // Draw the board.

  void Move();
  // Input a move from the user.

  int Playing();
  // Return 1 if the game is in progress.

private:
  int squares[MaxRow][MaxCol];
  int color;          // { empty, black, white }
  int status;         // { finished, playing }

  char * colorStr();   // get color of player
};
```

The `GoBoard::Move` function is the most complicated in the class. It inputs the next move from the player as two integers (`row`, `col`). It ensures that the values are legal and verifies that the target square is not already occupied. It then places the stone on the board.

2 Improving the Playing Board.   Revise the `GoBoard` class from the previous exercise so that it allows the user to input moves in the traditional Go notation. Looking at a board diagram, the horizontal rows are numbered from 1 to 19, starting at the bottom. The vertical columns are labeled A, B, C, . . . , T, starting from the left side. The letter I is omitted:

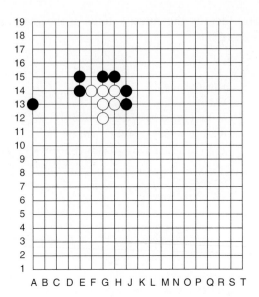

3 Checking for a Win.   Revise the GoBoard class from the previous two exercises. Add a function called CheckForWin that scans the board and looks for continuous sequences of five tiles of the same color. The five tiles could be arranged horizontally, vertically, or diagonally.

CHAPTER 5

Designing Classes

Previous chapters discussed the syntax and semantics of the C++ language, which comprise our basic tools for implementing programs. In this chapter, however, we concentrate on the design of classes and components (groups of classes) that make up an application. The object-oriented approach to design is fundamentally based on the object model, which we define. We describe a step-by-step approach to building components. Finally, we carry through the specifications, analysis, design, and implementation of an appointment-scheduling program for a doctor's office.

Terms Introduced in this Chapter:

abstraction	information hiding
base class	inheritance relationship
class interface	iterator
class implementation	link relationship
client	modifier
code reusability	modularity
component	mutator
composition relationship	object model
control abstraction	object-oriented analysis
conversion operator	object-oriented decomposition
derived class	object-oriented design
encapsulation	procedural abstraction

entity abstraction   selector
foundation operator   server
hierarchy   typing (type checking)

5.1 ANALYSIS, DESIGN, AND PROGRAMMING

Back in Chapter 1, we mentioned that *object-oriented* programming focuses on the physical entities that make up an application problem, and implements these entities as classes and objects. Here, we would like to distinguish between the analysis, design, and programming phases of program development, from an object-oriented point of view.

Object-oriented design is a design method that uses object-oriented decomposition and abstraction to implement a model of a system. *Object-oriented decomposition* is the process of using class and object abstractions to logically structure a system.

Object-oriented analysis is the process of examining application requirements from the perspective of the classes and objects found in the vocabulary of the problem domain. Once we understand what a program is supposed to accomplish, we discover the classes and objects appropriate to the problem.

The relationship between object-oriented analysis, design, and programming is this: The analysis produces the essential classes and objects relating to the problem we are trying to solve. The design decomposes the problem into specific objects and classes discovered during the analysis. The programming implements the design in a programming language.

5.2 THE OBJECT MODEL

5.2.1 Definition

Object-oriented programming has its roots in the *object model*. [Booch] points out that the object model is a way of looking at programs using principles of abstraction, encapsulation, modularity, hierarchy, and typing.[1] In the following sections, we will describe each of these principles.

The object model was developed and adopted by designers and programmers to deal with the complexity that results from placing greater demands on software. Users expect a lot more capabilities from software today than they did even ten years ago. Computer hardware has improved at an astounding rate, and the natural expectation by users has been for software to do the same. There have also been considerable pressures to reduce software development costs and bring products to market more quickly. [Yourdon], a leading expert on object-oriented design, writes:

---

[1] Two other principles, concurrency and persistence, are beyond the scope of our discussion.

The systems we build today are different than they were ten or twenty years ago. In every respect, they are larger and more complex; they are also more volatile and subject to constant change.

5.2.2 Abstraction

Abstraction clarifies the essential characteristics of an object, those that make it different from other types of objects. It is a way of providing a simplified view of what would otherwise be a complex entity. It is the outside view of an object. When describing a group of objects related by a common abstraction, we try to concentrate on their similarities rather than their differences.

The choice of abstraction depends greatly on the perspective of the viewer, or in practical terms, the requirements of the problem to be solved. For example, a mechanic would view an automobile in terms of its serviceable parts, whereas a driver would focus on the car's speed and manuverability.

A programming language is a good example of an abstraction. It shields the programmer from details of the computer's hardware and physical representation of data. For example, the `float` data type is an abstraction of a complicated binary real number representation. A variable is an abstraction of a chunk of memory stored at a physical address. A function declaration is an abstraction of a block of executable code, which has an interface consisting of its name, return type, and parameters.

A *class interface* is a simplified, coherent view of a class, containing the operations and data presented by the class to its users. A class interface might consist only of member functions that implement class operations, or it might include public data members that can be directly accessed by users. A class *implementation*, on the other hand, consists of program code that carries out the tasks associated with each operation, along with declarations of private and protected data members.

There is a practical aspect to this separation of interface and implementation: Once a class interface has been defined, users of a class can design their code around it. Meanwhile, development of the class implementation can proceed independently of the interface. Also, an existing class implementation can be improved over time, without affecting code that accesses the class.

5.2.3 Types of Abstractions

An abstraction can deal with how an object is manipulated, that is, how it responds to inputs. There are two general types of object-oriented abstractions: *control* (or action) abstractions and *entity* abstractions.

A *control abstraction* is a generalized set of operations, all of which perform the same kind of function, regardless of the context. One general example is a list-processing class, with operations such as *insert, remove,* and *find.* These operations might serve a variety of application domains, such as a bank teller simulation in which we use the operations *arrive, depart,* and *serve* to process customers.

An *entity* abstraction is based on a tangible element in a specific problem domain. The following would be typical entity abstractions:

```
Employee ( payroll data, calctax )
Student( id, calcgrade, register, drop, graduate )
Window (open, close, move, draw )
Machine( start, stop, temperature, status, reset )
```

Entity abstractions are the most obvious parts of a program design because they relate directly to the vocabulary of the problem domain. Control abstractions, on the other hand, are created by a program designer to actively manipulate other objects using well-known methods.

5.2.4 Encapsulation

Encapsulation is the enclosing of both variables and functions inside a class. In order for encapsulation to be useful in non-trivial programs, it is necessary to enclose both the class interface and implementation so that class users can interact with the class through its interface. [Booch] points out that encapsulation is achieved through *information hiding*, that is, the hiding of implementation details inside a class.

Why is information hiding so important? Without it, class users would know implementation details about a class, and might be tempted to directly modify data members without knowing how that might affect the rest of the class. Class implementations tend to change over time, and a class's creator must be free to modify its implementation as the need arises. Class users, on the other hand, should not have to alter their code when a class implementation is changed.

5.2.5 Modularity

Modularity, introduced into programming at least 20 years ago, is the encapsulation of related subroutines into independent compilation units, or modules. In C, for example, a module presents its interface through a header file containing function prototypes and global variable declarations. *Procedural abstraction*, the defining of a problem in terms of its operations, is the primary goal of modularity. C, like most other languages, does not require module interfaces to be exported, but C++ does. The primary advantage to exporting interfaces is that many programming errors can be caught at compile time, such as the passing of incorrect function argument types.

Using a modular approach, each module presents a protocol for handling communication to and from functions in the module. Variables and functions can be hidden in a module by assigning them internal linkage, and by providing access only through public functions. (In C and C++, the `static` keyword assigns internal linkage to identifiers.) Modularity was an important step in the direction of well-designed software; but, by itself, did not go far enough in supporting data abstraction.

5.2.6 Hierarchy

Hierarchy, or inheritance, describes a parent-child relationship between classes. This allows us to derive new classes from existing *base* classes, where the *derived* classes contain all the characteristics of their base classes.

For example, we might already have a class called `Point`. We could then derive a new class from `Point` called `Point3D`, containing the x and y data members of `Point` plus a new one called z. `Point` would be the base class, and `Point3D` would be the derived class:

Not only do derived classes inherit data, but they also inherit operations from their base classes. A *Draw* operation in `Point`, for example, would also be available in `Point3D`.

The chief advantage to deriving a new class from a base class is that you need only to define additional attributes and behaviors over and above those in the base. Instances of a derived class still inherit all characteristics of their base class.

5.2.7 Typing

Typing, or type checking, is the mechanism by which a language controls whether the values of objects can be interchanged. Strongly typed languages have strict rules that regulate the way objects of different types can be assigned, whereas weakly typed languages allow more flexibility in the way assignments are made.

C and C++ perform many type conversions automatically when an assignment operation takes place. For example, the value of the variable A can be assigned to a variety of types, possibly with loss of significant digits:

```
long A;
int B = A;
char C = A;
unsigned long D = A;
float E = A;
int F = E;
```

C++ does not, however, allow the arbitrary assignment of the value of a class object to another unrelated type of object. From this point of view, C++ is a strongly typed language. For example, a `Student` object cannot be assigned to an `Employee`:

```
Student S;
Employee E = S;   // error
```

Unless, that is, a specific member function has been added to either the `Student` or `Employee` class that makes this conversion possible. For example, the `Employee` class might contain a conversion constructor that specifically allows a `Student` to be assigned to an `Employee` that is in the process of being constructed:

```
class Employee {
public:
  Employee( const Student & S );
  //...
};
```

We might say that C++ offers the best of both worlds: The standard conversions between numeric types are carried over from the C language, but C++ classes control exactly how conversions take place between class objects. The net result is that a class user cannot incorrectly assign one class object to another because the error is caught by the compiler. In some cases, it might be desirable to prevent automatic conversions between numeric types, which could be accomplished by creating classes such as `Integer`, `Real`, `LongInteger`, and so forth.

It should also be mentioned here that automatic conversions can take place in C++ between objects whose classes are related by inheritance. The rules for this are quite specific and are spelled out in Section 7.2.

5.3 BASIC PRINCIPLES OF OBJECT-ORIENTED DESIGN

5.3.1 The Importance of Design

There is a lot more to becoming an effective object-oriented programmer than simply learning the syntax and semantics of C++. The most challenging aspect lies in the design of applications from an object-oriented point of view. Small programs can usually be designed as they are written. But non-trivial programs, particularly those involving multiple programmers, require considerable analysis and design in order to have a chance of success.

Is it possible to design and code a complicated program simultaneously? Almost never, and individuals with this level of talent are hard to keep around. Most often, the task of maintaining programs falls on individuals who may not have written the original code. If programs are correctly designed and documented, both their development and maintenance will be greatly simplified.

Let us proceed then with the assumption that nontrivial programs require analysis and design, and that object-oriented programs are best designed using object-oriented design methods.

5.3.2 Goals of Software Design

Well-designed software not only accomplishes the goals set out for it, but it has other distinguishing characteristics:

It is *simple* whenever possible. Rather than clutter a design with unnecessary features and obscure details, one aims for clarity. A simple, yet complete design is more likely to survive future program revisions. A simple design can also be more easily communicated between programmers and designers. Well-designed object-oriented programs generally have easy-to-understand class interfaces and clear relationships between classes.

Well-designed software is *flexible* enough to accomodate changes both at the design and programming levels. Ideally, one would prefer not to change a design after the program coding process had begun. But the reality is that changes are often necessary, and good designers try to leave room for change throughout the life of a program. In object-oriented programming, flexibility is enhanced when a designer can augment an existing class interface, and a programmer can revise a class implementation without causing changes to existing class users' code.

The best software is *extensible,* meaning that additions both at the large-scale level on down to the detailed level are possible without destroying the original program. Before formal methods of software design were widespread, we would often hear programmers complain about the difficulties of modifying existing software. In many cases, it was easier to completely rewrite programs rather than try to modify the originals. In object-oriented programming, extensibility is achieved by adding new classes to programs, and by using inheritance to refine the behavior of existing classes.

Where appropriate, well-designed software aims to be *portable,* meaning that the software can be recompiled and run on unrelated computer systems. Portability is often easier to achieve in an object-oriented environment. For example, classes can be clustered into libraries that allow cross-platform software development. This permits the same programs to be recompiled and run under different operating systems.

Well-designed software tries to be *reusable,* allowing it to be used with relatively few modifications in more than one program. Because of the tremendous time that goes into writing and debugging software, programmers have found that they can save money by reusing code from existing programs. Just as one might construct a computer from off-the-shelf parts that have already been tested, software developers try to do the same with their programs. [Stroustrup91] suggests that software designers could learn from automobile designers: When a new car is designed, every attempt is made to incorporate parts from the factory's own inventory. Not only does this greatly reduce the cost of the new car, but it improves the product's reliability by using parts that have already proven themselves under actual driving conditions.

Code reusability is improved in programs that use clusters of related classes that form cohesive units, called *components.* For example, foundation classes for graphical user interfaces (GUIs) are typically designed to be general enough to work in a variety of application programs. Some examples of GUIs are MS-Windows, X-Windows, and Motif.

Observing the goals of software design that we have described can help in producing better programs, but only if the designer has the experience and discipline to make it work. Object-oriented design methods by themselves do not guarantee success; they only provide a direction for designers to follow.

5.3.3 Designing Object-Oriented Programs

Above all, an object-oriented design should model the application problem that it is trying to solve. Every real-world problem has active players that can be used as a basis for creating the classes and objects in a program. [Stroustrup91] says, "Identify key concepts of an application, and give each class the responsibility for maintenance of all information relating to a single concept." It is not always easy to choose the classes that most closely correspond to the problem domain. You may find it helpful to participate in candid discussions with other programmers and designers about the design of a new program.

In the traditional method of top-down structured design, programs are designed around procedures. High-level tasks are divided into subtasks, and lower-level modules are added to the design until all low-level tasks are accounted for. The design is usually finished before a single line of code is written, because last-minute changes to a design drive up the costs of recoding modules affected by the changes. If flaws are discovered in the original design after the coding phase has begun, there is considerable economic pressure to work around the flaws rather than modify the design.

By contrast, object-oriented design is best viewed as an iterative process: After the initial design of classes and interfaces, individual components can be constructed. We can continue to refine the class design, possibly creating new classes from the common elements of existing ones, or by splitting complex classes into smaller ones. Even while a design is being completed, a great deal of coding and testing takes place. If some aspects of a design are found to be weak or unworkable in actual practice, the design is corrected. This flexibility is possible if we hide details inside classes and separately define the interfaces between classes; consequently, implementations can be revised without affecting a program's structure. Conversely, relationships between classes can be readjusted without affecting the code inside the classes.

5.4 DESIGNING COMPONENTS

A *component* is a group of related classes that work together. Sometimes a component will be a portion of a class library, such as a library dealing with graphical windows. When you are designing classes for an application, do not create a single class in isolation. Instead, design each class in terms of its interactions with other classes in the same component.

Some well-documented approaches to designing components can be found in [Booch], [Coad and Yourdon], [Martin and Odell], [Stroustrup91], and others. A good deal of analysis is done during the beginning stages, where one attempts to model the software after a real-world application. Stroustrup, for example, suggests four steps when designing components: find the classes, specify class operations, specify class dependencies, and specify class interfaces. We're going to explore these steps further.

5.4.1 Find the Classes

Find the classes that most closely resemble the real-world entities in the application. The phrase "find the classes" is significant because we did not say "create the classes." As designers, we are not creating something out of nothing; rather, we are discovering the inherent structure behind the application and adapting our program's design to that structure. When hearing an expert discuss an application, take note of the use of nouns, verbs, and adjectives. Perhaps the owner of a videotape rental store might discuss an inventory system as follows:

> When ordering new **videotapes** from a **supplier,** the store manager creates a **purchase order,** fills in the date, the supplier's name and address, and enters a **list of videotapes** to be ordered. The purchase order is added to a permanent **list of purchases.** When one or more videotapes are received from a supplier, a clerk locates the original purchase order and makes a record of each tape that was received. A record of the videotape is then added to the store's **inventory.** When all tapes listed on a particular purchase order have been received, the manager sends a **payment** to the supplier and the purchase order is given a completion date.

Notice that we highlighted important nouns such as *videotapes, supplier, purchase order, list of videotapes, list of purchases, inventory,* and *payment.* These might be good candidates for classes in the design of an inventory component. There might be other classes that are discovered during the early stages of the problem analysis. Verbs often translate into operations. In our discussion, we used verb phrases such as *create, fills in, added to, received from, locates, makes a record,* and *sends a payment.*

5.4.2 Specify Class Operations

We refine the classes in a component by specifying which operations each class can perform. This is a difficult task during the early stages of a design because it requires us to anticipate all the ways objects will interact. Operations performed by classes manifest themselves as member functions.

It is important to provide a basic set of operations such as the following, which make a class both usable and portable: one or more constructors, stream I/O operators, copy operations, and operations that get and set essential data members. Beyond these, we need operations that respond to messages from other class objects. We try not to overload each class, however, with lots of operations that do not contribute to the class's effectiveness.

Certain general categories of operations are provided by classes:

1. *Foundation operators* such as constructors and destructors, including copy constructors.
2. *Selectors,* which return the values of data members but do not allow the data to be changed.
3. *Modifiers*, or *mutators* that allow changes to data members.
4. *Conversion operators* that allow an instance of a class to be copied into another type of object.
5. *Iterators* that process data members containing collections of objects.

Many of the operations provided by a class can be specified during the analysis phase. In fact, the operations have a lot to do with the way we understand a class. An `InventoryList` class, for example, would probably have operations such as `AddNewItem`, `RemoveItem`, and `FindItem`.

Most class data members need not be specified during the analysis phase because they are part of the class implementation. This rule may be bent, however, as one C++ developer points out:

> Do not be alarmed if you, or others on the team, feel it necessary to describe a few of the data members in a very small number of classes in the design process. Even on the first day, it might be desirable to understand some of the details which will be fleshed out in the implementation in order to avoid what is sometimes referred as hand-waving or the mumble factor. Weeks, even months, of re-engineering the class tree can be avoided by spending a few hours early in the process thinking about and then documentating mission-critical details. [Kamenz]

5.4.3 Specify Class Dependencies

When specifying class dependencies, we attempt to show how the various classes in a component relate to each other. There are three types of dependencies, based on relationships between classes: *inheritance, composition,* and *link.* The first exists when a class is derived from another class. The second occurs when an object contains a copy of an object, or exerts control over a member object. The third occurs when an object passes messages to another object, but the objects are independent of one another.

For example, in a Student Registration program, each `Student` object contains an `Address` object, creating a composition relationship. Each `Student` object passes messages to a `CourseCatalog` object, creating a link relationship. A

`GraduateStudent` is a specialized type of `Student`, creating an inheritance relationship.

Often, a client-server relationship exists between two objects. A *client* is an object that uses the resources of another object, who in turn, is called the *server*. The server's interface lists the messages that it can receive from a client. A client requests operations or data by passing messages to a server.

5.4.4 Specify Class Interfaces

During the design phase, each class operation becomes a member function. When specifying a class interface, we create exact descriptions of the public members of each class. Function prototypes are supplied for member functions and comments describe the function's input/output values.

When the class interfaces are finished, they can be shared among a team of programmers who have been delegated the task of creating the class implementations. It is extremely important for the implementor of a class to test it in isolation. Otherwise, debugging a complex project would be nearly impossible.

Armed with the class interface, the user of a class can predict how such a class object will behave without knowing about the class's implementation. When a class interface changes, however, it causes a ripple effect through all classes that use it. These changes must be carefully planned by the project designer.

To help illustrate the principles we just presented on designing class components, we're going to design a simple program called *Doctor's Office Scheduling*, which schedules appointments for patients at a medical doctor's office. The scheduling component should be self-contained so that it could be inserted into any program without requiring modification.

5.5 CASE STUDY: DOCTOR'S OFFICE SCHEDULING

5.5.1 Specifications

We want to create a program that schedules appointments for patients in a doctor's office. The office has multiple doctors, each of which has a daily schedule divided into 15-minute appointment slots beginning at 8:00 a.m. and finishing at 6:00 p.m. In addition to scheduling appointments, we also want to print out a separate daily schedule for each doctor, listing the time and patient name of each appointment.

The program will be interactive with all output directed to the screen, except for the doctors' schedules, which will be written to a file for later printing. A restriction we have placed on the program for the moment is that only one appointment day is to be scheduled for each doctor. In the Chapter exercises, we suggest modifying this program so that each doctor has an array of schedules.

5.5.2 Analysis

In finding the classes for this application, we turn to nouns that were used in the specifications, such as doctor, patient, daily schedule, and appointment. Based on these, we will call the classes `Doctor`, `Patient`, `DailySchedule`, and `Appointment`. We will also have a class called `Scheduler` that performs the duties of the receptionist. Here is a likely script, or scenario for the appointment scheduling process:

- `Scheduler` requests the patient's name.
- `Patient` chooses a doctor.
- `Scheduler` displays doctor's schedule, showing available appointment slots.
- `Patient` requests a specific time slot.
- `Scheduler` adds the appointment to the doctor's schedule, and adds the appointment to the patient's records.
- `Scheduler` confirms the appointment.

5.5.2.1 *Class Dependencies.*   Class dependencies, or relationships, are an important part of the analysis of this application because they help us to understand how the objects in the program will interact. We know, for example, that a `Doctor` has a `DailySchedule`. The following diagram reflects the dependencies:

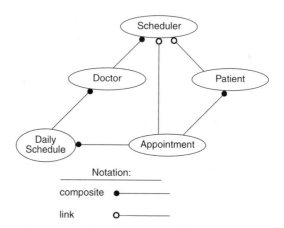

Composite relationships are shown by the lines beginning with solid circles: The `Scheduler` contains multiple doctors, and each `Doctor` contains a `DailySchedule`. A `DailySchedule` is made up of many `Appointment` objects. Each `Patient` contains an `Appointment`. Link relationships are shown by the lines beginning with open circles: The `Scheduler` requests information from a `Patient` and creates an `Appointment`.

The notation we use here and elsewhere in the book is loosely borrowed from [Booch] the so-called "Booch Lite" method.

5.5.2.2 Operations.   Also, as part of the analysis phase, we enumerate the operations that each class supports; the operations will later translate into class member functions. First, we assume that each class needs default constructors, stream I/O operators, and functions that get and set individual data members, so we don't list those operations here.

Doctor should support the following operations:

- AddToSchedule: Add an appointment to the doctor's schedule.
- ShowAppointments: Display all scheduled appointments.

DailySchedule should support the following operations:

- SetAppointment: Add an appointment to the schedule.
- IsTimeSlotFree: Find out if a particular time slot is available.
- ShowAppointments: Display scheduled appointments.

Appointment should support the following operations:

- Constructor: Create an Appointment object from a time slot, doctor number, and patient name.
- IsScheduled: Find out if an appointment has been scheduled for the current Appointment object.

Patient should support the following operations:

- InputName: Input the patient's name.
- ChooseDoctor: Select a doctor.
- ChooseTimeSlot: View a doctor's schedule and request an appointment time.
- SetAppointment: Schedule an appointment for the patient.

Scheduler should support the following operations:

- ScheduleOneAppointment: Schedule a single patient for a specific appointment time with a specific doctor.
- ScheduleAllAppointments: Input patient data, let patients request specific doctors and appointment times, update doctors' schedules.
- PrintAllAppointments: Display or print all scheduled appointments for all doctors.

5.5.2.3 Additional Classes. Let's visualize, for a moment, how the `Appointment` class will be implemented. We would like to display and input appointment times not as integers , but as time-of-day values such as 8:30, 10:45, and so on. For this, we create the `TimeSlot` class, which handles the translation and formatting of appointment times. We also use the `FString` class introduced in Chapter 4 for any string data members.

5.5.3 Design

During the design phase, we specify all of the class interfaces. The class operations and class dependencies produced by the analysis step provide the input to this phase. The output from the design phase is a header file containing all class definitions. We will show some of the class definitions here; a complete listing of all the source code for this program is in Appendix A.

5.5.3.1 The TimeSlot Class. The most useful operations in the `TimeSlot` class are performed by the stream I/O operators, which allow integers in the range 0-40 to be translated into specific appointment times. `StartHour` is a static data member that determines the earliest possible appointment time. The length of each appointment is determined by the static data member `ApptLen`:

```
class TimeSlot {
public:
  TimeSlot( const unsigned n = 0 );

  unsigned AsInteger() const;

  friend istream & operator >>(istream & inp, TimeSlot & T);

  friend ostream & operator <<(ostream & os, const TimeSlot & T);

private:
  static unsigned StartHour;
  static unsigned ApptLen;
  unsigned intValue;
};
```

The user is able to enter an appointment time in the 24-hour clock format *hh:mm*; this time is stored in the `TimeSlot` object as an unsigned integer. The time is redisplayed in the same 24-hour format.

5.5.3.2 The Appointment Class. The `Appointment` class ties together a doctor number, `TimeSlot` object, and patient name. It will itself be a member of the `DailySchedule` and `Patient` classes:

```
class Appointment {
public:
  Appointment();

  Appointment ( const TimeSlot & aTime,
        unsigned docNum, const Patient & aPatient );

  const FString & GetPatientName() const;

  const TimeSlot & GetTime() const;

  int IsScheduled() const;

  void SetTime( const unsigned n );

  friend ostream & operator <<( ostream & os,
        const Appointment & A );

private:
  enum { NoDoctor = 9999 };
  unsigned doctorNum;
  TimeSlot timeSlot;
  FString patientName;
};
```

5.5.3.3 *The Patient Class.*   The Patient class contains a patient's name and an Appointment object:

```
class Patient {
public:
  Patient();

  void InputName();

  unsigned ChooseDoctor() const;

  TimeSlot ChooseTimeSlot(const Doctor & D) const;

  const Appointment & GetAppointment() const;

  const FString & GetFirstName() const;

  const FString & GetLastName() const;

  int IsScheduled() const;
```

```
      void SetAppointment( const Appointment & A);

      friend ostream & operator <<( ostream & os,
         const Patient & P );

   private:
      FString lastName;
      FString firstName;
      Appointment nextVisit;
   };
```

When coding the `Patient` class, you will need to insert the following forward declaration for the `Doctor` class before defining the `Patient` class. This is required
because `Patient::ChooseTimeSlot` has a parameter of type `Doctor`:

```
      class Doctor;   // forward declaration
```

5.5.3.4 *The DailySchedule Class.*   The `DailySchedule` class contains an
array of `Appointment` objects. An instance of this class will be stored in each
`Doctor` object. It is responsible for checking individual time slots to see if they are
free, scheduling appointments, and showing all scheduled appointments:

```
      class DailySchedule {
      public:
        DailySchedule();

        int IsTimeSlotFree(const TimeSlot & aTime) const;

        void SetAppointment( const Appointment & app );

        void ShowAppointments( ostream & os ) const;

        friend ostream & operator <<( ostream & os,
             const DailySchedule & DS );

      private:
        enum { MaxTimeSlots = 40 };
        Appointment appointments[MaxTimeSlots];
      };
```

5.5.3.5 *The Doctor Class.*   The `Doctor` class contains an identification
number, last name, and a daily schedule. It is responsible for adding appointments
to its schedule and displaying the current daily schedule:

```
      class Doctor {
      public:
        Doctor();
```

```
        int AddToSchedule( const Appointment & app );

        const DailySchedule & GetSchedule() const;

        void SetId( unsigned n );

        void SetLastName( const FString & nam );

        const FString & GetLastName() const;

        void ShowAppointments( ostream & os ) const;

        static const FString & GetDoctorName(unsigned index);

        static void SetDoctorName( unsigned index,
                const FString & nam );
    private:
      unsigned id;
      FString lastName;
      DailySchedule schedule;
      static FString doctorName[NumDoctors];
    };
```

Notice that the class has a static data member called `doctorName`, which is an array containing all of the doctors' names. This array is loaded from a file at run time. We provide the static `GetDoctorName` and `SetDoctorName` access functions to make these names available globally.

The `AddToSchedule` member function attempts to schedule an appointment; it returns 1 if successful, or 0 if the requested appointment time is already taken.

5.5.3.6 The Scheduler Class.

The `Scheduler` class interacts with patients and doctors to set appointments. Its constructor initializes an array of `Doctor` objects with empty schedules:

```
        class Scheduler {
        public:
          Scheduler( Doctor * docs );

          void PrintAllAppointments( const char * fileName );

          int ScheduleOneAppointment();

          void ScheduleAllAppointments();

        private:
          Doctor * doctors;  // array of doctors
        };
```

In `ScheduleAllAppointments`, each patient's name is input, along with a requested time for an appointment. The doctor's schedule is consulted, and, if the time is available, the appointment is confirmed.

5.5.4 Main Program

The main program creates an instance of the `Scheduler` class, activating its constructor. We have attempted to keep our dealings with the objects at a high level of abstraction:

```
#include "doctors.h"

static Doctor doctorArray[NumDoctors];

int main()
{
  cout << "Doctors Office Scheduling Program\n\n";

  Scheduler officeSchedule( doctorArray );

  officeSchedule.ScheduleAllAppointments();

  officeSchedule.PrintAllAppointments( "appts.txt" );

  return 0;
}
```

The name `doctorArray` was declared with file scope, to avoid using up valuable stack space inside `main`. We also declare it with static linkage so that no statements outside of the main module can access it directly. In structured programming and in object-oriented programming, we try to avoid using global variables.

5.5.5 Class Implementations

We will present some highlights from the class implementations, with a reminder that the complete source code appears in Appendix A.

5.5.5.1 The TimeSlot Class.   The `TimeSlot` class implementation includes the stream input operator function. The user enters a 24-hour time in the format *hh:mm* and we store it in `buf`. We then create an input string stream and use it to read the hours and minutes from `buf`. Converting this to an integer time slot uses the following formula, where h = hour value, sa = the starting appointment time, aph = appointments per hour, m = minute value, and al = the appointment length in minutes:

$$timeSlot = (h - sa)^* aph + \frac{m}{al}$$

The number of appointments per hour is calculated as: $aph = \text{int}(60 / al)$. Here is the source code. We create an `istrstream` object and read the time from it to provide more robust input processing. This technique, and the reasons for using it, were demonstrated in Section 3.5:

```
istream & operator >>( istream & inp, TimeSlot & T )
{
  char buf[20];
  inp.getline( buf, 20 );     // get a line of input
  istrstream aStream( buf, 20 );
  int h, m;
  char ch;
  aStream >> dec >> h >> ch >> m;
  int aph = 60 / TimeSlot::ApptLen;
  if( h < T.StartHour )               // invalid hour?
    cerr << "\n Invalid hour value.\n";
  T.intValue = ((h - TimeSlot::StartHour)* aph)
             + (m / TimeSlot::ApptLen);
  return inp;
}
```

Note that we use the `dec` stream manipulator to guarantee that an input expression such as "09" will be interpreted as a decimal number.

The stream output operator takes an integer time slot value and converts it to a string in the 24-hour time format *hh:mm*. For example, if there were four appointments per hour and a starting hour of 08:00 for all appointments, then for a given time slot value *v*, we would calculate hours *h* as: $h = (v/aph) + 8$:

```
ostream & operator <<( ostream & os, const TimeSlot & T )
{
  int aph = 60 / T.ApptLen;
  int h = (T.intValue / aph ) + T.StartHour;
  int m = (T.intValue % aph ) * T.ApptLen;

  char oldfill = os.fill('0');
  os << setw(2) << h << ':' << setw(2) << m;
  os.fill( oldfill );
  return os;
}
```

We use the `ios::fill` function to set the default fill character to '0' so the hours and minutes will display with leading zeros (for example, "08:00"). Equally important, we restore the previous fill character before leaving this function to avoid having an unintended impact on stream output elsewhere in the program.

5.5.5.2 The Appointment Class.

An `Appointment` object can be constructed from a `TimeSlot`, a doctor number (docNum), and a `Patient`:

```
Appointment::Appointment ( const TimeSlot & aTime,
   unsigned docNum, const Patient & aPatient )
{
  timeSlot = aTime;
  doctorNum = docNum;
  patientName = aPatient.GetLastName();
  patientName.Append( ", " );
  patientName.Append( aPatient.GetFirstName() );
}

ostream & operator <<( ostream & os, const Appointment & A )
{
  os << "Dr. " << Doctor::GetDoctorName(A.doctorNum) << ", "
     << "Time: "
     << A.timeSlot;
  return os;
}
```

5.5.5.3 The Patient Class. ChooseTimeSlot displays the schedule of a doctor and asks the operator to enter a time in 24-hour format (hh:mm). The doctor's schedule is a DailySchedule object, which overloads the stream output operator. The function creates and returns a TimeSlot object:

```
TimeSlot Patient::ChooseTimeSlot( const Doctor & D ) const
{
  cout << '\n'
       << "Daily Schedule of Dr. " << D.GetLastName() << '\n'
       << "......................................." << '\n'
       << D.Schedule() << '\n'
       << "Enter a time (format hh:mm): ";
  TimeSlot aSlot;
  cin >> aSlot;
  return aSlot;
}
```

Here is the rest of the class implementation:

```
void Patient::InputName()
{
  cout << "Patient's last name: ";
  cin >> lastName;
  cout << "Patient's first name: ";
  cin >> firstName;
}

TimeSlot Patient::ChooseTimeSlot( const Doctor & D ) const
{
  cout << '\n'
       << "Daily Schedule of Dr. " << D.GetLastName() << '\n'
```

```
           << "......................................." << '\n'
           << D.GetSchedule() << '\n'
           << "Enter a time (format hh:mm): ";
     TimeSlot aSlot;
     cin >> aSlot;
     return aSlot;
   }


   ostream & operator <<( ostream & os, const Patient & P )
   {
     os << "Patient " << P.firstName << ' '
        << P.lastName << '\n'
        << "has been scheduled as follows:" << '\n'
        << P.nextVisit << endl;
     return os;
   }
```

5.5.5.4 *The DailySchedule Class.*

```
              DailySchedule::DailySchedule()
              {
                for(unsigned i = 0; i < MaxTimeSlots; i++)
                  appointments[i].SetTime( i );
              }
```

To verify that a particular appointment time is available, `IsFree` uses `aTime` to index into the `appointments` array and call `IsScheduled` for the appropriate time slot:

```
     int DailySchedule::IsFree( const TimeSlot & aTime ) const
     {
       unsigned n = aTime.AsInteger();
       return !appointments[n].IsScheduled();
     }
```

To schedule an appointment, `SetAppointment` gets the integer value of the appointment's time and uses this to index into the `appointments` array:

```
     void DailySchedule::SetAppointment( const Appointment & app )
     {
       unsigned n = app.GetTime().AsInteger();
       appointments[n] = app;
     }
```

`ShowAppointments` displays the appointment times and patient names of scheduled appointments:

```
void DailySchedule::ShowAppointments( ostream & os ) const
{
  for(unsigned  i = 0; i < MaxTimeSlots; i++)
  {
    if( appointments[i].IsScheduled())
      os << appointments[i].GetTime() << "    "
        << appointments[i].GetPatientName()
        << endl;
  }
}
```

The stream output operator displays a list of all appointment times and a notation showing which are available and which are taken:

```
ostream & operator <<( ostream & os, const DailySchedule & DS )
{
  for(unsigned  i = 0; i < DS.MaxTimeSlots; i++)
  {
    os << DS.appointments[i].GetTime();
    if( DS.appointments[i].IsScheduled())
      os << " ***     ";
    else
      os << "         ";
    if( i % 4 == 3 ) os << '\n';
  }
  os << endl;
  return os;
}
```

5.5.5.5 *The Doctor Class.*   In the `Doctor` class, the `AddToSchedule` function checks a time slot to make sure it is available, and if it is, adds an appointment to the doctor's schedule:

```
FString Doctor::doctorName[NumDoctors];
// static data member

int Doctor::AddToSchedule( const Appointment & app )
{
  if( schedule.IsTimeSlotFree( app.GetTime()))
  {
    schedule.SetAppointment( app );
    return 1;
  }
  return 0;
}
```

The `ShowAppointments` function outputs a list of scheduled appointments for a particular doctor:

```
void Doctor::ShowAppointments( ostream & os ) const
{
  os << "Appointments for Dr. "
     << lastName << '\n'
     << "................................"
     << endl;
  schedule.ShowAppointments( os );
  os << endl;
}
```

5.5.5.6 *Some Comments About Reusability.* The Doctor's Office Scheduling component was designed to be self-contained, allowing it to be re-used in related application programs. Unfortunately, reusability is often difficult to achieve. In other application programs for a doctor's office, for example, we might want to implement classes called `Doctor` and `Patient` differently.

In the `Patient` class of the current program, the stream output operator specifically displays a patient's name and appointment (time and doctor name). But, if the same `Patient` class were used in a program that tracked patients' immunization schedules, for example, the display we just mentioned would be inappropriate. A question we might ask is, just what type of stream output would be appropriate for all `Patient` objects? There probably is no correct answer to this question, because the nature of a patient changes according to the real-world application being solved. In Chapter 6, we will discover tools for creating alternate types of `Patient` objects (or other objects) that can customize their behavior according to an application's needs.

5.6 CHAPTER SUMMARY

We defined a number of terms in this chapter related to object-oriented analysis, design, and programming. We explained how analysis, design, and programming are complementary activities that produce better programs.

The *object model* is an essential way of looking at object-oriented programs that includes abstraction, encapsulation, modularity, hierarchy, and typing. Object-oriented analysis, design, and programming are based on the object model.

Abstraction clarifies the essential characteristics of an object that make it different from other types of objects. It is a way of providing a clarified, more solution-oriented view of what had previously been viewed as a complex, problematic entity.

Enclosing both the interface and implementation in a class is called *encapsulation*. *Information hiding* is a technique used to achieve encapsulation.

Modularity is the technique one uses to cluster related program code into separate compilation units.

Inheritance describes a parent-child relationship between classes. This allows us to derive new classes from existing ones, where the derived classes contain all characteristics of their parents plus additional features that make them unique. It is for this reason that a derived class is called a *superclass* in some object-oriented programming languages.

Typing, or *type checking* is the mechanism by which a language controls whether objects of different types can be interchanged.

In this chapter, we emphasize the importance of analysis and design because object-oriented programming involves a deeper understanding of the principles of object-oriented programming than just the syntax and semantics of C++. It usually takes professional programmers a considerable amount of time before they can internalize the principles of object-oriented design well enough to produce nontrivial applications.

Well-designed object-oriented programs generally have easy-to-understand class interfaces and clear relationships between classes. Portability is often easier to achieve in an object-oriented environment because classes can be clustered into libraries that allow cross-platform software development. In object-oriented programming, extensibility is achieved by adding new classes to programs, and using inheritance to refine the behavior of existing classes.

We discussed a number of design principles. First, an object-oriented design should model the application problem that it is trying to solve. Second, object-oriented design is best viewed as an iterative process, where design and programming work hand-in-hand.

We discussed ways of designing components (groups of related classes). The basic steps were:

- Find the classes that most closely resemble the real-world entities in the application.
- Specify which operations each class can perform, including its responses to messages sent by other objects.
- Specify class dependencies, showing how classes in the application depend on each other.
- Specify class interfaces, describing the public members of each class.

We finished the chapter with a complete case study, called Doctor's Office Scheduling. The specifications, analysis, design, and implementation steps were explained, showing how they fit in with the design principles from this chapter.

5.7 EXERCISES

5.7.1 Doctor's Office Scheduling

The following group of exercises relate to the Doctor's Office Scheduling program introduced in this chapter. It is suggested that you complete the exercises in sequence.

1 Using Member Accessor Functions.   Most textbook examples of classes allow member functions to directly access data members, probably for the sake of convenience.

But a good case can be made for requiring all member functions to call accessor functions to get and set the values of data members. For example, any future modification to the name of a data member such as `Patient::lastName` would require only two accessor functions to be modified: `GetLastName` and `SetLastName`. Every other function in the `Patient` class would continue to call the accessor functions rather than make direct references to the data members.

Try this approach on the `Doctor` and `Patient` classes in the Doctor's Office application. The only member functions that can directly access each data member should be the ones that get and set the member's value.

2 Saving Schedules to a File.   Enhance the Doctors' Office Scheduling program from this chapter so that schedules can be saved in a text file. Each time the program is run, have it load any existing schedules from a file before new appointments are added. Provide a user option to clear the existing schedules.

3 Array of Doctor Schedules.   Enhance the previous exercise so that each doctor has an array of five `DailySchedule` objects, one for each day of the work week. Allow patients to schedule on any day, and write out the entire week's schedule to a file.

4 Schedule Database.   The current design of the Doctor's Office Scheduling program makes inefficient use of memory because it must keep arrays of `DailySchedule` objects in memory. Redesign the `Appointment` class so that each object contains the following data members:

```
doctor number
date of appointment
time slot
patient name
```

Create a new class called `Schedule` that contains an array of `Appointment` objects. Provide the following basic operations, and add more as needed:

- `FindFirst`: Given a patient's name, return the index position of the first appointment containing the patient's name. Return -1 if no appointment can be found.

- `FindNext`: Return the index position of the next appointment made by the patient that was located by calling `FindFirst`. Return -1 if no appointment can be found.

- `AddAppointment`: Given an `Appointment` object, add it to the Schedule.

- `RemoveAppointment`: Given the index position of an `Appointment`, remove it from the `Schedule`.

- `SaveFile`: Save the `Schedule` to a file in such a way that it can be read from the file later.
- `LoadFile`: Load data for an existing schedule from a file into a `Schedule` object.

5.7.2 Employee Payroll

1 Employee Stack (1).   You are the manager of a data processing department that has the task of hiring and laying off employees. Seniority is important because you will lay off employees in the reverse order that they were hired (a *Last In, First Out* structure). This ensures that employees who were hired first will be the last to be laid off. Using the `Stack` class from the Chapter 2 exercises as a model, create a class that represents a stack of employees.

An `Employee` object should contain the following data members: ID, last name, first name, job title, years with company. Write a test program with a menu offering the following choices:

1. Hire new employee.
2. Let the user input a complete employee record.
3. Lay off employee(s).
4. Let the user select the number of employees to be be laid off. (The program should display all information about the employees that are removed from the stack.)
5. List all employees.
6. Exit program.

2 Employee Stack (2).   Enhance the previous exercise in the following ways:

- Save the employee stack in a file and reload the stack from the file each time the program is run.
- Assign a priority to employees based on their specialized skills. When laying off workers, exempt all employees with a priority level of 1.

5.7.3 Video Inventory

1 Video Inventory System.   Write a program that keeps track of videotapes owned and rented by a video store. The store needs to be able to display its inventory, add new tapes, remove tapes, search for a tape by its ID number or title, or search for all tapes matching a particular category, such as comedy or horror. Create a class called `VideoTape` containing the following data members:

```
long id;
FString title;
long supplierID;
float price;      // wholesale price
Category cat;     // action, comedy, horror, and so on
```

Create a class called `Inventory` that keeps track of an array of `VideoTape` objects. Hold the database in memory as an array, and write the entire array to a sequential file before exiting the program. The system should offer the user the following choices from a menu:

```
1) Initialize Inventory File
2) Add new title
3) Remove title
4) Search for title
5) List all titles
6) Exit program
```

2 Video Inventory System.   Continue the Video Inventory System from the previous exercise.

a. Automatically generate a unique tape ID whenever the user wants to add a new title.

b. Include error checking on user input that prevents any of the fields from being left empty.

5.7.4 Miscellaneous

1 Inventory Stack.   When a distributor stocks an inventory of items, the possibility always exists that suppliers' prices will change when new goods are received. Then, as orders from customers come in, the distributor has the option of selling off the old stock at the old prices, or selling the newest goods at the higher prices. The latter method follows a *Last In First Out* sequence. Using the `Stack` class from the Chapter 2 exercises as a model, create a `PartsStack` class. Each item in the `Stack` will be a `Part` object, defined as

```
class Part {
public:
  Part();

  Part( long pnum, int qty, long pDate, float aPrice );

  long GetPartNumber() const;

  float GetPrice() const;

  unsigned GetQuantity() const;

  void SetQuantity( unsigned n );

  friend ostream & operator <<( ostream & s,
```

```
      const Part & p );

   friend istream & operator >>( istream & s,
         Part & p );

 private:
   long  partNumber;   // part number
   unsigned quantity;  // quantity on hand
   long  date;         // date purchased (yymmdd)
   float price;        // price per item
};
```

Read the following `Part` records from a file and push them on the stack (add more data if you wish). The fields appear in the same order as the class data members:

```
100022  50 920101 100.00
100022  85 920505 105.00
100022  20 930101 125.00
100022  25 930610 135.00
100022 100 940101 140.00
100022  25 940801 150.00
```

Pop each `Part` object from the stack and display it on the screen.

2 Inventory Stack. Using the `Parts` inventory stack from the previous exercise, add the following features. In the test program, simulate the ordering of a large number of parts, 100, for example. Using a loop, pop each `Part` object from the stack until the order is filled. Any leftover parts should be pushed back on the stack for processing future orders. Calculate the total price of the order, based on the price stored in each `Part`. For example, an order for 100 `Parts` would break down as

```
25 parts @ 150.00 =  $3,750.00
75 parts @ 140.00 = $10,500.00
        Total price = $14,250.00
```

In this example, 25 items would still remain from the 940101 shipment, and would be pushed back on the stack. After filling the requested order, redisplay the stack to verify that the new quantities are correct.

3 AirBill Class. The `AirBill` class represents a form filled out by customers wishing to send a package from one destination to another. Find a way to divide the class into component classes that more effectively represent its individual parts. Draw a diagram showing class dependencies and create the class interfaces. Make a list of operations that might be supported by the `AirBill` class:

```
class AirBill {
public:
  enum PaymentMethodEnum
  { billSender, billReceiver, billThird, paidAdvance };
  enum ShipMethodEnum { ground, air };
  enum PackageTypeEnum { envelope, package };

private:
  FString id;                    // airbill number
  FString senderName;
  FString senderStreet;
  FString senderCity;
  FString senderState;
  FString senderZip;
  FString senderPhone;
  FString senderPhoneExtension;
  FString receiverName;
  FString receiverCity;
  FString receiverState;
  FString receiverZip;
  FString receiverPhone;
  FString receiverPhoneExtension;

  float packageWeight;
  float packageValue;
  PackageTypeEnum packageType;
  ShipMethodEnum shipMethod;

  PaymentMethodEnum paymentMethod;
  float paymentAmount;
};
```

CHAPTER 6

Derived Classes

In this chapter, we introduce inheritance and show how to create derived classes. Inheritance makes it possible to create hierarchies of related classes and reduce the amount of redundant code in class components. Support for inheritance is one of the capabilities that distinguishes *object-oriented* languages from *object-based* languages. We discuss constructors and destructors in classes related by inheritance. To show practical uses of inheritance, we develop a hierarchy of simple graphics drawing classes and a Company Vehicle Management system.

Terms Introduced in this Chapter:

abstract class
access declaration
base class
constructor-initializer
derived class
list, stack, queue

multiple inheritance
private inheritance
protected access specifier
scope resolution operator
single inheritance
virtual base class

6.1 INHERITANCE

6.1.1 Single Inheritance

In Chapter 1 we defined *inheritance,* or *is-a* as the relationship between two classes that results when a new class is derived from an existing class. The new class, called a *derived class*, includes the data members and operations of the *base class*. The term *is-a* arises from operational definitions of classes during the analysis phase of a project, such as "a graduate student *is a* student, who is also writing a thesis, taking qualifying exams, and so on."

The usual reason for using inheritance is to create a new class that extends the capabilities of some existing class. There will always be some additional data members and/or member functions in a derived class that distinguish it from its base class. For example, if we were to keep track of publications acquired by a library, we might find that books, magazines, and other publications have certain characteristics in common. All publications have a publisher and date of publication. Magazines have a certain number of issues per year and a circulation, and books have an ISBN number and author. We can express these similarities through a connected, directed graph, where the classes are nodes and the inheritance relationships are directed arcs:

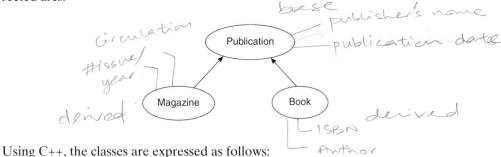

Using C++, the classes are expressed as follows:

```
#include "fstring.h"

class Publication {
public:
  void SetPublisher( const char * s );
  void SetDate( unsigned long dt );

private:
  FString publisher;
  unsigned long date;
};

class Magazine :public Publication {
public:
  void SetIssuesPerYear( unsigned n );
  void SetCirculation( unsigned long n );

private:
  unsigned issuesPerYear;
  unsigned long circulation;
};
```

```
class Book :public Publication {
public:
   void SetISBN( const char * s );
   void SetAuthor( const char * s );

private:
   FString ISBN;
   FString author;
};
```

A `Book` object contains data members and functions inherited from `Publication`, as well as an ISBN number and author. The following operations on `Book` objects are possible:

```
Book B;
B.SetPublisher( "Prentice Hall" );
B.SetDate( 970101 );
B.SetISBN( "0-02-359852-2" );
B.SetAuthor( "Irvine, Kip" );
```

The following operations can only be performed on `Magazine` objects:

```
Magazine M;
M.SetIssuesPerYear( 12 );
M.SetCirculation( 500000L );
```

Without the ability to use inheritance, we would have to make a copy of the source code for a class, give it a new name, and add new operations and/or data members. This would create a difficult maintenance situation, because whenever changes were made to the original class, corresponding changes would have to be made to any "copied" classes.

6.1.1.1 Differing Views of Employees.   Sometimes it is difficult to decide which inheritance relationship between classes is best for a program design. Let's use company employees as an example. We might classify them according to mode of payment, by full/part-time status, or by their permanent/temporary status. A view of employees based on mode of payment might separate them into employees earning a monthly salary, employees working on commission, and employees working for an hourly wage:

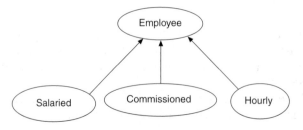

A view of employees based on full-time or part-time status might take into account differences in benefits packages:

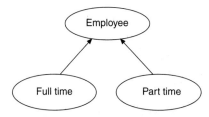

A view of employees based on permanent or temporary status would take into account differences in pension plans, seniority, and so forth:

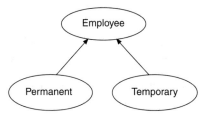

One difficulty we face is that the same employee might belong to several groups. A temporary full-time employee might be paid a monthly salary. A permanent part-time employee might be paid a commission. A permanent full-time employee might be paid an hourly wage. A question to ask is, which inheritance relationship describes the greatest amount of variation in the class attributes and operations? We would want this relationship to be the foundation of the class design. This question can only be answered when we know how the employee-related classes will be used in an actual application.

6.1.2 Declaring Derived Classes

The general form for declaring a derived class with single inheritance is

```
class class-name : access-specifier_opt base-class {
  member-list
};
```

where the optional *access-specifier* is `public`, `private`, or `protected`; *base-class* is the name of the class from which the current class is derived; and, *member-list* consists of data and function members. If the access-specifier is omitted, `private` is the default.

For example, let's derive a class called `Point3D` from `Point`, that represents a point in a 3-dimensional coordinate system. Each `Point3D` object inherits a complete copy of a `Point`, plus any new members declared in the derived class. A `Point3D` object, in other words, contains three data members: x, y, and z. Aside from constructors, it contains the member functions `SetX`, `SetY`, and `SetZ`:

```
class Point {
public:
  Point();
  Point( int xv, int yv );
  void SetX();
  void SetY();

private:
  int x;
  int y;
};

class Point3D :public Point {
public:
  Point3D();
  Point3D( int xv, int yv, int zv );
  void SetZ();

private:
  int z;
};
```

Private members in a base class can only be accessed by functions in the base class and designated friend functions. For this reason, the `Point3D` constructor cannot directly access x and y, but it is able to call `SetX` and `SetY`, which can, in turn, access x and y:

```
Point3D::Point3D( int xv, int yv, int zv )
{
  SetX( xv );
  SetY( yv );
  SetZ( zv );
}
```

`Point3D` users can call the same three functions and need not be concerned with whether member functions are in `Point` or `Point3D`:

```
Point3D P;
P.SetX( 100 );
P.SetY( 200 );
P.SetZ( 300 );
```

6.1.2.1 *Order of Constructor and Destructor Execution.*   Base class constructors are always executed first. If a base class itself is derived from another base

class, the latter's constructor is called first. In the next example, when we declare M, a `ManagementEmployee`, the first constructor to be executed is that of `Employee`; next is the `SalariedEmployee` constructor, and last is the `ManagementEmployee` constructor:

```
class Employee {
public:
  Employee();
  //...
};

class SalariedEmployee :public Employee {
public:
  SalariedEmployee();
  //...
};

class ManagementEmployee :public SalariedEmployee {
public:
  ManagementEmployee();
  //...
};

//...
ManagementEmployee M;
```

In derived classes that contain member objects, constructors for data members are executed after base class constructors. The body of the derived class constructor is executed last. In Example 6-1, for example, the `Sphere` class is derived from `Shape`, and `Point3D` is derived from `Point`. A `Sphere` contains a `Point3D` object marking its center. A `Point` contains two `Coordinate` objects, and a `Point3D` contains an additional `Coordinate`. When we declare a `Sphere` object, the program output is as follows:

```
Shape,Coordinate,Coordinate,Point,Coordinate,Point3D,Sphere
```

Because `Shape` is the base class of `Sphere`, its constructor executes first. Then, because a `Sphere` contains a `Point3D` object, the program prepares to execute the constructor of the base class of `Point3D`, which is `Point`. But a `Point` contains two `Coordinate` objects, so their constructors execute first. Finally, the `Point` constructor executes, followed by the `Point3D` and `Sphere` constructors.

Destructors execute in exactly the reverse order of constructors. The body of the derived destructor executes first, followed by the destructor of each nonstatic data member, followed by the destructor of the base class.

6.1.2.2 *Protected Access Specifier.*   A protected member of a base class can be accessed from both the base class and its derived classes. Protected access is

Example 6-1. The Coordinate, Point, Point3D, Shape, and Sphere Classes

```
#include <iostream.h>

class Coordinate {
public:
  Coordinate() { cout << "Coordinate,"; }
};

class Point {
public:
  Point() { cout << "Point,"; }
private:
  Coordinate x;
  Coordinate y;
};

class Point3D :public Point {
public:
  Point3D() { cout << "Point3D,"; }
private:
  Coordinate z;
};

class Shape {
public:
  Shape() { cout << "Shape,"; }
};

class Sphere :public Shape {
public:
  Sphere() { cout << "Sphere"; }
private:
  Point3D center;
};
```

used in two typical cases: The first is when we wish to allow a derived class to directly access members in a base class that would otherwise have been private. The second is when we wish to restrict access to base class members that might otherwise have been public.

6.1.2.3 Expanding Access to Base Class Members.   In the `Point` class, we can declare the `x` and `y` data members `protected`, in order to allow direct access to them by the `Point3D` class:

```
class Point {
    //...
protected:
    int x;
    int y;
};
```

From pg: 182 example program.

But this is not always a good idea. In fact, we prefer to force derived classes to call functions such as SetX and SetY, rather than grant them unrestricted access to base class data members. A simple change to the name of a data member in the base class could have a drastic effect on all of its derived classes, forcing the expensive and error-prone process of revising lots of source code. In general, a derived class should not be too dependent upon the implementation of its base class.

Sometimes, protected member access is undesirable but necessary. If an operation must be added to a base class, but the base class cannot be modified, the only choice is to derive a new class. The derived class may still require low-level access to data members that would otherwise be private. For example, the FString class has no operation to remove trailing spaces from a string. Assuming that we cannot modify FString, our alternatives might be one of the following:

- Copy the FString to a C-style string, trim the trailing spaces, and reassign the string back to the FString object.
- Derive a new class, which we will call FStringEnh from FString and add a member function that performs the trim operation.

The second alternative seems the more attractive of the two, particularly since we might want to add more operations to the FStringEnh class as the need arises. The derived class currently contains only one operation, RTrim:

```
class FString {
public:
    unsigned GetSize() const;
    //...
protected:
    char str[MaxSize+1];  // String characters
};

class FStringEnh :public FString {
public:
    FStringEnh & RTrim(); // Trim off trailing spaces.
};
```

When implementing the RTrim function, we find that direct access to the str[] array of characters is necessary. If str were private in the FString class, the following implementation would be impossible:

```
FStringEnh & FStringEnh::RTrim()
{
  unsigned len = GetSize();

  for(unsigned i = len-1; i > 0; i--)
    if( str[i] != ' ' ) break;

  str[i+1] = '\0';
  return *this;
}
```

Although close coupling between two classes is undesirable, it can be justified when there is no other acceptable alternative.

6.1.2.4 *Restricting Access to Base Class Members.*   We can also use the `protected` access-specifier to restrict access to base class members. Let's use an `Employee` base class as an example, from which we derive a `SalariedEmployee` class. We designate all member functions as `protected`, thus preventing `Employee` objects from being constructed or manipulated directly by user code:

```
class Employee {
protected:
  Employee();
  SetId( long id );
  SetLastName( const FString & lname );
  //...
};

class SalariedEmployee :public Employee
public:
  SalariedEmployee( long id, const FString & lname );
  //...
};
```

This means, for example, that `SetId` is only available to `SalariedEmployee` and any other classes derived from `Employee`. Therefore, an attempt to create an `Employee` and set its ID would fail:

```
Employee E;              // error: constructor inaccessible
E.SetId( 12345 );        // error: SetId() inaccessible
```

One reason for doing this might be that we do not intend to create `Employee` objects as such. Informally, we call `Employee` an *abstract class*.

6.1.3 Constructor-Initializers

A derived class constructor often receives arguments that must be passed on to its base constructor. The derived class has a *constructor-initializer*, which calls one or more base class constructors. The initializer appears immedately after the derived class constructor parameters, and is prefaced by a colon (:).

Using the `Point3D` class constructor name as an example, we can see the general format:

```
Point3D::Point3D( param-list ) : ctor-intializer
{
  // function body
}
```

In the implementation of the `Point3D` constructor, we pass xv and yv to the `Point` constructor:

```
class Point {
public:
  Point( int xv, int yv );
  //...
};

class Point3D :public Point {
public:
  Point3D( int xv, int yv, int zv );
  void SetZ();

private:
  int z;
};

Point3D::Point3D( int xv, int yv, int zv )
        :Point( xv, yv )
{
  SetZ( zv );
}
```

We have implemented `Point3D` outside the class definition to show that the constructor-initializer does not appear in the function prototype. If `Point3D` were implemented inside the class definition, the initializer would appear there.

6.1.3.1 Example: Magazine and Publication Classes.

Let's use a constructor-initializer in a more detailed example that involves both inheritance and compositon. We have a `Magazine` class which is derived from a `Publication` class, and the `Publication` class contains a `Date` class data member. Here are the `Date` and `Publication` classes:

```
#include <iostream.h>
#include "fstring.h"

class Date {
```

```
public:
  Date( int mo, int dy, int yr );
  //...
};

class Publication {
public:
  Publication( const FString & publshr,
               const Date & aDate );
private:
  FString publisherName;
  Date pubDate;
};

Publication::Publication( const FString & publshr,
      const Date & aDate ): pubDate( aDate ),
      publisherName( publshr )
{
  //...
}
```

The Publication constructor uses a constructor-initializer to initialize the publication date and publisher name.

The Magazine constructor uses a constructor-initializer to pass arguments to the constructor in Publication, its base class:

```
class Magazine :public Publication {
public:
  Magazine( const FString & publshr,
     const Date & aDate, unsigned issues );

private:
  unsigned issuesPerYear;
};

Magazine::Magazine( const FString & publshr,
    const Date & aDate, unsigned issues )
    : Publication( publshr, aDate )
{
  issuesPerYear = issues;
}
```

Some programmers would include issuesPerYear in the initializer, anticipating the possibility that it might later become a class object:

```
Magazine::Magazine( const FString & publshr,
    const Date & aDate, unsigned issues )
    : Publication( publshr, aDate ), issuesPerYear( issues )
{  }
```

Why use a constructor-initializer? Without it, the default constructor for the base class would be called, which would then have to be followed by calls to accessor functions to set specific data members. In general, this is a lot less efficient than using an initializer. For example,

```
Magazine::Magazine( const FString & publshr,
    const Date & aDate, unsigned issues )
{
  SetPublisherName( publshr );
  SetPublicationDate( aDate );
  issuesPerYear = issues;
}
```

Also, if the base class has no accessible default constructor, omitting the initializer causes a syntax error.

6.1.4 Public and Private Inheritance

When deriving a new class, it is possible to further restrict access to nonstatic base class members by using *private inheritance*. This causes all members of the base class to be assigned private status in the derived class. To do this, we use the `private` keyword in the base list of the derived class.

For example, SetX and SetY are declared public in Point, but they are made private in Point3D. The static function GetInstanceCount is unaffected by the private inheritance and remains public in both classes:

```
class Point {
public:
  void SetX();
  void SetY();
  static unsigned GetInstanceCount();
};

class Point3D :private Point {
  //...
};
```

The derived class's base-list can restrict access to base members, but cannot expand the access. A private member in a base class, for example, cannot become protected or public in a derived class.

One situation in which using private inheritance is advantageous is when the designer of a derived class is constrained by the design of an existing base class. It may not be possible or practical to modify a base class, particularly if other programs and classes are already using it. But, the derived class can choose to either augment or completely replace the base class's interface.

6.1.4.1 List Example.

An interesting example of inheritance is demonstrated by list, stack, and queue data structures. Informally, a *list* is an ordered collection of objects with two ends called *head* and *tail*, respectively. It supports operations such as the following:

- `IsEmpty`   Return 1 when the list is empty, otherwise return 0.
- `RemoveFirst`   Remove the first object in the list.
- `RemoveLast`   Remove the last object in the list.
- `PutFirst`   Add an object to the beginning of the list.
- `PutLast`   Add an object to the end of the list.

A *stack,* on the other hand, is an ordered list of objects that supports two primary operations. *Push* adds an object to the top of the stack, and *pop* removes and returns the object located at the stack top.

Finally, a *queue* is a specialized type of list in which objects are always removed from the head of the list and added to the tail. For example, customers lining up at a ticket booth form a queue. The *enqueue* operation adds a new customer to the tail, and the *serve* operation retrieves and removes the customer at the head of the queue.

Should stacks and queues be thought of as specialized forms of lists? This notion is not unusual, given that a list data structure is often used to implement a stack or queue. Below is a directed, connected graph showing inheritance relationships between three classes: `List`, `Stack`, and `Queue`. The arrows indicate that `Stack` and `Queue` are derived from `List`:

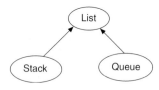

The `Item`, `List`, `Stack`, and `Queue` class interfaces might appear as follows:

```
class Item {
  //...
};

class List {
```

```
public:
  int IsEmpty() const;
  Item & RemoveFirst();
  Item & RemoveLast();
  void PutFirst( const Item & I );
  void PutLast( const Item & I );
  //...
};

class Stack :public List {
public:
  void Push( const Item & I );
  Item & Pop();
};

class Queue :public List {
public:
  void Enqueue( const Item & I );
  Item & Serve();
};
```

When implementing `Push` and `Pop` in the `Stack` class, we simply call the appropriate `List` functions:

```
void Stack::Push( const Item & I )
{
  PutFirst( I );
}

Item & Stack::Pop()
{
  return RemoveFirst();
}
```

A valid objection to this scheme is that `RemoveFirst` and `PutFirst` have no meaning in a `Stack` class. We can, however, restrict access to the `List` operations, using the `private` base class specifier when defining the `Stack` class. This ensures that a `Stack` user will not reach beyond the current level of abstraction and manipulate the list directly:

```
class Stack :private List {
public:
  void Push( const Item & I );
  Item & Pop();
  //...
};
```

If we create a stack and limit operations to `Push` and `Pop`, everything compiles. But we cannot access `List::RemoveFirst`, for example:

```
Item anItem;
Stack aStack;

aStack.Push( anItem );
anItem = aStack.RemoveFirst();   // error: inaccessible
```

On the other hand, we might want to call `IsEmpty` to determine if the `Stack` is empty. We can grant public access to `IsEmpty` by creating an *access declaration* for it in the public section of `Stack`:

```
class Stack :private List {
public:
  List::IsEmpty;   // grant public access

  void Push( const Item & I );
  Item & Pop();
};
```

This makes `IsEmpty` a public member in the `Stack` class. Now the following statements are valid:

```
Item anItem;
Stack aStack;
if( !aStack.IsEmpty() )
  Push( anItem );
```

We leave the implementation of the `Queue` class as a chapter exercise, with the assurance that it is no more difficult to implement than the `Stack` class.

6.1.5 Nested Class Scope

Member functions automatically have direct access to all data and function members within the current class. However, the name of a public or protected base class member may be hidden by the same name in a derived class. It is still possible to reference the base class member by overriding the current class scope with the scope resolution operator (`::`). In the next example, a statement in `Child::Print` calls `Parent::Print`. If we had omitted the `Parent::` qualifier from the call to `Print` inside `Child::Print`, the call would be recursive:

```
#include "fstring.h"

class Parent {
public:
  void Print() const;
  //...
};

class Child :public Parent {
public:
  void Print() const
  {
    Parent::Print();
    cout << age << '\n'
         << school << endl;
  }

private:
  int  age;
  FString school;
};
```

Is it possible for a statement in a base class to reference a member of one of its derived classes? Certainly not, because a base class has no knowledge of its derived classes. Using the `Parent` and `Child` classes again, it would be pure nonsense for the `Parent::Print` function to contain references to `Child` data members:

```
void Parent::Print()
{
  cout << name << '\n'
       << Child::age << endl;  // error
}
```

6.1.6 Friends in Derived Classes

A friend function is granted access to all public, private, and protected members of a class. But a friend of a base class is not automatically a friend of classes derived from that base. In the next example, `CalcPay` is a friend of `Employee`, but not of `SalariedEmployee`. In practical terms, we would use a different way of calculating pay for salaried employees anyway:

```
class Employee {
public:
  friend float CalcPay( Employee & E );
  //...
};
```

```
class SalariedEmployee :public Employee {
  //...
};
```

Instead, we could declare a different `CalcPay` function as a friend of `SalariedEmployee`:

```
class SalariedEmployee :public Employee {
public:
  friend float CalcPay( SalariedEmployee & E );
  //...
};
```

6.2 A GRAPHICS EXAMPLE

Let's explore derived classes through a graphics example, using the `Point`, `Rectangle`, and `Square` classes. A `Rectangle` contains a single `Point` (the up-per-left corner), and the `Square` class is derived from `Rectangle`. We can dia-gram the relationships as follows:

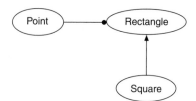

(Recall from Chapter 5 that the line connecter beginning with a solid circle implies a *has-a* relationship, and the line ending with an arrow implies an *is-a* relationship.)

When creating graphics classes for a program that will run in different envi-ronments, you must be particularly sensitive to the issue of portability. Graphics are implemented differently on various computer systems, such as X-Windows, MS-DOS graphics, MS-Windows graphics, and so on. Some popular C++ compilers in-clude some type of graphics interface, as in the case of the Borland Graphics Interface (BGI).

Fundamental to any graphics system is the ability to draw individual points, lines, and various other geometric shapes, such as circles and rectangles. To make a graphics application as portable as possible, we take advantage of the ability of C++ to encapsulate implementation-specific graphics functions in a single class.

For example, let's create a class called `GraphScreen` that provides a com-patibility layer between the graphic shape classes we plan to use, and specific graph-ics environments. This is a minimal list, but at this point, we would rather not clutter it up with a lot of unnecessary operations:

```
class GraphScreen {
public:
  static void DrawCircle( int x, int y, int r );
  static void DrawLine( int x1, int y1, int x2, int y2 );
  static void DrawPoint( int x, int y );
  static void DrawRect( int x1, int y1, int x2, int y2 );
  static int  Initialize();
  static void ShutDown();

private:
  GraphScreen() {  }
};
```

We need not create any instances of GraphScreen because it does not contain any nonstatic data members. In fact, the default constructor is private, preventing us from creating a GraphScreen object.

GraphScreen::Initialize must be executed before any other member function, and ShutDown must be the last function call that uses graphics. The remaining functions can be called in any order, as many times as needed.

6.2.1 The Point, Rectangle, and Square Classes

The Point class, which defines a point in a two-dimensional coordinate system, is supplied with only a minimal interface. It has a constructor, a Draw function, and functions to get and set the x and y data members:

```
class Point {
public:
  Point( int xVal, int yVal );
  void Draw() const;
  int  GetX() const;
  int  GetY() const;
  void SetX( int xVal );
  void SetY( int yVal );

private:
  int x;
  int y;
};
```

Point::Draw is implemented by passing its x and y coordinates to DrawPoint:

```
void Point::Draw() const
{
  GraphScreen::DrawPoint(x, y);
}
```

A `Rectangle` contains a `Point` that marks the position of its upper-left corner, as well as data members that store its height and width. We include a constructor, a `Draw` function, and selectors for `corner`, `height`, and `width`:

```
class Rectangle {
public:
  Rectangle( const Point & p, int wd, int ht );
  Point GetCorner() const;
  int   GetHeight() const;
  int   GetWidth()  const;
  void  Draw() const;

private:
  Point corner;   // upper-left corner
  int width;
  int height;
};

Rectangle::Rectangle( const Point & p, int wd, int ht )
         :corner(p), width(wd), height(ht)
{
  //...
}
```

`Rectangle::Draw` passes the coordinates of its upper-left and lower-right corners to `GraphScreen::DrawRect`:

```
void Rectangle::Draw() const
{
  Point p = GetCorner();
  int x = p.GetX();
  int y = p.GetY();
  GraphScreen::DrawRect(x,y,x+GetWidth(),y+GetHeight());
}
```

The `Square` class is derived from `Rectangle` because it is a specific type of rectangle in which the height and width are the same. It has no new data members, so it passes its constructor parameters to the base class:

```
class Square :public Rectangle {
public:
  Square( const Point & p, int side )
        : Rectangle(p, side, side) {  }
  void Draw() const;
};
```

```
void Square::Draw() const
{
  Point p = GetCorner();
  int x = p.GetX();
  int y = p.GetY();
  GraphScreen::DrawRect(x,y,x+GetWidth(),y+GetHeight());
}
```

We have redefined `Draw` in the `Square` class, although it is implemented exactly as in `Rectangle`. At a later time, we might decide to alter its implementation.

6.2.2 Test Program

The following is a short test program for the four graphics classes we just defined. `GraphScreen::Initialize` attempts to initialize the graphics system, and, if it returns 0 (indicating failure), we exit the program and return a prearranged error code.

We declare and draw a `Point`, a `Rectangle`, and a `Square`. This program links to the `graphscr` module, which contains the `GraphScreen` class:

```
#include <stdio.h>
#include "graphscr.h" // GraphScreen class
#include "graphex.h"  // Point, Rectangle, Square classes

int main()
{
  if( !GraphScreen::Initialize())
    return 255;                         // indicate an error

  Point P( 225, 275 );
  P.Draw();

  Rectangle R( Point(100,100), 150, 75 );
  R.Draw();

  Square S( Point(200,200), 35 );
  S.Draw();

  getchar();              // press Enter to quit
  GraphScreen::ShutDown();
  return 0;
}
```

6.3 CASE STUDY: VEHICLE MANAGEMENT SYSTEM

We discussed object-oriented design principles at some length in Chapter 5, and earlier in this chapter we introduced inheritance. We would now like to incorporate inheritance into the design process. Specifically, we're looking for ways to discover a class hierarchy that adequately expresses a problem domain. The problem domain is a Vehicle Management System for a company that owns a fleet of cars and trucks. First, we analyze the problem for class relationships; next, we design the interfaces for the essential classes. By commercial standards, this is a small program; by college classroom standards, it's somewhat long. Implementing the classes will be an interesting educational experience for the reader (we explain how in the chapter exercises).

6.3.1 Specifications

We would like to create a tracking program for company vehicles, identifying how and when vehicles are checked out for usage by employees. Some may be for cargo transportation. Others may be for periodic use by employees for business trips, for loaner cars, and so on.

For each vehicle that is checked out, we need to record its ID number, date checked out, driver name, mileage, and type of usage (personal or company), and its contents (passengers or cargo).

If a vehicle is checked out for company use, a record of each trip taken in the vehicle is required: it should list the date, time, miles driven, fuel cost, and the purpose of the trip. If a vehicle is checked out for personal use, no trip record is required, but the employee's automobile insurance information must be recorded. A vehicle carrying passengers should store a list of passenger names, whereas a vehicle carrying cargo should store an inventory of the vehicle contents.

6.3.2 Analysis

Our primary motivation should be to find the classes that are implied by the problem specifications. Expressed another way, our design should closely model the application domain. This application clearly presents two ways of classifying vehicles, either by usage (company and private), or by contents (passengers and cargo). Depending on which of these we choose first, the remaining class relationships will be greatly affected. Initially, we may not know which classification is best.

Regardless of how vehicles are classified, we can assume that a base class called `Vehicle` holds operations and attributes in common to all vehicles, such as the vehicle ID, driver name, date checked out, and so on.

6.3.2.1 Classify by Vehicle Usage.   If we elect to classify vehicles by usage, we can derive two classes from `Vehicle`, called `CompanyVehicle` and `PersonalVehicle`. A `CompanyVehicle` keeps a log of each trip, represented by the `TripLog` class. A `TripLog` contains the departure date and time, miles driven,

purpose of the trip, and fuel cost. A `PersonalVehicle` stores automobile insurance information. The following diagram shows the class dependencies:

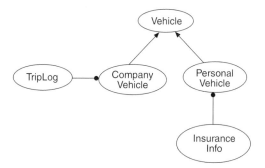

6.3.2.2 *Classify by Vehicle Contents.*   On the other hand, we might decide to classify vehicles by their contents (passenger or cargo). In that case, we derive the `PassengerVehicle` and `CargoVehicle` classes from `Vehicle`. Passenger vehicles are then divided into those for personal use (`PersonalVehicle` class) or for company use (`CompanyPassenger` class). Here is a diagram of the class relationships:

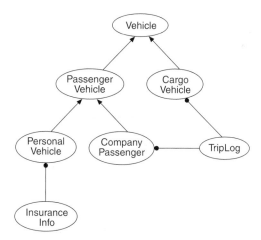

This choice of class relationships is more complicated than the first example, which divided vehicles by their usage. Note that we added a new class called `Company-Passenger` to deal with passenger vehicles used for company trips. Also, `TripLog` objects were placed inside both `CargoVehicle` and `CompanyPassenger` objects.

The choice as to which design to follow might be influenced by their possibilities for future expansion. For example, company vehicles might later be subdivided into passenger, delivery, long-range transport, and utility vehicles. On the other hand, we might later divide personal usage between short-term and long-term; or, we might divide company usage between internal and external. It might be necessary to generate completely different trip logs for passenger versus cargo vehicles. In any event, a good design should take these factors into account so that future expansion will disrupt the original design as little as possible.

6.3.3 Design

We're going to choose the design based on vehicle usage (company or personal), and create class interfaces for the Vehicle, TripLog, CompanyVehicle, PersonalVehicle, and InsuranceInfo classes. To simplify the design and implementation, we will not store passenger lists or vehicle inventories in company vehicles. But these could be added to the program, as suggested in the chapter exercises.

The Vehicle class, because it is the base class for both company and personal vehicles, contains data members common to all types of vehicles: the vehicle ID number, driver name, odometer reading, and date checked out. We also place in it a "tag" data member called vehicleType that indicates the current type of vehicle:

```
typedef unsigned long ulong;

class Vehicle {
public:
  enum VehicleEnum { personal, company };

  Vehicle( ulong idNum, VehicleEnum vtype );
  // Construct from an ID number and vehicle type.

  Vehicle & Input();
  // Input a Vehicle from the user.

  void SetOdometer( ulong odom );
  // Set the odometer value.

  friend ostream & operator <<( ostream & os,
      const Vehicle & v );

private:
  ulong id;             // vehicle ID
  FString driver;       // name of driver
  ulong odometer;       // total mileage
  Date chkDate;         // date checked out
  VehicleEnum vehicleType;
};
```

CompanyVehicle is derived from Vehicle and contains a record of the most recent trip taken in the vehicle:

```
class CompanyVehicle :public Vehicle {
public:
  CompanyVehicle( ulong idNum );

  CompanyVehicle & Input();
  // Input a Vehicle from the user.

  friend ostream & operator <<( ostream & os,
        const CompanyVehicle & cv );

private:
  TripLog tripRecord;  // a single trip record
};
```

In a more realistic version of this program, `tripRecord` would be a list of the most recent *n* trips, ordered by their dates and times.

`PersonalVehicle` is also derived from `Vehicle`, but it contains insurance information rather than a trip log:

```
class PersonalVehicle :public Vehicle {
public:
  PersonalVehicle( ulong idNum );

  PersonalVehicle & Input();

  friend ostream & operator <<( ostream & os,
        const PersonalVehicle & pv );

private:
  InsuranceInfo insurance;
};
```

`InsuranceInfo` contains the name of the employee's insurance company and the policy number:

```
class InsuranceInfo {
public:
  InsuranceInfo & Input();

  friend ostream & operator <<(ostream & os,
        const InsuranceInfo & I );

private:
  FString company;
  FString policyNumber;
};
```

TripLog contains information about a single trip taken in a company vehicle. It contains the date and time of the trip, the number of miles driven, the purpose of the trip, and the cost of fuel:

```
class TripLog {
public:
  TripLog();

  TripLog & Input();

  void SetMiles( unsigned m );

  void SetFuelCost( float f );

  friend ostream & operator <<( ostream & os,
        const TripLog & tLog );

private:
  Date tDate;          // date trip taken
  Time tTime;          // time trip taken
  unsigned miles;      // miles driven
  FString purpose;     // why the trip was taken
  float fuelCost;      // cost of fuel, in dollars
};
```

Date and Time are simple utility classes that input and display the date and time. They could easily be expanded to read and write a variety of standard formats. We did not anticipate the need for these in the analysis phase, but their use became clear as the Vehicle and TripLog classes were designed:

```
class Date {
public:
  Date( unsigned dy, unsigned mn, unsigned yr );

  Date & Input();

  friend ostream & operator <<( ostream & os,
        const Date & dType );

private:
  unsigned year;    // 0 - 2100
  unsigned month;   // 1 - 12
  unsigned day;     // 1 - 31
  void SetDay( unsigned dy );
  void SetMonth( unsigned mn );
  void SetYear( unsigned yr );
};
```

SetDay, SetMonth, and SetYear are declared private in the Date class to prevent a user from altering just one of these data members without checking its value against the others. We would not, for example, allow both month = 2 and day = 30. Similarly, SetHour and SetMinute are declared private in the Time class:

```
class Time {
public:
  Time( unsigned hr, unsigned mn );

  Time & Input();

  friend ostream & operator <<( ostream & os,
        const Time & tm );

private:
  unsigned hour;       // 0 - 23
  unsigned minute;     // 0 - 59
  void SetHour( unsigned hr );
  void SetMinute( unsigned mn );
};
```

6.3.4 Main Program

In the main program, we let the user decide whether to input a personal or company vehicle. We use a different function to create each type of vehicle (personal or company) and write it to a file. Create_PersonalVehicle lets the user input a vehicle for personal use, and Create_CompanyVehicle lets the user input a vehicle for company use:

```
#include "vehicle.h"
#include <fstream.h>

ofstream ofile( "vehicle.out", ios::app );

void Create_PersonalVehicle( ulong id )
{
  PersonalVehicle V( id );
  V.Input();
  ofile << V << endl;
}

void Create_CompanyVehicle( ulong id )
{
  CompanyVehicle V( id );
  V.Input();
  ofile << V << endl;
}
```

```
void Create_Vehicle()
{
 int usage;
 ulong id;
 cout << "Vehicle ID: ";
 cin >> id;
 cout << "Type of Usage (1)personal, (2)company:";
 cin >> usage;
 cin.ignore( 255, '\n' );

 if( usage == 1 )
   Create_PersonalVehicle( id );
 else if( usage == 2 )
   Create_CompanyVehicle( id );
}

int main()
{
  Create_Vehicle();
  return 0;
}
```

The following shows sample input as a user creates a `PersonalVehicle` object:

```
Vehicle ID: 1022033
Type of Usage (1)personal, (2)company: 1
Driver name [last,first]: Johnson, Joe
  Odometer reading: 15050
  Date checked out (mm/dd/yy format): 05/01/96
Insurance Information:
Insurance company: State Insurance Co.
Policy Number: A455 234 123
```

The following is sample file output produced from this example:

```
Vehicle ...................
  ID:       1022033
  Usage:    personal
  Driver:   Johnson, Joe
  Odometer: 15050
  Date out: 5-1-96
Insurance Information............
  Insurance provider: State Insurance Co.
  Policy number: A455 234 123
```

The following shows sample input as a user creates a `PersonalVehicle`:

```
Vehicle ID: 303003
Type of Usage (1)personal, (2)company: 2
Driver name [last,first]: Baker, Sam
   Odometer reading: 20500
   Date checked out (mm/dd/yy format): 06/01/96
Entering the trip log.
   Date of trip (mm/dd/yy format): 06/15/96
   Time (hh:mm format): 7:00
   Miles driven: 50
   Purpose: Business conference
   Fuel cost: 25
```

This is the output file produced by the program for the same vehicle:

```
Vehicle ...................
   ID:       303003
   Usage:    company
   Driver:   Baker, Sam
   Odometer: 20500
   Date out: 6-1-96
Trip Log..................
   Date:        6-15-96
   Time:        7:00
   Miles:       50
   Purpose:   Business conference
   Fuel cost: 25
```

6.3.4.1 Improvements to the Program. It would be possible to create an array containing both personal and company vehicles, but because of the strong type checking in C++, the array would have to contain pointers to either `PersonalVehicle` or `CompanyVehicle` objects. It would be necessary to cast each pointer to its appropriate type before attempting to display an object in the array. This is why we included the `vehicleType` data member in the `Vehicle` class to identify each object's type. Better methods exist for handling derived classes and pointers, but those will have to wait for Chapter 8, which explains virtual functions and polymorphism.

6.3.5 Class Implementations

We will just look at a few of the implementation details of the classes in this application. The complete program listing is in the instructor manual.

The stream output operator for the `Vehicle` class displays the properties common to all vehicle types:

```
ostream & operator <<( ostream & os, const Vehicle & V )
{
  const char * vstring[] = { "personal","company" };

  os << "  ID:        " << V.id << '\n'
     << "  Usage:     " << vstring[V.vehicleType] << '\n'
     << "  Driver:    " << V.driver << '\n'
     << "  Odometer:  " << V.odometer << '\n'
     << "  Date out:  " << V.chkDate << endl;

  return os;
}
```

The `CompanyVehicle` stream output operator function is able to take advantage of the `Vehicle` class stream output function by casting V, the function parameter, into a `Vehicle` object:

```
ostream & operator <<( ostream & os, const CompanyVehicle & V )
{
  os << "Vehicle ....................." << '\n'
     << Vehicle( V )
     << V.tripRecord << endl;
  return os;
}
```

We have avoided any direct references to `Vehicle` data members here for the following reason: If the data members in the `Vehicle` class should change at a later time, the `CompanyVehicle` function will not have to be modified.

The `Vehicle` class's `Input` member function prompts the user for the driver name, odometer reading, and date:

```
Vehicle & Vehicle::Input()
{
  cout << "Driver name [last,first]: ";
  driver.GetLine( cin );

  cout << "  Odometer reading: ";
  long n;
  cin >> n;
  SetOdometer( n );
  cin.ignore( 255, '\n' );

  cout << "  Date checked out ";
  chkDate.Input();
  return *this;
}
```

The `CompanyVehicle` class's `Input` function is simplified by being able to draw on the `Input` functions in the `Vehicle` and `TripLog` classes. The scope resolution operator (`::`) is used here to specify that we want to call the `Input` function in the `Vehicle` class:

```
CompanyVehicle & CompanyVehicle::Input()
{
  Vehicle::Input();
  tripRecord.Input();
  return *this;
}
```

6.4 MULTIPLE INHERITANCE

Sometimes, a single class contains attributes and properties inherited from two or more base classes. This creates a *multiple inheritance* relationship. For example, a graduate assistant in a university is both a student and a salaried employee. Such a person receives both a monthly salary and degree credits. The following connected graph shows the inheritance relationships:

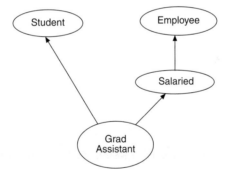

The differences between students and employees are nontrivial. An employee, for example, has tax withholding information, employee benefits, and a paycheck. A salaried employee has a monthly salary. A student has a major (a field of study), a grade point average, and a class schedule. A graduate assistant contains all of these properties, so it can benefit from multiple inheritance.

Example 6-2 contains declarations of the following classes: `Student`, `Employee`, `Salaried`, and `GradAssistant`. The multiple inheritance is created by the base class list of the `GradAssistant` declaration:

```
class GradAssistant :public Student, public Salaried
```

The data members in the base classes are declared private, so functions such as `GradAssistant::Display` have to call accessor functions in the base classes:

Example 6-2. Multiple Inheritance

```
#include <iostream.h>
#include "fstring.h"

typedef unsigned long ulong;

class Student {
public:
  unsigned GetAge() const;
  ulong GetId() const;
  unsigned GetMajor() const;
  void SetAge( unsigned n );
  void SetId( ulong n );
  void SetMajor( unsigned n );

private:
  ulong id;
  unsigned majorCode;
  unsigned degreeCode;
  float gpa;
  unsigned age;
};

class Employee {
public:
  unsigned GetAge() const;
  unsigned GetExemptions() const;
  const FString & GetBenefits() const;
  void SetAge( unsigned n );
  void SetBenefits( const FString benef );
  void SetExemptions( unsigned n );

private:
  unsigned age;
  unsigned exemptions;
  FString benefits;
};

class Salaried :public Employee {
public:
  float GetSalary() const;
  void SetSalary( float s );

private:
  float salary;
};

class GradAssistant :public Student, public Salaried {
public:
  void Display() const;
};
```

```
void GradAssistant::Display() const
{
  cout << GetId() << ','        // Student class
       << GetMajor() << ','     // Student class
       << GetSalary() << ','    // Salaried class
       << GetExemptions()       // Employee class
       << endl;
}
```

We can create a GradAssistant object, and then set and display selected data members:

```
int main()
{
  GradAssistant GA;
  GA.SetId( 12345 );
  GA.SetMajor( 108 );
  GA.SetExemptions( 2 );
  GA.SetSalary( 10000 );
  GA.Display();
}
```

A problem arises, however, if we try to set a GradAssistant's age by calling SetAge, because both the Student and Employee classes contain functions by this name. Ambiguity is resolved by specifying which base class is to be used:

```
GA.SetAge(22);              // error: ambiguous
GA.Student::SetAge(22);     // ok - specific
```

The situation is still awkward, because a class user calling GetAge might inadvertently retrieve the value of age from the Employee class rather than age from the Student class.

6.4.1 Virtual Base Classes

Occasionally, the same class name may appear multiple times in a class hierarchy, creating some ambiguity. We can label a class as a *virtual base class* to clear up the confusion.

Students and employees share certain attributes: both have a Social Security number, an age, a campus address, a department, and so forth. One problem that occurs in multiple inheritance relationships is that of duplicate names in the base classes. Suppose that the Student and Employee classes both contained member functions called GetAge and GetSocSecNum. References to these names would be ambiguous. A nice solution to this problem is to create a new base class called Person that contains common data members and operations, from which we derive both Student and Employee:

```
class Person {
public:
  unsigned GetAge() const;
  const FString & GetSocSecNum() const;
  void SetAge( unsigned n );
  void SetSocSecNum( const FString & ssn );

private:
  unsigned age;
  FString socSecNum;
};
```

The following connected graph shows the revised class relationships:

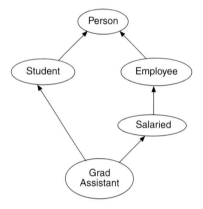

Here are the revised `Student` and `Employee` classes:

```
class Student :public Person {
public:
  unsigned GetMajor() const;
  void SetMajor( unsigned n );

private:
  unsigned majorCode;
  unsigned degreeCode;
  float gpa;
};

class Employee :public Person {
public:
  const FString & GetBenefits() const;
  unsigned GetExemptions() const;
  void SetBenefits( const FString & benef );
  void SetExemptions( unsigned n );
```

```
private:
  unsigned exemptions;
  FString benefits;
};
```

A common problem when deriving from a common class occurs when a base class member can be reached through more than one inheritance path. In the `GradAssistant` class, for example, if we call `GetAge`, the compiler does not know whether we want to call the `GetAge` function derived through the `Student-->Person` path, or the `GetAge` function derived through the `Salaried-->Employee-->Person` path:

```
void GradAssistant::Display() const
{
  cout << GetSocSecNum() << ','   // ambiguous
       << GetAge() << ','         // ambiguous
       //...
```

To resolve this ambiguity, we add the `virtual` specifier to the base class lists of `Student` and `Employee` to show that `Person` is a *virtual base class:*

```
class Student :public virtual Person {
//...
class Employee :public virtual Person {
//...
```

With these changes, it is now possible to call any function in the `Person` class without causing an ambiguous member reference.

6.5 CHAPTER SUMMARY

Single inheritance is the relationship between classes that results when a new class is created using the properties of an existing class. The new class, called the *derived* class, shares the structure and behavior of the original class, called the *base* class. Inheritance relationships enable derived classes to borrow attributes and operations from existing classes, thus reducing the amount of redundant code in programs.

One of the requirements for an object-oriented language to be called object-oriented is that it must support inheritance. An *inheritance tree* is a directed graph in which derived classes point toward their base classes.

A *base list* is a list of one or more classes from which the current class is derived. A *member list* is a list of data members and function members that make up a class definition.

Private inheritance is the term we use when a derived class restricts access to its base class members by making them private. This prevents users of the derived class from accessing the base class members.

Whenever possible, do not allow a derived class to directly access protected data members in a base class. Instead, make the members private, and provide public `Set` and `Get` functions for each data member. This helps to prevent a derived class from being overly dependent upon the implementation of its base class.

A derived class constructor often receives arguments that must be passed on to the constructor of a base class via a *constructor-initializer* list.

When a name in a base class is hidden by the same name in a derived class, you can use the `::` operator to reference the name in the base class (assuming that it is not private), as in `base::name`.

To help deal with the portability problems that appear when transferring a graphics application program from one system to another, we implemented a class called `GraphScreen` in this chapter. This was combined with classes that displayed points, rectangles, and squares.

Beginning C++ programmers often make mistakes when describing an *is-a* relationship between classes. In the case of the `Point` and `Line` classes, for example, it is better to let a `Line` object contain two points, rather than try to derive `Line` from `Point`. Similarly, we discussed the problems with using an inheritance relationship between the `List` and `Stack` classes.

Multiple inheritance results when a class is derived from two or more base classes. While this is a powerful tool, it can also create naming problems when identical names appear in more than one base class. In our `Student/Employee/Person` class hierarchy, we showed a specific problem that occurred when both `Student` and `Employee` were derived from the same base class, `Person`. We designated `Person` as a *virtual base class* to resolve the ambiguity caused by multiple paths through a class tree.

6.6 EXERCISES

6.6.1 Miscellaneous

1 Managing Time Zones.   Create a class called `Time` that contains hours, minutes, and seconds. Then derive a new class from `Time` called `ZonedTime` that also contains a time zone (Eastern Standard Time, Mountain Time, and so on). Create constructors for each class and overload the stream output operator. Create and display several `Time` and `ZonedTime` objects. Provide a member function that compares two `ZonedTime` objects, taking into account the time zones. To test your function, ask it to determine whether or not 20:05:00 Eastern Standard Time is equal to 17:05:00 Pacific Time. The time zones in the continental United States, from west to east are: Pacific Time, Mountain Time, Central Time, and Eastern Standard Time. If the time is 08:00:00 Eastern Standard Time, it is 07:00:00 Central Time, 06:00:00 Mountain Time, and 05:00:00 Pacific Time. In addition, each zone can have a *daylight savings* time, which places it one hour ahead of its usual time.

2 Queue Class Implementation.   Earlier in this chapter, we said that a *queue* is a specialized type of list, in which objects are always removed from the head of the list and added to the tail:

```
class Queue :private List {
public:
   void Enqueue( const Item & I );
   Item & Serve();
};
```

For example, customers lining up at a ticket booth form a queue. The *enqueue* operation adds a new element to the tail, and the *serve* operation retrieves and removes the element at the head of the queue. Implement a `Queue` class that contains these operations, and test it by inserting and removing objects from the queue.

3 Package Shipping.   A package being sent by a shipping company may be viewed differently depending on its location in the overall shipping cycle. At one point, it might be part of a shipping station's inventory awaiting either transport to another station or delivery to a customer. It might be aboard a delivery truck on its way to a customer. Or, it might be in a container during long-range transport from one city to another. The `StationPackage`, `CourierPackage`, and `TransportPackage` classes reflect those three situations, respectively.

Find data members and operations that are common to all three classes and place them in a base class called `Package`. Let the three original classes derive from `Package`. Write a short test program that constructs and displays each type of package:

```
class StationPackage {
  unsigned long packageId;
  unsigned long station;     // station ID
  unsigned long supervisor; // station supervisor ID
  char Adate[7];          // date of arrival at station
  char Ddate[7];          // date of departure
};

class CourierPackage {
public:
  enum ActionEnum { pickup, delivery };
private:
  unsigned long packageId;
  unsigned long courier;
  unsigned long route;
  unsigned date;            // date delivered
  unsigned time;            // time delivered
  FString customerName;
  int  customerSigned;      // 1=yes, 0=no
  ActionEnum action;        // pickup, delivery
};
```

```
class TransportPackage {
public:
  enum TransPortTypeEnum { truck, rail, air };

private:
  unsigned long packageId;
  unsigned long source;         // originating station ID
  unsigned long destination;    // destination station ID
  unsigned long supervisor;     // station supervisor ID

  unsigned date;                // date of transport
  unsigned time;                // time of transport
  TransPortTypeEnum transportType;
  FString carrier;
  FString transportID;
};
```

6.6.2 Vehicle Management System

The Vehicle Management System presented in this chapter was necessarily incomplete. The following exercises suggest interesting ways to enhance the program.

1 Selectors and Modifiers. Provide member functions that set and get each of the data members in the `Vehicle`, `PersonalVehicle`, and `CompanyVehicle` classes. For the `TripLog` class, provide a constructor that permits all data members to be initialized. Write a test program that demonstrates each of the new member functions.

2 Vehicle Management Stream I/O. Improve the Vehicle Management System program shown in this chapter as follows: Implement the `operator >>` function in each class, so that input is more flexible. In the main program, create an input file stream, and read all of the program's input from the file. Here is an example of an input file, with comments shown on the right side:

```
P                              (personal vehicle)
1000101                        vehicle ID
John Baker                     driver
25100                          odometer reading
05/10/97                       date checked out
Universal Protection Inc.      Insurance company
02-3320-4488-1982              Policy number
C                              (company vehicle)
1000101                        vehicle ID
Susan Smith                    driver
35200                          odometer reading
01/12/97                       date checked out
02/01/97                       date of trip
```

```
08:00                              time of trip
150                                miles driven
AZZ Conference                     purpose of trip
30                                 fuel cost
Z                                  end of file marker
```

The first character in each record is P, C, or Z. P identifies the following record as a PersonalVehicle, C identifies the record as a CompanyVehicle, and Z is a special marker used at the end of the input file.

Caution: The operator   >> functions for CompanyVehicle and PersonalVehicle both need to call the same function for their base class, Vehicle. There is a right way and a wrong way to do this. The right way is to cast the CompanyVehicle parameter into a Vehicle reference:

```
istream & operator >>( istream & inp, CompanyVehicle & v )
{
  inp >> (Vehicle &)v;  // get Vehicle data
  inp >> v.tripTaken;
  return inp;
}
```

The *wrong* way is to leave out the & and cause a temporary Vehicle object to be constructed and soon destroyed. The difference appears subtle, but the following code does not permit the Vehicle data members to be initialized:

```
istream & operator >>( istream & inp, CompanyVehicle & v )
{
  inp >> (Vehicle) v;  // calls copy constructor!
  inp >> v.tripTaken;
  return inp;
}
```

Without a doubt, this is one of C++'s well-known "gotchas."

3 Vehicle Constructors. Create constructors for the Vehicle, Company Vehicle, and PersonalVehicle classes that allow all data members to be initialized. Be sure to provide constructor-initializers for each class. For example, the PersonalVehicle constructor could be implemented as:

```
PersonalVehicle::PersonalVehicle( ulong id, const FString & driver,
  ulong odometer, const Date & chkDate, const InsuranceInfo & insur )
  :Vehicle( id, driver, odometer, chkDate, Vehicle::personal ),
  insurance(insur)
{ }
```

Write a program that tests each of the new constructors and redisplays each type of Vehicle object.

4 Vehicle Management: RentedVehicle Class. Derive a new class from `CompanyVehicle` called `RentedVehicle`. Vehicles of this type are rented from outside sources and provided to employees for company business. Additional data members are:

- `provider` (an `FString` object containing the name of a rental company)
- `invoiceNum` (unsigned long containing provider's rental invoice number)
- `dateRented` (a `Date` object)
- `returnDate` (a `Date` object)

Provide member functions that get and set each of these data members, and provide stream I/O operators for the new class. Add several new records to the input data file containing `RentedVehicle` objects.

5 Passenger Lists. In the original specifications for the Vehicle Management System, we mentioned the need to store a passenger list in each vehicle that carries passengers. Add a `PassengerList` object to the `CompanyVehicle` class, and implement the new class. Modify the test program accordingly.

6 Vehicle Inventory. In the original specifications for the Vehicle Management System, we said that an inventory list should be kept for vehicles carrying cargo. Add a `CargoList` object to the `CompanyVehicle` class, and implement the new class. Modify the test program accordingly.

7 Passenger and Cargo Vehicles. Combine the `PassengerList` and `CargoList` classes in the previous two exercises from a single class called `VehicleInventory`. Store a `VehicleInventory` object inside a `Company Vehicle`, and use a tag data member to identify which type of inventory is being used. (Notice, for example, how the `vehicleType` data member in the `Vehicle` class identifies the current type of vehicle.) Modify the test program to suit the changes you have made.

6.6.3 Multiple Inheritance

1 Students and Employees. Implement the `Student`, `Employee`, `Salaried`, and `GradAssistant` classes from Example 6-2. Run and test the program.

2 Virtual Base Class. Implement all classes shown in Section 6.4, including the virtual base class called `Person`. Run and test the program.

6.6.4 Graphics Classes

1 Colors for Point. Add a `color` data member to the `Point`, `Rectangle`, and `Square` classes. Write a program that demonstrates drawing these figures in different colors.

2 Filling Rectangles.   Create a `FilledRectangle` class, derived from the `Rectangle` class in this chapter. A `FilledRectangle` should be able to have a different color for the border than for the interior area. Write a test program that creates instances of `FilledRectangle` and displays rectangles of various colors and sizes.

3 GraphLine Class Design .   Design a class called `GraphLine` that represents a single line in a cartesian graph. A line may be interpreted as an array of y-values, such as the number of shares of a stock traded on a particular day. A `GraphLine` must have a color data member so that multiple lines in the same graph can be plotted in different colors.

4 XYGraph Class Design.   Design a class called `XYGraph` that defines a cartesian graph with an x-axis and a y-axis. It should contain information about the maximum values for x and y, as well as the physical ranges of the graphics window. It should also contain an array of `GraphLine` objects, designed in the previous exercise. Using information about the screen size, a point in a graph line can be scaled to fit within the screen. Suppose that the horizontal screen size were 1000, and suppose that the x-axis range were from 0 to 100. This would imply a ratio of 10:1. To plot an x-value of 50, the scaled x-value would equal 50 * 10.

5 XYGraph Class Implementation. Implement the `XYGraph` and `GraphLine` classes from the previous two exercises. Write a test program that reads a data file containing a list of integers and draws a line graph from the integers. *Extra:* Read several data sets and plot each graph line in a different color.

6 Polygon Class.   Create a class called `Polygon` that defines a graphical polygon. You might want to implement it either as an array of `Point` objects or as an array of `Line` objects. A `Polygon` should be able to store a polygon containing between 3 and 100 vertices. Implement and test the class by creating a number of polygons and drawing them (on a graphics screen, if possible).

7 Point and Line Classes.   One might suggest that the `Point` class serve as a base class for the `Line` class. This is not a good idea, because a `Line` is not just another type of `Point`; instead, the relationship between the `Point` and `Line` classes should be a *has-a* relationship. Let a `Line` contain two `Point` objects. Implement the `Point` and `Line` classes, and include functions such as `Draw` and `Move` that exist in both classes.

8 The Circle Class.   Assume that a graphical circle contains a `Point` for its center and an unsigned integer radius. Design and implement a `Circle` class. Write a test program that demonstrates the class operations. The following is a sample class definition:

```
class Circle {
public:
  Circle( const Point & P, unsigned r );
```

```
void Draw( unsigned color );
// Draw the circle in a given color.

void MoveTo( const Point & newPoint );
// Move the center to the location determined
// by newPoint.

const Point & GetCenter() const;
unsigned GetRadius() const;

void SetRadius( unsigned r );
void SetCenter( const Point & P );

private:
  Point center;
  unsigned radius;
};
```

6.6.5 Student Registration

1 Student Class Design. Design a class called Student that contains an ID number, a last name, and a first name. Derive another class from Student, called StudentRecord, which contains data members for total credits earned and total grade points. Define a constructor for each class that initializes its data members. The StudentRecord constructor should pass an initialization list to the Student constructor. Define stream output functions for both classes.

2 Student and StudentRecord Implementations. Implement the classes designed in the previous exercise and write a test program that initializes both Student and StudentRecord objects. Input the data from the user and display the objects on the screen.

3 College Transcript Design. Design a class called Course that includes the name of a course, credits awarded, and grade received for the course. Also, design a class called CourseList that contains an array of Course objects, and a count data member (the number of courses in the array). Specify class operations that allow a user to read a list of Course objects from a file, display the list, calculate a grade point average, and total credits for all courses.

4 Course and CourseList Implementations. Using the Course and CourseList classes designed in the previous exercise, implement the classes and write a program that tests the classes. Create a CourseList object, input a list of courses from a file, redisplay the CourseList, display the total credits for all courses, and calculate and display the student's grade point average.

5 Student Record with Course List. Using the StudentRecord and CourseList classes from the previous exercises, add a CourseList data member to the StudentRecord class. When a new Course is inserted into a student's

CourseList, update the total credits earned and the total grade points for the student. Input several student records from a file, with several courses per student. Display a registration report showing each student, along with his/her total credits and grade point average. For example,

ID	Name	Credits	GradePts	GPA
12345	Espinal,Luis	10	35	3.50
20000	Smith, Ann	15	45	3.00
(etc.)				

CHAPTER 7

Pointers
and Dynamic Allocation

Without question, pointers and dynamic memory allocation are among the most powerful tools available in C and C++. They allow us to build dynamic data structures that adapt to the application needs while a program is running. At the same time, pointers must also be used with care to avoid corrupting memory. In this chapter, we show how to safely allocate and dispose of memory for objects and arrays. We also show how the same pointer can point to objects of different classes, and how constructors and destructors are affected by dynamic allocation. Finally, we demonstrate a dynamic array class that expands automatically.

Terms Introduced in this Chapter:

adjacency matrix
allocate
casting away const
collection
copy constructor
const-qualified
dangling pointer
deallocate
deep copy
directed arc
directed path
dynamic allocation
exception

fixed allocation
fragmentation
graph
heap (free store)
memory exhaustion
memory leak
node, arc
object slicing
pointer to a constant
queue
ragged array
void pointer

7.1 CONSTANT POINTERS

7.1.1 Pointers to Constants

A *pointer to a constant* is a pointer that is declared in such a way that the object it points to cannot be modified via that pointer. This is one of the most useful features of data declarations in C++, because it combines the advantages of pointers with the protection given by the `const` qualifier. For example, cp contains the address of n and any attempt to modify n through cp fails:

```
int n = 0;
const int * cp = &n;
*cp = 30;              // error
n = 30;                // but this is ok
```

Notice that the object addressed by cp does not have to be declared const-qualified. In fact, in our example, n could still be modified directly.

We will use the term *constant* to mean *const-qualified*, indicating that the `const` qualifier was used in the declaration of a name. Whether or not the constant is protected by the operating system or hardware against changes is beyond the scope of our discussion.

When a function parameter is a pointer to a constant, the object addressed by the pointer cannot be modified. For example, the standard function `strlen` defined in the `string.h` header returns the length of a string. The string pointed to by parameter `str` will not be modified:

```
size_t strlen( const char * str);
```

The function can be called with either constant or non-constant arguments, as the following examples show:

```
const char * aStr = "AAAAAAAAA";
char name[] = "Johnson";

unsigned n;
n = strlen( aStr );
n = strlen( name );
```

On the other hand, you cannot pass a pointer to a constant to a function having a parameter that is a pointer to a non-constant. Doing so would allow the function to violate the *const*ness of the object. For example, the standard function `strcpy` copies a source string to a destination string, so its first argument cannot be const-qualified:

```
char * strcpy( char * dest, const char * source );
.
.
.
const char * dest;
const char * source;
strcpy( dest, source );   // error
```

There exists no implicit conversion in C++ from a pointer to a constant, to a pointer to a non-constant. On the other hand, performing the conversion explicitly is called *casting away const*, and is generally discouraged. In the following example, the Process function contains a const-qualified Student reference parameter, which we use to invoke the S.SetId member function:

```
class Student {
public:
  Student( long idNum );
  void SetId( long idNum );
  //...
};

void Process( const Student & S )
{
  S.SetId( 12345L );                 // error
  ((Student &)S).SetId( 12345L ); // bad style!
}
```

The first call to SetId generates an error, whereas the second does not. The second call to SetId unwisely uses the cast operator without knowing whether the argument passed to the function was declared const-qualified. It might have been a temporary object, or it might have been const-qualified, as in the following sample calls to Process:

```
int main()
{
  const Student aStudent(33333L);

  Process( Student(11111L) );   // temporary object
  Process( aStudent );          // const-qualified
  //...
```

Never cast away the const-qualified property of an object unless there is a strong justification for doing so. The object might be in either read-only memory or memory that is protected by the operating system.

7.1.2 Const-Qualified Pointers

In some instances, you may want to prevent the contents of a pointer itself from being modified. By placing the `const` qualifier in the pointer's declaration, we make the pointer itself const-qualified. In the next example, we are prevented from incrementing `sp`, although the string it addresses can be modified:

```
char message[80];
char * const sp = message;

sp++;                               // error
strcpy(sp, "A new message");   // ok
```

In this way, a const-qualified pointer has the same restriction as `message`, an array of characters, which is not an LValue and cannot be modified:

```
message++;   // error: LValue required
```

If neither the pointer nor the data it points to should be changed, we can use `const` twice to create a const-qualified pointer to a constant:

```
char message[80];
const char * const sp = message;

sp++;                               // error
strcpy(sp, "A new message");   // error
```

To summarize, there are four possible ways that we could have declared a pointer to `message`.

```
char * p1 = message;
char * const p2 = message;
const char * p3 = message;
const char * const p4 = message;
```

`p1` is completely non-constant, so the pointer and the string it points to can be modified. `p2` is a const-qualified pointer, so the pointer cannot be modified. `p3` is a pointer to a constant, so the string it points to cannot be modified. `p4` is a const-qualified pointer to a constant, so neither the pointer nor the string it points to can be modified.

7.1.3 Functions Returning Pointers to Constants

When a function returns a pointer to a constant, the variable (if any) receiving the return value must also be a pointer to a constant. In the following `Student` class, `GetName` returns a pointer to `name`, a data member:

```
class Student {
public:
  const char * GetName() const;
  //...
private:
  char name[30];
};
```

Predictably, we can only assign the function's return value to a pointer to a constant:

```
Student S;

char * ncName = S.GetName();      // error
const char * cName = S.GetName();  // ok
```

The reason for returning a pointer to a constant should be clear: We do not want a class user to directly modify a class data member via its pointer. This would violate the all-important principle of data encapsulation.

7.2 POINTER CONVERSIONS

7.2.1 Pointers to Array Elements

When memory is allocated for a pointer, C++ keeps track of the type of object to which the pointer points, which includes its implementation size. One advantage is that when the pointer points to an array element, increment and decrement operations on the pointer work correctly. This also allows a program to be recompiled and run on computer systems that implement different storage sizes for a given type. The compiler "knows" the size of the type on the target machine.

For example, we declare an array of float called flist, and assign the address of its first element to fp. When we increment fp, it points to the second array element:

```
float flist[] = { 10.5, 13.2, 4, 9.6 }; // array of float
float * fp = flist;                      // points to flist[0]
fp++;                                    // points to flist[1]
```

But what would happen if we tried to access the array with the wrong type of pointer? The compiler would make the wrong assumptions about the size of each array element. To illustrate, let's cast fp into an int* and increment the resulting pointer:

```
float flist[] = { 10.5, 13.2, 4, 9.6 };
float * fp = flist;
int * ip = (int *) fp;
++ip;
cout << *ip;              // unknown value
```

Having done this, we have no idea what value would be obtained by dereferencing ip. Clearly, this type of cast, although permitted, would only lead to confusion.

7.2.2 Void Pointers

C/C++ programmers use the void pointer type to achieve flexibility of types. Any pointer can be assigned to a void pointer. For example, the standard function memcpy, declared in the mem.h header, copies a block of nbytes bytes from a source to a destination:

```
void *memcpy(void *dest, const void *src, size_t nbytes);
```

The source and destination parameters are both *void pointers*, allowing the function to be used for objects of any type. For example, we could copy an array of long integers:

```
const unsigned ArraySize = 500;
long arrayOne[ArraySize];
long arrayTwo[ArraySize];

memcpy( arrayOne, arrayTwo, ArraySize * sizeof(long) );
```

But we might just as easily have copied an array of some other type.

C++, because of its stricter type-checking than C, requires an explicit cast when assigning a void pointer to a pointer of another type:

```
int * p;
void * v = p;   // ok
p = (int *) v;  // cast required
```

One must be cautious when performing an explicit cast, to make sure the cast matches the type of the object addressed by the pointer. C++'s type checking is intended to help the programmer avoid mistakes, not to prevent a deliberate type conversion.

7.2.3 References to Pointers

A reference to a pointer would seem to be a contradiction in terms, but it has practical value. A pointer can be passed to a function by reference in cases where the pointer must be modified by the function. For example, `FindNext` searches a string for a particular character. Its parameter p is left pointing to the character (or to the string's null terminator if the character is not found):

```
void FindNext( char * & p, char delim )
{
  while( *p && (*p != delim) )
    p++;
}
```

The function is useful when searching for substrings separated by a given delimiter. The next example shows a loop that calls `FindNext`, passing a pointer p that is updated after each call:

```
#include <iostream.h>

char str[] = "abc,def,ghi,jkl";

char * p = str;
do {
  cout << p << '\n';
  FindNext( p, ',' );
} while( *p++ != 0 );

cout << endl;
```

The program's output shows p making its way through the string:

```
abc,def,ghi,jkl
,def,ghi,jkl
,ghi,jkl
,jkl
```

7.2.4 Implicit Conversion of Derived Pointers to Base Pointers

Pointer variables offer the most flexibility in allowing the same variable to refer to different types of objects. The restriction is that the objects must be related by inheritance. Specifically, a base type pointer can point at either a base object or at a derived object. For example, using the `Point` and `Point3D` classes presented earlier, we could declare a pointer as type `Point *`, and assign it the address of a `Point3D` object:

```
Point3D center;
Point * p = &center;
```

A pointer to an object of a derived class can be implicitly converted to a pointer of its base type. Similarly, a reference to an object of a derived class can be implicitly converted to a reference of its base type:

```
Point3D * cp = new Point3D;
Point * p;
p = cp;
```

This type of pointer conversion usually takes place when a pointer of a derived type is passed to a function whose parameter is of a base type. For example, let's define the Student and GraduateStudent classes, in which Graduate Student is a Student with one additional data member:

```
class Student {
public:
  //...
private:
  long id;
  FString name;
};

class GraduateStudent :public Student {
public:
  //...
private:
  FString thesisTitle;
};
```

We can pass gp, a pointer to a GraduateStudent, to the CalcTuition function, which has a pointer-to-Student parameter. The pointer argument is implicitly converted to the parameter's type:

```
void CalcTuition( Student * sp )
{
  // sp points to Student or GraduateStudent
}
.

.
GraduateStudent * gp = new GraduateStudent;
CalcTuition( gp );
```

In fact, a pointer to an object of any class derived from Student would have been acceptable as a function argument. Providing an explicit cast would yield the same result as the implicit conversion, so it is considered unnecessary:

```
CalcTuition( (Student *)gp );
```

Our example using pointers would also have worked with references to Student and GraduateStudent objects:

```
void CalcTuition( Student & S )
{
  // S refers to a Student or GraduateStudent
}


GraduateStudent aGrad;
CalcTuition( aGrad );
```

Conceptually, passing an object's reference is the same as passing its address—only the notation is different.

If, however, we apply the cast operator to a GraduateStudent object, we get a completely different result:

```
GraduateStudent aGrad;
CalcTuition( Student(aGrad) );
```

This may look like a simple cast, but in fact, it calls the Student copy constructor and creates a temporary Student object. After the function call, the temporary object is destroyed. This type of error might go completely unnoticed until a call was made to a function that updated the object's data members. For instance, if CalcTuition updated one of the data members, aGrad would contain none of the changes made by the function.

7.2.5 Casting Base Pointers to Derived Pointers

A base pointer cannot be implicitly converted to a derived pointer. By a base pointer, we mean a pointer to an instance of a base class, and a derived pointer is a pointer to an instance of any class derived from the given base. Such an implicit conversion would be risky, because a derived object is a superset of a base object. Any attempt to reference nonexistent data or function members would result in unpredictable program results. Using the Student and GraduateStudent classes from Section 7.2.4, for example, imagine the following scenario where we attempt to display a nonexistent thesis title from a Student object:

```
void DoSomething( const GraduateStudent * GS )
{
  cout << GS->GetThesisTitle();
}


Student * sp = new Student;
//...
DoSomething( sp );    // syntax error
```

Of course, a really determined programmmer can cast the base pointer into the derived type. This is done, presumably, with full confidence that the cast is a sensible one, which in this case, it is not:

```
Student * sp = new Student;
//...
DoSomething( GraduateStudent(sp) );
```

In another situation, however, sp might actually point to a GraduateStudent object, and the cast would be appropriate:

```
Student * sp = new GraduateStudent;
//...
DoSomething( GraduateStudent(sp) );
```

7.2.5.1 Collection Class Example.

To show practical applications of both implicit and explicit pointer conversions, we will create a class called Item, which represents the base class of objects inserted into a Collection object. A *collection* is a general type of container for holding objects, typically implemented as an array or linked list. We also derive the Student class from Item, allowing Students to be added to a Collection:

```
class Item {
  //...
};

class Student :public Item {
  //...
};

class Collection {
public:
  void Append( const Item * ip );
  Item * Get() const;
};
```

The Append function takes a pointer to an Item and adds it to a Collection. We can pass a Student pointer to Append because it is implicitly converted to an Item pointer:

```
const unsigned Count = 10;
Collection studentList;
Student * p;
```

```
for(unsigned i = 0; i < Count; i++)
{
  p = new Student;
  studentList.Append( p );
}
```

To retrieve an item from the collection, we call the `Get` function, which returns an `Item` pointer. We explicitly cast that to a `Student` pointer, knowing full well that only `Student` objects were appended to the collection:

```
p = (Student *) studentList.Get();
```

Forcing class users to use explicit casts leads to ugly source code, so at some point, it may be worth it to wrap a shell around the `Collection` class by deriving a `StudentCollection`. Any casting can be done in the new class, making life easier for the class user:

```
class StudentCollection :public Collection {
public:
  Student * Get() const
  {
    return (Student *) Collection::Get();
  }
  //...
};

StudentCollection studentList;
Student * p;
//...
p = studentList.Get();   // no cast required
```

Of course, now we cannot insert other items (such as giraffes or umbrellas) in the collection, so we gain convenience at the expense of flexibility. In fact, we gain more in type checking and other conveniences of use than we lose in flexibility. You may wish to cast objects, but in general, the debugging time saved, and the absence of hard-to-find problems more than makes up for it.

7.3 ALLOCATING MEMORY

7.3.1 Fixed and Dynamic Allocation

Some years ago, language designers recognized the need for programmers to allocate storage for objects at run time. For example, when using an array with a fixed size to hold data read from a file, it was sometimes impossible at compile time to know how large a particular array should be. The term *fixed allocation* applies to an object whose size is determined at compile time.

The process of allocating memory for objects at run time is called *dynamic allocation*. Objects that use dynamic allocation need not have a specified size at compile time. A dynamic object's lifetime continues until either the program ends, or the object is explicitly deallocated.

Dynamic allocation allows you to write program statements that allocate and deallocate memory for individual objects on demand. Storage is allocated from a large chunk of memory called the *heap,* or *free store.* The heap can be used and reused as often as desired.

To *allocate* storage means to request a block of memory, the address of which is stored in a pointer variable. To *deallocate* storage means to release a block of memory whose address is in a pointer variable. We will also use the shorthand term *deleting a pointer* to mean that the storage addressed by the pointer is being deallocated, not the pointer itself.

Fragmentation is the condition where enough objects have been allocated and deallocated from the heap that gaps occur between allocated objects. If the heap is fragmented badly enough, an attempted allocation of a large object might fail because there is not enough available contiguous storage.

7.3.2 The New and Delete Operators

The `new` operator allocates a block of storage and returns the address of the storage. For example, the first of the following statements allocates a single integer and stores the address in the variable p. The second statement allocates space for 50 integers and places the address in `array`:

```
int * p = new int;
int * array = new int[50];
```

When an array is allocated, the program's runtime system keeps track of the array's size. The actual method for doing this is implementation-dependent.

Storage is deallocated by using the `delete` operator, which has two different formats, depending upon whether or not the object is an array. Deallocating an array requires the use of brackets, which tells C++ to look up the size of the array and deallocate the appropriate amount of storage:

```
delete p;          // a single object
delete [] array;   // an array
```

7.3.2.1 Storage Duration and Pointers.   Let's distinguish between the storage duration of a pointer itself, and the memory that it addresses. For example, a pointer may have automatic storage duration, while the memory it addresses has dynamic duration. In this case, the pointer can go out of scope while the dynamic memory remains allocated:

```
if( a > b )
{
  float * fp = new float;
  //...
}
```

In this example, since there exists no other pointer to the storage we allocated, the storage is left unavailable when fp goes out of scope at the end of the block. This is a common programming error called a *memory leak*.

Or, a pointer with static duration might contain the address of dynamic storage. The storage remains available until either it is deallocated by the delete operator, or the program ends. The static variable globalName is this type of pointer:

```
char * globalName;

void main()
{
  globalName = new char[50];

  //...
}
```

One advantage to this approach is that the size of the storage allocated to globalName can change throughout the lifetime of the program. All that is required is to deallocate the storage that globalName addresses, and then reallocate new storage as needed.

A pointer might be automatic and contain the address of another pointer which is declared static, which in turn contains the address of dynamic storage:

```
int main()
{
  static int * array = new int[100];
  int ** zp = &array;
  //...
}
```

The point of these examples is to show that there are many effective ways to combine pointers and dynamic memory allocation.

7.3.2.2 Dealing with Memory Exhaustion.   *Memory exhaustion* occurs when there is not enough available memory to satisfy a request made for dynamic memory by the new operator. In older versions of C++, it was necessary to test for a possible null pointer (value of 0) returned by new. More current C++ implementations throw an *exception*, which makes it possible for a program to gracefully handle the problem and decide whether or not to halt. Exception handling is not covered until Chapter 8, so our current course of action is to display a message indicating the

problem and halt the program. The worst thing a program could do would be to continue execution and try to dereference the invalid pointer.

A simple way to handle memory exhaustion is to create a function that is activated if memory allocation fails, and install it with the standard set_new_handler function. Our installed function must have a void return type with no parameters. Here is a simple example showing its use. The standard new.h header is required:

```
#include <new.h>    // for set_new_handler()

void allocation_handler()
{
  cout << "Out of memory. Aborting program.\n";

  // perform any necessary cleanup here...

  exit(1);
}

int main()
{
  set_new_handler( allocation_handler );

  while( 1 )
    char * P = new char[10000];  // eventually fails

  return 0;
}
```

A problem with this approach is that we don't know which files might be left open, or which class destructors have executed; but, for simple and non-critical applications, this approach is adequate.

7.3.3 Pointers to Class Objects

We frequently declare pointers to class objects and want to initialize them with the addresses of objects allocated by new. An object's constructor executes immediately after the new operator successfully allocates storage for the object. In fact, if the new operator fails to allocate storage, the constructor is not executed and the new operator returns a null address. In the next example, the first statement declares a pointer. If the second statement successfully allocates storage for a Student, the constructor will be called:

```
Student * P;      // declare a pointer
P = new Student;  // allocate storage
if( !P )
  // could not create a Student
```

When we create an array of class objects, the class's default constructor is called for each member of the array:

```
Point * figure = new Point[10];  // Calls Point() ten times.
```

The `delete` operator, when applied to a pointer containing the address of a class object, will cause the object's destructor to be called. If, for example, we deallocate the array of `Point` objects called `figure`, the class destructor will be called for each member of the array:

```
delete [] figure;
```

7.4 ARRAYS AND DYNAMIC ALLOCATION

7.4.1 One-Dimensional Arrays

Arrays are easily among the greatest consumers of memory in programs. When an array with storage class `static` has a fixed allocation, the memory used by the array cannot be used for any other purpose during a program's execution cycle. Instead, programmers often prefer the flexibility of dynamically allocating and deallocating storage for arrays, using the `new` and `delete` operators. The following example dynamically allocates space for a 1000-element array of `float`:

```
const unsigned ArraySize = 1000;
//...
float * myArray = new float[ArraySize];
```

As a matter of good style, we used a declared constant for the array dimension, to make all program statements relating to the array consistent in their references to the array size.

7.4.2 Two-Dimensional Arrays

A two-dimensional array may be thought of as an array whose elements are arrays. For example, the following statement dynamically allocates a contiguous two-dimensional array of integers in 3 rows and 10 columns:

```
int (*table)[10] = new int[3][10];
```

The notation `int (*table)[10]` indicates that `table` is a pointer to an array of 10 integers. The notation `int[3][10]` specifies a three-element array in which each element is an `int[10]` array.

In contrast to the complicated notation used when allocating the array, deallocating the array is simple because C++ already knows how many bytes of storage are used by the array:

```
delete [] table;
```

7.4.2.1 *Array of Pointers.*   Another way to dynamically allocate a two-dimensional array is to allocate each row of the array separately, and store its address in a pointer. To do this, we must declare an array of pointers, in which each pointer contains the address of a single row. The array of pointers itself can use either fixed or dynamic allocation.

For example, let's create a 50 × 1000 array of equipment readings called `samples`. The left side of the following diagram shows an array of pointers, each containing the address of a block of dynamic memory, shown along the right side:

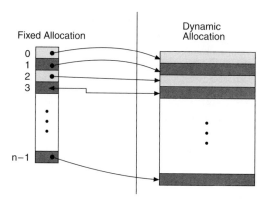

Here is a definition of the `samples` array:

```
const unsigned NumRows = 50;
const unsigned RowSize = 1000;
int * samples[NumRows];
```

We can allocate dynamic memory for each row, using the `new` operator:

```
for(unsigned i = 0; i < NumRows; i++ )
  samples[i] = new int[RowSize]
```

We can also initialize each element to 0, using subscripts in the same way as if the array had been statically allocated:

```
for(unsigned i = 0; i < NumRows; i++)
  for(unsigned j = 0; j < RowSize; j++)
    samples[i][j] = 0;
```

An excellent use for an array of pointers is when each row of a two-dimensional array varies in size. If we were creating a text-editing program, we might need to open a file and read each line of text into a buffer. Using the length of the line as a guide, we could allocate just enough space for the line and assign its address to a pointer. We call this type of array a *ragged array,* an example of which is shown by the following simple input routine:

```
ifstream infile( "ragged.cpp" );
if( !infile ) return 1;

const unsigned NumRows = 100;
const unsigned BufSize = 1024;

char * names[NumRows];
char buffer[BufSize];

unsigned j = 0;

while(!infile.eof())
{
  infile.getline( buffer, BufSize );
  names[j] = new char[ strlen(buffer)+1 ];
  strcpy( names[j], buffer );
  if( j++ >= NumRows ) break;
}
```

The program stops reading when either all rows have been filled, or the end of the input file is reached.

The ragged array approach makes efficient use of memory because it allocates only the minimum amount of storage needed for each row in the array. When the array is no longer needed, the program can also deallocate the storage. The following diagram depicts the ragged array we created:

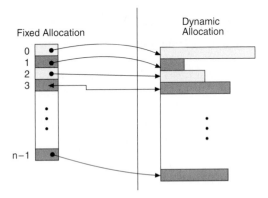

7.4.3 Graph Example

A *graph* is generally defined as a a collection of *nodes* (or *vertices*) that are connected by *arcs* (or *edges*). In our example that follows, each node is shown as a circle with an identifying number inside. Each arc is a line connecting two nodes, and a *directed arc* is an arc with a specific direction.

A graph can be used to show interrelationships between elements of a set by using nodes to indicate set members and arcs to show relationships between members. In our simple example, we number the nodes 0-4, and the arcs are marked with arrows to show direction. For example, there is a directed arc from node 1 to node 2, but not from node 2 to node 1:

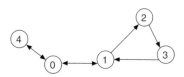

Informally, a *directed path* is made up of one or more directed arcs in sequence. In our diagram, for example, there is a directed path from node 1 to node 3 that includes node 2. There is also a 3-arc directed path from node 3 to node 4 (3, 1, 0, 4).

Graphs have many applications in computer science; among them are:

- A series of states and transitions between states. For example, each node might represent different possible moves by a computer playing chess, and each arc might represent the availability of a particular move.

- Relationships between independent entities; for example, each node might be a receiving station for parcels handled by a shipping company, and each arc might represent the availability of a shipping route between stations.

7.4.3.1 Adjacency Matrix.
Let's create a 5×5 *adjacency matrix M* of integers that serves as a reference to a graph. We use i as a row subscript, and j as a column subscript. In each position M_{ij}, a 1 indicates the presence of a directed arc from node i to node j. There is, for example, an arc from node 0 to node 1; another from node 0 to node 4, and so on:

```
          0    1    2    3    4
     ------------------------------
0:    0    1    0    0    1
1:    1    0    1    0    0
2:    0    0    0    1    0
3:    0    1    0    0    0
4:    1    0    0    0    0
```

A matrix might be implemented a number of different ways, but we choose to implement it as a two-dimensional array:

```
const int ROWS = 5;
const int COLS = 5;
int adjacent[ROWS][COLS] =
     { { 0,1,0,0,1 },
       { 1,0,1,0,0 },
       { 0,0,0,1,0 },
       { 0,1,0,0,0 },
       { 1,0,0,0,0 } };
```

Notice that the entire array is stored in contiguous memory starting with row 0 and ending with row 4:

0 1 0 0 1	1 0 1 0 0	0 0 0 1 0	0 1 0 0 0	1 0 0 0 0
row 0	row 1	row 2	row 3	row 4

We would like to count the number of directed arcs in the matrix by traversing the array and summing its elements. We could use a nested loop with subscripts, but this would require 25 iterations of the inner loop, in which the expression matrix[i][j] must be recalculated:

```
int sum = 0;

for(int i = 0; i < ROWS; i++)
  for(int j = 0; j < COLS; j++)
    sum += adjacent[i][j];
```

A better way to process the array would be by conceptually flattening it out, taking advantage of the way it is stored in memory (in row-major order). We calculate the location of the next byte beyond the end of the array and store it in last:

```
int sum = 0;
int * last = adjacent[0] + (ROWS * COLS);
for(int *p = adjacent[0]; p < last; p++)
  sum += *p;
```

The loop initializes p, a pointer to an integer, to the address of row 0, with the expression p = adjacent[0]. The single statement inside the loop is efficient because it requires only a single pointer dereference.

A note of caution is in order here: Flattening out an array and using a single loop is fine, as long as the array is in contiguous memory. The situation would be quite different for an array of pointers, each pointing to a disjunct block of memory. In that case, there would be absolutely no guarantee that the array's rows were stored in contiguous memory.

7.5 CONSTRUCTORS AND DESTRUCTORS

7.5.1 VString Class Example

Classes containing pointer data members frequently use the new operator in their constructors to allocate storage. This gives the class user some flexibility in being able to dictate the amount of storage used by each class instance at run time.

A useful example that comes to mind is a variable-length string class, which we will call VString. We can pass a length argument to the constructor, which determines the size of the VString. Or, we can pass a C-style string to the constructor when creating a VString object:

```
#include <string.h>

class VString {
public:
  VString( unsigned len = 0 );
  // Construct a VString of size <len>.

  VString( const char * s );
  // Construct a VString from a C-style string.

  ~VString();
  // Destructor

  unsigned GetSize() const;
  // Return the number of characters.

private:
  char * str;        // character array
  unsigned size;     // allocation size
};
```

The first constructor sets the size of the string, allocates storage equal to the size, and places a null byte at the beginning of the string. This doubles as a default constructor because of the default argument initializer that was in the function prototype:

```
VString::VString( unsigned len )
{
  size = len;
  str = new char[ size+1 ];
  str[0] = '\0';
}
```

The second constructor gets the size of the string parameter and uses it to allocate storage. It then copies the characters from the parameter into the `str` data member:

```
VString::VString( const char * s )
{
  size = strlen( s );
  str = new char[ size+1 ];
  strcpy( str, s );
}
```

The destructor deallocates the storage addressed by `str`:

```
VString::~VString()
{
  delete [] str;
}
```

We can declare a `VString` object of length zero, a 50-character empty `VString`, or a `VString` containing someone's name:

```
VString zeroLen;
VString emptyStr( 50 );
VString aName( "John Smith" );
cout << aName.GetSize();
```

The primary advantage to using `VString` rather than `FString`, as we have seen in the past, is that the size of a `VString` can be tailored to its application. An `FString`, on the other hand, is always fixed at an arbitrary size, imposing a severe restriction on its use and efficiency.

An actual variable-length string class would, of course, have to contain many more operations than those presented in `VString`. In the chapter exercises, we suggest some member functions that could be added. Also, the newest C++ draft standard contains two different string class specifications, which are shown in [Plauger].

7.5.2 Copy Constructors

A *copy constructor* is a special-purpose constructor that makes a duplicate copy of an object of the same type. In the next example, `Student B` and `Student C` are each assigned a copy of `Student A`:

```
Student A;
// ( Student A is initialized... )

Student B( A );
Student C = A;
```

The construction of Student C *appears* to use the assignment operator, but in fact, it calls the copy constructor using different notation.

A copy constructor is invoked automatically when a temporary object is constructed from an existing one. For example, if a Student were passed to a function that used a value parameter (rather than a reference), the compiler would construct a temporary copy of the passed argument, aStudent:

```
void RegisterStudent( Student S );
    .
    .
    .
Student aStudent();
RegisterStudent( aStudent );
```

Consider the short program in Example 7-1, which contains a Student class with a default constructor, copy constructor, destructor, and stream output opera-

Example 7-1. Student Class, with Construction of Temporary Object

```
#include <iostream.h>

class Student {
public:
  Student() { cout << "default constructor,"; }

  Student( const Student & s ) { cout << "copy constructor,"; }

  ~Student() { cout << "destructor,"; }

  friend ostream & operator <<( ostream & os, const Student & s )
  {
    cout << "Student,";
    return os;
  }
};

Student InputNewStudent()
{
  Student aStudent;
  //...
  return aStudent;
}

int main()
{
  cout << InputNewStudent();
  return 0;
}
```

tor. When we call the `InputNewStudent` function, it is instructive to follow the sequence of constructor and destructor calls:

1. `InputNewStudent` is called, and at the declaration of `aStudent`, the default constructor is executed.
2. The `return` statement invokes the `Student` copy constructor, creating a temporary `Student` object.
3. Upon leaving the `InputNewStudent` function, the `~Student` destructor is called as `aStudent` goes out of scope.
4. Back in `main`, the `operator <<` function displays the temporary `Student` object as "`Student`".
5. The `~Student` destructor is called, destroying the temporary `Student` object.

From this example, we can see that the temporary object is destroyed as soon as it is no longer referenced in `main`. The screen output is

```
default constructor, copy constructor, destructor, Student, destructor
```

In C++, it is important to understand the way that constructors and destructors are called, particularly when a considerable amount of execution time overhead is involved. To improve a program's efficiency, you may want to minimize the number of temporary objects that are created and destroyed.

7.5.2.1 Deep Copy Operation.
It is important to understand the difference between copying the contents of an object versus copying just the address of an object. The first approach is called a *deep copy* operation. For example, we allocate a block of memory and assign its address to `cp`. Next, we use the standard `strcpy` function to copy the characters in the name to the new location:

```
char name[] = "John Q. Citizen";
char * cp = new char[30];
strcpy( cp, name );
```

In the next statement, however, we copy only the address of `name` into `cp`:

```
char name[] = "John Q. Citizen";
char * cp = name;
```

The designers of C++ recognized from the start that the issue of deep copying would be important when copying class objects. Objects might contain data members that are pointers to objects, which themselves might contain pointers, and so forth. A copy constructor is responsible for making a deep copy of an object.

7.5.2.2 Student Copy Constructor.   If you don't explicitly define a copy
constructor, the compiler creates one for you, and by default, makes a bitwise copy
of an existing object. Up to this point in the book, we have assumed that a bitwise
copy would be appropriate for copying objects; but objects containing pointers
should not be copied this way.

In the Student class (Example 7-2), because coursesTaken is an array of
Course objects, the courses themselves are not physically inside a Student object. Copying a pointer is not the same as copying the object that it addresses. So, if
we constructed a new Student as a copy of an existing one, we would end up with
two Student objects containing pointers to the same storage:

Example 7-2. Student Class, Containing an Array of Course Objects

```
#include "fstring.h"

class Course {
public:
  Course( const FString & cname = " " );

private:
  FString name;
};

class Student {
public:
  Student( unsigned ncourses );
  ~Student();

private:
  Course * coursesTaken;
  unsigned numCourses;
};

Student::Student( unsigned ncourses )
{
  coursesTaken = new Course[ncourses];
  numCourses = ncourses;
}

Student::~Student()
{
  delete [] coursesTaken;
}
```

```
int ncourses = 7;        // number of courses
Student X( ncourses );
Student Y( X );          // make a copy
```

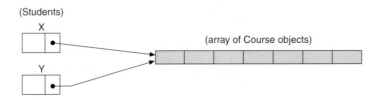

This cross-linking of two pointers causes all sorts of problems. Any change to Student Y's courses results in the same change to X. Worse yet, if X goes out of scope, its coursesTaken array is deallocated by the destructor; then, if Y subsequently goes out of scope, its destructor will try to deallocate the same array, resulting in an invalid pointer reference. The program might terminate abnormally, displaying a core dump and/or diagnostic message from the operating system.

If we create our own copy constructor for the Student class, we ensure that a separate copy of the coursesTaken array is made and no cross-linking occurs:

```
class Student {
public:
   Student( const Student & S );
   //...
};
```

A copy constructor always has a single parameter—a const-qualified reference to an object of the same class. To implement the constructor, we get the number of courses, allocate storage for coursesTaken in the current object, and copy the array:

```
Student::Student( const Student & S )
{
  numCourses = S.numCourses;
  coursesTaken = new Course[numCourses];
  for(unsigned i = 0; i < numCourses; i++)
    coursesTaken[i] = S.coursesTaken[i];
}
```

In some cases, we might never want to pass a Student to a function by value. In that case, we could declare the copy constructor private, preventing objects from being copied. For example, we could do this in the Student class:

```
class Student {
public:
  //...
private:
  Student( const Student & S );
  //...
};
```

Then, if we inadvertently passed a `Student` by value, the compiler would complain because it was unable to make a local copy of the `Student` argument:

```
void RoomAssign( unsigned rnum, Student S );
//...

unsigned roomNumber;
Student aStudent;
//...
RoomAssign( roomNumber, aStudent );   // error
```

7.5.2.3 *VString Copy Constructor.*   The `VString` class, introduced earlier in this chapter, is much more useful if it includes a copy constructor:

```
class VString {
public:
  VString( const VString & V );
  //...

private:
  char * str;        // character array
  unsigned size;     // allocation size
};
```

The copy constructor gets the size of the string in the source object, allocates storage, and copies the characters into the current string:

```
VString::VString( const VString & V )
{
  size = V.GetSize();
  str = new char[size+1];
  strcpy( str, V.str );
}
```

7.5.2.4 *Composite Classes with Copy Constructors.*   If a class contains other class objects and those classes contain pointers, we must create a copy constructor that copies class objects correctly. Let's assume that the `Student` class contains `Transcript` and `VString` objects, each of which contain pointers. Good

programming style dictates that we declare a copy constructor that includes `lastName` and `courses` in its constructor-initializer:

```
class VString { //... };

class Transcript { //... };

class Student {
public:
  //...
  Student( const Student & S )
          : lastName(S.lastName),     // copy last name
            courses(S.courses) { }    // copy transcript

private:
  VString lastName;
  Transcript courses;
};
```

As long as `VString` and `Transcript` have copy constructors, instances of those classes are correctly copied. And, even if we mistakenly leave the copy constructor out of the `Student` class, the default copy constructor generated by the compiler will still call the copy constructors of the member objects.

7.6 LONGARRAY CLASS EXAMPLE

We say that an array whose size is determined at compile time uses a *fixed allocation*. On the other hand, the size of an array using a *dynamic allocation* can be determined at run time. Dynamic allocation can be an advantage, for example, when an array must be initialized from an input file of unknown length. Using a dynamic array involves some amount of management, in the way of allocating and deallocating memory. We would like to show how array management can be encapsulated in a class, relieving the class user from having to deal with these issues.

7.6.1 Specifications

By default, C and C++ do not offer any protection against out-of-range subscripts for arrays. We might say that arrays are optimized for processing speed at the expense of safety. This provides us with a good reason for designing an array class that not only offers built-in range protection for subscripts, but allows us to specify the size of an array at run time, and even change the size after the array has been created. Here, we present a simple long integer array class (called `LongArray`) that offers the following operations:

- Lets the user allocate an array of arbitrary size.

- Deallocates the storage used by an array when it goes out of scope.

- Inserts integers into the array.

- Retrieves integers from the array.

- Constructs a copy of an existing array.

- Expands the array's size on demand.

7.6.2 Design

The `LongArray` class is shown in Example 7-3. The constructor lets the user choose the size of the array to be allocated and set an initial value for all elements. There is a copy constructor and a destructor. The `Get` function retrieves an array element, and the `Put` function inserts a number into the array.

The `GrowBy` function lets the user increase the array's size, `GetSize` returns the current size of the array, and `Init` sets each array element to the value passed as an argument. Three data members are required: `data` is a pointer to the storage used by the array, `size` indicates how many elements the array can hold, and `initv` holds the default initial value for all array elements.

7.6.3 Test Program

A simple test program for the `LongArray` class is shown in Example 7-4, which creates an array, fills it with random integers, constructs a new array as a copy of the first one, and displays the second array. By calling `set_new_handler`, we install an error-reporting function that displays a message if the program runs out of memory. We increase the array's size by calling `GrowBy`, and we call the `Put` function to insert a number in position 0:

```
Z.GrowBy( GrowValue );
Z.Put( 0, 9999 );
```

7.6.4 Class Implementation

The `LongArray` class implementation appears in Example 7-5. The constructor allocates storage for the array and calls `Init` to initialize the elements to default val-

Example 7-3. The LongArray Class Definition

```
#include <assert.h>

class LongArray {
public:
  LongArray( unsigned sz = 0, long defval = 0 );
  // Construct an array of size sz, initialize all
  // elements with defval.

  LongArray( const LongArray & L );
  // copy constructor

  ~LongArray();
  // destructor

  unsigned GetSize() const;
  // Return the current allocation size.

  void GrowBy( unsigned n );
  // Increase the allocation size by n elements.

  void Init( long defval = 0 );
  // Initialize all elements to defval.

  long Get( unsigned i ) const;
  // Retrieve element at index position i.

  void Put( unsigned i, long elt );
  // Insert element at index position i.

private:
  long * data;    // ptr to array containing elements
  unsigned size;  // current allocation size
  long initv;     // initial value
};
```

ues. The initial value for all array elements is saved in the `initv` data member, to be used later by the `GrowBy` function when it needs to initialize additional array elements.

The copy constructor allocates an array of exactly the same size as an existing array and makes a copy of its data. If the parameter for the copy constructor were declared simply as `LongArray L`, the copy constructor would invoke itself to make

Example 7-4. LongArray Test Program

```
#include <stdlib.h>
#include <iostream.h>
#include <new.h>    // for set_new_handler()
#includes "long.h"

void arraysize_error()
{
  cout << "Array too large. Aborting program.\n";
  exit(1);
}

int main()
{
  set_new_handler( arraysize_error );

  const unsigned ArraySize = 20;
  LongArray L(ArraySize, 0xFFFF );
  unsigned i;

  cout << "Initialized with default values:\n";
  for(i = 0; i < L.GetSize(); i++)
    cout << L.Get(i) << ',';
  cout << "\n--------------------------------\n";

  for(i = 0; i < L.GetSize(); i++)
    L.Put(i, rand());

  cout << "Initialized with random values:\n";
  for(i = 0; i < L.GetSize(); i++)
    cout << L.Get(i) << ',';
  cout << "\n--------------------------------\n";

  LongArray Z( L );  // copy constructor

  cout << "After copying the array:\n";
  for(i = 0; i < Z.GetSize(); i++)
    cout << Z.Get(i) << ',';
  cout << "\n--------------------------------\n";

  const unsigned GrowValue = 5;
  Z.GrowBy( GrowValue );
  Z.Put( 0, 9999 );

  cout << "After expanding by 5 and changing elt(0):\n";
  for(i = 0; i < Z.GetSize(); i++)
    cout << Z.Get(i) << ',';

  return 0;
}
```

Example 7-5. The LongArray Class Implementation

```cpp
#include "long.h"

LongArray::LongArray( unsigned sz, long defval )
{
  size = sz;
  data = new long[size];
  Init( defval );
}

LongArray::LongArray( const LongArray & L )
{
  size = L.size;
  initv = L.initv;
  data = new long[size];
  for(unsigned i = 0; i < size; i++)
    data[i] = L.data[i];
}

LongArray::~LongArray()
{
  delete [] data;
}

long LongArray::Get( unsigned i ) const
{
  assert( i < size );
  return data[i];
}

unsigned LongArray::GetSize() const
{
  return size;
}

void LongArray::GrowBy( unsigned growBy )
{
  unsigned tsize = size + growBy;
  long * temp = new long[tsize];

  // Copy the existing data.
  unsigned i;
  for(i = 0; i < size; i++)
    temp[i] = data[i];
```

Example 7-5 *(cont.)*

```
      // Set new positions to initial values.
      for(i = size; i < tsize; i++)
        temp[i] = initv;

      size = tsize;    // update the size value
      delete [] data; // delete the old array
      data = temp;     // save pointer to new data
    }

    void LongArray::Init( long defval )
    {
      initv = defval;
      for(unsigned i = 0; i < size; i++)
        data[i] = defval;
    }

    void LongArray::Put( unsigned i, long elt )
    {
      assert( i < size );
      data[i] = elt;
    }
```

a copy of the function argument. This would lead to infinite recursion as the copy
constructor was called again and again.

The `GrowBy` function allocates a new array, copies the existing array into a
new array, initializes the remaining elements to default values, and deallocates the
old array. Although this function requires extra effort to implement, it is well worth
it. The ability to change the size of an array at run time is a great convenience when
dealing with datasets of unknown size.

7.7 CHAPTER SUMMARY

Deleting a pointer means releasing all memory addressed by the pointer. Once this
has been done, you can no longer access the storage. A class destructor is usually responsible for deleting any dynamic storage used by instances of the class.

Casting a pointer to a base object into a pointer to a derived object is valid only when the exact type of the object being addressed is known. The converse, implicitly casting a pointer to a derived object into a pointer to a base object, is much
safer.

A *copy constructor* creates a new object that is a duplicate of an existing object
of the same class. A copy constructor runs automatically in three cases:

- When a class variable is used to initialize a newly defined variable of the same class.
- When a class variable is passed to a function as a value argument.
- When a function returns an object of the class type.

Cross-linking two pointers to the same storage location is dangerous at best, and can lead to serious runtime errors. To prevent that from happening, always provide a copy constructor for a class containing pointers.

The implementor of a class should never depend on users of the class to anticipate problems with copy and assignment semantics. That is purely the implementor's job.

7.7.1 Common Pointer Errors

We would like to highlight some of the more common mistakes made by programmers as they are learning to master pointers in C++.

7.7.1.1 Encapsulating the new Operator.   We're going to make a bold statement here: Avoid the use of the `new` operator in user code, that is, outside classes. Memory allocation errors can be introduced into programs when you allocate storage and later forget to release it. For example, something as simple as the following would cause a memory leak that could take considerable debugging time to track down:

```
void CreatesMemoryLeak()
{
  long * temp = new long[500];

  // lots of user code here...
}
```

The problem is, of course, that we neglected to release the dynamic memory addressed by `temp` before it went out of scope. On the other hand, if we had created a `LongArray` object, the class destructor would have taken care of the memory deallocation automatically, and there would be no memory leak:

```
void NoMemoryLeak()
{
  LongArray temp( 500 );

  // lots of user code here...
  // temp's destructor executes
}
```

The case for avoiding the direct use of the `new` operator will be even more compelling in Chapter 8, when we introduce exception handling. To produce programs that gracefully recover from memory allocation errors, the new operator should always be enclosed in a class.

7.7.1.2 Uninitialized Pointer.

Deleting storage indicated by a pointer that was never initialized is a serious error. So is deleting the same pointer twice. But deleting a null pointer is guaranteed in standard C++ not to have any effect. For this reason, we recommend setting a pointer to null when it does not point to actual data. In the next example, the second attempt to deallocate p will have no adverse effect:

```
int * p = new int;
.

.

delete p;   // release the memory block
p = 0;      // set pointer to null
delete p;   // harmless - no effect
```

Standard C/C++ libraries also include the malloc and free functions that allocate and release memory blocks. We recommend that you avoid mixing these with the new and delete operators. If you use malloc to create an array, for example, C++ doesn't guarantee that information about the array's size will be saved when the array is later deallocated. For example,

```
long * array = (long *) malloc( sizeof(long) * 50 );
//...
delete [] array;      // size unknown??
```

7.7.1.3 Null Pointer Assignment.

A common programming error is made when attempting to dereference a null pointer and use it to access memory. Memory may be corrupted, causing the program to behave strangely; a program may or may not run to completion, and if it does, the runtime system will usually display a "null pointer assignment" error message at the end. This type of error is difficult to track down because the error message does not identify the particular program statement that caused the problem. It is always a good idea to check a pointer for a null value. For example,

```
if( lp != 0 )
    *lp = 5000;    // assign a value
```

7.7.1.4 Dangling Pointer.

A *dangling pointer* is a pointer that no longer contains the address of allocated storage. One way to cause this error is to create a local variable and then try to use the variable's address outside the block. In the next example, the function returns a pointer to an automatic array called buffer. But the latter is destroyed when control passes out of the function:

```
char * Input()
{
  char buffer[128];

  cout << "Enter last name: ";
  cin.getline( buffer, 128 );
  return buffer;
}
```

The pointer returned by Input is a dangling pointer because it no longer refers to a valid address. Any attempt to use this pointer will be a serious program bug, often resulting in a memory protection error or core dump.

After the storage addressed by a pointer has been deallocated, it may even appear to contain valid data. We call these data *ghosts* because they appear to be real, but they only exist by accident, and accessing them can be a spooky experience. A good habit to develop is to set deallocated pointers to null if you think they might be mistaken for actual addresses. It is easy to test for a null pointer before dereferencing it.

On the other hand, simply setting a pointer to 0 does not by itself release the memory it addresses. The following would leave a useless block of storage allocated on the heap. If no other pointer contains the block's address, the memory cannot be deallocated until the end of the program, thus creating a memory leak:

```
float * p = new float[100];
p = 0;
```

7.8 EXERCISES

7.8.1 Miscellaneous

1 Allocating an Array of Float.   Write a function called makeArray that dynamically allocates *n* elements of an array of float, initializes all elements to 0, and and returns a pointer to the beginning of the array. Here is the prototype:

```
float * makeArray(unsigned n);
```

The function should return 0 if the array could not be allocated. Write a short program that tests makeArray.

2 Allocating an Array of Pointers.   Create an array of pointers to FString objects. Read each line from an input text file, allocate an FString object to hold the line, and assign the object's address to a pointer in the array. For example, an array of pointers could be declared as

```
const unsigned MaxRecs = 1000;

FString * fileRecs[MaxRecs];
```

3 Constant and Non-Constant Pointers.   Define a function with two pointer parameters. Experiment with statements that call the function, passing it a combination of pointers to constant and non-constant objects.

Find out which combinations are accepted by the compiler. In the function body, try modifying both the pointer parameters and the data they point to. Demonstrate that you understand the difference between a const-qualified pointer and a pointer to a constant.

4 Constant Function Return Value.   Define a function that returns `const float *`. Call the function and attempt to assign the result to the following variables. Which assignments are acceptable?

```
float * r1;
const float * r2;
```

Now, change the return type to `float *` and again attempt to assign the result to `r1` and `r2`. What conclusion can you draw from these experiments?

5 Comma-Delimited File.   Write a program that uses the `FindNext` function from Section 7.2.3 to read a comma-delimited text file. Each record in the file might contain payroll information such as employee ID, last name, first name, hourly pay rate, and pay period ending date.

7.8.2 VString Class

The following exercises are related to the `VString` class, which holds dynamically allocated strings. The class was presented in Section 7.5.1. In the following exercises, you will be asked to add more useful operations to the class.

1 Assigning a VString.   Implement a member function called `Assign` that copies another `VString` object into the current one. The function must allocate a new block of memory, copy the characters in the existing string, and deallocate the storage used by the current string. Make sure the user is not attempting to assign the same `VString` object to itself, as follows:

```
VString & Assign( const VString & V )
{
  if( this != &V )            // Not the same object?
  {
    // Allocate new storage, assign the string,
    // and deallocate the old storage.
  }
  return *this;
}
```

For more clues on how to do this, look at the `GrowBy` member function in the `LongArray` class presented in Example 7-5.

2 Assigning a C-Style String. Implement the following `Assign` function that makes a copy of a C-style string:

```
VString & Assign( const char * s );
```

3 Comparing two VString Objects. Implement the following `Compare` function for the `VString` class. Return the same values as for the standard `strcmp` function, defined in `string.h`:

```
int Compare( const VString & s ) const;
```

4 Stream I/O Functions. Implement the following stream I/O functions for the `VString` class:

```
VString & GetLine( istream & inp );
friend istream & operator >>( istream & inp, VString &  s);
friend ostream & operator <<( ostream & os, const VString & s );
```

5 Concatenation and Conversion. Implement the following functions for the `VString` class:

```
VString & Append( const VString & );
// Append another string to this one.

const char * CString() const;
// Convert this VString to const-qualified C-style string.
```

6 Delimited String Class. Derive a new class from `VString` that implements the `FindNext` function from Section 7.2.3. The class should let you store and extract items from delimited strings. Write a short program that creates several strings that use different delimiter characters (such as comma, slash, or spaces). Extract and display individual values from the delimited strings.

7.8.3 LongArray Class

1 Additional Operations. Add the following operations to the `LongArray` class presented in this chapter. Be sure to include range checking where appropriate. Write a test program that demonstrates each of these operations:

```
float Average() const;
// Return the average (arithmetic mean) of the array.

unsigned FindFirst( long n, int & wasFound ) const;
// Search for the first occurrence of n in the array.
// If n is found, set wasFound to 1 and return
// n's index position. Otherwise, set wasFound to 0.

long Sum() const;
// Return the sum of all array elements.
```

2 Ordered Array.   Derive a class called `OrderedArray` from the `LongArray` class that keeps elements in sorted order. Use a data member to determine whether the elements should be in ascending or descending order. When a new value is inserted into the array, create a space for it by moving all subsequent values back one position.

3 Circular Queue (Advanced).   A *queue* is a data structure that holds an ordered collection of elements. As with a line of people at a bank teller window, the person in front is served first, and arrivals are placed at the the back of the line. The two characteristic operations on a queue are *enqueue*, which adds a value to the end of a queue, and *serve*, which removes a value from the front of a queue.

Derive a `CircularQueue` class from the `LongArray` class from this chapter, and implement the `Enqueue` and `Serve` member functions. Write a short test program that creates a `CircularQueue` and tests each of the functions. Here are the important class operations:

```
void Clear();
// Empty the queue.

int Empty() const;
// Return 1 if the queue is empty, 0 if not.

int Full() const;
// Return 1 if the queue is full, 0 if not.

void Enqueue( long n );
// Append a value at the back of the queue.

long Serve();
// Remove a value from the front of the queue.
```

Implementation notes: You may want to keep two subscripts, called "head" and "tail," which point to the front and back of the queue, respectively. Both head and tail should wrap around to the beginning of the array when they reach the end. In other words, if the array has *n* elements, any subscript *i* is equal to *i mod n*.

7.8.4 Doctor's Office Scheduling

The following programming exercises are based on the Doctors Office Scheduling program from Chapter 5. At the time, we were constrained by having to use only fixed memory allocation. Now we can improve the program greatly by using dynamic allocation.

1 Dynamic Array of Appointments.   The original Doctor's Office Scheduling program used the `DailySchedule` class to hold all of the appointments for a particular doctor. Improve the implementation by changing the fixed array of appointments to a dynamically allocated array. Add a destructor to the `Daily Schedule` class that deallocates the array, and add a copy constructor to the same class. Run the original test program to make sure it still works correctly.

2 ScheduleArray Class. Create a new class called `ScheduleArray` that represents the array of appointments in a `DailySchedule` object. Using the `LongArray` class from the current chapter as a guide, implement the `Get` and `Put` operations with range checking. Be sure to implement a copy constructor. This new class will require some modification to classes that use `DailySchedule`, because the subscript operator [] is not implemented in `DailySchedule`. Revise the other classes as necessary and run the test program. *Optional:* Chapter 9 shows how to overload the subscript operator. You might want to try this in the `ScheduleArray` class.

3 Array of DailySchedule Objects. In the Doctor's Office Scheduling program, we stored only a single days' schedule for each doctor, partly because a larger schedule would have been impractical as a static data structure. Now that you know how to use dynamic allocation, revise the program so that each `Doctor` object contains a five-element array of pointers to `DailySchedule` objects representing Monday through Friday in the current week. Add a destructor to the `Doctor` class that deallocates the array, and implement a copy constructor. Make any other necessary changes to the classes and test the program.

7.8.5 Vehicle Management System

The Vehicle Management System that we designed and developed in Chapter 6 was forced into certain limitations at the time because we had not yet learned about dynamic memory allocation. Now, we can revisit the program and make the classes more useful and flexible. First though, it is suggested that you complete all exercises from Chapter 6 relating to the Vehicle Management System.

1 Multiple Trip Records. The `CompanyVehicle` class should be able to contain almost any number of trip records. In the input file, place an integer in each `CompanyVehicle` record that tells the program how many trip records are about to follow. Then, let the program dynamically allocate storage for the trip records. Here is an example of a `CompanyVehicle` record in the input file (comments are shown on the right-hand side):

```
C                           (company vehicle)
1000101                     vehicle ID
Bertha Smith                driver
35200                       odometer reading
01/12/97                    date checked out
2                           (number of trip records)
```

```
02/01/97                  date of trip #1
08:00                     time
150                       miles driven
AZZ Conference            purpose
30                        fuel cost
02/03/97                  date of trip #2
09:30                     time
75                        miles driven
XYZ Meeting               purpose
20                        fuel cost
```

2 Arrays of Vehicles.   Make the following modifications to the original version of the Vehicle Mangagement System program:

- Add at least ten more vehicle records to the input data file.
- Dynamically allocate an array of `CompanyVehicle` objects, and another array of `PersonalVehicle` objects.
- As the input file is read, insert each vehicle record in the appropriate array.
- Print two separate reports—one of personal vehicles, and another of company vehicles. Call each report a "Vehicle Usage Report."

7.8.6 Two-Dimensional Arrays

1 Traversing a Cube.   Create a class called `Cube` that represents a geometric cube as a graph. Each cube vertex will be a graph node. Provide the following operations:

```
void PathsBetween( int n, char node1, char node2 )
// Display a list of all n-edged paths between node1 and node2.

void PathsFrom( int n, char node )
// Display all n-edged paths originating from node that
// are not cycles.

int PathExists( int n, char node1, char node2 )
// Return 1 if an n-edged path exists between node1 and node2.
```

We avoid any paths containing more than one occurrence of the same node; these are called *cycles*.

To represent the cube as a graph, label the cube nodes with letters A through H, which are also the nodes in the graph:

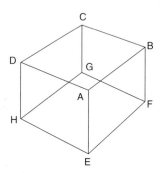

The graph may be represented as adjacency matrix M; in any row i and column j, a 1 in position M_{ij} indicates that an edge (arc) exists between node i and node j. A 0 indicates that no edge exists. Use this matrix to perform the operations specified by the Cube class:

	A	B	C	D	E	F	G	H
A	0	1	0	1	1	0	0	0
B	1	0	1	0	0	1	0	0
C	0	1	0	1	0	0	1	0
D	1	0	1	0	0	0	0	1
E	1	0	0	0	0	1	0	1
F	0	1	0	0	1	0	1	0
G	0	0	1	0	0	1	0	1
H	0	0	0	1	1	0	1	0

To find all non-cyclical two-edged paths from node A to node F, for example, make a list of the nodes connected by edges to A. They are B, D, and E. For each of these, note whether it is connected by an edge to F. In fact, both nodes B and E are connected to F; so, the two paths are A-B-F and A-E-F. A quick inspection of the cube diagram shows this to be true.

CHAPTER 8

Polymorphism and Exceptions

With the completion of this chapter, we will have covered the essential techniques of object-oriented programming in C++. Object-oriented programming is often defined in terms of inheritance and polymorphism. In these features lie the ability to create flexible class interfaces that allow for a variety of implementations. In this chapter, we introduce polymorphism, implemented through the use of virtual functions. We demonstrate the use of these in a package shipping application program. We then tackle exception handling, a recent and important addition to the C++ language.

Terms Introduced in this Chapter:

abstract class	pure virtual function
catch clause	pure-specifier
code reusability	stack unwinding
context	static binding
dynamic binding	throwing an exception
exception	throw expression
exception handler	throw point
exception handling	try block
memory exhaustion	virtual destructor
polymorphism	virtual function

8.1 POLYMORPHISM

8.1.1 Static and Dynamic Binding

When a variable is bound to a specific type at compile time, we call this *static binding*. To a limited degree, C++ also permits *dynamic* binding, where a pointer or reference can address objects of different types, as long as their classes are related by inheritance. We introduced this idea in Section 7.2.4, with an example using the `Point` and `Point3D` classes. Not all languages permit dynamic binding. On the other hand, some languages allow dynamic binding of all types, not just related ones. Such flexibility carries the risk that unintentional or erroneous assignments might occur at runtime. Such errors can be difficult to anticipate and prevent.

8.1.2 Defining Polymorphism

[Booch] defines *polymorphism* as the concept where a single name may denote objects of different classes that are related by some common base class. To implement polymorphism, a language must support dynamic binding.

The reason why polymorphism is so useful is that it gives us the ability to manipulate instances of derived classes through a set of operations defined in their base class. Each derived class can implement the operations defined in the base class differently, while retaining a common class interface provided by the base class.

For example, let us assume that the `SalariedEmployee` class is derived from `Employee`, and that both classes contain a `CalcPaycheck` member function. `CalcPaycheck` is a simple example of the "common class interface" that we just described:

```
class Employee {
public:
  void CalcPaycheck();
  //...
};


class SalariedEmployee :public Employee {
public:
  void CalcPaycheck();
  //...
};
```

Next, let's declare `ep` as an `Employee` pointer and assign it the address of a `SalariedEmployee` object. Our intention is for the `CalcPaycheck` function in the `SalariedEmployee` class to be called:

```
Employee * ep;
ep = new SalariedEmployee;
ep->CalcPaycheck();
```

Invoking a member function such as `CalcPaycheck` via ep raises interesting questions: Will `CalcPaycheck` in the `Employee` class be called, or will `CalcPaycheck` in the `SalariedEmployee` class be called? One would hope that the latter would be true, because ep currently points to a `SalariedEmployee`. Unfortunately, as the example is written, the `CalcPaycheck` function in the `Employee` class is called. In order to cause the right function to be called from the right class, we have to declare `CalcPaycheck` as a virtual function. The next section shows how to do this.

8.1.3 Virtual Function Example

A *virtual function* is a nonstatic member function prefaced by the `virtual` specifier. It tells the compiler to generate code that looks up an object's type at runtime and uses this information to select the appropriate version of the function. If this explanation seems a little fuzzy, consider the `CalcPaycheck` function from the previous example: If the program somehow "knew" that ep pointed to a `SalariedEmployee`, it could have called the `CalcPaycheck` function in the `SalariedEmployee` class.

A virtual function may optionally be overridden by functions in derived classes having the same signature. The virtual specifier needs only to appear with the base class function, but it's a good idea to duplicate the virtual specifier in the derived classes as well.

Let's suppose that we have derived both the `SalariedEmployee` and `HourlyEmployee` classes from `Employee`:

```
class Employee {
public:
  virtual void CalcPaycheck();
};

class HourlyEmployee :public Employee {
public:
  virtual void CalcPaycheck();
};

class SalariedEmployee :public Employee {
public:
  virtual void CalcPaycheck();
};
```

We declare p0, p1, and p2 as `Employee` pointers, and assign them the addresses of `Employee`, `SalariedEmployee`, and `HourlyEmployee` objects, respectively:

```
Employee * p0 = new Employee;
Employee * p1 = new SalariedEmployee;
Employee * p2 = new HourlyEmployee;

p0->CalcPaycheck(); // calls Employee::CalcPaycheck()
p1->CalcPaycheck(); // calls SalariedEmployee::CalcPaycheck()
p2->CalcPaycheck(); // calls HourlyEmployee::CalcPaycheck()
```

Finally, we will just mention a few facts that could prove useful: Any nonstatic member function except a constructor can be virtual. Virtual functions can also be friends of other classes. Some compilers require the class destructor to be virtual if a class contains any virtual functions.

8.1.3.1 *Combinations of Virtual and Non-Virtual Functions.* The question often arises: What if a non-virtual function calls a virtual function? For example, we can define the `Employee` and `SalariedEmployee` classes as follows:

```
class Employee {
public:
  void Display() const;        // non-virtual
  virtual void CalcPaycheck();  // virtual
};

class SalariedEmployee :public Employee {
public:
  void Display() const;
  virtual void CalcPaycheck();
};

void Employee::Display()
{
  CalcPaycheck();
  //...
}

void SalariedEmployee::Display()
{
  CalcPaycheck();
  //...
}
```

In the following example, we invoke `Display` through the pointer `ep`. This causes `Employee::Display` to be called, which in turn calls `SalariedEmployee::CalcPaycheck`:

```
Employee * ep = new SalariedEmployee;
//...
ep->Display();
```

In other words, `CalcPaycheck` still works as a virtual function, although it is called by a non-virtual function.

On the other hand, what if a virtual function calls a non-virtual function? In the next example, `Display` is virtual and `CalcPaycheck` is non-virtual:

```
class Employee {
public:
  virtual void Display() const;  // virtual
  void CalcPaycheck();           // non-virtual
};

class SalariedEmployee :public Employee {
public:
  virtual void Display() const;
  void CalcPaycheck();
};
```

The following example calls `SalariedEmployee::Display`, which in turn calls `SalariedEmployee::CalcPaycheck`:

```
Employee * ep = new SalariedEmployee;
//...
ep->Display();
```

8.1.4 A Common Interface

Typically, virtual functions appearing in a base class are intended to provide a common interface for all of its derived classes. In the `Employee` class, for example, we might want to define a general set of operations that get and set data member values, display an `Employee`, input an `Employee`, and process an `Employee`'s paycheck:

```
class Employee {
public:
  long GetDepartment() const;
  long GetId() const;
  void SetDepartment( long deptId );
  void SetId();

  virtual void CalcPaycheck() const;
  virtual void Input();
  virtual void CalcPaycheck();

private:
  long id;
  long deptNum;
};
```

The only member functions that should be virtual are those that will be implemented in derived classes. `GetId`, for example, is not virtual because it only refers to a private data member. `CalcPaycheck`, on the other hand, is implemented differently for each type of `Employee`, including those paid a monthly salary and those paid on an hourly basis.

8.1.4.1 Passing Objects by Address.

Another situation in which virtual functions are useful is when a function parameter's type is a pointer or reference to a base class. When calling the function, we can pass a pointer or reference to an object that is of any type derived from the base class. Assuming that `CalcPaycheck` is a virtual function, the particular instance of `CalcPaycheck` to be called is determined at run time:

```
void ProcessAnyEmployee( Employee & er )
{
    long anId = er.GetId();    // non-virtual
    er.CalcPaycheck();         // virtual
}
```

On the other hand, `GetId` is not a virtual function, and will be called directly from the `Employee` class.

Because C++ supports polymorphism, we can pass an `Employee`, a `SalariedEmployee`, or any other type derived from `Employee` to the `Process AnyEmployee` function. This offers the advantage of letting us write a single function that handles all types of employees:

```
SalariedEmployee S;
HourlyEmployee H;
//...
ProcessAnyEmployee( S );
ProcessAnyEmployee( H );
```

The effect is the same if `ProcessAnyEmployee` has an `Employee *` parameter:

```
void ProcessAnyEmployee( Employee * ep )
{
    long anId = ep->GetId();    // non-virtual
    ep->CalcPaycheck();         // virtual
}

SalariedEmployee S;
HourlyEmployee H;
//...
ProcessAnyEmployee( &S );
ProcessAnyEmployee( &H );
```

8.1.5 Virtual Destructors

A *virtual destructor* is preceded by the `virtual` specifier and behaves like a virtual function. If we assume that a base class and one or more of its derived classes have destructors, we must make sure that the correct destructor is called for a base pointer that currently points to a derived object. Calling the wrong destructor could be disastrous, particularly when it contains a `delete` statement; the wrong size chunk of memory might be deallocated. For this reason, we recommend that any class containing virtual functions should also have a virtual destructor. Although the base class destructor is usually empty, there is always a strong possibility that one of its derived class destructors will need to do meaningful work.

In the next example, the `BookItem` class is derived from `Item`, and we have a pointer in `BookItem` that must be deallocated:

```
class Item {
public:
  virtual ~Item();
  //...
};

class BookItem :public Item {
public:
  virtual ~BookItem();

private:
  char * title;
};
```

By making the destructors virtual, we ensure that the `BookItem` destructor is called when we apply the `delete` operator to p:

```
Item * p;            // base pointer
p = new BookItem;    // point to derived object
//...

delete p;    // calls the BookItem destructor
```

Destructors are not inherited, so it is wise to define one for each derived class. In our example, if we omitted the destructor from `BookItem`, a default destructor would automatically be created for the class, but it would not contain statements to deallocate storage pointed to by class data members.

8.1.6 Abstract Classes

An *abstract class* is a class that can only be a base class for other classes. You cannot create an instance of an abstract class. Instead, it serves as a base for other classes, containing operations that are common to all of its derived classes. An abstract class either contains or inherits at least one pure virtual function. A *pure virtual function* is a virtual function that contains a *pure-specifier*, designated by the "= 0" following the `Draw` function prototype:

```
class Shape {
public:
  virtual void Draw() = 0;
  //...
};
```

A pure virtual function is not implemented in the base class, but it serves as a prototype for derived classes that implement the function. In fact, a derived class must implement all pure virtual functions declared in its base class if instances of the derived class are to be created; otherwise, the derived class is automatically an abstract class.

Consider the case of the `SalariedEmployee` and `HourlyEmployee` classes. We already know that certain operations are common to both classes, such as `Display`, `Input`, and `CalcPaycheck`. We create an abstract class called `Employee` containing pure virtual member functions:

```
class Employee {
public:
  virtual void Display() = 0;
  virtual void Input() = 0;
  virtual void CalcPaycheck() = 0;
  //...
};
```

We would probably derive a number of different classes from `Employee`. Each of those classes would share the common interface defined here. Also, to be sure that the derived classes do not duplicate the same operations in `Employee` using different function names, we force those classes to override the pure virtual functions and implement the operations.

[Stroustrup91] points out that abstract classes are an ideal vehicle for presenting a class interface without letting users see the class implementation. One might decide not to place any private members in an abstract class. Only operations that comprise the interface would be described in the header file for the abstract class.

8.1.6.1 Shape Class Example.   The following `Shape` abstract class includes three operations, `Draw`, `MoveTo`, and `Rotate`, which are common to its derived classes:

```
class Shape {
public:
  virtual ~Shape();
  virtual void Draw() const = 0;
  virtual void MoveTo( int x2, int y2 ) = 0;
  virtual void Rotate( int degrees ) = 0;
};
```

The `Circle` class, derived from `Shape`, must override each of the pure virtual functions, or it too will be considered an abstract class:

```
class Circle : public Shape {
public:
  Circle();
  Circle( const Point & aCenter, float aRadius );
  virtual ~Circle();
  virtual void Draw() const;
  virtual void MoveTo( int x2, int y2 );
  virtual void Rotate( int degrees );

private:
  Point center;
  float radius;
};
```

The `Polygon` class, on the other hand, is an abstract class because we have not implemented all of the pure virtual functions from the `Shape` class:

```
class Polygon :public Shape {
public:
  Polygon();
  Polygon( Point & cent, Point * verts );
  virtual ~Polygon();

private:
  Point center;
  Point * vertices;   // array of Points
};
```

Pure virtual functions provide a good mechanism to prevent the inadvertent omission of a essential operations in derived classes. If we tried, for example, to create an instance of `Circle`, and if `Circle` did not contain a `Rotate` function, the compiler would issue an error saying that it could not create an instance of an abstract class.

Next, we would like to apply virtual functions and polymorphism to the analysis, design, and implementation of a software tracking system for package shipping.

8.2 CASE STUDY: PACKAGE SHIPPING SERVICE

8.2.1 Specifications

The Acme Package Shipping Service has customers that bring in packages to be shipped to other locations. The company's package management software needs to keep a list of all packages that are waiting to be sent, in a form that allows for easy update and retrieval. The program has to uniquely identify each package with a tracking number. Each record from the input file will contain a tracking number, origination ZIP Code, destination ZIP Code, shipping date, cost, and weight. For example,

```
100101 31313 33130 960402 15.00  8.0
```

The output should appear as follows. A list of packages should be loaded and displayed, along with a calculation of their total weight:

```
0: [100101,31313,33130,960402,15.00,8.00]
1: [102001,20000,96535,960403,7.50,4.50]
2: [100311,10101,12110,960405,5.00,3.00]
3: [101400,10000,70515,960410,5.30,3.20]
4: [110510,22222,33133,960412,15.00,10.50]


Total weight of 5 packages = 29.20
```

The table should then be sorted in ascending order by tracking number and redisplayed:

```
0: [100101,31313,33130,960402,15.00,8.00]
1: [100311,10101,12110,960405,5.00,3.00]
2: [101400,10000,70515,960410,5.30,3.20]
3: [102001,20000,96535,960403,7.50,4.50]
4: [110510,22222,33133,960412,15.00,10.50]
```

We let the user enter a package tracking number. The program searches for the matching package and displays both its index position and details about the package:

```
Searching for package 110510
Found at position 4
. . . . . . . . . . . . . . . . . . . . .
Tracking number: 110510
Origination ZIP code: 22222
Destination ZIP code: 33133
Date sent: 960412
Shipment cost: 15.00
Package weight: 10.50
```

8.2.2 Analysis

Recognizing that keeping track of lists of packages is similiar to many other applications, we would like to create a set of general classes that could be used elsewhere. This concept, called *code reusability,* is an important consideration in the software industry because of the high cost of writing new software. To this end, we will create an abstract class called `Table` that defines useful operations on tables such as adding new items, clearing a table, counting items, searching, retrieving items, and sorting. The table could be implemented as an array or linked list, but the exact implementation will be chosen only in classes that are derived from `Table`.

Because we don't know in advance exactly which types of objects will be stored in a `Table`, it is useful to create an abstract base class called `Item` that defines basic operations supported by all table items such as construction, comparison, assignment, and stream I/O.

From `Item` we will derive a class called `Package` that keeps specific information about each package; it supports construction, assignment, stream I/O, and comparison to other packages. Finally, it will be useful to have a class called `TableAsArray` that allows `Package` objects to be stored in an array.

We can make a simple diagram of the class relationships. The `Package` class is derived from the `Item` class, a `Table` (abstractly) contains `Item` objects, `TableAsArray` is derived from `Table`, and a `TableAsArray` contains `Package` objects:

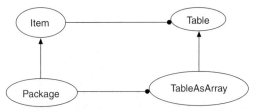

8.2.3 Design

8.2.3.1 Table Class.   During the design phase, we create interfaces for the classes that were suggested during the analysis phase. The `Table` class supports the following operations: adding items, clearing the table, counting items, retrieving items, searching, and sorting. The key field used for sorting and searching is undefined here, and must be specified by classes that are derived from `Item`. Here is the class definition:

```
#include "item.h"
#include "limits.h"

class Table {
public:
  virtual ~Table() {  };
```

```
    virtual void AddItem( Item * I ) = 0;
    // Add a new item to the table.

    virtual void Clear() = 0;
    // Empty the table.

    virtual unsigned GetCount() const = 0;
    // Return the number of entries in the table.

    virtual Item * GetItemPtr( unsigned i ) const = 0;
    // Retrieve pointer to item at position i.

    virtual unsigned IndexOf( const Item * P ) const = 0;
    // Search for a matching item in the table;
    // if found, return its index position,
    // otherwise return UINT_MAX.

    virtual void Sort() = 0;
    // Sort the table in ascending order.
};
```

We cannot create instances of `Table` because it is an abstract class. Every member is a pure virtual function, requiring it to be overridden in a non-abstract derived class. As a matter of good programming style, we use the `const` qualifier so derived classes overriding these functions must also make the functions const-qualified.

8.2.3.2 Item Class.

`Item` is the abstract base class for any object that will be inserted in a `Table`. Instances of classes derived from `Item` will be inserted in instances of classes derived from `Table`:

```
class Item {
public:
  virtual ~Item() {  }

  virtual int Compare( const Item & I2 ) const = 0;
  // Compare *this to Item I2; return -1 if
  // *this is less than I2, 0 if *this is equal,
  // and 1 if *this is greater than I2.

  friend ostream & operator <<( ostream & os, const Item & I );
  friend istream & operator >>( istream & inp, Item & I );

private:
  virtual void printOn( ostream & os ) const = 0;
  virtual void readFrom( istream & inp ) = 0;
};
```

Any object inserted in a `Table` must support the `Compare` operation, which is used by `Table::IndexOf` and `Table::Sort`.

8.2.3.3 Stream I/O Operators.   The inclusion of both `operator <<` and the `printOn` function at first seems redundant, and it is hard to see how we could perform I/O in an abstract class. But this was done so `operator <<` could behave as if it were a virtual function. `Package::printOn` is virtual, and is called from `Item::operator <<`:

```
ostream & operator <<( ostream & os, const Item & I )
{
  I.printOn( os );
  return os;
}
```

`Package::printOn` writes a `Package` to an output stream, for example:

```
void Package::printOn( ostream & os ) const;
```

Therefore, an `Item` pointer that currently addresses a `Package` can invoke `operator <<` as if it were virtual:

```
Item * p;
p = new Package;
//...
cout << *p;
```

The same relationship exists for `operator >>` and `Package::readFrom`. Both `printOn` and `readFrom` are private because they need not be called directly by class users.

8.2.3.4 Package Class.   The `Package` class, shown in Example 8-1, is perhaps the easiest class to design because its data members and operations are closely tied to the program specifications. It is derived from `Item`, so `Package` objects can be inserted in any object whose class is derived from `Table`. Notice that the `Compare` function still has a `const Item &` parameter, because the function must have the same signature as its namesake in the `Item` class.

8.2.3.5 TableAsArray Class.   From the `Table` class we derive a new class called `TableAsArray` and override the former's pure virtual functions. This class is implemented as an array of pointers to `Item` objects. Here is the class definition:

```
#include <iostream.h>
#include <iomanip.h>
#include <assert.h>
#include "table.h"
```

```
class TableAsArray : public Table {
public:
  TableAsArray( unsigned tableSize );

  virtual ~TableAsArray();

  virtual void AddItem( Item * )I;

  virtual void Clear();

  virtual unsigned GetCount() const;

  virtual Item * GetItemPtr( unsigned i ) const;

  virtual unsigned IndexOf( const Item * P ) const;

  virtual void Sort();

  friend ostream & operator <<( ostream &,
        const TableAsArray & );

private:
  Item ** data;     // array of pointers to Items
  unsigned size;   // allocation size
  unsigned count; // number of Items

private:
  void swap( Item * & p1, Item * & p2 );
};
```

Documentation for the virtual functions (`AddItem`, `Clear`, `GetCount`, `GetItemPtr`, `IndexOf`, and `Sort`) may be found in the `Table` class declaration. The private `swap` member function is not really part of the class interface, and is called only by `TableAsArray::Sort`.

It's difficult to imagine how `TableAsArray` can search and sort, given that it contains no references to `Packages` or other specific types of items. The key to this puzzle is in the `Package` class: it implements the `Compare` function, which in turn is called by `IndexOf` and `Sort`.

8.2.4 Main Program

Here we will only present excerpts from the main program, but a complete listing of the main program can be found in Appendix A. The main program opens an input file stream and declares a table capable of holding packages. We also create an output file stream called `outfile`:

Example 8-1. The Package Class Definition

```cpp
#include <iostream.h>
#include "item.h"

class Package :public Item {
public:
  Package();

  Package( long trackNumP, long originP,
           long destinP, long dateP,
           float costP, float weightP );

  long GetDestination() const;
  long GetTrackingNumber() const;
  float GetWeight() const;
  void PrintLong( ostream & os ) const;

  int Compare( const Item & I2 ) const;
  // Compare *this to Package I2,
  // return -1 if *this is less than I2,
  // return 0 if *this is equal to I2,
  // and return 1 if *this is greater than I2.

  // Functions that set data member values:

  void SetTrackNum( long trackNumP );
  void SetOrigin( long originP );
  void SetDestination( long destinP );
  void SetDate( long dateP );
  void SetCost( float costP );
  void SetWeight( float weightP );
  void Init();

private:
  long  trackNum;    // tracking number
  long  origin;      // originating ZIP code
  long  destin;      // destination ZIP code
  long  date;        // date sent (yymmdd)
  float cost;        // shipping cost
  float weight;      // weight in kilograms

  virtual void printOn( ostream & os ) const;
  virtual void readFrom( istream & is );
};
```

```
ifstream input( "PACKAGES.TXT" );
if( !input )
{
  cout << "Input file not found; halting program.\n";
  abort();
}

unsigned numRecords;
input >> numRecords;

input.ignore( 1, '\n' );
ofstream outfile( "OUTFILE.TXT" );
```

We create a `Package` and, using a loop, input each package from the file and add it to `ptable`, a table of packages. We write the table to the output file stream:

```
TableAsArray ptable( numRecords );
Package * pkg;
unsigned i;

for(i = 0; i < numRecords; i++)
{
  pkg = new Package;
  input >> *pkg;
  ptable.AddItem( pkg );
  if( input.eof() ) break;
}
outfile << ptable << endl;
```

To calculate the total weight of the packages, we iterate over the table, use `GetItemPtr` to retrieve each `Package`, and add its weight to a total:

```
Package * z;
float sum = 0.0;

for(i = 0; i < ptable.GetCount(); i++)
{
  z = (Package *) ptable.GetItemPtr( i );
  sum += z->GetWeight();
}

outfile << "Total weight of packages = "
        << sum << "\n\n";
```

In this example, note that `GetItemPtr` returns an `Item` pointer, and `Item` is the base class for `Package`. To assign a value to z, we must cast the return value of `GetItemPtr` to a `Package` pointer.

Alternatively, we could declare `z` as an `Item` pointer and cast it into a `Package *` when calling `GetWeight`:

```
Item * z;
//...
z = ptable.GetItemPtr( i );
sum += ((Package *)z)->GetWeight();
```

The extra parentheses are required because the -> operator has a higher precedence than the cast operator. Recall that `GetWeight` is not part of the `Item` class interface, and therefore cannot be called in the same way as a virtual function.

The following statements sort and redisplay the table, then search for a specific package and display its index position:

```
TableAsArray ptable( numRecords );
Package * pkg;
//...

ptable.Sort();
outfile << ptable << endl;

long id = 101400L;
pkg->Init();
pkg->SetTrackNum( id );
unsigned n = ptable.IndexOf( pkg );


outfile << "Searching for package " << id << '\n';
if( n != UINT_MAX )
{
  outfile << "Found at position " << n << '\n';
  pkg = (Package *)ptable.GetItemPtr( n );
  pkg->PrintLong( outfile );
}
else
  outfile << "Package " << id << " not found.\n";
```

8.2.5 Class Implementations

We will not show all class implementations here, but a complete listing of the program appears in Appendix A. The `Table` class, incidentally, has no implementation because it contains only pure virtual functions.

8.2.5.1 *Item Class.*   The `Item` class implements two operator functions:

```
ostream & operator <<( ostream & os, const Item & I )
{
  I.printOn( os );
  return os;
}

istream & operator >>( istream & inp, Item & I )
{
  I.readFrom( inp );
  return inp;
}
```

8.2.5.2 Package Class. The `Package` default constructor calls `Init`, which in turn calls member functions that initialize each data member:

```
Package::Package()
{
  Init();
}

void Package::Init()
{
  SetTrackNum( 0 );
  SetOrigin( 0 );
  SetDestination( 0 );
  SetDate( 0 );
  SetCost( 0.0f );
  SetWeight( 0.0f );
}
```

A `Package` can also be constructed from a tracking number, origination, destination, shipping date, cost, and weight:

```
Package::Package(
    long trackNumP,
    long originP,
    long destinP,
    long dateP,
    float costP,
    float weightP )
{
  SetTrackNum( trackNumP );
  SetOrigin( originP );
  SetDestination( destinP );
  SetDate( dateP );
  SetCost( costP );
  SetWeight( weightP );
}
```

The `Compare` function compares two `Package` objects, making it possible for `TableAsArray` to search and sort packages. The function returns -1 if this package's tracking number is less than `Package I2`. It returns 0 if the tracking numbers are equal, or it returns 1 if this package's number is greater than that of `Package I2`:

```
int Package::Compare( const Item & I2 ) const
{
  if( trackNum < ((Package &)I2).trackNum )
    return -1;
  else if( trackNum == ((Package &)I2).trackNum )
    return 0;
  else  // if( trackNum > ((Package &)I2).trackNum )
    return 1;
}
```

The notation `((Package  &)I2).trackNum` casts `I2` from an `Item` to a `Package` before accessing the `trackNum` data member.

The `readFrom` and `printLong` member functions handle input and output, respectively, of packages from streams:

```
void Package::readFrom( istream & inp )
{
  Init();
  inp >> trackNum >> origin >> destin
      >> date >> cost >> weight;
  inp.ignore( 10, '\n');
}

void Package::PrintLong( ostream & os ) const
{
  unsigned svflags = os.setf( ios::showpoint | ios::fixed );
  int svprecision = os.precision(2);

  os << "........................\n"
     << "Tracking number: "
     << trackNum << '\n'
     << "Origination zip code: "
     << origin   << '\n'
     << "Destination zip code: "
     << destin << '\n'
     << "Date sent: "
     << date << '\n'
     << "Shipment cost: "
     << cost << '\n'
     << "Package weight "
     << weight << endl;
```

```
    os.precision( svprecision );
    os.flags( svflags );
}
```

Notice that we carefully save the current flags and precision of the output stream before changing them. This prevents the changes we make here from affecting other functions that use the same output stream. Another function, `printOn`, displays the data members without descriptive labels.

8.2.5.3 TableAsArray Class.

The `TableAsArray` class implements the pure virtual functions that were declared in the `Table` class. The table contains an array of pointers, giving us the ability to store objects of different types in the table. The objects must, however, be derived from the `Item` class.

The constructor takes a size argument and uses this to dynamically allocate the array:

```
TableAsArray::TableAsArray( unsigned sz )
{
  size = sz;
  assert( size < UINT_MAX );
  count = 0;
  data = new Item *[size];
  for(unsigned j = 0; j < size; j++)
    data[j] = 0;
}
```

`AddItem` checks for available array positions before storing an item's pointer in the table. We cannot make `P` a pointer to constant because the `data` pointer is not declared that way:

```
void TableAsArray::AddItem( Item * P )
{
  if( count < size )
    data[count++] = P;
  else
    cout << "Error: Table full; item not added.\n";
}
```

The `Clear` function deletes the items addressed by the array of pointers. This fact must be well documented so users do not try to reference the pointers after the table has been destroyed:

```
void TableAsArray::Clear()
{
  for(unsigned i = 0; i < count; i++)
    delete data[i];
```

```
         delete [] data;
         count = 0;
         size = 0;
     }
```

IndexOf tries to locate an item in the table, and if successful, returns the index position in the array where it was found. Otherwise, the function returns UINT_MAX, a standard constant defined as the largest possible unsigned integer in limits.h:

```
unsigned TableAsArray::IndexOf( const Item * P ) const
{
  for(unsigned i = 0; i < count; i++)
    if( P->Compare(*data[i]) == 0 ) return i;

  return UINT_MAX;
}
```

The Sort function orders the table in ascending order using a simple (but inefficient) *selection sort*. Notice that we call the overloaded Compare function defined in the Item class without knowing exactly what type of items are being compared:

```
void TableAsArray::Sort()
{
  for(unsigned curr = 0; curr < count-1; curr++)
  {
    unsigned minIndex = curr;

    for(unsigned k = curr+1; k < count; k++)
      if( data[k]->Compare(*data[minIndex]) < 0 )
        minIndex = k;

    if( minIndex != curr )
      swap( data[curr], data[minIndex] );
  }
}
```

8.3 EXCEPTION HANDLING

In C++, errors such as memory exhaustion, subscript range errors, or division by zero are called *exceptions*. The range and definition of these errors, as well as the way the errors are handled, can be programmer-defined. *Exception handling* is the mechanism provided by C++ for handling exceptions. Exception handling first officially became part of C++ about 1990.

Inadequate error trapping has always been a problem in software. Part of the problem is that error trapping is very labor-intensive on the part of programmers. Also, one is faced with choices as to where errors should be trapped and how they should be handled. Upon encountering an error, a program has several choices: it can immediately terminate; it can ignore the error with the hope that nothing disastrous happens; or, it can set an error flag, which will (presumably) be checked by other program statements. Under the last option, each time a particular function is called, the caller must check the function's return value, and if an error is detected, determine a way of either recovering from the error or terminating the program.

In practice, programmers don't do this consistently, partly because it is a lot of work, and because error-checking statements often obscure the understanding of the rest of the code. Also, it is difficult to remember to catch every possible error condition every single time a particular function is called. Often, exceptional efforts must be made by the programmer to invoke destructors, deallocate memory, and close data files before halting a program.

The solution to such problems in C++ is to call on mechanisms in the language that support error handling, relieving us of having to add complex, artificial error-handling code to every program. In C++, when an exception is generated, the error cannot be ignored or the program will terminate. If error handling code is in place for a particular type of error, the program has the option of recovering from the error and continuing execution. This approach helps to ensure that no error will simply slip through the cracks and cause a program to behave erratically.

A program *throws* an exception at the point where an error is first detected. When this happens, a C++ program automatically searches for a block of code called an *exception handler,* which responds to the exception in some appropriate way. This response is called *catching an exception.* If an exception handler cannot be found, the program simply terminates.

8.3.1 Throw, Catch, and Try

Many different types of exceptions can occur, so when an exception is thrown, a throw *expression* (or throw *point*) identifies the type of exception. For example, the following throws an exception when a subscript is out of bounds:

```
const unsigned ArraySize = 500;
unsigned i;
    .
    .
    .
if( i >= ArraySize )      // subscript valid?
   throw RangeError();    // no: throw an exception
```

Essentially, a throw expression is like a function call in which the argument is a newly created RangeError object. In our example, RangeError is not a standard exception class, so it must be defined within the current scope. This version of `RangeError` has no data or function members, but other exeception classes often do:

```
class RangeError{ };  // exception class
```

The `try` keyword, along with statements falling within { . . . } braces is called a *try block.* It must be immediately followed by one or more *exception handlers.* Each exception handler begins with the `catch` keyword, followed by a block containing statements. The following shows the format of a `try` block followed by two handlers:

```
try {
   statement-list
}
catch ( parameter-list ) {
   statement-list
}
catch ( parameter-list ) {
   statement-list
}
```

The most likely parameter is an exception object, usually passed by constant reference, such as: `const RangeError & R`.

An exception can only be thrown after a program's execution has entered a `try` block. The `throw` expression might be physically inside the block, or it might be nested in functions called from the `try` block. For example, the following `try` block contains a call to `UpdateArray`, which in turn may throw an exception:

```
void UpdateArray( int i )
{
  if( i < 0 ) throw RangeError();
  //...
}

void TestTheArray()
{
  try {
    UpdateArray( -1 );
  }
  catch( const RangeError & R ) {
    cout << "Range error exception occurred!\n";
    abort();
  }
}
```

The `catch` parameter is a const-qualified `RangeError` object, a reference to the one passed by the `throw` expression. The sample handler displays an error message and halts the program. Doing this leaves a program in an unpredictable state; files might still be open, memory allocated, and so on. Alternatively, a handler could attempt to recover from an exception by notifying the user and passing a new subscript value to the `UpdateArray` function.

In the next example, `TestTheArray` calls `InsertValue` from a `try` block. Inside `InsertValue`, if `i` is too large, a `RangeError` exception is thrown and control immediately passes to the handler in `TestTheArray`. An error message is displayed and the program continues without having corrupted memory with an out-of-range subscript:

```
const unsigned ArraySize = 50;
int array[ArraySize];
//...

void InsertValue( unsigned i, int value )
{
  if( i >= ArraySize ) throw RangeError();
  array[i] = value;
}

void TestTheArray()
{
  unsigned j;
  int anInt;
  cout << "Enter a subscript and a value: ";
  cin >> j >> anInt;
  try {
    InsertValue( j, anInt )
  }
  catch( const RangeError & ) {
    cout << "Range error in TestTheArray()";
    throw;
  }
}
```

In this example, the handler throws the same exception object backward to the previous context, which is the function that called `TestTheArray`. This re-throwing of the exception is optional, but helpful when the program must back up through nested function calls, possibly all the way to `main`.

It can be argued that this type of subscript range error is easily caught by traditional means, such as by having `InsertValue` return a status value. For example, `InsertValue` could return -1, thus indicating a subscript range error:

```
int InsertValue( unsigned i, int value )
{
  if( i >= ArraySize ) // range error
    return -1;
```

```
        else
        {                        // subscript ok
          array[i] = value;
          return i;
        }
    }
```

The `TestTheArray` function could take an appropriate action based on the status code after calling `InsertValue`:

```
void TestTheArray()
{
  //...
  int status = InsertValue( j, anInt );
  if( status == -1 )
    cout << "Range error in TestTheArray()";
}
```

But will every programer who writes code that calls `InsertValue` remember to check the return value and take appropriate action? Probably not, and the consequences of not doing so might be disastrous.

Well-designed function libraries, whether object-oriented or not, typically return status codes from functions that indicate success or failure. User programs are supposed to check these codes and respond appropriately. Unfortunately, users often neglect to test function return codes because of the extra work involved. The problem might not be one of laziness; it might have to do with the clutter of extra error-checking statements. A thrown exception, on the other hand, demands to be handled, or the program terminates. A function library that throws exceptions virtually guarantees that no serious errors will go unnoticed.

Returning to our example, we might prefer to handle range errors in a higher context, perhaps at the point where `TestTheArray` was called. Without exception handling, we would have to take the value returned by `InsertValue` and pass it back to the caller of `TestTheArray`. Writing the extra statements to do this in complicated programs can be both time-consuming and error-prone.

Exception handling makes it easy to pass a thrown exception backward to the previous caller, or *context*. Failing to find a handler there, a C++ program backs up through each context until a handler is found. If a program backs up all the way to `main` without finding a handler, it automatically calls `terminate`, a standard function defined in the `except.h` header. By default, `terminate` calls `abort`, which stops the program. For example, if `TestTheArray` were called by `main`, we could place the handler there:

```
void TestTheArray()
{
  unsigned j;
  int anInt;
```

```
      cout << "Enter a subscript and a value: ";
      cin >> j >> anInt;
      InsertValue( j, anInt );
   }


   int main()
   {
     //...
     try {
       TestTheArray();
     }
     catch( const RangeError & ) {
       cout << "Range error in main()";
     }
     //...
```

In fact, much of the power of exception handling lies in its ability to handle errors at different levels of abstraction. It often happens that an error occurs at a level that contains no information about the context in which the error occurred. As [Stroustrup91] points out,

> The author of a library can detect run-time errors but does not in general have any idea what to do about them. The user of a library may know how to cope with such errors but cannot detect them - or else they would have been handled in the user's code and not left for the library to find.

So, a library user will ordinarily surround one or more library function calls with a `try` block, and then catch any exceptions that are thrown by the library. The `catch` clauses in the user's code will take whatever action that is appropriate to the application.

8.3.1.1 Unwinding the Execution Stack.   When a program throws an exception, the destructor is called for each object that was constructed from the time the program entered a `try` block. This process is called *stack unwinding*, and it is a major strength of the exception handling mechanism. In the next example, if an exception is thrown while creating the `LongArray` object, the file stream's destructor is called first, then the handler executes:

```
        try {
          ofstream log("log.txt");
          LongArray L(30000);
        }
        catch( xalloc )  {
          cout << "Unable to create LongArray";
        }
```

When an exception is thrown during the construction of a composite object, destructors will be invoked only for those data members that have already been constructed. Similarly, if an exception is thrown during the construction of an array of objects, destructors are invoked only for those array elements that have already been constructed.

In the following example, the `Student` class contains `VString` and `Transcript` data members. The student's name will be constructed first, followed by the `records` data member:

```
class VString { ... };

class Transcript { ... };

class Student {
private:
  VString lastName;
  Transcript records;
};

int main()
{
  try {
    VString collegeName("Miami-Dade");
    Student S;
  }
  catch( ... ) {
    //...
  }
```

Let's assume that an exception is thrown by the `Transcript` constructor. First, the `VString` destructor is invoked for `collegeName`, followed by the same destructor for `S.lastName`. But the `Transcript` destructor is not invoked because the `records` data member was only partially constructed.

If an exception is thrown again while a destructor is executing, `terminate` is called. Also, if a handler cannot be found for a thrown exception, `terminate` is called. Most important, when `terminate` is called, standard C++ does not specifiy whether or not the stack is unwound, so destructors for existing class objects might not be called.

8.3.2 LongArray Class Example

In Chapter 7 we created the `LongArray` class, a dynamically allocated array of long integers. We showed how to call the standard C++ `set_new_handler` function to install a user-defined function that would execute whenever memory could not be allocated. If an error occurred, the function displayed a message and halted the program. For example,

```
void allocation_handler()
{
  cout << "Out of memory. Aborting program.\n";
  exit(1);
}

int main()
{
  set_new_handler( allocation_handler );
  // ...
```

This approach was about like pushing the 'panic' button. It was virtually impossible to invoke class destructors in an orderly, consistent manner because the same runtime error could occur in many different situations. Another problem with this approach was that we had no information about the context in which an error occurred, and we therefore were left with no practical way to relay this information to the user.

8.3.2.1 Memory Exhaustion.
When a C++ program discovers that sufficient memory cannot be allocated by a call to the new operator, the resulting condition is called *memory exhaustion*. The program automatically throws a standard exception called xalloc. If an exception handler is prepared to catch the exception, it can deal with the problem in an appropriate manner, perhaps by allocating less memory or by displaying a message to the user. On the other hand, if no exception handler is available, the program terminates. The xalloc exception class is defined in the except.h header.

For example, an xalloc exception might be thrown by the LongArray constructor. No explicit throw expression is necessary:

```
LongArray::LongArray( unsigned sz )
{
  size = sz;
  data = new long[size];
}
```

When creating a LongArray object, if an xalloc exception is thrown, the handler executes, displaying an error message, and the call to ProcessTheArray never takes place:

```
int main()
{
  const unsigned arraySize = 30000u;

  try {
    LongArray L( arraySize );
    ProcessTheArray( L );
```

```
  }
catch( xalloc )  {
  cout << "Unable to create LongArray";
}
//...
```

This example also shows that statements attempting to allocate memory need not be physically located inside the `try` block, but must be within the block's execution scope in order for exceptions to be caught.

8.3.2.2 Subscript Errors.

It's no secret that an out-of-bounds array subscript can have disastrous effects on a program. In the original version of the `LongArray::Get` function, we used an `assert` macro to check the subscript range. Let's rewrite the function so it throws a `RangeError` exception:

```
long LongArray::Get( unsigned i ) const
{
  if( i >= size ) throw RangeError();
  return data[i];
}
```

In a program that creates a `LongArray` object, we enclose a call to `Get` inside a `try` block, followed by a handler that takes appropriate action. The parameter for the handler is a const-qualified `RangeError` object. We use a loop that continues asking for a subscript until until one that is in range is entered by the user:

```
LongArray L(20);

int ok = 0;
while( !ok ) {
  long n;
  cout << "Enter an array subscript (0-19): ";
  cin >> i;
  try {
    n = L.Get(i);
    ok = 1;
  }
  catch( const RangeError & R ) {
    cout << "Illegal subscript.\n";
  }
}
```

As a mater of habit, we designate `R` as a reference parameter, to avoid the automatic creation of a copy of the `RangeError` parameter.

8.3.2.3 Multiple Handlers.

Most programs performing exception handling have to handle more than one type of exception. A single `try` block can be followed by multiple handlers, each configured to match a different exception type. For example, we can begin by defining the RangeError and InputFileError exception classes, along with the same LongArray class we have been using:

```
class RangeError {  };
class InputFileError {  };
class LongArray {
  //...
};
```

The ReadFile function attempts to open an input file, throwing an Input-FileError exception if unsuccessful:

```
void ReadFile( ifstream & infile, LongArray & L )
{
  infile.open( "INDATA.TXT" );
  if( !infile ) throw InputFileError();
  //...
}
```

The GetArrayElement function calls LongArray::Get, which in turn might throw a RangeError exception:

```
void GetArrayElement( const LongArray & L )
{
  unsigned i;
  cout << "Enter subscript: ";
  cin >> i;
  long n = L.Get( i );
}
```

In main, we enclose all function calls in a try block and follow it with a separate handler for each type of exception:

```
int main()
{
  unsigned ArraySize = 50;

  try {
    ifstream infile;
    LongArray L( ArraySize );
    ReadFile( infile, L );
    GetArrayElement( L );
    cout << "Program completed normally.\n";
  }
  catch( xalloc ) {
    cout << "Memory allocation error\n";
```

```
    }
    catch( const RangeError & R ) {
      cout << "Subscript out of range\n";
    }
    catch( const InputFileError & F ) {
      cout << "Unable to open input file\n";
    }
    catch( ... ) {
      cout << "Unknown exception thrown\n";
    }

    return 0;
  }
```

We also included a handler that handles any type of exception, identified by the (...) parameter list. Any previously unhandled exception will be caught by this handler.

8.3.3 Improved RangeError Class

There are improvements to the RangeError class that can supply more information about where and how an exception was thrown. For example, we can add a constructor with parameters holding the source file name and line number where the exception was thrown, plus the subscript value that caused the exception. RangeError also contains a stream output operator that displays relevant information:

```
    const unsigned FileNameSize = 40;

    class RangeError {
    public:
      RangeError( const char * fname,
                  unsigned line,
                  unsigned subscr )
      {
        strncpy(fileName, fname, FileNameSize);
        lineNumber = line;
        value = subscr;
      }

      friend ostream & operator <<( ostream & os,
            const RangeError & R )
      {
        os << "RangeError exception thrown: "
           << R.fileName
           << ", line " << R.lineNumber
```

```
            << " value = " << R.value
            << endl;
        return os;
      }

    private:
      char fileName[FileNameSize+1];
      unsigned lineNumber;
      unsigned value;
    };
```

In `LongArray::Get`, for example, we pass the appropriate parameters to the `RangeError` constructor:

```
long LongArray::Get( unsigned i ) const
{
  if( i >= size )
    throw RangeError( __FILE__, __LINE__, i );
  return data[i];
}
```

Note that we include information about how and where the exception occurred. The standard __FILE__ macro returns a string containing the current source file name, and the standard __LINE__ macro returns an integer identifying the source line number.

Example 8-2 contains a complete program that demonstrates the new `RangeError` class. In `GetArrayElement` we ask for an array subscript, and if an exception is thrown, we notify the user and ask for another subscript:

```
void GetArrayElement( const LongArray & L )
{
  int ok = 0;
  while( !ok )
  {
    unsigned i;
    cout << "Enter an array subscript (0-"
         << ( L.GetSize()-1 ) << "): ";
    cin >> i;

    long n;
    try {
      n = L.Get( i );
      ok = 1;
      cout << "Element contains " << n << endl;
    }
    catch( const RangeError & R ) {
      cout << R;
```

```
        cout << "Caught at: " << __FILE__
            << ", line " << __LINE__
            << endl;
        throw R;
      }
    }
  }
```

In the handler, we display both the location where the exception was thrown, and the location of the handler. Note that the last line of the handler throws the same exception again, passing it along to the previous context, which in this case is `main`. Here is an example of the output:

```
Number of Array elements? 30
Enter an array subscript (0-30): 31
RangeError exception thrown: EXCEPT.CPP, line 71, value = 31
Caught at: EXCEPT.CPP, line 121
Exception caught in main().
```

The `RangeError` class can be used not only by programs using `LongArray` objects, but in any program that needs to report range errors.

8.4 DEBUGGING TIPS

8.4.1 Avoiding Calls to new in User Code

Consistent with block scope rules, any object declared in a `try` block is not accessible outside the block. This creates an interesting problem when statements within a `try` block perform memory allocation. In the next example, if the first array of characters is successfully allocated but the second array allocation fails, `pc1` goes out of scope without letting us deallocate the memory it addresses:

```
const unsigned size1 = 500;
const unsigned size2 = 30000;

try {
  char *pc1 = new char[size1];
  char *pc2 = new char[size2];
}
catch( xalloc )  {
  cout << "Allocation error";
}
```

To prevent this type of problem, we can avoid directly calling the `new` operator in user code. This point was mentioned in Chapter 7, but its purpose can now be

Example 8-2. Exception Handling Example

```cpp
#include <iostream.h>
#include <except.h>
#include <fstream.h>
#include "fstring.h"

class RangeError {
public:
  RangeError( const FString & fname,
              unsigned line,
              unsigned subscr )
  {
    fileName = fname;
    lineNumber = line;
    subscript = subscr;
  }

  friend ostream & operator <<( ostream & os, const RangeError & R )
  {
    os << "RangeError exception thrown: " << R.fileName
       << ", line " << R.lineNumber << endl;
    return os;
  }

private:
  FString fileName;
  unsigned lineNumber;
  unsigned subscript;
};

class LongArray {
public:
  LongArray( unsigned sz = 0 );
  ~LongArray();

  unsigned GetSize() const;
  long Get( unsigned i ) const;
  void Put( unsigned i, long item );

private:
  long * data;    // array of long integers
  unsigned size; // allocation size
};
```

Example 8-2 *(cont.)*

```
void LongArray::Put( unsigned i, long item )
{
  if( i >= size )
    throw RangeError( __FILE__ ,__LINE__, i );
  data[i] = item;
}


long LongArray::Get( unsigned i ) const
{
  if( i >= size )
    throw RangeError( __FILE__ ,__LINE__, i );
  return data[i];
}


//----------------( test program )----------------------

unsigned GetArraySize()
{
  unsigned n;
  cout << "Number of array elements? ";
  cin >> n;
  return n;
}


// Fill the array with random integers.

void FillArray( LongArray & L )
{
  int i;
  try {
    for( i = 0; i < L.GetSize(); i++ )
      L.Put( i, rand() );
  }
  catch( const RangeError & R ) {
    cout << R;
    throw R;
  }
}


// Retrieve an array element.
```

Example 8-2 *(cont.)*

```cpp
void GetArrayElement( const LongArray & L )
{
  int ok = 0;
  while( !ok )
  {
    unsigned i;
    cout << "Enter an array subscript (0-"
         << ( L.GetSize()-1 ) << "): ";
    cin >> i;

    long n;
    try {
      n = L.Get( i );
      ok = 1;
      cout << "Element contains " << n << endl;
    }
    catch( const RangeError & R ) {
      cout << R;
      cout << "Caught at: " << __FILE__
           << ", line " << __LINE__ << endl;
      throw R;
    }
  }
}

int main()
{
  try {
    LongArray L( GetArraySize() );
    FillArray( L );
    GetArrayElement( L );
  }
  catch( ... ) {
    cout << "Exception caught in main().\n";
    return 1;
  }

  return 0;
}
```

shown more clearly in the context of exception handling. Wrap all memory allocations inside classes, so whenever an exception is thrown, each object's destructor takes care of its own memory deallocation.

Let's rewrite the foregoing example, this time using `DynString` objects to hold the two character arrays (see Example 8-3). In a test run of the program, object `pc1` was allocated successfully, but `pc2` was not. The output from the program was

```
Created string at: 0x0dc2
Deleted string at: 0x0dc2
Allocation error caught.
```

By comparing the program to its output, we see that an exception was thrown while attempting to allocate `pc2`, so the destructor for `pc1` was called. Finally, the handler was executed. On the other hand, if the program had successfully allocated both strings, the following message would have been displayed: `Both allocations successsful.`

8.5 CHAPTER SUMMARY

Static binding means that the address of an object is known at compile time. A statically bound function's address is known at compile time. On the other hand, *dynamic binding* means that a single pointer can point to objects of different types. A dynamically bound function must have its address looked up at run time. A call to a statically bound function results in faster execution than a call to a dynamically bound one.

Once declared *virtual* in a base class, a member function remains virtual in its derived classes. You do not need to declare a function virtual if the exact type of an object pointer invoking the function is known at compile time.

Destructors are not inherited, so we usually define one for each derived class. Destructors cannot be overloaded because they have no parameters. Destructors can be *virtual*. A base class should contain a virtual destructor even if the function does nothing.

An *abstract* class is one that contains at least one pure virtual function. A *pure virtual function* is a member function that is declared using a *pure-specifier,* which means the function prototype ends with "`= 0`". The function must be implemented in any derived class before instances of the class can be created. Pure virtual functions provide a good mechanism to prevent the inadvertent omission of essential operations in derived classes.

Exception handling is a sophisticated way to handle runtime errors in C++. Rather than aborting a program and leaving objects in an undefined (or corrupted) state, exception handling gives us the ability to perform a more graceful recovery from errors. Exception handling lets us handle an error at different levels, providing context-specific information that can be used as an aid to fixing the problem that caused the exception.

Example 8-3. Dynamic Allocation Example

```
#include <iostream.h>
#include <except.h>

const unsigned size1 = 500;
const unsigned size2 = 30000;

class DynString {
public:
  DynString( unsigned strSize );
  ~DynString();

private:
  char * str;
  unsigned size;
};

DynString::DynString( unsigned strSize )
{
  size = strSize;
  str = new char[strSize];
  cout << "Created string at:"
       << hex << &str << endl;
}

DynString::~DynString()
{
  delete [] str;
  cout << "Deleted string at:"
       << hex << &str << endl;
}

int main()
{
  try {
    DynString pc1( size1 );
    DynString pc2( size2 );
    cout << "Both allocations successsful\n";
  }
  catch( xalloc )  {
    cout << "Allocation error caught.";
  }
  return 0;
}
```

A program *throws* an exception at the point where an error is first detected. An exception handler responds to the exception by *catching* the exception. If an appropriate exception handler cannot be found, the program terminates. A `try` block, introduced by the `try` keyword, identifies the execution scope of statements that might throw an exception. A `try` block is always followed by a *handler*, which begins with the `catch` keyword.

Most exception handlers identify a specific type of exception that they are able to catch; others can catch any type of exception. Some exception handlers attempt to fix the problem that caused an exception, and then resume the program's execution.

Using the `LongArray` class, we showed how to detect and handle memory exhaustion, when the `new` operator failed to allocate storage for an array. An `xalloc` exception is automatically thrown in such cases.

We also showed how to throw an exception when an array subscript was out of bounds, and we created a custom exception class called `RangeError` that displayed information about the location where the exception occurred.

8.6 EXERCISES

8.6.1 Vehicle Management System

Use the Vehicle Managment System and the modifications made to the program in the Chapter 6 and Chapter 7 exercises as a starting point for the exercises in this section.

1 Abstract Vehicle Class.   Make the `Vehicle` class an abstract class, with at least one pure virtual function. In the `main` program declare a pointer to a `Vehicle`, and alternately initialize it with both `CompanyVehicle` and `PersonalVehicle` constructors. Add the appropriate virtual functions to the two classes so that the following statements in the test program will correctly input and display both types of vehicles:

```
void InputAndShow( Vehicle * p )
{
  cin >> *p;
  cout << *p;
}

int main()
{
  Vehicle * p;
  p = new CompanyVehicle;
  InputAndShow( p );
```

```
p = new PersonalVehicle;
InputAndShow( p );
```

2 CompanyVehicle Table.   Using the `Table` and `TableAsArray` classes presented in this chapter as a guide, create a table of `CompanyVehicle` objects. Make it possible for the user to view a listing of all vehicles checked out on or before a specified date. The listing should show the checkout date, the name of the person checking out the vehicle, and the vehicle ID number.

3 TripLog Table.   In each `CompanyVehicle`, store the `TripLog` objects in a table. Use the `Table` and `TableAsArray` classes presented in this chapter as a guide. Provide functions to search for trips by date. In other words, the user should be able to retrieve a list of all trips taken on a particular date, regardless of whom the cars were checked out to.

8.6.2 Package-Shipping Service

The followng exercises relate to the Package-Shipping Service program presented in Section 8.2.

1 Finding Packages.   Write statements in the test program for the Package-Shipping Service application that find and display all packages bound for the same destination. Let the user choose the destination by typing a string of digits, possibly containing a '*' wildcard character for partial matches. For example, "331*" would match ZIP Codes such as 33111, 33132, and 33165.

2 Table Class.   Add a function to the `Table` class that lets the user remove a specific item from the `Table`. Here is a suggested prototype:

```
void RemoveAt( unsigned index );
```

Implementing this function is not as simple as it might seem. You will have to make a decision about what to do about deleted table positions. Two approaches come to mind:

One approach is to set the deleted item's pointer to null in the array of pointers used by the `TableAsArray` class. The `operator` `<<` function would have to be modified so that it skips null table entries. When new entries are added to the table, the `AddItem` function could look for the first empty table position and use it first before appending a new entry to the end of the array.

Another approach is to slide foreward all pointers to items that occur after the deleted item in the array. The `TableAsArray::count` data member would also have to be decreased by 1. This method requires some execution time when a table is large. This method will also render invalid all indexes to table items that were moved during the `Remove` operation.

3 Address and Person Classes.   Enhance the Package-Shipping Service program as follows:

1. Create an `Address` class, containing street, city, state, and ZIP Code.
2. Create a `Person` class, containing the last name and address of a customer who will receive a package.
3. Add a recipient data member to the `Package` class, showing the receiving person's name and address. The recipient is a `Person` object. Modify the stream I/O operator functions in the `Package` class to handle the new data member.

Use the following declaration for the `Address` and `Person` classes and create your own implementations:

```
class Address {
public:
  Address( const FString & streetv,
    const FString & cityv,
    const FString & statev,
    const FString & zipv );
  const FString & GetStreet();
  const FString & GetCity();
  const FString & GetState();
  const FString & GetZip();

private:
  FString street;
  FString city;
  FString state;
  FString zip;
};

class Person {
public:
  Person();
  Person( const FString & lname,
        const Address & addr );
  friend istream & operator >>( istream & inp,
        Person & P );
  friend ostream & operator <<( ostream & os,
        const Person & P );

private:
  FString lastName;
  Address homeAddress;
};
```

Use the same `main` program that was presented in this chapter. Run and test the program, using the following sample input file as a guide. Add at least five more records:

```
100101 31313 33130 960402 15.00  8.0 A 200   Holmes    221 Baker St.   London       England  1E6 2B4
102001 20000 96535 960403  7.50  4.5 O 42    McGarrett 305 Oneawa St.  Honolulu     HI       96222
100311 10101 12110 960405  5.00  3.0 A 3000  Magnum    4442 Kam Hwy.   Waimanalo    HI       96732
101400 10000 70515 960410  5.30  3.2 S 1000  Columbo   321 Nob Hill    San Francisco CA      98222
110510 22222 33133 960412 15.00 10.5 S 500   Friday    202 Sunset Blvd Los Angeles  CA       98123
```

4 Adding Shipment Type and Insured Value. Make the following modifications to the `Package` class: add a *type of shipment* data member, defined as an enumerated type (air, surface, overnight); also, add an *insured value* data member, type `float`.

Modify the stream I/O operator functions to take advantage of the new data members.

5 Transferring Packages Between Stations. Assume that you have three different stations in your shipping company, each with a separate collection of packages in their possession. Write a program that simulates the transfer of individual packages from one station to another. Assume that each station has a ZIP Code, which should match the destination ZIP Code on one of the packages. When a `Package` object is sent from Station A to Station B, it must be removed from A's list and added to B's list. *Extra:* Send all packages bound for a single station as a group.

8.6.3 Exception Handling

1 The TableAsArray class. Add exception handling to all appropriate functions in the `TableAsArray` class (Section 8.2). For example, the `AddItem` and `GetItemPtr` functions can throw `RangeError` exceptions, and the `TableAs Array` constructor can throw an `xalloc` exception. Modify the main program so it can handle these exceptions. Also, `main` can throw an `InputFileError` exception when opening the Package File.

2 Doctors Office Scheduling. Add exception handling to the Doctors Office Scheduling program, introduced in Chapter 5, and enhanced in the exercises for Chapter 7. You might want to throw both `RangeError` and `InputFileError` exceptions. If you are using dynamic memory allocation, be sure to catch `xalloc` exceptions. Modify the test program so that it tests each of the possible exceptions.

CHAPTER 9

Operator Overloading

Operator overloading makes it possible to manipulate class objects with standard C++ operators such as +, *, [ ], and <<. In this chapter we will demonstrate overloading both unary and binary operators, including the cast operator for implicit and explicit type conversion, relational operators, the assignment operator, and the subscript operator. In the second half of the chapter we will introduce bit manipulation and implement a useful class called BitArray.

Terms Introduced in this Chapter:

binary operator   operator overloading
bit array   unary operator
operator function

9.1 OVERLOADING BASICS

9.1.1 How Operators Are Overloaded

Operator overloading refers to the technique of ascribing new meaning to standard operators such as +, >>, and = when used with class operands. This is a great convenience because it lets us work with objects in an intuitive way. We have already used overloaded stream operators, beginning in Chapter 3. More a convenience than a necessity, overloaded operators represent an elegant yet often misunderstood part of C++.

In both C and C++, a *unary* operator is an operator that has only a single operand. The ++ operator, for example, is unary. A *binary* operator, on the other hand, has two operands. The / operator, for example, is binary. Some operators such as + are both unary and binary, depending on their usage:

```
n++;        // unary
x / y;      // binary
+x;         // unary
x + y;      // binary
```

Because we are already accustomed to using unary and binary operators in expressions, there is an advantage to using these same operators with class objects. When overloading an operator for a particular class, we must try to choose a meaning that is consistent with the operator's customary usage. For example, the + operator is well-suited to concatenating two FString objects:

```
FString s1("one");
FString s2("two");
FString s3 = s1 + s2;    // "onetwo"
```

On the other hand, overloading the < operator for this operation would only confuse class users.

An operator function is a function whose name consists of the keyword operator followed by a unary or binary operator, in the form

operator *operator*

You can overload any of the following operators:[1]

Unary:

```
new    delete    new[]    delete[]

++      increment
--      decrement
()      function call
[]      subscript
+       plus
-       minus
*       dereference
```

---

[1] The names given in this list are meant to be descriptive, but not necessarily universal.

```
&       address of
!       logical NOT
~       bitwise NOT
,       comma
```

Binary:

```
+       addition
-       subtraction
*       multiplication
/       division
%       modulus


=       assignment
+=      addition with assignment
-=      subtraction with assignment
*=      multiplication with assignment
/=      division with assignment
%=      modulus with assignment


&       bitwise AND
|       bitwise OR
^       bitwise exclusive OR
^=      bitwise exclusive OR with assignment
&=      bitwise AND with assignment
|=      bitwise OR with assignment


==      equal
!=      not equal
>       greater than
<       less than
>=      greater than or equal
<=      less than or equal


||      logical OR
&&      logical AND

<<      left shift
<<=     left shift with assignment
>>      right shift
>>=     right shift with assignment


->      pointer
->*     pointer to member
```

The following operators cannot be overloaded:

```
       .      member access
       .*     member access-dereference
       ::     scope resolution
       ?:     arithemtic-IF
```

Except for operator `new`, operator `delete`, and operator `->`, operator functions can return any data type. The precedence, grouping, and number of operands cannot be changed. Except for the `()` operator, operator functions cannot have default arguments.

An operator function must be either a non-static member function or a nonmember function having at least one parameter whose type is a class, reference to a class, enumeration, or reference to an enumeration. This rule prevents us from changing the meanings of operators that operate on intrinsic data types. For example, the following would be invalid:

```
int operator +( int x, int y )
{
   return x * y;
}
```

On the other hand, the following nonmember function is valid because at least one parameter is a class type:

```
class Integer {
//...
public:
   int value;
};

int operator +( const Integer & x, int y )
{
   return x.value + y;
}
```

9.1.2 Arithmetic Operators

9.1.2.1 Unary Operators in the Time Class.
The unary `++` and `--` operators can be overloaded either as prefix or postfix operators.

In Example 9-1, for example, we define a class called `Time` that performs range checking and operations on time values. This class could be useful in any program that needs to display and format time values. The `Time` class prevents users from assigning illegal values to hours and minutes, and provides a convenient way

Example 9-1. The Time Class, with Overloaded Operators

```
// Time of day, expressed in hours and minutes,
// using a 24-hour clock.

#include <iostream.h>
#include <iomanip.h>
#include "range.h"    // RangeError class

const unsigned HourMax = 23;
const unsigned MinuteMax = 59;

class Time {
public:
  Time( unsigned c = 0 );
  Time( const Time & t );

  void SetHours( unsigned h );
  void SetMinutes( unsigned m );

  // prefix and postfix increment operators
  // increment the minutes.
  const Time & operator ++();
  Time operator ++(int);

  const Time & operator +=( unsigned n );
  // Add n minutes to the current Time object.

  friend ostream & operator <<( ostream & os, const Time & h );

private:
  unsigned hours;
  unsigned minutes;
};

// Construct from unsigned integer.

Time::Time( unsigned tv )
{
  SetHours(tv / 100);
  SetMinutes(tv % 100);
}

// Copy constructor.

Time::Time( const Time & t2 )
```

Example 9-1 *(cont.)*

```
{
  minutes = t2.minutes;
  hours = t2.hours;
}

void Time::SetHours( unsigned h )
{
  if( h > HourMax )
    throw RangeError(__FILE__,__LINE__,h);
  hours = h;
}

void Time::SetMinutes( unsigned m )
{
  if( m > MinuteMax )
    throw RangeError(__FILE__,__LINE__,m);
  minutes = m;
}

// prefix increment: add 1 to minutes; if
// end of hour reached, reset to beginning
// of next hour.

const Time & Time::operator ++()
{
  if( ++minutes > MinuteMax )
  {
    minutes = 0;
    hours = (hours + 1) % (HourMax + 1);
  }
  return *this;
}

// postfix increment: return the current
// time value, then add 1 to the time.

Time Time::operator ++( int )
{
  Time save( *this );   // construct a copy
  operator ++();        // increment the time
  return save;          // return the copy
}

// Add n minutes to the time.
```

Example 9-1 *(cont.)*

```
const Time & Time::operator +=( unsigned n )
{
  unsigned t = minutes + n;
  minutes = t % (MinuteMax + 1);   // remaining minutes
  hours += t / (MinuteMax + 1);    // add to hours
  hours = hours % (HourMax + 1);   // roll over to next day
  return *this;
}


// Display in "hh:mm" format.

ostream & operator <<( ostream & os, const Time & t )
{
  os.fill('0');
  os << setw(2) << t.hours << ':' << setw(2) << t.minutes;
  return os;
}
```

for incrementing the minutes in an hour. Most importantly, the class overloads the prefix and postfix ++ operators.

To test this class, we create several Time objects, initialize them with a variety of values, increment them, and display their new values:

```
void Test()
{
  Time a;
  Time b(1845);

  cout << ++a << '\n'       // 00:01
       << b++ << endl;      // 18:45
```

Notice that Time a is incremented before it is written to the output stream; Time b, on the other hand, is written to the stream before being incremented. This happens because the prefix operator returns the Time value after it was incremented, and the postfix operator returns the Time value before it was incremented.

The class also overloads the binary += operator, allowing us to add two Time objects and display the result:

```
Time c(2359);
cout << (c += 15) << '\n';   // 00:14
```

We also have to be sure that the increment operator works correctly when the minutes are incremented past 59:

```
// Increment a Time object in a loop:

Time d(1230);
for(unsigned i = 0; i < 50; i++)
  cout << ++d << ',';
cout << endl;
```

In order to implement exception handling, we surround the call to the Test function with a `try` block, and catch `RangeError` exceptions:

```
int main()
{
  try {
    test();          // Test the Time class.
  }
  catch( const RangeError & R ) {
    cout << R;
  }
  return 0;
}
```

We encourage the reader to overload the prefix and postfix `--` operators as an exercise.

9.1.2.2 Implementing the Operators.

To implement the prefix `++` operator, we add 1 to the minutes and check to see if they have exceeded 59. If so, we increment the hour. If the hour exceeds 23, we roll it over to zero with the modulus (%) operator:

```
const Time & Time::operator ++()
{
  if( ++minutes > MinuteMax )
  {
    minutes = 0;
    hours = (hours + 1) % (HourMax + 1);
  }
  return *this;
}
```

In order to implement the postfix `++` operator, we have to save the current Time, call the prefix `++` operator, and return the saved Time:

```
Time Time::operator ++( int )
{
  Time save( *this );   // construct a copy
  operator ++();        // increment the time
  return save;          // return the copy
}
```

A `RangeError` exception can be thrown by the `SetHours` and `SetMinutes` functions.

9.1.2.3 Overloading Binary Operators.

Some of the binary arithmetic operators that are more commonly overloaded are +, +=, -, -=, /, /=, *, and *=. As long as their meanings are not distorted, these operators can be a convenience.

For example, the `Time` class in Example 9-1 has an addition-assignment operator that adds n minutes to the current time. After adding n to the minutes, we check for possible overflow by using modulus and integer division:

```
const Time & Time::operator +=( unsigned n )
{
  unsigned t = minutes + n;
  minutes = t % (MinuteMax + 1);   // remaining minutes
  hours += t / (MinuteMax + 1);    // add to hours
  hours = hours % (HourMax + 1);   // roll over to next day
  return *this;
}
```

If the current time were 12:50 and we added 25 minutes, for example, t would become 75 (50 + 25), `minutes` would become 15 (t mod 60) and `hours` would become 13 (12 += t / 60).

It would also be a good idea to overload the += operator so the parameter can be a `Time` object. We leave this function as an exercise:

```
const Time & operator +=( const Time & T )
```

9.1.3 FString Class Example

The `FString` class was first presented in Chapter 4; but now we have an opportunity to improve the class by adding operator functions such as = and +=. The complete `FString` class definition is listed in Example 9-2, but we have excerpted a few of the member function prototypes here:

```
class FString {
public:
  //...                                        // #
  FString & operator +=( const char * s );     // 1.
  FString & operator +=( char c );             // 2.
  FString & operator +=( const FString & s );  // 3.
  FString & operator =( const char * s );      // 4.
  FString & operator =( char c );              // 5.
  FString & operator =( const FString & s );   // 6.
  //...
};
```

Example 9-2. Fstring Class Definition

```
#include <iostream.h>
#include <strstream.h>
#include <iomanip.h>
#include <string.h>
#include <stdlib.h>  // for strtol()

class FString {
public:
  // Constructors
  FString();
  FString( const char * s );
  FString( const FString & s );
  FString( const char ch );

  // Assignment operators
  FString & operator =( const char * s );
  FString & operator =( const FString & s );
  FString & operator =( char c );

  // Append & Concatenate operators
  FString & Append( const FString & s );
  FString & operator +=( const FString & s );
  FString & operator +=( const char * s );
  FString & operator +=( char c );
  FString operator +( const FString & s2 );

  // Cast operators
  operator const char *() const; // cast to C-style string
  operator long() const;         // cast to long integer

  // Comparison operators and functions
  int operator ==( const FString & s ) const;
  int operator !=( const FString & s ) const;
  int operator < ( const FString & s ) const;
  int operator > ( const FString & s ) const;
  int operator <=( const FString & s ) const;
  int operator >=( const FString & s ) const;

  // Stream I/O operators and functions
  void GetLine( istream & inp );
  friend istream & operator >>(istream & inp, FString & s);
  friend ostream & operator <<(ostream & os, const FString & s);

private:
  enum { MaxSize = 255};
  char str[MaxSize+1];
};
```

(The reference numbers next to each of the function names will be used in the examples that follow.)

The += operator appends either an FString, a C-style string, or a character to the current FString. The = operator assigns either an FString, a C-style string, or a single character to the current FString. This operator also replaces the Assign function used in the first version of this class shown in Chapter 4. The following examples show how each operator can be used. Note that the examples are labeled with the same reference numbers that we placed next to the function declarations:

```
FString s1;
FString s2("Lincoln");
s1 += "Abe";                        // 1.
s1 += ' ';       // "Abe "          // 2.
s1 += s2;        // "Abe Lincoln"   // 3.
s1 = "Cleveland";                   // 4.
s1 = 'X';                           // 5.
s2 = s1;                            // 6.
```

Beginners often confuse a copy constructor call with a call to the operator = function. The following two statements both call the copy constructor. Despite its appearance, the second statement does not call operator =:

```
FString s2( s1 );
FString s2 = s1;
```

On the other hand, the following statement calls operator =:

```
s2 = s1;
```

By convention, operator = returns a reference to the current FString, allowing it to be used in nested expressions such as

```
s1 = s2 = "Fillmore";
```

If the function returned an FString object (rather than a reference), the function would have to construct a temporary FString and return a copy of the current FString object. This would waste processing time and memory.

9.1.3.1 Implementing Append and the += Operator. In the FString class from Chapter 4, the Append function attaches another string to the end of the current one. We have improved it here by having it throw a `RangeError` exception if the combined length of the two strings exceeds `MaxSize`, the enumerated constant that appears in the class definition:

```
FString & FString::Append( const FString & s )
{
  size_t n = strlen( str ) + strlen( s.str );
  if( n >= MaxSize )
    throw RangeError(__FILE__, __LINE__, n);
  strcat( str, s.str );
  return *this;
}
```

We can also overload the += operator and implement it by calling `Append`:

```
FString & FString::operator +=( const FString & s )
{
  return Append( s );
}
```

This is an example of adding to a class interface without disturbing any other classes that might depend on the `Append` function. If we removed `Append` from the class, a great deal of existing code might have to be modified.

9.1.3.2 Implementing the Assignment Operator.   The = operator, used for assigning a new string to the current one, is overloaded for both `FString` and C-style string parameters. The first implementation assigns the `FString` parameter to the current string, making sure that the current string and `s` are not the same object:

```
FString & FString::operator =( const FString & s )
{
  if( *this == s ) // Cannot assign object to itself.
    return *this;

  size_t n = strlen( s.str );
  if( n > MaxSize )
    throw RangeError( __FILE__, __LINE__, n );
  strcpy( str, s.str );
  return *this;
}
```

The second implementation converts a `const char *` parameter to an `FString` and calls the first `operator` = function:

```
FString & FString::operator =( const char * s )
{
   return *this = FString(s);
}
```

The third implementation stores the character parameter in the first position of the string and appends a null byte:

```
FString & FString::operator =( char ch )
{
  str[0] = ch;
  str[1] = '\0';
  return *this;
}
```

9.1.4 Non-Member Operator Functions

Whenever possible, operator functions should be class members, because operations performed on instances of the class should be encapsulated there. However, if making an operator a member function would result in awkward expressions involving the operator, we make an exception to the rule.

The stream output operator, for example, is customarily placed at the right of a stream object or reference to a stream object, and at the left of an expression being written to the stream:

```
Point p;
cout << p;
```

But this order of operands would not be possible if the `operator` `<<` function were a class member. This is what the declaration would look like:

```
class Point {
public:
   ostream & operator << ( ostream & os );
   //...
};
```

Using the `<<` operator in an expression would be awkward because either a `Point` object would have to invoke the operator function, or a `Point` would have to appear as the left-hand operand in a binary expression. For example,

```
Point p;
p.operator <<( cout );   // function call
p << cout;               // (same effect)
```

Both uses of the operator are awkward and non-intuitive. Instead, it is customary to declare this operator as a non-member function, in which the first argument is a stream and the second is a `Point`. This allows the operands to appear in the "normal" order with the stream at the left and the `Point` at the right:

```
Point p;
cout << p;
```

Here is a sample implementation of the `operator` `<<` function for `Point` objects. In this particular case, the function does not have to be a friend of the `Point` class, because it requires no direct access to private or protected class members:

```
ostream & operator << ( ostream & os, const Point & p )
{
  os << p.GetX() << ',' << p.GetY();
  return os;
}
```

On the other hand, if the function required direct access to the private `Point` data members, we could declare it as a friend of the `Point` class:

```
class Point {
public:
   friend ostream & operator << ( ostream & os,
          const Point & p );
   //...
};
```

Although we might be tempted to make `operator` `<<` a non-member, non-friend function, this would not be a good idea. Its prototype would not appear in the `Point` class definition, so a reader might not realize how closely the function was tied to the class structure.

9.1.5 Cast Operator

A cast operator is useful for performing conversions between a class object and some other type. Unless two types are related by inheritance, C++ will not automatically convert from one type to another.

For example, we might want to provide a way of converting an `FString` object containing a string of digits into a `long`. The `FString` class would include the following declaration of a member function that casts into a `long`:

```
class FString {
public:
   operator long() const;
   //...
};
```

The declaration syntax is unusual in that it does not show a return type; the return type is understood to be the target type of the cast, in this case, long.

The long() cast operator is implemented by calling the standard strtol function, declared in the stdlib.h header:

```
#include <stdlib.h>

FString::operator long() const
{
   return strtol( str, 0, 0 );
}
```

Because the cast operator has been implemented, an FString can be assigned to either an int or a long, assuming that the converted value's range fits the destination type:

```
FString F("12345");
long z = F;
int n = F;
```

A cast operator can also use a pointer as its target type. For example, we might need to convert an FString object to char * in order to pass it to a function:

```
class FString {
public:
   //...
   operator char *();
   //...
};
```

The cast operator is invoked automatically if we pass an FString to a function requiring a char * parameter, or if we assign an FString to a char *. For example, the standard strlen function defined in string.h returns the length of a C-style string. When we pass it an FString object, the cast operator is automatically called, converting the argument to char *:

```
FString filename;
cin >> filename;
if( strlen( filename ) == 0 )
   // (filename is empty...)
```

The cast operator can also be invoked explicitly:

```
void trim( char * st );
//...
FString filename;

trim((char *)filename );
```

9.1.5.1 *General Comments About Conversions.* There are a few important things to remember about conversions:

1. A cast operator is absolutely required when converting from a class type to a standard type such as `int`, `char *`, `float`, or `double`.

2. There cannot be an implicit conversion from a new type to an existing type unless we pursue one of two alternatives: either add a new constructor to the existing class, or add a cast operator to the new class. The first alternative involves changing the interface of an existing class, which can cause far-reaching changes to user code. The second alternative, adding a cast operator to the new class, is preferable because it affects only the new class. For example, when creating a `Student` class, we might want to provide a cast operator that converts a `Student` to an `FString`. The following shows how the cast operator might be used:

```
Student s( 12345, "George Washington" );
FString f = (FString) s;
```

3. A constructor with a single parameter will always be used by the compiler for implicit conversions. For example, the `FString` class contains a constructor with a `const char *` parameter. This constructor is automatically invoked when we pass a C-style string to the `OpenFile` function:

```
class FString {
public:
  FString( const char * s );
  //...
};

int OpenFile( const FString & fileName );
.
.
.
int result = OpenFile( "infile" );
```

9.1.6 Equality and Relational Operators

When it is reasonable to compare two instances of the same class, it is a good idea to overload the equality (== and !=) and relational (<, >, <=, >=) operators. In the following example, we declare two operators that compare `Student` objects by their ID numbers:

```
class Student {
public:
   int operator ==( const Student & s ) const;
   int operator <( const Student & s ) const;
   //...
private:
   long id;
};

int Student::operator ==( const Student & s ) const
{
   return id == s.id;
}

int Student::operator <( const Student & s ) const
{
   return id < s.id;
}
```

Although there is just a single Student parameter, the operator really compares two objects: the Student that invoked the function, and the Student identified by the parameter.

9.1.6.1 FString Class Example.   Let's add the <, >, <=, >=, ==, and != operators to the FString class and show how they might be implemented. (The complete class implementation appears in Example 9-3.) We assume here that strings will be compared in the usual way, using the host computer's character set (ASCII, for example) and collating sequence. Here are the operator function declarations:

```
class FString {
public:
   int operator ==( const FString & s ) const;
   int operator !=( const FString & s ) const;
   int operator < ( const FString & s ) const;
   int operator > ( const FString & s ) const;
   int operator <=( const FString & s ) const;
   int operator >=( const FString & s ) const;
   //...
};
```

For example, the == operator calls the standard strcmp function declared in string.h and compares it to zero. This is a *case-sensitive* comparison, meaning that uppercase letters are not considered same as lowercase:

```
int FString::operator ==( const FString & s ) const
{
   return strcmp( str, s.str ) == 0;
}
```

Example 9-3. Fstring Class Implementation

```
#include "fstring.h"
#include "range.h"

FString::FString()
{
  str[0] = '\0';
}

FString::FString( const char ch )
{
  str[0] = ch;
  str[1] = '\0';
}

FString::FString( const FString & s )
{
  *this = s;
}

FString::FString( const char * s )
{
  size_t n = strlen( s );
  if( n > MaxSize )
    throw RangeError( __FILE__, __LINE__, n );
  strcpy( str, s );
}

FString & FString::operator =( const FString & s )
{
  size_t n = strlen( s.str );
  if( n > MaxSize )
    throw RangeError( __FILE__, __LINE__, n );
  strcpy( str, s.str );
  return *this;
}

FString & FString::operator =( const char * s )
{
  return *this = FString(s);
}

FString & FString::operator =( char ch )
{
  str[0] = ch;
```

Example 9-3 *(cont.)*

```
  str[1] = '\0';
  return *this;
}

FString & FString::Append( const FString & s )
{
  size_t n = strlen( str ) + strlen( s.str );
  if( n >= MaxSize )
    throw RangeError( __FILE__, __LINE__, n );

  strcat( str, s.str );
  return *this;
}

FString & FString::operator +=( const char * s )
{
  return *this += FString(s);
}

FString & FString::operator +=( char c )
{
  return *this += FString(c);
}

FString & FString::operator +=( const FString & s )
{
  return Append( s );
}

FString FString::operator +( const FString & s2 )
{
  FString temp( *this );
  return temp += s2;
}

FString::operator const char *() const
{
  return str;
}

FString::operator long() const
{
  return strtol( str, 0, 0 );
}
```

Example 9-3 *(cont.)*

```
int FString::operator ==( const FString & s ) const
{
  return strcmp( str, s.str ) == 0;
}

int FString::operator !=( const FString & s ) const
{
  return strcmp( str, s.str ) != 0;
}

int FString::operator < ( const FString & s ) const
{
  return strcmp( str, s.str ) < 0;
}

int FString::operator > ( const FString & s ) const
{
  return strcmp( str, s.str ) > 0;
}

int FString::operator <=( const FString & s ) const
{
  return !(*this > s);
}

int FString::operator >=( const FString & s ) const
{
  return !(*this < s);
}

void FString::GetLine( istream & inp )
{
  inp.getline( str, MaxSize+1 );
}

istream & operator >>( istream & inp, FString & s )
{
  inp >> setw(s.MaxSize+1) >> s.str;
  return inp;
}

ostream & operator <<( ostream & os, const FString & s )
{
  os << s.str;
  return os;
}
```

The < operator returns 1 when the value returned by strcmp is less than zero:

```
int FString::operator < ( const FString & s ) const
{
  return strcmp( str, s.str ) < 0;
}
```

Other operators can be implemented by calling existing operator functions. Here is the >= operator, for example:

```
int FString::operator >=( const FString & s ) const
{
  return !(*this < s);
}
```

Saying that a string *has a smaller value* implies that the string ocurrs earlier in the character collating sequence. String comparisons always begin with the first letter in each string, moving to the next position only if the current characters are identical. If two strings are the same except that one is shorter, the shorter string will have a smaller value because its trailing null is less than any other character. For example, "abc" has a smaller value than "abca".

9.1.7 Assignment Operators and Copy Constructors

When a class contains members that are pointers to dynamic storage, we know from Chapter 7 that the class requires both a copy constructor and an overloaded assignment operator, to prevent C++ from performing a default bitwise copy of the class data members.

For example, each Transcript object contains a dynamically allocated array of course names, represented as FString objects. A bitwise copy of a Transcript would only copy the pointer called courses, not the actual courses in the array:

```
class Transcript {
public:
  Transcript();
  Transcript( const Transcript & T );
  ~Transcript();
  Transcript & operator =( const Transcript & T );

private:
  enum { MaxCourses = 20 };
  FString * courses;   // pointer to list of course names
  unsigned count;
};
```

The following is an implementation of the copy constructor for the Transcript class. Because each Transcript should contain a separate copy of the courses array, we allocate dynamic storage and copy the courses one by one:

```
Transcript::Transcript( const Transcript & T )
{
  count = T.count;
  courses = new FString[MaxCourse];
  for(unsigned i = 0; i < count; i++)
    courses[i] = T.courses[i];
}
```

The = operator is similar to a copy constructor, except that it must first deallocate the array of courses in the current Transcript. Before doing so, we prevent the user from accidentally assigning the same Transcript object to itself. Otherwise, the function would deallocate the very storage that we were about to copy:

```
Transcript & Transcript::operator =( const Transcript & T )
{
  if( this != &T )         // Not the same object?
  {
    delete [] courses;
    courses = new FString[MaxCourse];
    count = T.count;
    for(unsigned i = 0; i < count; i++)
      courses[i] = T.courses[i];
  }
  return *this;
}
```

Because a number of lines in the copy constructor and assignment operator are identical, these lines could be placed in a separate private member function, to reduce the amount of duplicated code. The private function could be called by both the copy constructor and assignment operator. This is suggested in the chapter exercises.

The following are examples that call either the copy constructor or the assignment operator function:

```
Transcript t1;
Transcript t2( t1 );   // copy constructor
Transcript t3 = t1;    // copy constructor
t2 = t1;               // assignment operator
```

Aside from the issue of allocating dynamic memory, other good reasons exist for overloading the assignment operator. For example, we might want to validate attempted changes to data members; we might want to recalculate the values of selected data members; or, we might want to notify the rest of the program that an object is being copied.

9.1.8 Subscript Operator

A useful binary operator that we can overload is the subscript operator, declared in the form

$$classname::\texttt{operator[]}(\ type\ y\ )$$

where the parameter y is a subscript. When the operator appears in an expression such as x[y], x is the invoking class object and y is the function argument.

9.1.8.1 LongArray Example.   The LongArray class, introduced in Chapter 7, allows users to dynamically allocate array objects. Let's add the [] operator to this class:

```
class LongArray {
public:
  long & operator []( unsigned i );
  long & operator []( unsigned i ) const;
  //...

private:
  long * data;
  unsigned size;
};
```

Operator [] returns a reference to an array element, allowing it to be used for both retrieval and insertion. It replaces the Get and Put member functions we used in the previous version of this class. For example, when retrieving a value from the array, the operator simply returns a long integer:

```
const unsigned Size = 10;
LongArray L( Size );
unsigned i = 0;
cout << L[i];   // retrieve element i
```

But, when assigning a new value to an array element, the operator returns a reference that is an alias for the element. The following statement reads the input stream into element i of LongArray L:

```
cin >> L[i];  // Read stream into element i
```

The following copies element i to element j:

```
L[j] = L[i];
```

Ordinarily, member functions should not return non-constant references to private data members, because doing so violates class encapsulation. But the [] operator must return a reference if assignment to array elements is to be permitted. For an array class that overloads the [] operator in the C++ Draft Standard, see the <dynarray> class in [Plauger].

It is useful to define both constant and non-constant versions of this function, so the operator can be invoked by a const-qualified LongArray object. In the next example, ShowArray requires operator[] to be a constant member function:

```
void ShowArray( const LongArray & L )
{
  for(unsigned i = 0; i < L.GetSize(); i++)
    cout << L[i] << ',';
  cout << endl;
}


LongArray L( Size );
//...
ShowArray( L );
```

The implementation of operator[] checks the range of parameter i and throws a RangeError exception if it is out of range:

```
long & LongArray::operator[]( unsigned i )
{
  if( i >= size )
    throw RangeError( __FILE__,__LINE__,i );
  return data[i];
}
```

9.2 OPTIONAL: BITWISE OPERATORS

In Section 9.3 we will introduce a class called BitArray that makes extensive use of bitwise operators. Before doing so, we will review the bitwise operators common to both C and C++. We assume that all values are unsigned, thus avoiding differences between the way compilers implement signed integers. Using unsigned integers n and j, here is a quick summary of the operators:

```
n << j      n is shifted j bits to the left
n >> j      n is shifted j bits to the right
n & j       n is ANDed with j
n | j       n is ORed with j
n ^ j       n is exclusive ORed with j
~n          n is NOTed
```

9.2.1 Shifting Bits

The shift operators move all bits in an operand either left or right. For example, let's suppose that n is of type `unsigned char`, and is represented by eight bits. As n is shifted to the left, the highest bit disappears, each of the other bits moves one position to the left, and the lowest bit position is cleared (set to 0):

```
unsigned char n;
n = 0xCF;                 // n = 11001111
n = n << 1;               // n = 10011110
```

When n is shifted to the right, the lowest bit disappears, other bits are moved to the right, and the highest position is cleared:

```
unsigned char n;
n = 0xCF;                 // n = 11001111
n = n >> 1;               // n = 01100111
```

9.2.2 Bitwise AND

When two integers are bitwise ANDed together, each bit in the first is matched to its corresponding bit in the second. The resulting bit is 1 only if the two input bits were 1. For unsigned character values n and j,

```
    n = 11001111
    j = 00001111
    ...............
n & j = 00001111
```

9.2.3 Bitwise OR

When two numbers are bitwise ORed together, each bit in the same position of the numbers are matched up. The resulting bit is always 1 unless both of the input bits were 0. For example,

```
    n = 11001111
    j = 00001111
    . . . . . . . . . . . . . . . .
n | j = 11001111
```

9.2.4 Bitwise Exclusive OR

When two numbers are exclusive ORed together, the bits in the numbers are matched up. The resulting bit is 1 only if the two input bits were different:

```
    n = 11001111
    j = 00001111
    . . . . . . . . . . . . . . . .
n ^ j = 11000000
```

The exclusive OR can be used to reverse, or toggle the bits in a number. This is done by exclusive ORing a number with all 1's:

```
n       = 11001111
j       = 11111111
    . . . . . . . . . . . . . . . .
n ^ j = 00110000
```

9.2.5 Bitwise NOT

The bitwise NOT operator also toggles all bits in a number:

```
 n = 11001111
~n = 00110000
```

9.3 BITARRAY CLASS EXAMPLE

9.3.1 Uses of Bit Mapping

In this section, we will present a class called `BitArray` that shows how operator overloading can be put to good use. The `BitArray` class is loosely modeled after the `<bitset>` class described in the C++ Draft Standard [ANSI-95].

There are many occasions when it is useful to use an array of bits to efficiently represent a set of integers. We call these *bit arrays* or *bit sets*, because each bit in an ordered sequence of binary bits contains a 1 or 0. Each bit maps onto a number that belongs to the set of integers, making it easy to add and remove members, test for set membership, form the unions and intersections of sets, and so on.

For example, the C++ `ios` class uses a number of formatting flags that control numeric formatting for input/output. Some of these are: `showpoint`, `scientific`, `showpos`, `showbase`, and `fixed`. In most C++ implementations, each flag is mapped onto a different power of 2, allowing the flags to be combined in various ways. Suppose the values for these flags were as follows, shown in both hexadecimal (base 16) and binary (base 2). Each has a 1 bit in a different position:

```
    flag            hexadecimal       binary
..............................................................
 showpoint          0x0001            0000000000000001
 scientific         0x0002            0000000000000010
 showpos            0x0004            0000000000000100
 showbase           0x0008            0000000000001000
 fixed              0x0010            0000000000010000
```

To combine values such as these, we use the bitwise OR operator (|) to produce an integer that is passed to the `ios::setf` function. The following expression produces an integer equal to binary `0000000000000111`:

```
    ios::setf( ios::showpoint | ios::scientific | ios::showpos );
```

Enumerated constants are useful here so that a user of the `ios` class does not have to remember specific numeric values for the flags.

Bitwise operations have drawbacks when performed directly on C++ built-in integral types. We must specify each flag value carefully so that it does not overlap with any other. If the number of flags exceeds the bits in some standard data type (such as unsigned long), the checking of flag values becomes much more difficult. We must, in these cases, calculate the index offset into an array of integers and locate a particular binary bit. The drawbacks we have mentioned can be overcome by creating a class that contains an array of integers. In this class, we let the mapping of individual bit numbers to their physical positions be encapsulated in member functions.

9.3.2 BitArray Class Definition

The `BitArray` class definition appears in Example 9-4. An important feature is that a user can specify the size of the array at run time; we allocate dynamic memory for the array storing the bits. The class includes a default constructor, another constructor that lets the caller determine the array size, a destructor, assignment operator (=), set union operator (|=), set intersection operator (&=), as well as <<

Example 9-4. BitArray Class Definition

```
// Each bit is mapped to an ordinal value between
// 0 and N-1, where N is the set size. N may be 1 to 65,536.

#ifndef BITARRAY_H
#define BITARRAY_H

#include <iostream.h>
#include "range.h"

// The type of a single component of the array holding
// the bits can be unsigned char, unsigned int,
// or unsigned long.

typedef unsigned int elttype;


class BitArray {
public:
  BitArray();
  // Default constructor.

  BitArray( size_t sz = 0 );
  // Construct a bit array of size sz.

  ~BitArray() { delete [] bits; }
  // Destructor.

  size_t Count() const;
  // Return the number of '1' bits.

  BitArray & operator =( unsigned long n );
  // Construct a bit array from n. This is a
  // departure from the draft standard.

  BitArray & operator |=( const BitArray & S );
  // Form the union of bits in current array
  // with those in Bit array S.

  BitArray & operator &=( const BitArray & S );
  // Form the intersection of bits in current array
  // with those in Bit array S.

  friend ostream & operator <<( ostream &, const BitArray & );
  // Stream output.
```

Example 9-4 *(cont.)*

```
friend istream & operator >>( istream & inp, BitArray & BA );
// Stream input.

void Reset();
// Clear all bits.

void Reset( size_t n );
// Clear bit n.

void Set( size_t n );
// Set bit n.

int Test( size_t n ) const;
// Return value of bit n.

void Toggle( size_t n );
// Toggle bit n.

private:
  enum { BitsPerByte = 8,
         NumBits = sizeof(elttype) * BitsPerByte };

  size_t size;         // maximum number of bits
  size_t numElements;  // size of bits[] array

  elttype * bits;      // array of bits
};
```

and >> stream I/O operators. The `Reset` function clears one or all bits, the `Set` function sets one or all bits, the `Test` function checks a single bit to see if it has been set, and the `Toggle` function reverses a single bit.

9.3.3 BitArray Class Implementation

9.3.3.1 Arrangement of Bits.   From the class data members and enumerated constants (refer back to Example 9-4), we see that each array component is of type `elttype`, which we currently define as `unsigned int`. The constant `BitsPerByte` determines the number of bits that may be stored in a single byte. `NumBits` counts the total number of bit positions in each array component, based on the number of bytes in a component, and `BitsPerByte`. Notice that `size_t` is used throughout the class; this is a standard synonym for the `unsigned int` type.

A listing of the `BitArray` class implementation appears in Example 9-5. The most important aspect of the implementation is the mapping of logical array positions onto the physical sequence of packed bits. A 256-bit array, for example, uses just 32 bytes of memory (assuming eight bits per byte). The lowest bit of the first byte is element 0. To illustrate, if we created a 16-element array and added 0, 4, 6, and 10 to the array, the bits would be arranged as follows:

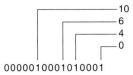

```
0000010001010001
```

This array would require only two bytes of storage. This is just one possible implementation, as we might just as easily have decided to reverse the order of the bits.

The `BitArray` class implements exception handling by implicitly throwing `xalloc` exceptions and explicitly throwing `RangeError` exceptions. An `xalloc` exception might be thrown by the constructor when allocating a new array. A `RangeError` exception might be thrown by the `Reset`, `Set`, `Test`, and `Toggle` functions.

The `BitArray` constructor has a parameter that specifies the number of bit positions in the array. We subtract 1 from this number, divide by `NumBits`, and add 1 to determine the required number of array components:

```
BitArray::BitArray( size_t sz )
{
  size = sz;
  numElements = ((size -1) / NumBits) + 1;
  bits = new elttype[ numElements ];
  Reset();
}
```

The `Count` function tests each bit position and returns the number of bits that are set:

```
size_t BitArray::Count() const
{
  size_t tally = 0;
  for(size_t i = 0; i < size; i++)
  {
    if( Test(i) )
      tally++;
  }
  return tally;
}
```

Example 9-5. BitArray Class Implementation

```
#include "bitarray.h"

size_t min( size_t t1, size_t t2 )
{
  if( t1 < t2 )
    return t1;
  return t2;
}

BitArray::BitArray()
{
  size = 0;
  numElements = 0;
  bits = 0;
}

BitArray::BitArray( size_t sz )
{
  size = sz;
  numElements = ((size -1) / NumBits) + 1;
  bits = new elttype[ numElements ];
  Reset();
}

BitArray::~BitArray()
{
  delete [] bits;
}

size_t BitArray::Count() const
{
  size_t tally = 0;
  for(size_t i = 0; i < size; i++)
  {
    if( Test(i) )
      tally++;
  }
  return tally;
}

BitArray & BitArray::operator |=( const BitArray & B2 )
{
  size_t count = min( numElements, B2.numElements );
  for(size_t i = 0; i < count; i++)
    bits[i] |= B2.bits[i];
  return *this;
}
```

Example 9-5 *(cont.)*

```
BitArray & BitArray::operator &=( const BitArray & B2 )
{
  size_t count = min( numElements, B2.numElements );
  for(size_t i = 0; i < count; i++)
    bits[i] &= B2.bits[i];
  return *this;
}

BitArray & BitArray::operator =( unsigned long n )
{
  Reset();
  for(size_t i = 0; i < size, n != 0; i++, n >>= 1)
    if(n & 1)
      Set(i);
  return *this;
}

ostream & operator <<( ostream & os, const BitArray & BA )
{
  for(size_t i = BA.size; 0 < i;)
    os << (BA.Test(--i) ? '1':'0');
  return os;
}

istream & operator >>( istream & inp, BitArray & BA )
{
  BA.Reset();
  char ch;
  for(size_t i = BA.size; 0 < i;)
  {
    --i;
    inp >> ch;
    if( ch == '1' )
      BA.Set(i);
  }
  return inp;
}

void BitArray::Reset()
{
  for(size_t i = 0; i < numElements; i++)
    bits[i] = 0;
}

// Clear bit n.
```

Example 9-5 *(cont.)*

```
void BitArray::Reset( size_t n )
{
  if( n >= size )
    throw RangeError(__FILE__,__LINE__,n);

  bits[n / NumBits] &= ~((elttype)1 << n % NumBits);
}

void BitArray::Set( size_t n )
{
  if( n >= size )
      throw RangeError(__FILE__,__LINE__,n);

  bits[n / NumBits] |= ((elttype)1 << n % NumBits);
}

int BitArray::Test( size_t n ) const
{
  if( n >= size )
    throw RangeError(__FILE__,__LINE__,n);

  int z = bits[n / NumBits] & ((elttype)1 << n % NumBits);
  return z != 0;
}

void BitArray::Toggle( size_t n )
{
  if( n >= size )
    throw RangeError(__FILE__,__LINE__,n);

  bits[n / NumBits] ^= ((elttype)1 << n % NumBits);
}
```

9.3.3.2 Set Union and Intersection Operations. The |= operator performs a bitwise OR of each bit in the current array with another array called B2. This operator is useful for computing the union of two sets:

```
BitArray & BitArray::operator |=( const BitArray & B2 )
{
  size_t count = min( numElements, B2.numElements );
  for(size_t i = 0; i < count; i++)
    bits[i] |= B2.bits[i];
  return *this;
}
```

(The `min` function returns the smaller of two unsigned integers.)

The `&=` operator performs a bitwise AND of each bit in the current array with another array. This is useful for computing the intersection of two sets:

```
BitArray & BitArray::operator &=( const BitArray & B2 )
{
  size_t count = min( numElements, B2.numElements );
  for(size_t i = 0; i < count; i++)
    bits[i] &= B2.bits[i];
  return *this;
}
```

9.3.3.3 Calculating Bit Offsets.

The most difficult part about working with packed bits is calculating the offset, or location of a particular bit. Suppose that we want to implement the `Test` member function, which returns 1 if a particular bit has been set. The array of integers holding the bits is called `bits`. Let's assume that `NumBits` equals 8 and we want to locate and test bit n. First, we divide n by `NumBits` to get the array subscript j that indicates which array element is to be examined:

```
unsigned j = n / NumBits;
```

Next, we isolate the correct bit by constructing a *mask*, or bit pattern. The expression n `%` `NumBits` tells us how many positions to shift 1 to the left to align with n's bit position within the current array component:

```
elttype mask = (elttype)1 << (n % NumBits);
```

Next, we AND `bits [j]` with the mask and return 1 if the resulting value is not 0:

```
int z = bits[j] & mask;
return z != 0;
```

Suppose that the array contained the following values and we wanted to check bit 17:

The bits[] Array

```
        bit 17
          ↓
00000010 10000110 00000000
  [2]       [1]       [0]
```

Using the sample values, the calculations would proceed as follows:

```
j = 17 / 8
  = 2

mask = 1 << (17 % 8)
     = 1 << 1
     = 2

z = bits[2] & 2
  = 2                    // answer: bit 17 is set
```

The foregoing steps can be folded into a single expression that isolates bit n, shown here in the implementation of the Test function:

```
int BitArray::Test( size_t n ) const
{
  if( n >= size )
    throw RangeError(__FILE__,__LINE__,n);

  int z = bits[n / NumBits] & ((elttype)1 << n % NumBits);
  return z != 0;
}
```

Similarly, the Toggle function reverses a single bit at position n by XORing it with 1:

```
void BitArray::Toggle( size_t n )
{
  if( n >= size )
    throw RangeError(__FILE__,__LINE__,n);

  bits[n / NumBits] ^= ((elttype)1 << n % NumBits);
}
```

The Set function sets a single bit at position n:

```
void BitArray::Set( size_t n )
{
  if( n >= size )
    throw RangeError(__FILE__,__LINE__,n);

  bits[n / NumBits] |= ((elttype)1 << n % NumBits);
}
```

The stream output operator incorporates the Test operation into translating the bit array into a string of 1 and 0 characters:

```
ostream & operator <<( ostream & os, const BitArray & BA )
{
  for(size_t i = BA.size; 0 < i;)
    os << (BA.Test(--i) ? '1':'0');
  return os;
}
```

9.3.4 Testing the BitArray Class

A short program that tests the `BitArray` class is shown in Example 9-6. Here, we will discuss a few highlights of the program. First, `main` calls several test funtions, enclosing the calls in a `try` block. This permits the program to catch the two types of exceptions that can be thrown:

```
int main()
{
  try {
    Test1();
    Test2();
    Test3();
    Test4();
  }
  catch( const RangeError & re ) {
    cout << re;
  }
  catch( const NoFileError & nf ) {
    cout << nf;
  }
  return 0;
}
```

The following statements assign a bit-mapped long integer to a `BitArray` object and display the bits:

```
BitArray X( 20 );
X = (1 + 4 + 8 + 32 + 128 + 1024 );
cout << X << '\n';
```

The following statements set and reset bit 12 in `BitArray X`:

```
X.Set( 12 );
cout << X << '\n';
X.Reset( 12 );
cout << X << '\n';
```

The following statements find the union and intersection of `BitArray` objects A and B:

Example 9-6. Test Program for the BitArray Class

```
#include <iostream.h>
#include <iomanip.h>
#include <fstream.h>
#include <conio.h>
#include "bitarray.h"
#include "fstring.h"
#include "nofile.h"    // NoFileError exception class


void Test1()
{
  // Assign a long integer to a BitArray.

  BitArray X( 20 );
  X = (1 + 4 + 8 + 32 + 128 + 1024 );
  cout << X << '\n';

  // Set and reset an individual bit.

  X.Set( 12 );
  cout << X << '\n';
  X.Reset( 12 );
  cout << X << '\n';
}

void Test2()
{
  // Read a string of bits from a file.

  FString fileName( "bits.txt" );

  cout << "Reading file: " << fileName << '\n';
  ifstream bfile( fileName );
  if( !bfile ) throw NoFileError( fileName );

  BitArray filebits(16);
  bfile >> filebits;
  cout << filebits << '\n';
}

void Test3()
{
  // Add several integers to a set.
```

Example 9-6 *(cont.)*

```cpp
const size_t SetSize = 16;
BitArray B( SetSize );
B.Set(1);    // add several elements
B.Set(5);
B.Set(8);
B.Set(15);

cout << '\n'
     << "BitArray B:     " << B << '\n';

// Test for set membership.

for( int i = 0; i < SetSize; i++ )
  if( B.Test(i) )
    cout << setw(2) << i << " is a member" << '\n';

// Perform union and intersection operations.

BitArray A( SetSize );
A.Set(3);
A.Set(4);
A.Set(9);
cout << "\nBitArray B:     " << B
     << "\nBitArray A:     " << A;

A |= B;
cout << "\nA union B:      " << A;

A.Toggle(4);
cout << "\nToggled bit 4: " << A << '\n';
}

void Test4()
{
  // Create a room scheduling application, and
  // determine which rooms are both requested
  // and available.

  enum { _101,_110,_112,_114,_120,_190,_192,_200,
         _201,_205,_208,_210,_220,_221,_225,_230 };

  const size_t RoomMax = 16;

  BitArray rooms( RoomMax );
  rooms.Set(_101 );
```

Example 9-6 *(cont.)*

```
  rooms.Set(_110 );
  rooms.Set(_120 );
  rooms.Set(_220 );
  rooms.Set(_221 );
  rooms.Set(_225 );
  cout << "\nrooms:              " << rooms;

  BitArray requests( RoomMax );
  requests.Set(_101);
  requests.Set(_110);
  requests.Set(_120);
  requests.Set(_225);
  requests.Set(_230);
  cout << "\nrequests:           " << requests;

  BitArray approved( RoomMax );
  approved |= requests;        // union
  approved &= rooms;           // intersection
  cout << "\nrequests approved: " << approved
       << endl;
}

int main()
{
  cout << "Examples using the BitArray class."
       << endl;

  try {
   Test1();
   Test2();
   Test3();
   Test4();
  }
  catch( const RangeError & re ) {
    cout << re;
  }
  catch( const NoFileError & nf ) {
    cout << nf;
  }
  return 0;
}
```

```
A |= B;   // Union of A and B.
A &= B;   // Intersection of A and B.
```

A `BitArray` called `filebits` is read from an input file stream and displayed on the screen:

```
ifstream bfile( filename );
//...
BitArray filebits(16);
bfile >> filebits;
cout << filebits << '\n';
```

The `Test4` function in the test program simulates the scheduling of college classrooms. We create an array called `rooms`, and set individual bits matching rooms that happen to be available:

```
enum { _101,_110,_112,_114,_120,_190,_192,_200,
       _201,_205,_208,_210,_220,_221,_225,_230 };

const size_t RoomMax = 16;

BitArray rooms( RoomMax );
rooms.Set(_101);
rooms.Set(_110);
rooms.Set(_120);
rooms.Set(_220);
rooms.Set(_221);
rooms.Set(_225);
```

Similarly, we construct a `BitArray` called `requests` that represents requests for available rooms that could be used for college courses. We then form a third `BitArray` called `approved` that represents the intersection between available and requested rooms:

```
BitArray requests( RoomMax );
requests.Set(_101);
requests.Set(_110);
requests.Set(_120);
requests.Set(_225);
requests.Set(_230);

BitArray approved( RoomMax );
approved |= requests;          // union
approved &= rooms;             // intersection
```

9.4 CHAPTER SUMMARY

Operator overloading permits us to ascribe new meaning to standard operators. C++ allows both unary and binary operators to be overloaded as either member or non-member functions. It is important to associate an operator with an operator that is consistent with the way the operator is used with other objects.

An operator function can be a non-static member function, or it can be a non-member function having at least one parameter whose type is a class, reference to a class, an enumeration, or a reference to an enumeration.

Whenever possible, operator functions should be class members because operations performed on instances of the class should be encapsulated there. However, if making an operator a member function would result in awkward expressions involving the operator, we make an exception to the rule.

A cast operator is absolutely required when converting from a class type to a basic (predefined) type such as `int`, `float`, or `double`. A constructor with a single argument will always be used by the compiler for implicit conversions.

We created a `Time` class, in which the unary `++` and `--` operators were overloaded, and range checking was performed on minute and hour values.

We showed how overloaded operators could be used to improve the `FString` class, by allowing the concatenation and assignment of strings.

In this chapter, we explained how the standard bitwise operators work on unsigned integers: `<<` (left shift), `>>` (right shift), `|` (OR), `&` (AND), `~` (NOT), and `^` (XOR).

We created the `BitArray` class, modeled after the `<bitset>` class in the C++ Draft Standard. This class has operator functions for performing unions, intersections, adding elements, and removing elements.

9.5 EXERCISES

9.5.1 Miscellaneous

1 The Point Class.   In previous chapters we demonstrated the `Point` class, which defines the location of a point on a two-dimensional cartesian plane. Design and implement a `Point` class that includes the subtract (`-`) operator function for finding the distance between two points. Also, include a conversion function that converts a point to a C-style string (`char *`). Write a program to test your revised `Point` class.

2 The LongMatrix Class.   Create a class called `LongMatrix` that contains an array of `LongArray` objects. Add an operator function that multiplies two matrices. For example,

```
LongMatrix A;
LongMatrix B;
LongMatrix C;
   .

   .

C = A * B;
```

Define a stream input function and stream output function. Write a test program that initializes two or more `LongMatrix` objects by reading them from a file, adds them, multiplies them, and writes them to both the screen and a disk file.

Let's say that we want to multiply matrices A and B, producing C. Matrix A has m rows and n columns, and matrix B has n rows and p columns. We will assume that the number of columns in A matches the number of rows in B. Rows and columns are numbered starting at zero. Each element in C (called *Cij*) is the product of the ith row of A and the jth column of B:

```
c[i][j] = 0;
for(int k = 0; k < n; k++)
   c[i][j] += a[i][k] * b[k][j];
```

Using the following sample values in matrices A and B, matrix C would be calculated as

A			**B**		**C**	
1	2	3	1	4	14	32
4	5	6	2	5	32	77
			3	6		

Row 0 of matrix C was calculated as follows:

```
1*1 + 2*2 + 3*3          1*4 + 2*5 + 3*6
```

Row 1 of matrix C was calculated as follows:

```
4*1 + 5*2 + 6*3          4*4 + 5*5 + 6*6
```

3 Cast Operator with Temperatures. Create two classes: `Celsius` and `Fahrenheit`, each of which can hold a single temperature. Implement a cast operator in the `Fahrenheit` class that converts to `Celsius`, and implement a cast operator in `Celsius` that converts to `Fahrenheit`. Use statements such as the following to test your classes:

```
Fahrenheit F( 451 );
Celsius C;

C = F;              // cast to Celsius
C = (Celsius) F;    // same
C = Celsius(F);     // same
F = C;              // cast to Fahrenheit
```

Use the following class definitions as a starting point, and add operators for stream I/O:

```
class Fahrenheit;

class Celsius  {
public:
  Celsius( float n = 0.0 );

  operator Fahrenheit();
  // Cast into a Fahrenheit object.

private:
  float temp;
};

class Fahrenheit {
public:
  Fahrenheit( float n = 0.0 );

  operator Celsius();
  // Cast into a Celsius object.

private:
  float temp;
};
```

Notice that Fahrenheit had to be forward-declared, so that its name could be used in the Celsius class definition.

4 The Transcript Class.   In Section 9.1.7, the Transcript class contained both a copy constructor and an assignment operator function. We pointed out that duplicate code exists in these functions:

```
Transcript::Transcript( const Transcript & T )
{
  count = T.count;
  courses = new FString[MaxCourse];
  for(unsigned i = 0; i < count; i++)
    courses[i] = T.courses[i];
}

Transcript & Transcript::operator =( const Transcript & T )
{
  if( this != &T )          // not the same object?
  {
    delete [] courses;
```

```
      count = T.count;
      courses = new FString[MaxCourse];
      for(unsigned i = 0; i < count; i++)
        courses[i] = T.courses[i];
    }
    return *this;
  }
```

Create a new private member function called `MakeCopy` that contains the identical code. Let this function be called by both the copy constructor and `operator =`. Test the class by writing a short program that uses these operators.

9.5.2 Student Registration Application

The exercises in this section have to do with the Student Registration application program that was first introduced in Chapter 2, and then developed in the exercises of subsequent chapters.

    1 The StudentTable Class.   Create a class called `StudentTable` that contains an array of `Student` objects. Include a data member that keeps track of the number of students in the table, since the constructor will allow each instance of a `StudentTable` to be a different size. Define a subscript operator so that students can be retrieved and modified by a client program (be sure to perform range checking on the subscript). Finally, `StudentTable` should contain an `Append` function that appends students to the array. Write a test program that reads a list of students from a file, appends them to a `StudentTable`, and accesses students using the subscript operator.

    2 Searching a StudentTable.   Using the `StudentTable` class from the previous exercise, implement a `Find` function that accepts a student ID and returns a reference to a `Student` object. Write a test program that reads a list of students from a file and appends them to a table. The program should prompt the user for a student ID number, search for the student, and display the student if found. Let the user search for students repeatedly until a blank student ID is entered.

    3 Sorting the StudentTable.   Using the `StudentTable` class from the previous two exercises, add a `Sort` function that sorts the table. Implement the table as an array of pointers to students. Write a test program that reads a table from a disk file, sorts the table, and writes it to another disk file. If possible, use the *quickSort* algorithm to do the sort.

    4 Students with Arrays of Courses.   Using the `Student` class from previous exercises, add an array of `FString` objects to each `Student` object, containing the names of the courses the student has taken. Each student will have taken a different number of courses, so the array must be allocated dynamically when the student record is read from a file. Write a test program that reads ten or more students from a file, each containing a variable-length list of zero to eight courses. Display all Student objects on the console.

5 Students with Disabilities.   The following Student and StudentRecord classes will be used as a basis for this exercise, along with the VString class presented in Section 7.5.1. Add more member functions as needed:

```
class Student {
public:
  Student( const VString& stNum,
           const VString& lName,
           const VString& fName );
  virtual ~Student();
  virtual void print_on( ostream & os );

private:
  VString stuNum;
  VString lastName;
  VString firstName;
};

class StudentRecord :public Student {
public:
  StudentRecord( const VString& stNum,
      const VString& lName, const VString& fName,
           unsigned cred, float grPts);
  ~StudentRecord();
  void print_on( ostream & os );
  float gpa();

private:
  unsigned credits;    // credits earned
  float    gradePts;   // grade points
};
```

Add a data member to StudentRecord called disability, which is a BitArray object. The enumerated type to be used for this set should at least contain the following, with any additional enumerators you would like to add:

```
enum DisabilityEnum { visual, hearing, speech };
```

Include a member function called AddDisability that allows values to be added to the disability set, and another called CheckDisability that returns 1 if a particular disability is a member of the student's disability set. Modify the printOn member function so that it displays any disabilities the student has (as integers). Write a test program that initializes several StudentRecord objects, adds disability information to each, and writes the records to an output stream.

Optional enhancements:

a. Instead of displaying student disabilities as integers, display them as strings, such as "hearing impaired", "visually impaired", and so on.

b. Read a text file containing ten or more student records into an array of `StudentRecord` objects. Count the number of students with each type of disability and display the counts at the end of the program.

9.5.3 The BitArray Class

1 Set Comparison.   Implement an operator `==` function in the `BitArray` class that returns 1 if two sets are identical. Also, implement an operator – function that returns a new set C containing all the elements in A that are not also in B (called the *set difference*):

```
C = A - B;
```

CHAPTER 10

Templates

The introduction of templates into C++ created a sensation in the C++ community during the early 1990's because they greatly magnified the power of the language. Using templates, the compiler can generate new source code for functions and classes. Many excellent commercial C++ libraries were built using templates, so it is important to understand how they work.

Terms Introduced in this Chapter:

class template	generic class
dictionary	lookup table
function template	parameterized class
generated class	template
generated function	template parameters

10.1 INTRODUCTION

A *template* may be thought of as a blueprint, or framework for a function or class. C++ recognizes two types of templates: class templates and function templates. A *class template* is a framework for generating the source code for any number of related classes. Class templates are also called *generic classes* or *parameterized classes*. A *function template* is a framework for generating related functions.

When a C++ compiler uses a template to produce a new class, the result is called a *generated class*. Similarly, a function generated by a function template is called a *generated function.*

Function templates were added to the C++ language to relieve the programmer of the burden of having to write multiple versions of the same function just to carry out the same operation on different data types. In a function template, the data types of one or more of its parameters are themselves parameters. When the function is called, the data types of the arguments dictate the types of the function parameters. The compiler constructs a specific instance of the function, inserting the required type specifiers wherever they are needed.

Templates are a relatively new addition to C++, and have grown in stature to the point that the latest C++ standard specifies a Standard Template Library (STL). This library is implemented by a number of C++ compiler vendors, and it will probably be used by most professional C++ programmers.

Imagine creating a class that was custom-designed for a particular data type, such as an array of integers. You might also want to use the class with an array of float, but that would require duplicating the class's source code and changing all references from int to float. Class templates provide an elegant solution to this problem.

In a class template, data types are passed as *template parameters*. These parameters may be used both in the class definition and in the implementation of all member functions.

In this chapter we first show how to create function templates, using an example of a table lookup function. We also show how class templates are created, using an array class template as an example. Finally, we will present a class template in the form of a dictionary class that retrieves information using key values.

10.2 FUNCTION TEMPLATES

10.2.1 Introduction

A function template must have at least one type parameter, but it can have more. The format for a function template having only a single template parameter is

```
template<class T>
return-type function-name( T param )
```

T is called a *template parameter* because it refers to a data type that will be supplied when the function is called. T must also be used as the data type of at least one function parameter. The following is an example:

```
template <class T>
void Display( const T & val )
{
  cout << val;
}
```

A function template can have additional parameters which are not template parameters. For example,

```
template <class T>
void Display( const T & val, ostream & os )
{
  os << val;
}
```

The same template parameter may also appear multiple times in the function's parameter list. The following template exchanges the values of two variables:

```
template <class TParam>
void Swap( TParam & x, TParam & y )
{
  //...
}
```

There can be multiple template parameters, each of which must appear at least once in the function's parameter list. In the following example, T1 and T2 are template parameters and can represent different types:

```
template <class T1, T2>
void MyTemplate( T1 x, T2 y )
{
  //...
}
```

10.2.1.1 Example: The Swap Function.   The function template called Swap exchanges the values of two objects, regardless of their type. This is a handy function in programs that perform sorting operations, for example:

```
template <class TParam>
void Swap( TParam & x, TParam & y )
{
  TParam temp;
  temp = x;
  x = y;
  y = temp;
}
```

If objects are passed to this template, they must be capable of being copied correctly by the = operator. Particularly if the objects contain pointers, the definition of an operator = function in their class is mandatory.

A generated function is only created when the function template is called in user code. For example, the following calls to Swap cause two separate instances of the function to be generated:

```
int m, n;
Student S1;
Student S2;
//...
Swap( m, n );       // call with integers
Swap( S1, S2 );     // call with Students
```

The two generated functions (which we never actually see) are

```
void Swap( int & x, int & y )
{
   int temp;
   temp = x;
   x = y;
   y = temp;
}

void Swap( Student & x, Student & y )
{
   Student temp;
   temp = x;
   x = y;
   y = temp;
}
```

There is an important difference between using macros, a mainstay of the C language, and templates: Macros rely on text substitution performed by the C preprocessor, with no type checking of macro arguments. Template arguments, on the other hand, are checked for correct syntax and semantics by the C++ compiler before any generated functions are created.

10.2.1.2 Multiple Template Parameters.   Let's create a function template with multiple template parameters. In the next example, T1 and T2 both appear in the ArrayInput parameter list. T1 is assumed to be an array and T2 is an integral type:

```
template <class T1, class T2>
void ArrayInput( T1 array, T2 & count )
{
   for(T2 j = 0; j < count; j++)
```

```
        {
          cout << "Value: ";
          cin >> array[j];
        }
     }

     const unsigned tempCount = 3;
     float temperature[TempCount];

     const unsigned stationCount = 4;
     int station[stationCount];

     // T1 = float *, T2 = unsigned
     ArrayInput( temperature, tempCount );

     // T1 = int *, T2 = unsigned
     ArrayInput( station, stationCount );
```

10.2.1.3 Declaring Templates.   A function template should be placed in a header that is included in a source program ahead of any statements that call the function. Suppose the `ArrayInput` template were stored in the `array.h` header. Then, a program calling the function would have the following statement sequence:

```
     #include array.h
     //...

     const unsigned tempCount = 50;
     float temperatures[tempCount];
     ArrayInput( temperatures, tempCount );
```

10.2.2 Example: Table Lookup

A practical template function is one that performs a table lookup. Due to the flexibility of templates, a table lookup can be performed on tables containing different types of objects.

For example, the following `indexOf` function scans an array for a single value, returning the index of the first matching entry or -1 if a match is not found:

```
template <class T>
long indexOf(const T & searchVal, const T * table, unsigned size)
{
   for(unsigned i = 0; i < size; i++)
      if( searchVal == table[i] )
         return i;
   return -1;
}
```

Of course, any type T object passed to this template must recognize the == operator.

We could call indexOf by passing it a float along with an array of float; we might also do the same for integers:

```
const unsigned iCount = 10;
const unsigned fCount = 5;

int iTable[iCount] = { 0,10,20,30,40,50,60,70,80,90 };
float fTable[fCount] = { 1.1, 2.2, 3.3, 4.4, 5.5 };

cout << indexOf( 20, iTable, iCount )  << '\n'
     << indexOf( 2.2f, fTable, fCount ) << endl;
```

10.2.2.1 Argument Matching. C++ has a specific way of matching template parameters: The first parameter appearing in a function call dictates the data type of the corresponding template parameter. For example, when we pass a double as the first argument to indexOf, T is replaced by double. When T is replaced, the second parameter becomes a pointer to double. The processing of type parameters is by first use, rather than by any attempt at "best fit":

```
long indexOf(const T & searchVal,const T* table,unsigned size);
//...

const unsigned fCount = 5;
float fTable[fCount];
double x = 2.2;
cout << indexOf( x, fTable, fCount );
```

The following function would be generated and the second parameter would not match the data type of fTable. A syntax error would result:

```
long indexOf(const double & searchVal, const double* table,
             unsigned size)
```

A solution is to use two different template parameters, T1 and T2, so searchVal and table can be different types:

```
template <class T1, class T2>
long indexOf(const T1 & searchVal, const T2 * table,
    unsigned size)
{
  //...
}
```

10.2.2.2 Pointer Arguments. An easy trap to fall into is the one that appears when a function template uses relational and/or equality operators. Not all objects can be meaningfully compared. For example, what if we call `indexOf`, passing it an array of C-style strings? The following function call returns -1 (no match found):

```
const unsigned nameCount = 5;
char * names[nameCount] = { "John","Mary","Sue","Dan","Bob" };
cout << indexOf( "Dan", names, nameCount );
```

The problem here is that `indexOf` is comparing pointers, not the strings they point to. It's easier to see this if we manually substitute `char*` for T:

```
long indexOf( const char * & searchVal, const char ** table,
              unsigned size )
{
  for(unsigned i = 0; i < size; i++)
    if( searchVal == table[i] )   // compare pointers?
      return i;
  return -1;
}
```

As a general rule, we must implement the == operator in any class that we plan to pass to this function template. For example, here is an abbreviated version of the `Student` class, showing the implementation of the `operator ==` function:

```
class Student {
public:
  Student( long idVal );
  int operator ==( const Student & S2 ) const
  {
    return id == S2.id;
  }
private:
  long id;
  //...
};
```

Next, we create `sTable`, a table of `Student` objects, pass it to `indexOf`, and display the return value:

```
const unsigned sCount = 5;
Student sTable[sCount] = { 10000, 11111, 20000, 22222, 30000 };
Student s( 22222 );
cout << indexOf( s, sTable, sCount );      // '3'
```

10.2.3 Explicit Function Implementations

Depending on the argument types passed to a function template, the generated function may not be useful; this was the case when we tried to pass C-style strings to the `indexOf` function template. A possible remedy is to create an explicit function that overrides the template, as we do here for `indexOf`:

```
long indexOf( const char * searchVal, const char * table[],
              unsigned size )
{
  for(unsigned i = 0; i < size; i++)
    if( strcmp(searchVal, table[i]) == 0 )
      return i;
  return -1;
}
```

This version of `indexOf` is called only when the passed arguments are an exact match to the function parameters. The reason we can use an explicit function is because of the way the compiler searches for a matching function when a function is called. The following sequence of steps is followed:

1. Search for an exact match of the function call arguments to an existing function signature. Note that a non-constant argument is considered an exact match with a const-qualified parameter. For example, a `char *` argument matches a `const char *` parameter.

2. Search for a function template from which a function can be generated with exactly matching arguments.

3. Use function overloading resolution, with implicit conversions (discussed in Section 3.4). This could include standard conversions, such as `int` to `float`, or conversions using cast operators in classes.

Of course, the greater the number of overloaded versions of a function exist, the more time one spends on program maintenance. That is why function templates should be used whenever possible.

10.3 CLASS TEMPLATES

Class templates offer the ability to generate new classes, just as function templates generate new functions. We're most interested in using class templates in those cases where we would otherwise be forced to create multiple classes with the same attributes and operations. The most common types of templates are container classes, such as arrays, lists, and sets. As templates, each of these classes could work with a variety of data types. The basic format for defining a class template with one parameter is

```
template <class T>
class MyClass {
  //...
};
```

The template parameter T can be either a type or an expression. For example, we might pass different data types to the template, creating two different classes:

```
MyClass<int>     X;
MyClass<Student> aStudent;
```

A class template can have multiple parameters, as in the following Circle template example, which has parameters T1 and T2:

```
template<class T1, class T2>
class Circle {
  //...
private:
  T1 x;
  T1 y;
  T2 radius;
};


//...
Circle<int, long>  C;
Circle<unsigned, float> D;
```

Let us design our first class template by solving a common problem, manipulating arrays.

10.3.1 Example: Array Class Template

In our discussions of operator overloading in Chapter 9, we presented the LongArray class that encapsulated an array of long integers. Here is a simplified version of the class:

```
class LongArray {
public:
  LongArray( unsigned sz );
  ~LongArray();
  long & operator[]( unsigned i );

private:
  long * values;
  unsigned size;
};
```

But, if we needed an array of float, we would have to duplicate the LongArray class, give it another name, and change the internal data type from int to float:

```
class FloatArray {
public:
  FloatArray( unsigned sz );
  ~FloatArray();
  float & operator[]( unsigned i );

private:
  float * values;
  unsigned size;
};
```

When we compare the two classes (LongArray and FloatArray), very little difference is seen between their class definitions (we highlighted them in FloatArray). This provides an incentive for creating a class template called Array:

```
template <class T>
class Array {
public:
  Array( unsigned sz );
  ~Array();
  T & operator[]( unsigned i );

private:
  T * values;
  unsigned size;
};
```

The compiler uses the class template to generate specific variants of the Array class. We declare the arrays by appending the data type (in brackets) to the Array template name:

```
Array<int>      X;   // array of int
Array<float>    Y;   // array of float
Array<FString>  Z;   // array of fixed-length strings
Array<Point>    W;   // array of graphic points
```

The Array class template uses the identifier T as a type argument, so T is replaced by a specific data type in each generated class. The compiler generates each of these classes on an "as needed" basis. So, if we declared a class template that was never used, the compiler would just leave it out of the executable program.

10.3.1.1 Array Class Implementation.
Out-of-line member functions appear in the same header as the template class definition. The name of the class is written as Array<T>. Here is the class constructor, for example, that allocates dynamic storage for the data member holding the array values:

```
template<class T>
Array<T>::Array( unsigned sz )
{
  values = new T[sz];
  size = sz;
}
```

Notice that the first line is identical to the first line of the class template: "template<class T>". Here is the implementation of the [] operator, with exception handling included:

```
template<class T>
T & Array<T>::operator[] ( unsigned i )
{
  if( i >= size )
    throw RangeError(__FILE__,__LINE__,i);
  return values[i];
}
```

Here is the destructor implementation:

```
template<class T>
Array<T>::~Array()
{
  delete [] values;
}
```

10.3.1.2 Sample Program.   Let's look at a short program that uses the Array class template. We create three arrays for a springboard diving competition: diveNum (array of int), difficulty (array of float), and diveName (array of FString). Each array has five members. The program inputs five sets of data from the user and redisplays the dive names:

```
#include "array.h"      // Array class template
#include "fstring.h"    // FString class declaration

int main()
{
  const unsigned numDives = 5;

  Array<int>      diveNum( numDives );
  Array<float>    difficulty( numDives );
  Array<FString>  diveName( numDives );

  int j;
  for(j = 0; j < numDives; j++)
  {
    cout << "Enter dive #, difficulty level, dive name ";
```

```
        cin >> diveNum[j] >> difficulty[j] >> ws;
        diveName[j].GetLine( cin );
    }

    for(j = 0; j < numDives; j++)
        cout << diveName[j] << '\n';
    cout << endl;

    return 0;
}
```

Alternatively, we could place the three arrays inside a class called DiveList:

```
class DiveList {
//...
private:
    enum { numDives = 5 };
    Array<int>     diveNum( numDives );
    Array<float>   difficulty( numDives );
    Array<FString> diveName( numDives );
};
```

Or, we could create an array of Dive objects, assuming that each dive has an ID number, difficulty level, and name:

```
class Dive {
//...
private:
    int     diveNum;
    float   difficulty;
    FString diveName;
};

const unsigned numDives = 5;

Array<Dive> diveList( numDives );
```

In each case, we used the Array class template only with classes having simple copy semantics. To insert class variables containing pointer members, we would have to provide appropriate copy constructor and assignment operator functions.

10.3.2 FTString Class Template

We first introduced the FString (fixed string) class in Chapter 4 as a convenient way to deal with string assignment, copying, input, and output. The class was easy to implement, but we had to compromise in one respect—all strings had to be the same length. In practice, this can be a waste of memory, since some strings (such as a ZIP Code) are shorter than others.

One alternative is to use a class template to generate strings of specific sizes. Whereas the `Array` class template had a data type as its template parameter, the `FTString` class template has an unsigned integer parameter that specifies the string length. The parameter `MaxSize` is of type `size_t`, which is an unsigned integer:

```
#include <iostream.h>
#include <iomanip.h>
#include <string.h>
#include "range.h"

template <size_t MaxSize>
class FTString {
public:
  FTString();

  FTString( const char * s );

  void GetLine( istream & inp );

  int Length() const;

  FTString & operator =( const char * s );

  operator char *();

  int operator ==( const FTString & s2 ) const;

  friend istream & operator >>( istream & inp,
        FTString<MaxSize> & s )
  { /*...*/ }
  friend ostream & operator <<( ostream & os,
        const FTString<MaxSize> & s )
  { /*...*/ }
private:
  char str[MaxSize+1];
};
```

When declaring `FTString` objects, we supply a length argument so that each declaration generates a different class:

```
FTString<30> name;
FTString<40> street;
FTString<15> city;
FTString<2>  state;
FTString<5>  zip;
```

A disadvantage to this approach is that each of the above generates a separate class, increasing the program's compiled code size. We would ordinarily try to limit the number of different FTString classes in order to avoid this problem. It should also be pointed out that FTString objects of different sizes cannot be compared to each other, using operators such as ==, <, or >.

The constructor implementations from FTString are shown here. We throw a RangeError exception if an attempt is made to copy a longer string into a shorter one:

```
template<size_t MaxSize>
FTString<MaxSize>::FTString()
{
   str[0] = '\0';
}

template<size_t MaxSize>
FTString<MaxSize>::FTString( const char * s )
{
   size_t n = strlen(s);
   if( n >= MaxSize )
     throw RangeError(__FILE__,__LINE__,n);
   strcpy( str, s );
}
```

The remaining member functions appear with the complete class listing in Appendix A.

10.4 DICTIONARY CLASS TEMPLATE

10.4.1 Dictionary Class Template

A great many application programs use a data structure called a *dictionary* or *lookup table,* in which one can use a key value to retrieve its associated data value. For example, we might want to associate automobile part numbers with the names of corresponding parts:

```
        Keys              Values

        100000 --->       tire
        100001 --->       wheel
        100002 --->       distributor
        100003 --->       air filter
```

A dictionary can be implemented as a class template, which we will call Dictionary. Because this is a class template, the dictionary keys and values can be a variety of types. The `Dictionary` template is declared with the template parameters `TKey` and `TVal`. Its data members include an array of keys and an array of associated values. The `keys` array can be searched to find a matching value from the `values` array. `TKey` and `TVal` can be any classes or data types that define the `=` and `==` operators, and the `<<` operator for stream output:

```
template<class TKey, class TVal>
class Dictionary {
public:
  Dictionary( unsigned maxEntries );
  ~Dictionary();

  int Add( const TKey & tk, const TVal & tv );
  // Add new key and value to dictionary.

  int Find( const TKey & tk );
  // If a key matching tk is found, set current to
  // the key's location and return 1. Otherwise,
  // return 0.

  int IsFull() const;
  // Return 1 if the dictionary is full, 0 otherwise.

  TVal Get() const;
  // Retrieve a copy of value at current key position.

  friend ostream & operator <<( ostream & os,
          const Dictionary<TKey, TVal> & D );

private:
  TKey * keys;        // array of dictionary keys
  TVal * values;      // array of dictionary values
  unsigned avail;     // index of next unused element
  unsigned size;      // size of the arrays
  unsigned current;   // current index position
};
```

The `Dictionary` class includes such fundamental operations such as `Find`, `Add`, `Get`, `IsFull`, and stream output.

The data member `current` holds the index position of the last attempted search for a key value. If `TKey` is a class rather than an intrinsic data type, it must implement the comparison (`==`) operator.

10.4.2 Creating a Dictionary

To create a `Dictionary` object, one must supply two template arguments: the first is the type of the keys; the second is the type of the values associated with the keys.

Here are some examples: D1 is a dictionary that can hold up to 50 integer keys associated with long integer values; D2 can hold up to 20 long integer keys associated
with FString values; and, D3 associates 100 FString keys with long integers:

```
#include "dict.h"      // Dictionary template
#include "fstring.h"   // FString class

Dictionary<int, long> D1( 50 );
Dictionary<long, FString> D2( 20 );
Dictionary<FString, long> D3( 100 );
```

10.4.3 Dictionary Class Implementation

Because Dictionary is a class template, its implementation appears in the same
source file as the definition. A complete listing of the Dictionary class template
can be found in Appendix A.

The constructor allocates arrays for the keys and values arrays (type TKey
and TVal). The other data members, avail, size, and current, identify (1) the
next available array position, (2) the maximum index of any key that can be stored
in the dictionary, and (3) the current index position after a Find operation:

```
template<class TKey,class TVal>
Dictionary<TKey,TVal>::Dictionary( unsigned maxEntries )
{
  keys = new TKey[ maxEntries+1 ];
  values = new TVal[ maxEntries+1 ];
  avail = 0;
  size = maxEntries;
  current = 0;
}
```

The destructor deletes the keys and values arrays:

```
template<class TKey, class TVal>
Dictionary<TKey,TVal>::~Dictionary()
{
  delete [] keys;
  delete [] values;
}
```

The Find function uses a simple sequential lookup to locate a given key in the
keys array. It returns 1 if successful, or 0 if the key was not found. It also updates
current:

```
template<class TKey,class TVal>
int Dictionary<TKey,TVal>::Find( const TKey & tk )
{
  for(unsigned i = 0; i < avail; i++)
    if( tk == keys[i] )
    {
      current = i;    // save current position
      return 1;
    }
  return 0;   // no matching key found
}
```

The Add function accepts two arguments: the key being inserted, and its associated value. The arguments are based on the TKey and TVal data types:

```
template<class TKey,class TVal>
int Dictionary<TKey,TVal>::Add( const TKey & tk,
                                const TVal & tv )
{
  if( !Find( tk ) ) // not already in dictionary?
  {
    if(IsFull())              // dictionary full?
      throw DictionaryFull();
    unsigned i = avail++;  // save position
    keys[i] = tk;             // add new key
    values[i] = tv;           // add associated value
    return 1;                 // success!
  }
  throw DuplicateKey(); // attempt to add duplicate key
}
```

We throw two types of exceptions from the Add member function. The first, called DictionaryFull, is thrown when no more keys can be added:

```
class DictionaryFull {
public:
  friend ostream & operator <<(ostream & os,
        const DictionaryFull & F)
  {
    os << "Dictionary is full.";
    return os;
  }
};
```

A `DuplicateKey` exception is thrown when one tries to add the same key to a
`Dictionary` more than once:

```
class DuplicateKey {
public:
  friend ostream & operator <<(ostream & os,
        const DuplicateKey & F)
  {
    os << "Attempt to add duplicate key.";
    return os;
  }
};
```

The stream output function outputs each of the key and value pairs to the console. This will work only if both data types recognize the stream output operator:

```
template<class TKey, class TVal>
ostream & operator <<( ostream & os,
        const Dictionary<TKey, TVal> & D )
{
  for(unsigned i = 0; i < D.avail; i++)
    cout << D.keys[i] << " -> "
          << D.values[i] << '\n';

  return os;
}
```

The `Dictionary` class could contain a number of other useful functions, which will
be suggested in the exercises at the end of the chapter.

10.4.4 Demonstration Program

In a demonstration program (see Example 10-1) for the `Dictionary` class that
we've created, two dictionaries are created: the first is a list of customer accounts,
and the second is a list of automobile parts.
    We declare a `Dictionary` object that can hold as many as 100 customer ac-
counts, add some entries, and display the dictionary. The customer accounts dictionary associates account numbers with file record numbers:

```
Dictionary<unsigned, long> accounts( 100 );
cout << "Customer Accounts:\n";

try {
  accounts.Add( 101, 287 );
  accounts.Add( 152, 368 );
  accounts.Add( 173, 401 );
```

```
    accounts.Add( 185, 368 ); // duplicate value is ok
    accounts.Add( 152, 399 ); // duplicate key forbidden
  }
catch( const DuplicateKey & dk ) {
  cout << dk << endl;
}
cout << accounts << endl;  // display the list
```

By handling the `DuplicateKey` exception here, the program can recover from the error without having to back up to `main`.

To find an account number, we assign it to a variable and call the `Find` function. It returns 1 if successful, and sets the dictionary's internal pointer to the matching dictionary value (which is returned by `Get`):

```
          cout << "Account number to find? ";
          unsigned n;
          cin >> n;
          if( accounts.Find( n ))
            cout << "Account number " << n
                 << " may be found at record "
                 << accounts.Get() << '.' << endl;
          //...
```

10.4.4.1 *Automobile Parts Dictionary.*   The Automobile Parts Dictionary associates part numbers with part descriptions. First, we open an input file containing the keys and values to be added to the dictionary:

```
          FString filename( "parts.txt" );
          ifstream infile( filename );
          if( !infile ) throw NoFileError( filename );
```

A `NoFileError` exception is thrown if the input file cannot be opened, and control returns to `main`. Here is a sample `parts.txt` file read by the program:

```
100000 tire
100001 wheel
100002 distributor
100003 air filter
100004 carburetor
100005 fuel pump
100006 flywheel
100007 clutch plate
```

Example 10-1. Dictionary Test Program

```
#include <iostream.h>
#include <fstream.h>
#include <except.h>  // xalloc exception
#include "dict.h"    // Dictionary class
#include "fstring.h" // FString class
#include "nofile.h"  // NoFileError Exception class

// Create a Dictionary of customer account numbers
// (int) and file record numbers (long).

void create_customer_accounts()
{
  Dictionary<unsigned, long> accounts( 100 );
  cout << "Customer Accounts:\n";

  try {
    accounts.Add( 101, 287 );
    accounts.Add( 152, 368 );
    accounts.Add( 173, 401 );
    accounts.Add( 185, 368 ); // duplicate value is ok
    accounts.Add( 152, 399 ); // duplicate key forbidden
  }
  catch( const DuplicateKey & dk ) {
    cout << dk << endl;
  }
  cout << accounts << endl;  // display the list

  cout << "Account number to find? ";
  unsigned n;
  cin >> n;
  if( accounts.Find( n ))
    cout << "Account number " << n
         << " may be found at record "
         << accounts.Get() << '.' << '\n';
  else
    cout << "Account not found." << '\n';
  cout << endl;
}

// Create a dictionary of automobile part
// numbers (long) and part descriptions (String).

void create_parts_list()
```

Example 10-1 *(cont.)*

```
{
  FString filename( "parts.txt" );
  ifstream infile( filename );
  if( !infile ) throw NoFileError( filename );

  // Add part numbers and descriptions to a dictionary.

  unsigned long partNum;
  FString descrip;
  const unsigned plistSize = 200;

  cout << "Automobile parts list:\n";
  Dictionary<unsigned long, FString> pList( plistSize );

  try {
  infile >> partNum;
    while( !infile.eof())
    {
      descrip.GetLine( infile );
      pList.Add( partNum, descrip );
      infile >> partNum;
    }
  }
  catch( const DuplicateKey & dk ) {
    cout << dk << endl;
  }
  cout << pList;

  cout << "Part number to find? ";
  cin >> partNum;

  if( pList.Find( partNum ))
    cout <<
      "Part " << partNum << " is a "
          << pList.Get() << '.' << endl;
  else
    cout << "Part number not found." << endl;
}

// main: create two dictionaries, handle all
// uncaught exceptions.

int main()
```

Example 10-1 *(cont.)*

```
{
  cout << "Dictionary Template Demo Program\n\n";
  try {
    create_customer_accounts();
    create_parts_list();
  }
  catch ( xalloc ) {
    cout << "Memory allocation error\n";
  }
  catch ( const DictionaryFull & df ) {
    cout << df;
  }
  catch ( const NoFileError & nf ) {
    cout << nf;
  }
  catch ( ... ) {
    cout << "Unknown exception caught.\n";
  }
  return 0;
}
```

If the file is opened successfully, we create a `Dictionary` object and use a loop to read each part number and description from the file:

```
const unsigned plistSize = 200;

Dictionary<unsigned long, FString> pList(pListSize);

try {
  infile >> partNum;
  while( !infile.eof())
  {
    descrip.GetLine( infile );
    pList.Add( partNum, descrip );
    infile >> partNum;
  }
}
catch( const DuplicateKey & dk ) {
  cout << dk << endl;
}
```

We also display the dictionary:

```
        100000 -> tire
        100001 -> wheel
```

```
100002 -> distributor
100003 -> air filter
100004 -> carburetor
100005 -> fuel pump
100006 -> flywheel
100007 -> clutch plate
```

The user inputs a part number; the `Find` function searches the dictionary and displays the part's description if the part number is found:

```
Part number to find? 100005
Part 100005 is a fuel pump.
```

In `main`, it is important to catch any exceptions that have not already been caught at lower levels. This ensures a graceful program termination and cleanup if an exception is thrown:

```
int main()
{
  cout << "Dictionary Template Demo Program\n\n";
  try {
    create_customer_accounts();
    create_parts_list();
  }
  catch ( xalloc ) {
    cout << "Memory allocation error\n";
  }
  catch ( const DictionaryFull & df ) {
    cout << df;
  }
  // (etc.)
```

10.5 CHAPTER SUMMARY

A *function template* is a framework for a function that can adapt itself to the data types of the arguments passed to it. Function templates were added to the C++ language to relieve the programmer of the burden of having to write multiple versions of the same function just to carry out the same operation on different data types. The compiler generates instances of the function when the function is called. A function template must have at least one argument, and that argument must be used in the function.

A *class template* is a generic framework that forms the basis for creating specific classes. One of the major goals of class templates is to eliminate the needless duplication of effort that would be required if separate versions of the same class had to be written and maintained. The generated classes differ only in those places where the template parameters appear in the template source code. Function and class templates are ordinarily placed in headers that are included by programs that call the functions or create class objects.

We demonstrated a function template called `indexOf` that searches a table of any nonpointer data type. We explained how arguments are matched in function calls to arguments in function declarations, and we also showed how to create specific template functions when needed.

We presented an `Array` class template that could be useful in a wide range of applications. The `Array` template can hold a variety of data types, and performs range checking on subscripts, exception handling, and dynamic memory allocation. We showed how to use the `Array` template in the Springboard Diving Competition program. We also presented a fixed-string class template called `FTString` and a `Dictionary` class template that compared keys to their associated values. These class templates were used to show how class templates relieve programmers of the burden of having to write and maintain multiple versions of nearly identical classes.

When distributing software that uses templates, it is important to realize that class users need to have copies of all of your template source code. Unfortunately, this presents a temptation for users to tinker with the code, possibly introducing errors.

10.6 EXERCISES

10.6.1 Miscellaneous

1 The Max and Min Function Templates.   Create two simple and useful function templates:

Max   Return a reference to the larger of two objects.
Min   Return a reference the smaller of two objects.

Test the function by passing it predefined scalar types such as `int`. Pass it several types of class objects, including `FString`, `Student`, or other classes of your own design. Any type of object passed to this function must support the < and > operators, so you must implement these operators in your own classes.

10.6.2 Array Class Template

1 The Student Registration Program.   In the Student Registration program presented in Chapter 3, the `Registration` class contained an array of `Course` objects:

```
class Registration
{
  //...
  Course courses[10];
};
```

Now, we want to substitute the `Array` class template from the current chapter when declaring the `courses` array. Modify and test the program accordingly.

2 Array of Students.   Modify the Student Registration program from Chapter 3 by creating an array of students. Use the `Array` class template and generate a report that lists all of the students, and for each student, his/her list of courses.

3 Array of Robots.   The Robot Wars simulation program from Chapter 4 stored an array of robots in the `Grid` class. Modify this program by using the `Array` class template to implement the array of robots.

4 Array Subscript Ranges.   The `Array` class template currently requires all subscripts to be zero-based, meaning that the lowest subscript value is always 0. However, we would like the class to be more flexible. Modify the class so that subscripts can also be negative numbers. Let the class user pass the minimum and maximum subscript values to the class constructor:

```
Array( long min, long max );
// Construct an array with subscripts
// in the range [min..max].
```

5 The Doctor's Office Scheduling Program.   Chapter 5 contained a case study dealing with a Doctor's Office Scheduling program. The `DailySchedule` class contained an array of appointments declared as

```
Appointment appointments[MaxTimeSlots];
```

For this exercise, implement the `appointments` array with the `Array` class template. It should be declared as

```
class DailySchedule
{
  //...
  Array<Appointment> appointments;
};
```

Because the `Array` class constructor requires a single argument (the size of the array), we suggest that you add this argument to the member initialization list of the `DailySchedule` constructor.

6 Expanding an Array.   Modify the `Array` class template presented in this chapter so that it is expandable. Implement the `Grow` function and write a test program that demonstrates the function:

```
int Grow( int n );
// Expand the array by n positions. Return 1 if
// successful, 0 if not.
```

7 Matrix Class Template.   Create a class template for a two-dimensional array called `Matrix`. Implement a constructor, destructor, subscript operator, and stream output operators. Write a test program and create several `Matrix` objects that hold integers, strings, students, and so on.

10.6.3 Dictionary Class Template

1 The Dictionary::Find Function.   The `Dictionary` class template uses the `Find` function to update an internal variable called `current`, and the `Get` function to return the value at `values[current]`. Revise the class so that `Find` returns an index to the position where a given key is located. Then, modify the `Get(n)` function so that it returns the value at index position n. In the following example, `aDict.Get(n)` returns the value associated with key 1000:

```
int wasFound = 0;
unsigned n = aDict.Find( 1000, wasFound );
if( wasFound )
  cout << aDict.Get( n ) << endl;
```

2 Dictionary Value Search.   Rather than search for a key in a dictionary, it is sometimes useful to find the first key that matches a particular value. Add a function to the `Dictionary` class called `FirstKeyOf` that performs this operation:

```
TKey FirstKeyOf(TVal & v) const;
// Find the first key that matches the value
// contained in v. Set current position to the
// position of the key. Return 1 if successful,
// 0 if not.
```

3 Automatic Dictionary Expansion.   The `Dictionary` class template aborts the program if we try to add too many objects to the dictionary. A better approach would be to let the dictionary grow automatically, by a specified size increment. Write and test a member function that does this, with the following specification:

```
int Grow( int n );
// Attempt to increase the dictionary size by n elements.
// Return 1 if successful, 0 if not.
```

4 The Get Function.   The current implementation of `Dictionary::Get` returns a copy of the object at the current position. This choice was made in the interest of data security, to prevent class users from being able to directly modify dictionary values. This involves a trade-off, since it means that dictionaries containing large objects will incur the overhead of making temporary copies of objects when `Get` is called. Re-implement the `Get` function so that it returns a constant reference to a `TVal` object. Alter the test program supplied in this chapter so it will work with your modified `Dictionary` class.

5 The Remove Function.   One problem that we did not address in this chapter was that of removing dictionary entries. Add a function called `Remove` to the `Dictionary` class and add statements to the Dictionary Test program to make sure `Remove` works correctly. You may want to mark removed entries with a predefined key value, or you may want to slide subsequent dictionary entries forward to take up the space used by a removed entry. Justify your choice, citing the advantages and disadvantages of each approach.

6 Multi-Value Dictionary.   Make the `TVal` template parameter of the `Dictionary` class a `LongArray`. A single key should be associated with a list of values. For example, the `Dictionary` keys might be client ID numbers for a software consulting company; the values associated with each key might be job codes for tasks for each client. Here are some sample input data, where each row begins with a client ID and continues with the list of associated job codes:

ClientId	Job Codes
10000	49053, 49055, 50124
10001	36021, 36039, 49100, 51240

Write a program that implements such a dictionary, and add more data for client IDs and job codes, using the sample format. Client IDs and job codes should be unsigned long integers.

7 Nesting an Array Within a Dictionary.   Implement the previous exercise using the `Array` class template for the list of job codes. That is, each `TVal` in the dictionary is an `Array` template. This is how `clientList` could be declared:

```
Dictionary<long, Array<long> >  clientList;
```

8 Data Handles (Dictionary Application).   Multitasking computing environments must manage their own memory resources, and one of the difficulties in this lies in providing reliable access to data by application programs. Let's suppose that variable `P` is a pointer to data allocated at address `N`. But, in the process of reorganizing memory, the data at addresss `N` is moved to a new location; consequently, `P` is no longer a valid pointer. A well-known solution to this problem is to store an integer *handle* to the data inside `P` that can be used to look up the location of `N` in an address table. If `N` is moved, the address table is modified accordingly, and `P` can still be used to locate N. The handle associated with N, on the other hand, never changes until N is deallocated.

Write a program that creates two dictionaries: the first one should contain a list of variable names and their associated handles; the second should contain handles associated with physical addresses:

Variable	Handle
P	10246
Q	00215
R	20439
count	21052
stuRec	30552

Handle	Address
10246	0A6F
00215	1B49
20439	6D2E
21052	0042
30552	19B6

P is currently at address 0A6F
Q is currently at address 1B49
(etc.)

Demonstrate the process of searching for a variable, obtaining its handle, and searching for the handle in the address table.

CHAPTER 11

Object-Oriented Containers

A *container i*s a general type of data structure that holds a collection of objects. Arrays, lists, graphs, and dictionaries are examples of containers. In this chapter, we present object-oriented containers that use dynamic memory allocation. This allows them to expand and contract as needed to make more efficient use of memory. We present both singly and doubly linked lists, a graph searching example, and an iterator class.

Terms Introduced in this Chapter:

ancestor node	linked list
container	link pointer
control abstraction	list
depth-first search	non-intrusive list
descendant node	object-based list
doubly linked list	sibling node
dummy head pointer	singly linked list
dummy tail pointer	state space
intrusive list	traverse
iterator	

11.1 LINKED LISTS

Informally, a *list* is a set of sequentially organized elements. Lists usually store similarly typed data. The following are examples of lists:

```
15,4,96,22,85,4,0,-1,17,2
apple,orange,pear,banana,plum
Bob,Mary,Jan
elephants
```

In earlier chapters we discussed the graph data structure, which was a collection of nodes connected by arcs. A list is a specific type of graph, where each node except the first has a single preceding node, and each node except the last has a single following node. A list can contain from 0 to *n* nodes, where *n* is limited in practical terms by the available memory in a program.

A list can be implemented in different ways, the two most common of which are as an array or as a linked list. A *linked list* is a list in which each element in the list is called a *node*, and a connection between any two nodes is called a *link*. Most linked list implementations use dynamic memory allocation to reserve storage for nodes, and use pointer variables to represent the links between nodes.

Unlike an array, a list need not be pre-allocated. Instead, it takes up only the amount of room needed for the nodes it currently contains. As each new item is added to a list, a new node is created and attached to other list nodes. When an item is removed, its node is deallocated. Linked lists have an important limitation: nodes must be accessed sequentially by following pointers embedded in each node.

A list data structure can be useful in any number of applications where an ordered collection of information must be kept in memory. Lines of text in a document, for example, can be stored in a list that expands dynamically according to the number of lines in the document. List-processing applications usually have to add and remove nodes, and search for data in nodes. Here are some common operations, grouped according to similar functions:

Append	Add a node to the end of a list.
Prepend	Insert a node at the beginning of a list.
Insert	Insert a node in the middle of a list.
Find	Find a particular node.
Get	Get the node at the current position.
Replace	Replace the contents of a node.
IsEmpty	Find out if the list is empty.
Remove	Remove a single node.
Clear	Remove all nodes.

The inclusion of a key field in each list node makes it easier to search for individual nodes. Each item in a list of student records, for example, could contain a student ID field that would serve as a key.

11.1.1 Singly Linked Lists

In a singly linked list, each node contains a *link pointer* that points to the next node in the list. To *traverse* a list means to move from one end of the list to the other, following the links between nodes. A singly linked list can only be traversed in one direction, from the beginning to the end.

To simplify the inserting and deleting of nodes, we place empty nodes at the beginning and end of the list, called *head* (H) and *tail* (T), respectively. The empty nodes are often called *dummy nodes.* [1] Each node contains a *link pointer*, also called *next,* that contains the address of the node that follows it:

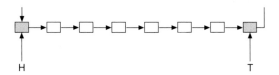

In this diagram, the tail node's link pointer points to the head node, making the list circular. Alternatively, the tail node's link pointer could point to the tail node itself or to NULL.

11.1.1.1 Inserting a Node.   A common operation with lists is inserting a new node. For example, to insert node X at the beginning of a list containing nodes A and B, we find the dummy head pointer and attach it to node X. We also attach X's link pointer to node A:

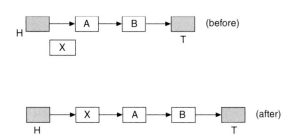

---

[1] Dummy nodes result in a small amount of excess storage, which is only noticeable in a program that has a large number of short lists. Also, some list implementations do not require a tail node.

It is easy to insert a node after any existing list node. For example, to insert X between A and B, we locate node A, attach A's link pointer to X, and attach X's link pointer to B:

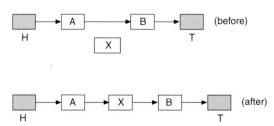

It is easier to insert a new node after an existing node than before it, because the links between nodes point in a single direction. In the previous example, if we had an existing pointer to node B and wanted to insert node X before B, we would have to start at the head of the list and follow all nodes up to node A, the predecessor of B. The longer the list ahead of B, the more processing time this would take. For that reason, our linked list implementation will have an `InsertAfter` function, and we leave the writing of an `InsertBefore` as a chapter exercise.

11.1.1.2 Removing a Node.
When removing node X from a list, we reroute the link pointer from X's previous node to the node that follows X. For example, we locate node A and attach its link pointer to node B. Then, the storage used by node X can be released:

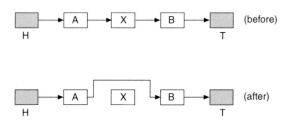

11.1.2 A Linked List Class

There are two general approaches to creating linked lists in C++. The first approach is to use a class template to generate list classes that are tied to specific node types. The second approach is to create a base class for all list nodes, a generic list-handling class, and require that any class objects inserted in a list be derived from the list node class. We will explore both approaches, starting with templates.

In order to show how to use a class template, we will create a singly linked list class called `Tlist<T>`. Each node will be a `Tnode<T>` object, also created from a class template. As always, a complete listing of the class along with a test program can be found in Appendix A.

11.1.2.1 *Tnode and Tlist Class Templates* .   The Tnode class template

defines objects stored in a Tlist. The template parameter T can be of any type.
Tnode<T> objects are only created by functions inside the Tlist<T> class:

```
template <class T>
class Tnode {
  friend class Tlist<T>;

public:
  Tnode():next(0){ }

  Tnode( const T & val );

  Tnode<T> * Next() const;

  friend ostream & operator <<(ostream & os,
        const Tnode<T> & N);

private:
  T value;          // data stored in node
  Tnode * next;     // points to next node
};
```

The data member called next is the link pointer that connects a node to its successor. Because Tlist functions need to access Tnode private members, Tlist is a
friend class.

By making the Tnode operations public, we allow nodes to be created and
manipulated in user code. This means that a user can call the Next function to obtain the successor of a node, and can use the << operator to output a node to a
stream. The convenience of these operations must be balanced against the tighter
encapsulation that would be achieved by making all Tnode members private.

The Tlist class includes a standard set of basic operations on lists. The template parameter T can be any data type:

```
template <class T>
class Tlist {
public:
  Tlist();
  ~Tlist();

  int Advance();
  // Return 0 if current position is already at
  // the end of the list; otherwise, increment
  // current and return 1.
```

```
    void Append( const T & nodeVal );
    // Add a new node to the end of the list.


    void Clear();
    // Remove all nodes.


    T Get() const;
    // Get data at the current position.


    void GoLast();
    // Set current to the last node in the list.


    void GoTop();
    // Set current to the header node.


    void InsertAfter( const T & nodeVal );
    // Insert new node after current one.


    int IsEmpty() const;
    // Return 1 if the list is empty; otherwise,
    // return 0.


    void Prepend( const T & nodeVal );
    // Insert a node at the beginning of the list.


    void Replace( const T & newVal );
    // Replace data in the current node.


    friend ostream & operator <<( ostream & os,
          const Tlist<T> & S );

private:
  Tnode<T> * head;        // dummy head node
  Tnode<T> * tail;        // dummy tail node
  Tnode<T> * current;     // current position
};
```

11.1.2.2 The NoCurrentNode Exception Class.
The one type of exception that can be explicitly thrown by `Tlist` functions is called `NoCurrentNode`. When calling `Get`, for example, we retrieve the node at the position called `current`. If this does not point to an actual node, an exception is thrown. The class contains a stream output function that may be used by the exception handler to display the cause of the exception:

```
class NoCurrentNode {
public:
  friend ostream & operator <<( ostream & os,
        const NoCurrentNode & nc )
  {
    os << "List exception: No current node.";
    return os;
  }
};
```

11.1.2.3 Testing the Tlist class.
Example 11-1 contains a short test program that creates different types of lists. First, we create a list of `float` values called `scores`. Then, we fill the list with random numbers and redisplay it. We also create a list of names, stored in `FString` objects.

We could also insert class objects in a `Tlist`. In the Doctor's Scheduling program, for example, we could manage a linked list of `Patient` objects. The following statements read a file containing patient records and store them in a list:

```
#include "tlist.h"

Tlist<Patient> patients;

ifstream infile( "patient.txt" );
Patient P;

while( !infile.eof() )
{
  infile >> P;
  patients.Append( P );
}
```

11.1.2.4 Class Implementations.
We will discuss most of the `Tlist` member functions here, and you can see the complete class implementation in Example 11-2. First, the default constructor allocates dummy head and tail nodes, and attaches them to each other to create a circular linked list:

Example 11-1. Testing the Tlist Class

```cpp
#include <stdlib.h>
#include <except.h>
#include "fstring.h"
#include "tlist.h"      // Tlist<T> class

void CreateRandomScores()
{
  Tlist<int> scores;
  cout << "Creating a random list of scores:\n";

  for(int i = 0; i < 10; i++)
  {
    int n = rand() % 100;
    scores.Append( n );
  }
  cout << scores << endl;

  scores.GoLast();
  cout << "Last item: " << scores.Get() << '\n';

  scores.GoTop();
  scores.Advance();
  cout << "First item: " << scores.Get() << '\n';

  cout << "\nReplacing first node with value 101...\n";
  scores.Replace( 101 );
  cout << scores;

  cout << "\nClearing the list...";
  scores.Clear();
  if( scores.IsEmpty())
    cout << "the list is now empty.\n";
}

void CreateNameList()
{
Tlist<FString> names;

// Append some names to the list,
// display the current name, and
// display the entire list.
```

Example 11-1 *(cont.)*

```
names.Append( "Baker" );
names.Append( "Johnson" );
names.Append( "Chong" );
names.Append( "Hamamoto" );
names.Append( "Kawai" );
names.Append( "Figueroa" );
cout << "current: " << names.Get() << endl;
cout << names;

// Replace the name at the beginning
// of the list, insert a name at the
// end, insert a name at the beginning,
// and redisplay the list.

names.GoTop();
names.Advance();
names.Replace( "Allton" );
names.GoLast();
names.InsertAfter( "Gonzalez" );
names.Prepend( "Abraham" );
cout << names << endl;

// Clear the list.

cout << "Clearing the list...";
names.Clear();
if( names.IsEmpty())
  cout << "the list is empty.\n\n";
}

int main()
{
  try {
    CreateRandomScores();
    CreateNameList();
  }
  catch( xalloc ) {
    cout << "Memory allocation error.\n";
  }
  catch( const NoCurrentNode & nc ) {
    cout << nc;
  }
  return 0;
}
```

Example 11-2. Tnode and Tlist Class Implementations

```cpp
//............Tnode<T> class ............

template <class T>
Tnode<T>::Tnode( const T & val ): value(val)
{
  next = 0;
}

template <class T>
Tnode<T> * Tnode<T>::Next() const
{
  return next;
}

template <class T>
ostream & operator <<( ostream & os, const Tnode<T> & N )
{
  os << N.value << ',';
  return os;
}

//........... Tlist<T> class ............

template <class T>
Tlist<T>::Tlist()
{
  head = new Tnode<T>;
  tail = new Tnode<T>;
  head->next = tail;
  tail->next = head;
  current = head;
}

template <class T>
Tlist<T>::~Tlist()
{
  Clear();
  delete head;
  delete tail;
}

template <class T>
int Tlist<T>::Advance()
{
  if( !current ) throw NoCurrentNode();
  if( current->next != tail )
```

Example 11-2 *(cont.)*

```
  {
    current = current->next;
    return 1;
  }
  return 0;
}

template <class T>
void Tlist<T>::Append( const T & nodeVal )
{
  GoLast();
  InsertAfter( nodeVal );
}

template <class T>
void Tlist<T>::Clear()
{
  current = head->next;
  while( current != tail )
  {
    head->next = current->next;
    delete current;
    current = head->next;
  }
  current = head;
  head->next = tail;
}

template <class T>
int Tlist<T>::IsEmpty() const
{
  return head->next == tail;
}

template <class T>
T Tlist<T>::Get() const
{
  if( !current ) throw NoCurrentNode();
  return current->value;
}

template <class T>
void Tlist<T>::GoLast()
{
  if( !current ) throw NoCurrentNode();
  while( current->next != tail )
    current = current->next;
}
```

Example 11-2 *(cont.)*

```cpp
template <class T>
void Tlist<T>::GoTop()
{
  current = head;
}

template <class T>
void Tlist<T>::InsertAfter( const T & nodeVal )
{
  if( !current ) throw NoCurrentNode();
  Tnode<T> * p = new Tnode<T>( nodeVal );
  p->next = current->next;
  current->next = p;
  current = p;
}

template <class T>
void Tlist<T>::Prepend( const T & nodeVal )
{
  GoTop();
  InsertAfter( nodeVal );
}

template <class T>
void Tlist<T>::Replace( const T & newVal )
{
  if( !current ) throw NoCurrentNode();
  current->value = newVal;
}

template <class T>
ostream & operator <<( ostream & os, const Tlist<T> & S )
{
  if( S.IsEmpty()) return os;

  Tnode<T> * p = S.head->Next();
  while( p != S.tail )
  {
    os << *p;
    p = p->Next();
  }
  os << endl;
  return os;
}
```

```
template <class T>
Tlist<T>::Tlist()
{
   head = new Tnode<T>;
   tail = new Tnode<T>;
   head->next = tail;
   tail->next = head;
   current = head;
}
```

The destructor calls the `Clear` function, which deallocates all nodes containing data, and then deletes the dummy head and tail nodes:

```
template <class T>
Tlist<T>::~Tlist()
{
   Clear();
   delete head;
   delete tail;
}
```

The `Advance` function moves the current position to the node that follows it, unless `current` is already at the end of the list. We use the return value to alert a calling program that the end of the list has been reached:

```
template <class T>
int Tlist<T>::Advance()
{
   if( !current ) throw NoCurrentNode();
   if( current->next != tail )
   {
      current = current->next;
      return 1;
   }
   return 0;
}
```

The `Append` function goes to the end of the list and inserts a node:

```
template <class T>
void Tlist<T>::Append( const T & nodeVal )
{
   GoLast();
   InsertAfter( nodeVal );
}
```

The `Clear` function removes and deallocates all nodes in the list except the dummy head and tail. Unlike an array, where a single `delete` statement can delete a contiguous block of memory, a linked list must be traversed from beginning to end and each node deleted separately:

```
template <class T>
void Tlist<T>::Clear()
{
  current = head->next;
  while( current != tail )
  {
    head->next = current->next;
    delete current;
    current = head->next;
  }
  current = head;
  head->next = tail;
}
```

The list is considered empty when the head points to the tail:

```
template <class T>
int Tlist<T>::IsEmpty() const
{
  return head->next == tail;
}
```

The GoLast function moves the current position to the end of the list:

```
template <class T>
void Tlist<T>::GoLast()
{
  if( !current ) throw NoCurrentNode();
  while( current->next != tail )
    current = current->next;
}
```

The InsertAfter function constructs a new node p, attaches the current node to p, and attaches p to the node following current:

```
template <class T>
void Tlist<T>::InsertAfter( const T & nodeVal )
{
  if( !current ) throw NoCurrentNode();
  Tnode<T> * p = new Tnode<T>( nodeVal );
  p->next = current->next;
  current->next = p;
  current = p;
}
```

The `Prepend` function goes to to the beginning of the list and inserts a new node following the dummy head node:

```
template <class T>
void Tlist<T>::Prepend( const T & nodeVal )
{
  GoTop();
  InsertAfter( nodeVal );
}
```

The stream output operator locates the first data node, assigns it to p, displays each node, and advances through the list using the `Tnode::Next` function:

```
template <class T>
ostream & operator <<( ostream & os, const Tlist<T> & S )
{
  if( S.IsEmpty()) return os;
  Tnode<T> * p = S.head->Next();
  while( p != S.tail )
  {
    os << *p;
    p = p->Next();
  }
  os << endl;
  return os;
}
```

In writing the statement

```
os << *p;
```

we assume that class `Tnode<T>` defines the `<<` operator for stream output.

This function also helps to show why we made the `Next` function in the `Tnode` class public. As it traverses the list, `operator <<` needs to move to the next node in the list. It cannot directly access the `next` data member of `Tnode`. `Tlist` is a friend of `Tnode`, and `operator <<` is a friend of `Tlist`, but that doesn't make `operator <<` a friend of `Tnode`.

11.2 CASE STUDY: SEARCHING A GRAPH

In Chapter 7 we introduced the graph data structure, which is a set of nodes connected by arcs. We represented a graph as an adjacency matrix, using an array implementation, and showed how to count the number of directed arcs in a graph. Now we would like to show how to create an adjacency matrix using linked lists, and how to search for a specific path between any two given nodes.

11.2.1 The Depth-First Search Algorithm

Some of the more interesting applications in computer science involve searching for a solution to a problem when a direct path to the solution is unknown. Such problems may often be represented by a graph (called a *state space*). For example, a *directed graph* can be used to represent a one-way shipping network, which we would use as a guide when sending a package from one location to another:

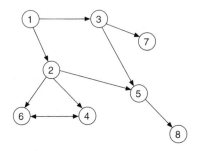

In a directed graph, the arcs connecting nodes always show a specific direction. For example, nodes 2 and 3 follow node 1. Nodes 5, 7, and 8 follow node 3, and node 3 precedes them.

The *depth-first search* algorithm is one of the most common ways to search a graph. Simply put, in a depth-first search, each path is explored to its limit before pursuing another path. For example, suppose that we want to find a path from node 1 to node 8, and we can examine only one node at a time. We might randomly choose to examine node 3; from there, we could choose node 7. But upon discovering that node 7 is a dead end, we would backtrack to node 3 and try node 5, discovering that node 5 is followed by node 8, thus completing the search. Of course, if we knew ahead of time that path 1-3-5-8 existed, no search would have been necessary.

Using the same graph, we could construct an adjacency matrix as an array of linked lists, and use it to conduct a depth-first search. In the adjacency matrix, each node number is followed by a list of zero or more nodes attached to the node. Nodes 6, 4, and 5, for example, are attached to node 2:

```
1: 2, 3
2: 6, 4, 5
3: 5, 7
4: 6
5: 8
6: 1
7:
8:
```

The order in which the numbers appear in each list is arbitrary, but it does affect the searching order. We track each list from left to right, backtracking when an empty list is found. In order to know which nodes have already been visited, we use an array of integers called `visited`, where `visited[v]` equals 1 only when node v has been visited. Using this adjacency matrix and searching for a path from node 1 to node 5, the depth-first search performs the following steps, in order:

1. Visit node 1 by moving to row 1 in the table.
2. Get the first number in row 1, which is 2.
3. Visit node 2 by moving to row 2.
4. Get the first number in row 2, which is 6.
5. Visit node 6 by moving to row 6.
6. Get the first number in row 6, which is 1.
7. Node 1 has already been visited and there are no more entires in row 6, so backtrack to row 2.
8. Get the second number in row 2, which is 4.
9. Visit node 4 by moving to row 4.
10. Node 6 has already been visited, so backtrack to row 2.
11. Get the third number in row 2, which is 5.
12. Visit node 5 by moving to row 5. This is the goal of our search, so we stop.

This represents just one possible depth-first search from node 1 to node 5. Depending on the order of nodes in the adjacency lists, any of the following would have been valid depth-first searches of the same graph, starting at node 1 and ending at node 5:

```
1,2,5
1,2,6,5
1,2,4,6,5
1,2,6,4,5
1,3,5
1,3,7,5
```

A depth-first search may result in a relatively large number of operations because the search is blind. The program using it has no way of knowing how close it is to the goal, and may have to backtrack many times before finding a solution path.

Most real-world problems are much larger than our sample graph, so it's useful to consider a graph with a large number of nodes, in which most nodes might have only a few attached arcs. An adjacency matrix for such a graph would be mostly empty. If an array were used to store the matrix, memory would not be used efficiently. But, a linked-list representation allocates only as much memory as is needed for each list of nodes attached to a starting node.

11.2.1.1 Graph Class.
We going to create a `Graph` class that implements a depth-first search. Each `Graph` object contains an array of lists, in which each node

in each list contains an integer. The integer might be a record identification number, or possibly a subscript into an array of much larger objects not physically stored in the graph. The two main operations supported by the class are AddArc, which adds a new arc to the matrix, and Search, which looks for a path from one node to another:

```
#include <iostream.h>
#include <iomanip.h>
#include "range.h"    // RangeError class
#include "tlist.h"    // Tlist class template

class Graph {
public:
  Graph( unsigned n );
  // Create a Graph capable of containing
  // as many as n nodes.

  ~Graph();
  // Destructor.

  void AddArc( unsigned v1, unsigned v2 );
  // Add an arc between nodes v1 and v2.

  int Search(unsigned v1,unsigned v2,Tlist<unsigned>& path);
  // If a path can be found from v1 to v2,
  // return 1 and display the path; otherwise, return 0.

  friend ostream & operator <<( ostream & os, const Graph & T);
  // Stream output operator.

private:
  unsigned size;                // number of nodes
  unsigned * visited;           // array of visited nodes
  Tlist<unsigned> * adjList;    // array of lists

  int searchDFS( unsigned v1, unsigned v2,
      Tlist<unsigned> & path );
  // Internal DFS search.
};
```

A Graph object with *n* nodes contains an array[0..*n*-1] of lists, each holding the ID numbers of nodes attached to that particular node.

11.2.1.2 Class Implementation.
The complete implementation of the Graph class appears in Appendix A. The array of Tlist<int> objects is dynamically allocated by the Graph class constructor, which gives us some flexibility at run time:

```
Graph::Graph( unsigned n )
{
  size = n;
  adjList = new Tlist<unsigned>[size];
  visited = new unsigned[size];
}
```

The graph can contain as many as UINT_MAX nodes; this constant is defined in the limits.h header.

To add an arc between nodes v1 and v2, we find row v1 and add v2 to its adjacency list. A RangeError exception is thrown if either parameter is larger than the maximum number of nodes:

```
void Graph::AddArc( unsigned v1, unsigned v2 )
{
  if( v1 >= size )
    throw RangeError(__FILE__,__LINE__,v1);
  if( v2 >= size )
    throw RangeError(__FILE__,__LINE__,v2);
  adjList[v1].Append( v2 );
}
```

The Search function takes three arguments: the starting node, the goal node, and an empty unsigned integer list. If the search is successful, the list will be filled with the node numbers found on the path. We clear the visited array and initialize the call to searchDFS, a private member:

```
int Graph::Search( unsigned v1, unsigned v2,
    Tlist<unsigned> & path )
{
  for(unsigned i = 0; i < size; i++)
    visited[i] = 0;

  if( searchDFS( v1, v2, path ))
  {
    path.Prepend( v1 );
    return 1;
  }
  return 0;
}
```

The recursive searchDFS function is the most interesting part of the class. First, we check to see if v1 and v2 are the same; this would indicate that the goal has been found. Next, we mark node v1 as visited, and check its adjacency list (assigned to L). If L is not empty, we retrieve the first node in the list; if it has not been visited, we recursively call searchDFS, passing it the new node number. If this succeeds, we add the current node number to the path list and the function returns. If we haven't found the goal yet, we move to the next list node by calling Advance and we try again:

```
int Graph::searchDFS( unsigned v1, unsigned v2,
    Tlist<unsigned> & path )
{
  if( v1 == v2 ) return 1;
  if( v1 >= size )
    throw RangeError(__FILE__,__LINE__,v1);
  if( v2 >= size )
    throw RangeError(__FILE__,__LINE__,v2);

  visited[v1] = 1;
  Tlist<unsigned> & L = adjList[v1];

  if( !L.IsEmpty() )
  {
    L.GoTop();
    L.Advance();
    do {
      unsigned n = L.Get();
      if( !visited[n] )                   // If node not already visited,
        if( searchDFS( n, v2, path )) // search the following nodes.
        {
          path.Prepend( n );              // Insert node on the path list.
          return 1;
        }
    } while( L.Advance() );
  }
  return 0;  // No path found.
}
```

The local variable L was used for notational convenience as a reference to adjList[v]. Because L is a reference, no copy constructor is called, and no class destructor is invoked when L goes out of scope.

11.2.1.3 Test Program.
A short test program for the Graph class is shown in Example 11-3. It reads a text file containing nodes, constructs a graph, displays it, and searches for a path. It's important to handle RangeError exceptions when adding new nodes to the graph and when searching for a path. Here is a sample input file that generates an adjacency matrix for the graph we presented earlier:

Example 11-3. Test Program for the Graph Class

```cpp
#include <fstream.h>
#include "graph.h"

void GraphTest( ifstream & input )
{
  unsigned grsize;
  input >> grsize;
  Graph G( grsize );

  unsigned v1, v2;
  input >> v1 >> v2;

  try {
    while( !input.eof() )
    {
      G.AddArc( v1, v2 );
      input >> v1 >> v2;
    }
  }
  catch( const RangeError & R ) {
    cout << R;
  }

  cout << G; // Display graph as adjacency list.

  // Create an empty path list, and search for a
  // path; if found, display the path.

  cout << "Searching for a path. Enter first and\n"
       << "last nodes, separated by a space: ";

  unsigned first, last;
  cin >> first >> last;
  Tlist<unsigned> path;

  try {
    if( G.Search( first, last, path ))
      cout << "Path found: " << path << endl;
    else
      cout << "Path not found." << endl;
  }
  catch( const RangeError & R ) {
    cout << R;
  }
}
```

Example 11-3 *(cont.)*

```
int main()
{
  ifstream input( "TREE.TXT" );
  if( !input )
    return 1;

  try {
    GraphTest( input );
  }
  catch( ... ) {
    cout << "Unknown exception thrown.\n";
  }
  return 0;
}
```

```
8
1 2
1 3
2 6
2 4
2 5
3 5
3 7
5 8
```

11.3 OBJECT-BASED LIST

We found that the `Tlist` class template caused a new list class to be generated for each type of list, and that each list contained objects of the same type. List templates are called *non-intrusive* because they do not require any change to be made to classes that define objects inserted in lists. When we created the `Tlist<FString>` class, for example, we did not have to modify the `FString` class.

Another way of creating lists of different types is to create an *object-based*, or *intrusive* list class; any object placed in the list must be derived from the same base class. Before templates were added to C++, this was the only practical way to create lists of different types. Many commercial C++ compilers are supplied with both template and object-based list classes.

We're going to create an object-based list class and implement it as a doubly linked list. Object-based lists certainly do not have to be doubly linked, but we will use this opportunity to demonstrate how a doubly linked list can be implemented.

A *doubly linked list* is a linked list in which each node has a link to its predecessor node, as well as a link to its successor node. Implementing a doubly linked list requires more pointer manipulation, but the list permits both forward and backward traversals:

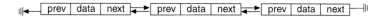

Additional memory is used by the extra pointer in each node, but depending on the size of each node, the storage used by the pointer may not be significant. The ability to traverse the list backwards is a major benefit that permits searching backward for nodes, and easier insertions of nodes in a list.

In the upcoming examples, The base class for all list nodes will be `DblNode`, and the list class will be `DblList`. `DblNode` is an abstract class, so no instances of `DblNode` will be created. The list will contain pointers to objects, where the objects' classes are derived from `DblNode`. If we wish, the same list could contain pointers to different types of objects. The following diagram shows a list containing pointers to `Student`, `Faculty`, and `Administrator` objects:

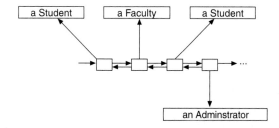

The flexibility afforded by a list containing pointers gives us a great advantage when dealing with objects that are related by a class hierarchy and that have similar operations.

11.3.1 DblNode Class

Because a `DblNode` is inserted in a doubly linked list, it must have pointers to both its preceding and following nodes. `DblNode` has a member function called `Detach` that detaches a node from its neighbors. This relieves the `DblList` class from some of the burden of manipulating these pointers:

```
#include <iostream.h>

class DblNode {
   friend class DblList;
   friend class DblIterator;
```

```
public:
  DblNode();
  virtual ~DblNode() {  }


  DblNode * Next() const;
  // Return pointer to next node.


  DblNode * Prev() const;
  // Return pointer to previous node.


  DblNode * Detach();
  // Detach node from its neighbors.


  virtual int operator ==( const DblNode & N )
           const = 0;
  // Compare nodes for equality.


  friend ostream & operator << (ostream & os,
        const DblNode & N );
  friend istream & operator >> (istream & inp,
        DblNode & N );


private:
  virtual void printOn( ostream & os ) const = 0;
  virtual void readFrom( istream & inp ) = 0;

  DblNode * next;      // pointer to next node
  DblNode * prev;      // pointer to previous node
};
```

The DblList and DblIterator classes are friends of DblNode, so they can directly manipulate the prev and next pointers in each node. The DblIterator class will be discussed in Section 11.4.1.

11.3.2 DblList Class

11.3.2.1 DblList Class Definition.   The DblList class definition is shown in Example 11-4. Each DblList object contains two pointers: first points to the first node in the list, and last points to the last node. Having a pointer to the end of the list makes it easier to add and remove nodes from the end. The destructor removes each node from the list and releases its storage. The Find member function searches for a node, and if it is found, returns a pointer to the matching list item.

Example 11-4. The DblList Class Definition

```
#ifndef DBLLIST_H
#define DBLLIST_H

#include "dblnode.h"

class DblList {
  friend class DblIterator;

public:
  DblList();
  // Construct an empty list.

  ~DblList();
  // Destructor: delete all nodes.

  void Append( DblNode * N );
  // Add node to end of the list.

  void DeleteAll();
  // Delete all nodes in the list.

  DblNode * Find( const DblNode & N ) const;
  // Find a node in the list.

  DblNode * Remove( DblNode * N );
  // Remove a node from the list.

  int IsEmpty() const;
  // Return 1 if the list is empty.

  DblNode * First() const;
  // Return pointer to first node.

  DblNode * Last() const;
  // Return pointer to last node.

  long GetSize() const;
  // Return the number of nodes.

  friend ostream & operator << ( ostream & os,
        const DblList & L );

private:
  virtual void printOn( ostream & ) const;

  DblNode * first;  // first node in the list
  DblNode * last;   // last node in the list
  long size;        // number of elements
};

#endif
```

The `DblNode` class does not keep a pointer to the current list position. However, the class user can retrieve the previous and next pointers from a `DblNode`. For example, a program using a list of `Package` objects might traverse the list and display each package's destination:

```
class Package :public DblNode {
public:
  //...
  FString GetDestination() const;


private:
  virtual void printOn( ostream & os ) const;
  virtual void readFrom( istream & inp );
};


DblList packages;

Package * P = (Package *) packages.First();

while( P )
{
  cout << P->GetDestination() << endl;
  P = (Package *)P->Next();
}
```

Unfortunately, `First` and `Next` return `DblNode *` values, which we want to assign to `Package *` variables. So, the user has to cast the return values of these functions into type `Package *`.

11.3.2.2 DblList Class Implementation.

The complete `DblList` class implementation appears in Example 11-5. We will highlight a few of the more important member functions here. The `Append` function's parameter is a pointer to a `DblNode` (or an object derived from `DblNode`). If the list is empty, we simply attach the new node to the `first` and `last` data members. Otherwise, we attach the forward link pointer of the `last` node to the new node and attach the new node's backward link pointer to `last`:

```
void DblList::Append( DblNode * P )
{
  if( !P ) return;
```

```
if( last )         // is there a last node?
{
  last->next = P;   // yes: attach new node to it
  P->prev = last;
}
else                // no: attach new node to first
  first = P;

last = P;          // last points to appended node
size++;            // increment size of list
}
```

The `Find` member function searches for the first node that matches node `N`. We start at the beginning of the list, move through the nodes one at a time, and return a pointer to the first node that matches:

```
DblNode * DblList::Find( const DblNode & N ) const
{
  DblNode * P = first;
  while( P )
  {
    if( N == *P )
      return P;
    P = P->next;
  }
  return 0;
}
```

This function requires the class of any object inserted in the list to have defined the == operator. Notice, however, that it is not necessary to know the exact type of the pointer, as long as it is derived from `DblNode`.

The `Remove` function locates the forward link from the previous node and attaches it to the node that follows `P`. Similarly, the backward link of the node following `P` is reattached to the preceding node:

```
DblNode * DblList::Remove( DblNode * P )
{
  if( !P ) return 0;

  if( P == first )        // removing the first node?
    first = first->next;
  if( P == last )         // removing the last node?
    last = last->prev;

  P->Detach();   // detach node from its neighbors
  size—;         // decrement list size
  return P;
}
```

Example 11-5. The DblList Class Implementation

```
#include "dbllist.h"

DblList::DblList()
{
  first = 0;
  last = 0;
  size = 0;
}

DblList::~DblList()
{
  DeleteAll();
}

void DblList::Append( DblNode * P )
{
   if( !P ) return;

   if( last )        // is there a last node?
   {
     last->next = P;   // yes: attach new node to it
     P->prev = last;
   }
   else              // no: attach new node to first
     first = P;

  last = P;           // last points to appended node
  size++;             // increment size of list
}

void DblList::DeleteAll()
{
  while( first )
    delete Remove( first );
}

// Find a node. If successful, return a pointer to the
// list element that matches P; otherwise, return 0.
// Requires definition of operator ==().

DblNode * DblList::Find( const DblNode & N ) const
{
  DblNode * P = first;
  while( P )
```

Example 11-5 *(cont.)*

```
  {
    if( N == *P )
      return P;
    P = P->next;
  }
  return 0;
}


DblNode * DblList::First() const
{
  return first;
}


long DblList::GetSize() const
{
  return size;
}


int DblList::IsEmpty() const
{
  return first == 0;
}


DblNode * DblList::Last() const
{
  return last;
}


// Private member function that outputs the
// list to a stream.

void DblList::printOn( ostream & os ) const
{
  DblNode * N = first;
  while( N )
  {
    os << (*N);
    N = N->next;
  }
}


DblNode * DblList::Remove( DblNode * P )
{
  if( !P ) return 0;
```

Example 11-5 *(cont.)*

```
  if( P == first )        // removing the first node?
    first = first->next;
  if( P == last )         // removing the last node?
    last = last->prev;

  P->Detach();    // detach node from its neighbors
  size—;          // decrement list size
  return P;
}

ostream & operator << (ostream & os,
    const DblList & aList)
{
  aList.printOn( os );
  return os;
}
```

The `Detach` member function in the `DblNode` class takes care of some of the low-level pointer details, simplifying the code in `Remove()`.

11.3.2.3 *Deriving a New List Class.*   It's not usually necessary to derive a new class from `DblList` in order to use it. But a more specialized list class can be a convenience, to avoid the inconvenient casting of pointers when calling `DblList` functions such as `First` and `Next`. For example, we create a `StudentList` class that wraps a "shell" around `DblList` and returns pointers to `Student` objects:

```
    class StudentList :public DblList {
    public:
      Student * Find( const Student & P ) const;
      Student * Remove( Student * P );
      Student * First() const;
      Student * Last() const;
    };
```

This makes creating a `StudentList` very convenient for a client program. For example, the return value of `Find` can be directly assigned to a `Student` pointer:

```
    StudentList college;
    //...
    Student * sp = college.Find( Student(10015) );
```

11.3.3 Object-Based vs. Template-Based Lists

There are both advantages and disadvantages to using object-based versus template lists. One issue is runtime efficiency. In an object-based list, nodes are created outside the list, so an insertion operation simply involves pointer manipulation. A template list, on the other hand, allocates storage for a new node whenever an object is inserted in the list, and releases storage for a node when it is removed from the list. Because of the extra overhead of allocating and deallocating memory, the object-based approach is often faster.

Another issue is convenience. When creating a list of int, float, or some other standard data type, a simple declaration of Tlist<int> does the trick. On the other hand, creating an object-based list of integers would require creating a new class that derives from DblNode. We would also have to implement each of the pure virtual functions in DblNode.

Another issue is flexibility. Whereas a list class generated by a template is restricted to objects of the same type, an object-based list can easily store objects of different types, as long as they are derived from the same base node class. Suppose that we derived the Student, Employee, and Doctor classes from DblNode. Then objects of each type could be inserted in the same list:

```
class Student :public DblList { ... };
class Employee :public DblList { ... };
class Doctor :public DblList{ ... };

DblList allInOne;
Student * stuP;
Employee * empP;
Doctor * docP;

allInOne.Append( stuP );
allInOne.Append( empP );
allInOne.Append( docP );
```

Creating a list containing different types of objects has its risks: unless each object keeps track of its own type, a program might have a hard time trying to decipher the type of each list member and processing it correctly. However, the C++ language implements run-time type identification (called RTTI) for just this purpose. See [ANSI-95] for a complete description.

11.4 ITERATOR CLASSES

An *iterator* class belongs to a general category of classes called *control abstractions*. A control abstraction provides some degree of manipulation (or control) over objects of another class. For example, an iterator class is a tool for traversing List objects. The iterator might be thought of as an extension of the List class. An important reason for using an iterator is that it can be used to encapsulate the standard operations of traversing lists into a class. Then, multiple instances of iterators can be used with any list.

11.4.1 DblIterator Class

We are going to create the DblIterator class, which defines the properties and operators of iterators associated with DblList objects. The basic operations for an iterator class include moving to the beginning or end of a list, moving forward or backward, getting the iterator's current list position, and applying a user-supplied function to each list member. A DblList may have multiple iterators, but a DblIterator can be associated with only one DblList. Each iterator retains its state (position) in its associated list, and each iterator is independent of all other iterators. Here is the class definition:

```
typedef void (* IterFtype)( DblNode * );

class DblIterator  {  // friend of DblNode, DblList classes
public:
  DblIterator( const DblList & L );

  DblNode * Advance();
  DblNode * BackUp();
  DblNode * GoFirst();
  DblNode * GoLast();

  DblNode * GetCurrPos() const;
  // Return pointer to node at current position.

  void Apply( IterFtype );
  // Pass each list member to a function.

private:
  const DblList * aList;  // the list being iterated
  DblNode * currPos;      // current position in list
};
```

The data members are aList, a pointer to the iterator's associated list, and currPos, a pointer to the current position in the list. A typedef defines IterFtype, a pointer to a function having a DblNode pointer parameter.

11.4.2 DblIterator Class Implementation

Let's look at some highlights of the DblIterator class implementation. The complete listing is in Appendix A. The constructor takes a constant reference to an existing `DblList` and saves its address in `aList`, a pointer-to-constant data member. By default, the iterator points to the beginning of the list:

```
DblIterator::DblIterator( const DblList & L ):aList(&L)
{
  currPos = aList->first;
}
```

The `GoFirst` function moves to the first node in the list by copying the list's `first` pointer to the iterator's current position:

```
DblNode * DblIterator::GoFirst()
{
  return currPos = aList->first;
}
```

The `Advance` function moves the current position forward and returns a pointer to the current node. If we have reached the end of the list, we just return 0:

```
DblNode * DblIterator::Advance()
{
  if( currPos->next )
    return currPos = currPos->next;
  else
    return 0;
}
```

The `Apply` function makes it easy for an iterator to pass each member of a list to a function:

```
void DblIterator::Apply( IterFtype fp )
{
  GoFirst();
  do
    fp( currPos );  // call the function
  while( (*this).Advance() );
}
```

Its only parameter is of type `IterFtype`, which was defined along with the `DblIterator` class. `IterFtype` is a pointer to a function that returns `void`, and that has a single parameter of type `DblNode *`:

```
typedef void (* IterFtype)(DblNode *);
```

11.4.3 Application: Bookstore List with an Iterator

Let's write a short program that creates a bookstore sales list. It creates a linked list of books and uses an iterator to traverse the list several times. We will create a

`Book` class that contains an ISBN number, author, title, cost, and year of publication. The author and title will be `FTString` objects, based on the string template
class from Chapter 10.

The following diagram helps to show the class relationships we have in mind:
`Book` is derived from `DblNode`; a `DblList` contains a collection of `Book` objects; a
`Book` contains several `FTString` objects (20, 30, and 50 characters, respectively); a
`DblIterator` contains a pointer to a `DblList`, as well as a pointer to the current
`DblNode` object in the list:

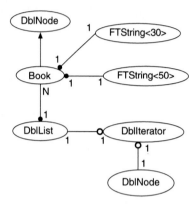

Because books will be inserted in a `DblList`, we derive `Book` from `DblNode`
and override the virtual `printOn`, `readFrom`, and operator `==` functions. The
`Book` class is defined here, and its implementation appears in Appendix A:

```
#include <iostream.h>
#include "dblnode.h"
#include "ftstring.h"

class Book : public DblNode {
public:
  Book();
  Book( const FTString<20> & isbnV,
        const FTString<30> & authorV,
        const FTString<50> & titleV,
        int yearV, float costV);

  virtual ~Book();

  Book & operator =( const Book & B );

  float GetCost() const;

  virtual int operator == (const DblNode &) const;
  virtual void printOn( ostream & os ) const;
  virtual void readFrom( istream & is );
```

```
private:
  FTString<20> isbn;
  FTString<30> author;
  FTString<50> title;
  int year;
  float cost;
};
```

When comparing two books for equality, we use the titles:

```
int Book::operator ==( const DblNode & B ) const
{
  return title == ((Book &)B).title;
}
```

11.4.3.1 Main Program.   The Bookstore program, shown in Example 11-6, reads a file containing book ISBN numbers, titles, authors, dates, and prices, and appends Book objects to a list:

```
input >> (*B);          // input a book
while( !input.eof() )
{
  titles.Append( B ); // add it to the list
  B = new Book;        // create a book node
  input >> (*B);       // input a book
}
```

Next, we create a DblIterator object and tie it to the book list. The iterator traverses the list and applies CalcPrice to each member:

```
DblIterator I( titles );  // create an iterator
I.Apply( CalcPrice );
```

CalcPrice simply multiplies the wholesale cost of each book by a standard markup (20%) and displays the retail price. Then, we traverse the list in reverse order and display each book:

```
I.GoLast();
do {
  Book * B = (Book *) I.GetCurrPos();
  cout << *B;
} while( −I );
```

Example 11-6. The BookStore Program

```cpp
#include <iostream.h>
#include <fstream.h>
#include <except.h>
#include "nofile.h"    // NoFileError exception class
#include "dbllist.h"   // DblList class
#include "dbliter.h"   // DblIterator class
#include "book.h"

const char inFileName[] = "books.txt";

ofstream log( "iter.txt" );

void CalcPrice( DblNode * np )
{
  float retailPrice = ((Book *)np)->Cost() * 1.20;
  log << *np << "Retail Price = " << retailPrice
      << '\n' << endl;
}

void IteratorTest()
{
  DblList titles;
  ifstream input( inFileName );
  if( !input ) throw NoFileError( inFileName );

  Book * B = new Book;  // allocate a new book
  input >> (*B);        // input a book

  while( !input.eof() )
  {
    titles.Append( B ); // add it to the list
    B = new Book;       // create a book node
    input >> (*B);      // input a book
  }

  DblIterator I( titles );  // create an iterator

  cout << "\nCalculating Retail Prices:\n\n";
  I.Apply( CalcPrice );

  cout << "\n\nTitles in reverse order:\n\n";
  I.GoLast();

  do {
    Book * B = (Book *) I.GetCurrPos();
```

Example 11-6 *(cont.)*

```
    cout << *B;
  } while( --I );
}

int main()
{
 try {
  IteratorTest();
 }
 catch( xalloc ) {
   cout << "Memory allocation exception.\n";
 }
 catch( const RangeError & R ) {
   cout << R << endl;
 }
 catch( const NoFileError & nf ) {
   cout << nf << endl;
 }

 return 0;
}
```

11.4.3.2 Program Input-Output.   The input file consists of the ISBN number, title, author, date, and cost for each book, on separate lines. For example,

```
02-3030204-343
Turbo Pascal
Guaneri
1996
38.00
03-20204-3434
Programming in ANSI C
Amati
1995
42.00
.
.
```

The program's output is almost identical, except that each list member has been passed to the `CalcPrice` function:

```
Turbo Pascal
Guaneri
1996
02-3030204-343
38
Retail Price = 45.6
Programming in ANSI C
Amati
1995
03-20204-3434
42
Retail Price = 50.4

.

.
```

We could easily create multiple iterators for the same list, each retaining its own state from call to call. Each iterator could point to a different position in the same list, or each iterator could point to a different list:

```
DblList titles;
DblIterator J( titles );
DblIterator K( titles );

.

.

J.GoLast();
K.GoFirst();
```

11.5 CHAPTER SUMMARY

A *linked list* is a set of items organized sequentially, where each member of the list is a *node* and the connection between any two nodes is a *link*. A linked implementation of a list is flexible because it uses almost no storage until nodes are added to the list. It expands and shrinks dynamically according to the number of nodes, and generally makes efficient use of memory.

Some common operations on lists are as follows: *Append* adds a node to the end of a list; *Insert* inserts a node in the middle of a list; *Empty* indicates if a list is empty; *Find* searches for a node; *Get* retrieves a node; *Clear* removes all nodes; *Prepend* inserts a node at the beginning of a list; *Remove* removes a node; and *Replace* replaces the contents of a node.

In this chapter, we showed how to create two types of lists: template-based lists (called *non-intrusive*) and object-based lists (called *intrusive*).

In a *singly linked* list, each node contains a *link pointer* that points to the next node in the list. A *doubly linked* list consists of nodes having both forward and backward links. To *traverse* a list means to begin at one end of a list and follow the links between nodes to move to the other end.

A template-based list uses a type parameter to determine what types of objects will be stored in the list. In this chapter, we created the Tlist<T> class template, where T can be int, float, Student, Package, or any other class type. This type of list requires no knowledge of the internal list structure by the class user. We wrote a simple test program that created several lists: a list of test scores, a list of names and a list of patients.

In this chapter we continued our study of graphs that was begun in Chapter 7, with a program that creates an adjacency matrix. We implemented the matrix using an array of linked lists, and showed how to search for a specific path between any two given nodes. We introduced the depth-first search algorithm for searching a graph, and created a Graph class that implemented the search.

We created an object-based list class called DblList that implemented a doubly linked list. We also created the DblNode class, the base class for all objects inserted in a DblList. We showed that this type of intrusive list is efficient, but its use requires some modifications to existing classes. We wrote a test program that demonstrated the DblList class.

We explained how to create and use an iterator class for list processing called DblIterator. We demonstrated the iterator in a short program that processed a list of books. Iterator objects have an advantage in programs that do complex manipulation of list pointers, because the same list can have multiple iterators and the iterators can be completely independent.

11.5.1.1 Inheritance Considerations.
An interesting issue comes up when using an object-based list class such as DblList. Suppose that, in a given project, an application class hierarchy already exists, and we are contemplating building a linked list of an existing type. We might, for example, like to insert SalariedEmployee objects in a list:

Because any object inserted in the list must derive from DblNode, we would have to derive either Employee or SalariedEmployee from DblNode. If we chose the former, we could subtly alter the class hierarchy supported by Employee. If we chose the latter, we would be using multiple inheritance:

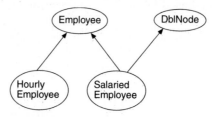

The latter option might be the most attractive, particularly if we do not have access to the source code for the Employee class and its derived classes. One of the primary reasons for including multiple inheritance in C++ was to allow for situations like this.

11.6 EXERCISES

11.6.1 List Template Enhancements and Applications

The exercises in this section all use the Tlist class template presented earlier in the chapter as a starting point. In general, the exercises are mutually independent, unless we specifically suggest completing another exercise first.

1 InsertBefore Function. Write an Insert function for the Tlist class template that inserts a new node immediately before the current node:

```
void Tlist<T>::InsertBefore( const T & nodeVal );
```

You will have to back up to the head of the list and follow each link until you locate the node just before the current node. Write a short program that tests the function.

2 Find Function. Add a Find function to the Tlist class template that searches the list for a specific value. The function should return 1 and update the current position in the list if it finds the value, or return 0 if it does not:

```
int Tlist<T>::Find( const T & val );
```

3 Stack Class Template. From Chapter 2, we know that a *stack* is a data structure that supports the LIFO (*last in, first out*) ordering of inserting and removing data. The *push* operation adds a value to the top of the stack, and *pop* removes the value currently at the top. Create a Stack class template by using a Tlist<T> to hold the stack's data:

```
void Stack<T>::Push( const T & val );
T Stack<T>::Pop();
```

Your class should also provide both a constructor and functions called `Empty` and `Full` that return the stack's status. Write a short test program that creates several stacks containing integers, strings, and class objects.

4 List with No Duplicates.   The current implementation of the `Tlist` class allows duplicate items to be inserted in a list. This approach can be very inefficient, particularly in large lists. Instead, you can add an instance count to the `Tnode` class:

```
template <class T>
class Tnode {
  //...
private:
  T value;
  int instanceCount;
  Tnode * next;
};
```

Before adding a new node to the list, search the list for the same value. If the value is found, increment its corresponding `instanceCount`. You can use the `Find` function from Exercise 2 in this section to locate a value in the list. Write a test program that reads a text file and inserts words into the list. At the end, display the list and show the instance count for each word.

5 Tlist Concatenation Operator.   Add an `operator +=` function to the `Tlist` class template that concatenates another list to the current one. Write a program that creates two lists, concatenates them, and displays the result. A suggested declaration for the operator functions is:

```
Tlist<T> & operator +=( const Tlist<T> & T2 );
```

6 Tlist Copy Constructor.   Add a copy constructor to the `Tlist` class template that allows an existing list to be copied into the list being constructed. The two lists must have separate memory allocations; if one list goes out of scope, for example, the other must not be affected. Here is a suggested declaration for the constructor:

```
Tlist( const Tlist<T> & T2 );
```

7 Iterator for the Tlist Class.   Create an iterator class template called `TIterator<T>` that manipulates any `Tlist`-generated class. Use the `DblIterator` class presented earlier in this chapter as a model. You will not be able to implement the `operator −` function because the `Tlist` nodes do not point backward.

Write a program that demonstrates the iterator as a class data member. For example, you could create a simple `Course` class that holds transcript information about a single college course:

```
class Course {
  //...
private:
  FTString<10> courseName;  // e.g., "BIO 1052"
  FTString<5> semester;     // e.g., "94/1"
  float grade;              // e.g., 3.50
};
```

Next, create a `Student` class that contains a list of courses and an iterator data member that keeps track of the current position in the list:

```
class Student {
public:
  Student( long idNum, const FTString<30> & lname )
           :lastName(lname), iter(transcript);
  //...
private:
  long id;
  FTString<30> lastName;
  Tlist<Course> transcript;
  TIterator<Course> iter;
};
```

8 Doubly Linked List Class Template. Create a class template for doubly linked lists. Implement the same operations as the `DblList` class from this chapter. Write a short program that tests the list operations.

9 Queue Class. A queue data structure is a specialized type of list based on the *first-in/first-out* (FIFO) model, which requires that the first item inserted in a list be the first processed. Customers waiting in line at a store cash register, for example, are served according to the FIFO model. Ordinarily, it is not possible for someone in the middle of the line to be processed before someone who arrived earlier.

Create a `Queue` class (template or object-based) by using a linked list to hold the queue's data, and provide the following operations: *enqueue* adds an item to the end of the list; *serve* removes an item from the beginning of the list; *empty* returns true if no items are found in the list; and, *clear* removes all items from the list. Write a simple test program that creates at least two queues: one containing integers and another containing class objects.

11.6.2 Hospital Waiting Room

1 Hospital Waiting Room (Priority Queue). A priority queue is a queue in which items are either ordered or selected according to some criteria. In a hospital emergency room, for example, patients are classified according to the severity of their illness or injury, and those in most need are helped first. [Stubbs/Webre] call such a queue a *highest-priority-in/first-out queue* (HPIFO).

Create a `Patient` class in which each patient object contains an identification number, last name, first name, injury severity index (1-5, with 1 being the highest), and time of arrival (*hh:mm*).

Read a list of patients from a file and process them in order of priority level (based on the injury severity index). In this context, processing a patient means removing the person's record from the priority queue and displaying the record. If two or more waiting patients have the same priority level, choose the one with the earliest arrival time.

2 Hospital Waiting Room (Enhanced).   Using the program from the previous exercise, improve the program in the following ways:

1. Each time a patient is about to be processed, input the current time from the user and scan the queue, looking for patients that have been waiting for more than two hours; automatically add 1 to their priority.
2. When processing the next patient, scan the queue and pick the patient with the highest priority.
3. The hospital's quality control department has given you a table containing the maximum acceptable waiting time for each patient priority level:

Patient Priority	Max. Wait Time (Minutes)
1	1
2	5
3	15
4	30
5	60

In your hospital waiting room simulation, keep track of the number of patients from each priority level that exceeded the maximum allowable wait time, and calculate the average wait time for patients in each category. To make the simulation meaningful, you should create at least ten patient records for each category.

11.6.3 Retail Store Simulation

The following exercises use the `Queue` class from the earlier exercises in this chapter to create a simulation of customers who arrive and are served by a store clerk at a cash register. We will assume that each arriving customer goes to the back of the line, and each customer is served from the front of the line.

1 Single Customer Queue.   Use a loop to simulate a time interval of one minute, during which *n* customers arrive and a single customer is served. The value of *n* is determined by a random number that is generated during each loop iteration, and should be in the range 0..*Max*. Run the simulation and display the length of the queue during each time interval.

Experiment with different values for *Max;* for each of these, repeat the simulation loop 500 times and generate the following statistics: shortest queue (after the first 30 minutes), average queue length, longest queue length, and number of customers served.

2 Retail Store Simulation (Enhanced).　　Using the simulation from the previous exercise as a basis, enhance the program in the following ways: create four lines of customers, where one customer from each line is processed during each loop iteration (called a *round-robin* approach) assume that customers arriving at the store automatically join the shortest line. Run the simulation and generate the same statistics that were requested for the previous exercise.

11.6.4 Office Supply Store

The following exercises are modifications to programs written for the Office Supply Store application that appeared in the exercises of Chapter 2.

1 Product List.　　The Office Supply Store program in Chapter 2 reads a list of `Product` objects from an input file. Modify this program so that the products are stored in a linked list (template or object-based).

2 Manufacturer List.　　As was done for the product list in the previous exercise, read the file containing manufacturers into a linked list.

3 Inventory List.　　As was done for the product and manufacturer lists in the previous exercises, read the file containing inventory records into a linked list.

4 Locating Product Information.　　Using the linked lists of products, manufacturers, and inventory, write a program that searches for an inventory record and displays all related information. Let the user enter a product ID number; the program should display the product name, price, quantity on hand, and manufacturer.

5 Adding New Products.　　Building on the previous four exercises, let the user add a new product to the product list, and specify how many items of the product the store has on-hand. Verify that the user has entered an existing manufacturer ID, and display an error message if the ID is not found in the manufacturer list. Write the modified product and inventory lists to new data files in the same format as the corresponding input files (this will allow the new files to be used as input the next time you run the program).

6 Adding New Manufacturers.　　Building on the previous five exercises, let the user add a new manufacturer to the manufacturer list and write the information to a new data file.

7 Multiple Manufacturers.　　In the Office Supply Store application, we assumed that each product had only a single manufacturer and price. Let's broaden that view by allowing the same product to be supplied by any number of manufacturers, each with a different price. Each `Product` object should contain a product ID and a linked list that contains the following information in each node:

```
long manufId;   // manufacturer ID
float price;     // wholesale price
float markup;    // markup from wholesale (.nn)
```

Add more records to the product data file (Chapter 2) so that each product has between 1 and 10 manufacturers. Modify the `Product` class and write a program that reads and displays all product and manufacturer information from the Product File.

11.6.5 Student Registration

The following exercises are based on the `Student` Registration program presented as a case study in Chapter 3.

1 List of Courses.   In the Student Registration program from Chapter 3, modify the `Registration` class so that it contains a linked list of courses. Run and test the main program shown in Chapter 3.

2 List of Students.   Building on the previous exercise, create a class called `StudentList` that contains a linked list of `Student` objects. Read student registration data from an input file, build a linked list, and display a list of students and courses taken. Here is a diagram of the class dependencies:

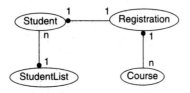

3 Registration Report.   Building on the previous two exercises, create a class called `RegistReport` that formats and produces a registration report. For each student, display the person's name, a list of courses taken, number of credits registered for by the student, tuition rate, and tuition amount owed by the student. At the end of the report, display the total credits registered for by all students and the total tuition amount collected.

4 Adding New Courses.   Build on the Student Registration program from the previous exercises by allowing individual students to add new courses to their registration lists. After reading the input file of student registration data, let the user enter a student ID. Display the matching student's list of courses. Let the user add a new course to the student's course list. Write the updated information back to the same data file, in the same format as the input file. Continue accepting student IDs until the user wants to quit. Run the program again and verify that the courses were added correctly.

5 Dropping Courses.   Build on the Student Registration program from the previous exercises by allowing individual students to drop courses from their registration lists. After reading the input file of student registration data, let the user enter a student ID. Display the matching student's list of courses. Let the user choose a course to be dropped. After confirming the drop, write the updated information back to the same data file, in the same format as the input file. Continue accepting student IDs until the user wants to quit. Run the program again and verify that the courses were added correctly.

6 Creating Class Rolls.   Build on the Student Registration program from Exercises 1 and 2 in this section. Create a new class called `ClassRoll` that contains a linked list of student IDs for students that have signed up for a particular course. Each course record contains the following:

```
FTString<10> courseName;    // course name
int numSeats;               // number of seats
```

(For a description of the FTString class, see Section 10.3.2.)

Create a class called `ClassRollList` that holds a linked list of `ClassRoll` objects, and read a list of `ClassRolls` from an input file. Using the linked lists of students and courses from Exercises 1 and 2 in this section, for each course taken by a student, add the student's ID to the appropriate class roll. Produce a listing of each class roll, with the ID numbers of all students registered for the course. *Extra:* Display the name, as well as the ID number of each student.

Program Listings

CHAPTER 2: STUDENT REGISTRATION

Class Definitions

```
//*********************************************
// COURSE.H - Course and Registration Classes
//*********************************************

#include <iostream.h>
#include <fstream.h>

const unsigned CnameSize = 10;

class Course {
public:
  Course();
  void Input( ifstream & infile );
  void Output( ofstream & ofile ) const;

private:
  char name[CnameSize]; // course name
  char section;         // section (letter)
  unsigned  credits;    // number of credits
};
```

```
const unsigned MaxCourses = 10;

class Registration {
public:
  Registration();
  void Input( ifstream & infile );
  void Output( ofstream & ofile ) const;

private:
  long studentId;          // student ID number
  unsigned semester;       // semester year, number
  unsigned count;          // number of courses
  Course courses[MaxCourses]; // array of courses
};
```

Class Implementations

```
//***************************************************
// REGIST.CPP - Course and Registration Class
//                 Implementations
//***************************************************

#include "course.h"

Course::Course()
{
  name[0] = '\0';
}

void Course::Input( ifstream & infile )
{
  infile >> name >> section >> credits;
}

void Course::Output( ofstream & ofile ) const
{
  ofile << "  Course:  " << name << '\n'
        << "  Section: " << section << '\n'
        << "  Credits: " << credits << endl;
}

Registration::Registration()
{
  count = 0;
}

void Registration::Input( ifstream & infile )
```

```
{
  infile >> studentId >> semester >> count;

  for(int i = 0; i < count; i++)
    courses[i].Input( infile );
}

void Registration::Output( ofstream & ofile ) const
{
  ofile << "Student ID: " << studentId << '\n'
        << "Semester:   " << semester << '\n';

  for(int i = 0; i < count; i++)
  {
    courses[i].Output( ofile );
    ofile  << '\n';
  }
}
```

Main Program

```
//***********************************************
// MAIN.CPP - Main Registration Program
//***********************************************

#include "course.h"

int main()
{
  // Read a Registration object from an
  // input file and write it to an output file.

  ifstream infile( "rinput.txt" );
  if( !infile ) return -1;

  Registration R;
  R.Input( infile );

  ofstream ofile( "routput.txt", ios::app );
  if( !ofile ) return -1;

  R.Output( ofile );

  return 0;
}
```

CHAPTER 3: STUDENT REGISTRATION

Class Definitions

```
//**************************************
// COURSE.H - Course Class Definition
//**************************************

#ifndef COURSE_H
#define COURSE_H

#include <iostream.h>
#include <string.h>

const unsigned CourseNameSize = 10;

class Course {
public:
  Course();
  Course( const char * nam, char sect, unsigned cred );
  // Construct a course from a name, section letter,
  // and number of credits.

  unsigned GetCredits() const;
  // Get the number of credits.

  void SetCredits( unsigned cred );
  // Set the number of credits.

  friend ostream & operator <<( ostream & os, const Course & C );
  friend istream & operator >>( istream & input, Course & C );

private:
  char name[CourseNameSize];  // course name
  char section;    // section (letter)
  int  credits;    // number of credits
};

inline unsigned Course::GetCredits() const
{
  return credits;
}

inline void Course::SetCredits( unsigned cred )
{
  credits = cred;
}

#endif
```

```
//***********************************************
// REGIST.H - Registration Class Definition
//***********************************************

#ifndef REGIST_H
#define REGIST_H

#include <iostream.h>
#include "course.h"

const unsigned MaxCourses = 10;

class Registration {
public:
  Registration();
  unsigned GetCredits() const;
  unsigned GetCount() const;
  friend ostream & operator <<( ostream & os,
        const Registration & R);

  friend istream & operator >>( istream & input,
        Registration & R );

private:
  long studentId;            // student ID number
  unsigned semester;         // semester year, number
  unsigned count;            // number of courses
  Course courses[MaxCourses]; // array of courses
};

inline unsigned Registration::GetCount() const
{
  return count;
}

#endif
```

Course Class Implementation

```
//***********************************************
// COURSE.CPP - Course Class Implementation
//***********************************************

#include "course.h"
```

```
Course::Course()
{
  name[0] = '\0';
}

Course::Course( const char * nam, char sect,
                unsigned cred )
{
  strncpy( name, nam, CourseNameSize );
  section = sect;
  credits = cred;
}

istream & operator >>( istream & input, Course & C )
{
  input >> C.name >> C.section >> C.credits;
  return input;
}

ostream & operator <<( ostream & os, const Course & C )
{
  os << "  Course:  " << C.name << '\n'
     << "  Section: " << C.section << '\n'
     << "  Credits: " << C.credits << '\n';
  return os;
}
```

Registration Class Implementation

```
//****************************************************
// REGIST.CPP - Registration Class Implementation
//****************************************************

#include "regist.h"

Registration::Registration()
{
  count = 0;
}

unsigned Registration::GetCredits() const
{
  unsigned sum = 0;
  for(int i = 0; i < count; i++)
    sum += courses[i].GetCredits();
```

```
    return sum;
}


istream & operator >>( istream & input, Registration & R )
{
    input >> R.studentId >> R.semester >> R.count;

    for(int i = 0; i < R.count; i++)
        input >> R.courses[i];

    return input;
}


ostream & operator <<( ostream & os, const Registration & R )
{
    os << "Student ID: " << R.studentId << '\n'
        << "Semester:   " << R.semester << '\n';

    for(int i = 0; i < R.count; i++)
        os << R.courses[i] << '\n';

    return os;
}
```

Main Program

```
//****************************************
// MAIN.CPP - Main Registration Program
//****************************************

#include <iostream.h>
#include <fstream.h>
#include "course.h"  // Course class definition
#include "regist.h"  // Registration class definition

int main()
{
    ifstream infile("rinput.txt");
    if( !infile ) return -1;

    Registration R;
    infile >> R;

    ofstream ofile("routput.txt");

    ofile << R
        << "Number of courses = " << R.GetCount() << '\n'
```

```
               << "Total credits     = " << R.GetCredits() << '\n';

      // Declare and initialize a Course, and modify
      // its credits.

      Course aCourse( "MTH_3020", 'B', 2 );
      aCourse.SetCredits( 5 );
      cout << aCourse << endl;

      return 0;
   }
```

CHAPTER 4: FSTRING CLASS

Definition

```
//****************************************
// FSTRING.H - FString Class Definition
//****************************************

#ifndef FSTRING_H
#define FSTRING_H

#include <iostream.h>
#include <iomanip.h>
#include <string.h>

class FString {
public:
  FString();

  FString( const char * s );
  // Construct from a C-style string.

  FString( const FString & s );
  // Construct from another FString.

  FString & Append( const FString & s );
  // Append another FString to current object.

  FString & Assign( const char * s );
  // Assign a C-style string to current object.

  FString & Assign( const FString & s );
  // Assign an FString to current object.
```

```
  const char * CString() const;
  // Convert current object to a C-style string.

  int Compare( const FString & s ) const;
  // Implement the standard strcmp() function.
  // case-sensitive

  int IsLess( const FString & s ) const;
  // Return 1 if current object is less than s.

  int IsGreater( const FString & s ) const;
  // Return 1 if current object is greater than s.

  int IsEqual( const FString & s ) const;
  // Return 1 if current object is equal to s.

  FString & GetLine( istream & inp );
  // Get a line of input from a stream.

  friend istream & operator >>( istream & inp,
        FString & s );

  friend ostream & operator <<( ostream & inp,
        const FString & s );

  enum { MaxSize = 256 };  // Maximum allowable string size

private:
  char str[MaxSize+1];  // String characters
};

#endif
```

Implementation

```
//*********************************************
// FSTRING.CPP - FString Class Implementation
//*********************************************

#include "fstring.h"

FString::FString()
{
    str[0] = '\0';
}


FString::FString( const char * S )
```

```
{
  strncpy( str, S, MaxSize );
  str[MaxSize] = '\0';
}

FString & FString::Append( const FString & S )
{
  strncat( str, S.CString(), MaxSize );
  return *this;
}

FString & FString::Assign( const char * S )
{
  strncpy( str, S, MaxSize );
  return *this;
}

FString & FString::Assign( const FString & S2 )
{
  strncpy( str, S2.str, MaxSize );
  return *this;
}

const char * FString::CString() const
{
  return str;
}

int FString::Compare( const FString & S2 ) const
{
  return strcmp( str, S2.str );
}

FString & FString::GetLine( istream & inp )
{
  inp.getline( str, MaxSize+1 );
  return *this;
}

istream & operator >>( istream & inp, FString & S )
{
  inp >> setw(S.MaxSize+1) >> S.str;
  return inp;
}

ostream & operator <<( ostream & os, const FString & S )
{
```

```
  os << S.str;
  return os;
}
```

CHAPTER 4: ROBOT SIMULATION

Class Definitions

Screen Class
```
//********************************************************
// SCREEN.H - Non-portable Video and Keyboard Functions
//********************************************************

// Some or all of the following functions may be available
// in your C++ configuration. Enable the #define directive
// that applies to your compiler and insert the appropriate
// implementation code.

#ifndef SCREEN_H
#define SCREEN_H

#define __BCPLUSPLUS__ // select Borland C++

class Screen {
public:
  void SetCursorPosition( int x, int y );
  void ClearScreen();
  void ClearToEol();
  int KbHit();
};

#ifdef __BCPLUSPLUS__    // Borland C++ implementation
#include <conio.h>

inline void Screen::SetCursorPosition( int x, int y )
{
  gotoxy( x, y );
}

inline void Screen::ClearScreen()
{
  clrscr();
}

inline void Screen::ClearToEol()
{
```

```
    clreol();
}

inline int Screen::KbHit()
{
  return kbhit();
}

#endif  // end of BCPLUSPLUS definitions
#endif  // end of ifndef condition
```

Position Class

```
//*****************************************
// POSITION.H - Position Class Definition
//*****************************************

// A Position is a reference to an object's
// position in a 2-dimensional cartesian space.

#ifndef POSITION_H
#define POSITION_H

#include <stdlib.h>    // for rand()

enum Direction { up, down, left, right, none };

class Position {
public:
  enum { xMax = 80, yMax = 22 };
  Position();

  unsigned GetX() const;
  unsigned GetY() const;
  // Get the X and Y coordinates.

  void SetX( unsigned newX );
  void SetY( unsigned newY );
  // Set the X and Y coordinates.

  void Move( Direction dir, unsigned xMax, unsigned yMax );
  // Move in direction dir, to maximum X-position xMax,
  // and maximum Y-position yMax.

  static Direction ChooseRandomDirection();
  // Choose a random direction in which to move.
```

```
private:
  unsigned x;        // x-position
  unsigned y;        // y-position
};

// Inline functions belong in the header file.

inline unsigned Position::GetX() const
{
  return x;
}

inline unsigned Position::GetY() const
{
  return y;
}

inline void Position::SetX( unsigned newX )
{
  x = newX;
}

inline void Position::SetY( unsigned newY )
{
  y = newY;
}

#endif
```

Robot Class

```
//**********************************
// ROBOT.H - Robot Class Definition
//**********************************

#ifndef ROBOT.H
#define ROBOT.H

#include "position.h"

class Robot {
public:
  Robot();

  Position & Move();
  // Move to a new position, return its value.
```

```
  unsigned IsActive() const;
  // Return 1 if this Robot is alive.

  void Fight();
  // Fight with any robots in the same cell.

  unsigned GetX() const;
  unsigned GetY() const;
  // Get the X and Y coordinates.

  void static SetEnergyStart( unsigned n );
  // Set the starting energy level of all Robots.

private:
  Position  where;         // shield x,y position
  Direction direction;     // 0,1,2,3
  unsigned  energy;            // energy level
  static unsigned energyStart; // starting energy level

  Direction chooseRandomDirection() const;
};


inline unsigned Robot::GetX() const
{
  return where.GetX();
}

inline unsigned Robot::GetY() const
{
  return where.GetY();
}

#endif
```

Grid Class

```
//*******************************
// GRID.H - Grid Class Definition
//*******************************

// Each cell contains 0-n robots. When robots share the same
// cell, they fight and are weakened. We display the grid
// after each battle, and count the number of remaining
// robots.
```

```
#ifndef GRID_H
#define GRID_H

#include <iostream.h>
#include "screen.h"      // for clearScreen()
#include "position.h"   // Position class
#include "robot.h"       // Robot class

class Grid {
public:
  Grid( Robot * robotArray, unsigned numRobots );
  // Construct a Grid from an array of robots
  // and a count of the number of robots.

  void Battle();
  // Simulate one round of battle.

  unsigned CountActive() const;
  // Return the number of active robots.

  void Draw() const;
  // Draw the grid on the screen.

private:
  Robot * robots;            // array of robots
  unsigned cells[Position::xMax][Position::yMax];
  unsigned robotCount;       // starting number of robots
  unsigned activeCount;      // number of active robots
  unsigned timeCount;        // elapsed seconds
  void clearCells();         // clear all cells
};

#endif
```

Class Implementations

```
//*************************************************
// POSITION.CPP - Position Class Implementation
//*************************************************

#include "position.h"

Position::Position(): x(0),y(0)
{   }

// Update the current object's position. Do not
// go below 0, and stay below xMax and yMax.
```

```
void Position::Move( Direction dir, unsigned xMax,
    unsigned yMax )
{
    if( (dir == up) && ( y > 0) )
      y--;
    else if( dir == down )
      y++;
    else if( (dir == left) && (x > 0) )
      x--;
    else if( dir == right )
      x++;
    x = x % xMax;
    y = y % yMax;
}


// Static member function that returns a randomly
// chosen direction. The ordering of constants in
// the Dir[] array here must match those in the
// Direction enumerated type.

Direction Position::ChooseRandomDirection()
{
  const unsigned dcount = 4;
  Direction Dir[dcount] = {up, down, left, right};
  unsigned n = /rand % dcount;
  return Dir[n];
}



//******************************************
// ROBOT.CPP - Robot Class Implementation
//******************************************

#include "position.h"
#include "robot.h"

unsigned Robot::energyStart = 10; // starting energy level

Robot::Robot()
{
  energy = energyStart;
  unsigned x = /rand % Position::xMax
  unsigned y = /rand % Position::yMax
  where.SetX( x );
  where.SetY( y );
  direction = Position::ChooseRandomDirection();
}
```

```
unsigned Robot::IsActive() const
{
  return energy > 0;
}

void Robot::SetEnergyStart( unsigned n )
{
  energyStart = n;
}

void Robot::Fight()
{
  if (energy > 0) energy--;
}

Position & Robot::Move()
{
  direction = Position::ChooseRandomDirection();
  where.Move( direction, Position::xMax, Position::yMax );
  return where;
}


//****************************************
// GRID.CPP - Grid Class Implementation
//****************************************

#include "grid.h"
extern Screen theScreen;

Grid::Grid( Robot * robotArray, unsigned numRobots )
{
  robots = robotArray;
  activeCount = robotCount = numRobots;
  timeCount = 0;
}

// Clear all cells in the Grid to 0.

void Grid::clearCells()
{
  for(unsigned x = 0; x < Position::xMax; x++)
    for(unsigned y = 0; y < Position::yMax; y++)
      cellsX[y] = 0;
}

// Count the number of active robots in the Grid.
```

```
unsigned Grid::CountActive() const
{
  unsigned sum = 0;
  for(unsigned i = 0; i < robotCount; i++)
    if( robots[i].IsActive() )
      sum++;
  return sum;
}


// Update the positions of all robots in the Grid. For each
// robot entering an occupied cell, it is weakened by
// fighting the other robot.

void Grid::Battle()
{
  Position p;
  unsigned x, y;
  clearCells();

  for(unsigned j = 0; j < robotCount; j++)
  {
    if( robots[j].IsActive() )  // is the robot alive?
    {
      p = robots[j].Move();
      x = p.GetX();              // get its position
      y = p.GetY();
      (cellsX[y])++;             // increment cell count

      if( cellsX[y] > 1 )     // cell occupied?
        robots[j].Fight();    // robots fight!
    }
  }
  timeCount++;
}


// Draw the Grid, showing the number
// of living robots in each cell.

void Grid::Draw() const
{
  theScreen.SetCursorPosition( 1,1 );
  cout << "                                      ";
  theScreen.SetCursorPosition( 1,1 );
  cout
    << "Active: " << CountActive()
    << "     "
    << "Time: " << timeCount
```

```
        << '\n'
        << "............................................"
            "............................"
        << '\n';

  for(unsigned y = 0; y < Position::yMax; y++)
    for(unsigned x = 0; x < Position::xMax; x++)
    {
      unsigned n = cellsX[y];
      if( n )
        cout << n;
      else
        cout << ' ';
    }
}
```

Main Program

```
//********************************************************
// MAIN.CPP -  Robot Battle Simulation, Main Program
//********************************************************

#include <assert.h>
#include "grid.h"     // Grid class
#include "robot.h"    // Robot class

Screen theScreen;      // Screen functions

// Set the startup configuration for the simulation.

void configure( unsigned & startE, unsigned & stopC )
{
  theScreen.ClearScreen();
  cout << "ROBOT WARS (battle simulation)\n\n"
       << "Starting energy level of each robot? ";
  cin >> startE;
  cout << "Stop when population reaches which number? ";
  cin >> stopC;
}


// NumRobots can be any integer 1 - 5000.
const unsigned NumRobots = 2000;
Robot robots[NumRobots];  // array of robots

int main()
{
```

```
    unsigned startEnergy, stopCount;

    configure( startEnergy, stopCount );
    assert( stopCount < NumRobots );

    Robot::SetEnergyStart( startEnergy );


    Grid G( robots, NumRobots );  // construct the grid

    // Repeat the simulation loop until the robot
    // population dwindles to desired level.

    do {
      G.Battle();              // carry out one battle cycle
      G.Draw();                // draw the grid
    } while ( G.CountActive() > stopCount );

    return 0;
}
```

CHAPTER 5: DOCTOR'S OFFICE SCHEDULING

Class Definitions

```
//***************************************************
// DOCTORS.H - Doctor's Office Scheduling Program
//
// TimeSlot, Appointment, Patient, DailySchedule,
// Doctor, and Scheduler Class Definitions
//***************************************************

#ifndef DOCTORS_H
#define DOCTORS_H

#include <iostream.h>
#include <fstream.h>
#include <strstream.h>
#include "fstring.h"    // custom string class

const unsigned NumDoctors = 5;
extern int getYN( const char * );

class Doctor;      // forward definitions
class Patient;
```

```cpp
class TimeSlot {
public:
  TimeSlot( const unsigned n = 0 );

  unsigned AsInteger() const;

  friend istream & operator >>(istream & inp, TimeSlot & T);

  friend ostream & operator <<(ostream & os, const TimeSlot & T);

private:
  static unsigned StartHour;
  static unsigned ApptLen;
  unsigned intValue;
};

class Appointment {
public:
  Appointment();

  Appointment ( const TimeSlot & aTime,
        unsigned docNum, const Patient & P);

  const FString & GetPatientName() const;

  const TimeSlot & GetTime() const;

  int IsScheduled() const;

  void SetTime( const unsigned n );

  friend ostream & operator <<( ostream & os,
        const Appointment & A );

private:
  enum { NoDoctor = 9999 };
  unsigned doctorNum;
  TimeSlot timeSlot;
  FString patientName;
};

class Patient {
public:
  Patient();

  void InputName();
```

```
   unsigned ChooseDoctor() const;

   TimeSlot ChooseTimeSlot(const Doctor & D) const;

   const Appointment & GetAppointment() const;

   const FString & GetFirstName() const;

   const FString & GetLastName() const;

   int IsScheduled() const;

   void SetAppointment( const Appointment & A );

   friend ostream & operator <<( ostream & os,
      const Patient & P );
private:
  FString lastName;
  FString firstName;
  Appointment nextVisit;
};

class DailySchedule {
public:
  DailySchedule();

  int IsTimeSlotFree( const TimeSlot & T ) const;

  void SetAppointment( const Appointment & A );

  void ShowAppointments( ostream & os ) const;

  friend ostream & operator <<( ostream & os,
        const DailySchedule & DS );

private:
  enum { MaxTimeSlots = 40 };
  Appointment appointments[MaxTimeSlots];
};

class Doctor {
public:
  Doctor();

  int AddToSchedule( const Appointment & A );
  // Try to schedule an appointment. Return 1 (true) if
```

```
    // successful, 0 (false) if not.

  const DailySchedule & GetSchedule() const;

  void SetId( const unsigned );

  void SetLastName( const FString & L );

  const FString & GetLastName() const;

  void ShowAppointments( ostream & ) const;

  static const FString & GetDoctorName( unsigned index );

  static void SetDoctorName(unsigned, const FString & nam);

private:
  unsigned id;
  FString lastName;
  DailySchedule schedule;
  static FString doctorName[NumDoctors];
};


class Scheduler {
public:
  Scheduler( Doctor * docs );

  void PrintAllAppointments( const char * fileName );

  int ScheduleOneAppointment();

  void ScheduleAllAppointments();

private:
  Doctor * doctors;  // points to first element in array of doctors
};

//............ Inline Functions .................

inline TimeSlot::TimeSlot( const unsigned n )
{
  intValue = n;
}


inline unsigned TimeSlot::AsInteger() const
{
```

```
  return intValue;
}

inline const DailySchedule & Doctor::GetSchedule() const
{
  return schedule;
}

inline void Doctor::SetId( const unsigned n )
{
 id = n;
}

inline void Doctor::SetLastName( const FString & aName )
{
  lastName = aName;
}

inline const FString & Doctor::GetLastName() const
{
  return lastName;
}

inline const FString & Doctor::GetDoctorName( unsigned i )
{
  return doctorName[i];
}

inline void Doctor::SetDoctorName( unsigned i, const FString & aName )
{
  doctorName[i] = aName;
}

inline const FString & Appointment::GetPatientName() const
{
  return patientName;
}

inline int Appointment::IsScheduled() const
{
  return doctorNum != NoDoctor;
}

inline void Appointment::SetTime( const unsigned n )
{
  timeSlot = n;
}
```

```
inline const TimeSlot & Appointment::GetTime() const
{
  return timeSlot;
}

inline const FString & Patient::GetFirstName() const
{
  return firstName;
}

inline const FString & Patient::GetLastName() const
{
  return lastName;
}

inline Appointment::Appointment()
{
  doctorNum = NoDoctor;
}

inline const Appointment & Patient::GetAppointment() const
{
  return nextVisit;
}

inline Patient::Patient() {   }

inline void Patient::SetAppointment( const Appointment & app )
{
  nextVisit = app;
}

inline int Patient::IsScheduled() const
{
  return nextVisit.IsScheduled();
}

#endif
```

Class Implementations

```
//****************************************************
// DOCTORS.CPP - Doctor's Office Scheduling Program
//
// TimeSlot, Appointment, Patient, DailySchedule,
// Doctor, and Scheduler Class Implementations
//****************************************************
```

```cpp
#include <stdlib.h>
#include "doctors.h"


//.............Global Function ..............

// Display a question, ask for yes or no answer;
// return 1 if Y pressed, otherwise return 0.

#include <ctype.h>   // for toupper()

int getYN( const char * st )
{
  char ch;
  cout << st << " [Y/n]: ";
  cin >> ch;
  cin.ignore(80,'\n');
  if( toupper(ch) == 'Y' ) return 1;
  return 0;
}

//................. TimeSlot ......................

unsigned TimeSlot::StartHour = 8;
unsigned TimeSlot::ApptLen = 15;

istream & operator >>( istream & inp, TimeSlot & T )
{
  char buf[20];
  inp.getline( buf, 20 );     // get a line of input
  istrstream aStream( buf, 20 );
  unsigned h, m;
  char ch;
  aStream >> dec >> h >> ch >> m;
  unsigned aph = 60 / TimeSlot::ApptLen;
  if( h < T.StartHour )            // invalid hour?
    cerr << "\n Invalid hour value.\n";
  T.intValue = ((h - TimeSlot::StartHour)* aph)
            + (m / TimeSlot::ApptLen);
  return inp;
}

ostream & operator <<( ostream & os, const TimeSlot & T )
{
  unsigned aph = 60 / T.ApptLen;        // 4 = 60 / 15
  unsigned h = (T.intValue / aph ) + T.StartHour;  // (S / 4) + 8
  unsigned m = (T.intValue % aph ) * T.ApptLen;    // (S % 4) * 15
```

```
  char oldfill = os.fill('0');
  os << setw(2) << h << ':' << setw(2) << m;
  os.fill( oldfill );
  return os;
}


//............... DailySchedule ...................

DailySchedule::DailySchedule()
{
  for(unsigned i = 0; i < MaxTimeSlots; i++)
    appointments[i].SetTime( i );
}

int DailySchedule::IsTimeSlotFree( const TimeSlot & aTime ) const
{
  unsigned n = aTime.AsInteger();
  return !appointments[n].IsScheduled();
}

void DailySchedule::SetAppointment( const Appointment & app )
{
  unsigned n = app.GetTime().AsInteger();
  appointments[n] = app;
}

void DailySchedule::ShowAppointments( ostream & os ) const
{
  for(unsigned i = 0; i < MaxTimeSlots; i++)
  {
    if( appointments[i].IsScheduled())
      os << appointments[i].GetTime() << "    "
         << appointments[i].GetPatientName()
         << endl;
  }
}

ostream & operator <<( ostream & os, const DailySchedule & DS )
{
  for(unsigned i = 0; i < DS.MaxTimeSlots; i++)
  {
    os << DS.appointments[i].GetTime();
    if( DS.appointments[i].IsScheduled())
      os << " ***    ";
    else
      os << "         ";
    if( i % 4 == 3 ) os << '\n';
```

```
  }
  return os;
}

//.................... Doctor ......................

FString Doctor::doctorName[NumDoctors]; // static data member

Doctor::Doctor()
{
  id = 0;
}

int Doctor::AddToSchedule( const Appointment & app )
{
  if( schedule.IsTimeSlotFree( app.GetTime()))
  {
    schedule.SetAppointment( app );
    return 1;
  }
  return 0;
}

void Doctor::ShowAppointments( ostream & os ) const
{
  os << "Appointments for Dr. "
     << lastName << '\n'
     << "................................"
     << '\n';
  schedule.ShowAppointments( os );
  os << endl;
}

//................. Appointment ......................

Appointment::Appointment ( const TimeSlot & aTime,
    unsigned docNum, const Patient & aPatient )
{
  timeSlot = aTime;
  doctorNum = docNum;
  patientName = aPatient.GetLastName();
  patientName.Append( ", " );
  patientName.Append( aPatient.GetFirstName() );
}

ostream & operator <<( ostream & os, const Appointment & A )
{
```

```
  os << "Dr. " << Doctor::GetDoctorName(A.doctorNum) << ", "
     << "Time: "
     << A.timeSlot;
  return os;
}

//.................... Patient .........................

void Patient::InputName()
{
  cout << "Patient's last name: ";
  cin >> lastName;
  cout << "Patient's first name: ";
  cin >> firstName;
}

// Display list of doctor names and numbers. Let user
// enter a number, and return this as the function result.

unsigned Patient::ChooseDoctor() const
{
  for(unsigned i = 0; i < NumDoctors; i++)
    cout << i << ": " << Doctor::GetDoctorName(i) << '\n';

  unsigned n = 0;
  int ok = 0;
  do {
    cout << "Enter a doctor number: ";
    cin >> n;
    cin.ignore(255,'\n');
    if( n >= NumDoctors )
      cout << "Number out of range!\n";
    else
      ok = 1;
  } while( !ok );

  return n;
}

TimeSlot Patient::ChooseTimeSlot( const Doctor & D ) const
{
  cout << '\n'
       << "Daily Schedule of Dr. " << D.GetLastName() << '\n'
       << "......................................" << '\n'
       << D.GetSchedule() << '\n'
       << "Enter a time (format hh:mm): ";
  TimeSlot aSlot;
```

```
  cin >> aSlot;
  return aSlot;
}


ostream & operator <<( ostream & os, const Patient & P )
{
  os << "Patient " << P.firstName << ' '
     << P.lastName << '\n'
     << "has been scheduled as follows:" << '\n'
     << P.nextVisit << endl;
  return os;
}

//.................. Scheduler .....................

// Initialize the id numbers and names of the
// array of doctors from a file.

Scheduler::Scheduler( Doctor * docs )
{
  doctors = docs;
  ifstream dnameFile( "doctors.txt" );
  if( !dnameFile )
  {
    cout << "Cannot open input file! Aborting program.\n";
    abort;
  }
  FString temp;
  for(unsigned i = 0; i < NumDoctors; i++)
  {
    doctors[i].SetId( i );
    temp.GetLine( dnameFile );
    doctors[i].SetLastName( temp );
    Doctor::SetDoctorName(i, temp);
  }
}

// Write each doctor's list of appointments,
// showing time and patient name for each.

void Scheduler::PrintAllAppointments(const char * fileName)
{
  ofstream ofile( fileName );
  if( ofile )
    for(unsigned i = 0; i < NumDoctors; i++)
      doctors[i].ShowAppointments( ofile );
```

```
}


void Scheduler::ScheduleAllAppointments()
{
  while( ScheduleOneAppointment() )
    continue;
}

// Choose a doctor, input patient name, and
// ask for a particular time slot. Make the
// appointment and display the results.

int Scheduler::ScheduleOneAppointment()
{
  // Get patient name, let patient request a doctor.

  Patient aPatient;
  aPatient.InputName();
  unsigned doctorNum = aPatient.ChooseDoctor();

  Doctor & theDoc = doctors[doctorNum];

  while( !aPatient.IsScheduled() )
  {
    // Patient chooses a time slot. Construct an appointment
    // from the time slot, doctor number, and patient name.

    TimeSlot aTime = aPatient.ChooseTimeSlot( theDoc );
    Appointment app( aTime, doctorNum, aPatient  );

    // Try to schedule the patient for a particular time
    // slot with the chosen doctor. If successful, add the
    // appointment time to the patient's record; if not,
    // display an error message.

    if( theDoc.AddToSchedule( app ))
      aPatient.SetAppointment( app );
    else
      cout << "Sorry, Dr. " << theDoc.GetLastName()
           << " is not available at that time. " << endl;
  }
  cout << aPatient;
  return getYN("Continue?");
}
```

Main Program

```
//**************************************************
// MAIN.CPP - Doctor's Office Scheduling Program
//**************************************************

#include "doctors.h"

/*
Ordinarily, we would not want the array of doctors to be
global. Unfortunately, if it were declared inside main(),
it might exceed the available runtime stack space in some
C++ environments. The global data space is usually larger than
the runtime stack, so we've made the array global.

In Chapter 7 we show how to dynamically allocate the
array, removing the memory size restriction so the array can
be declared inside main().
*/

static Doctor doctorArray[NumDoctors];

int main()
{
  cout << "Doctors Office Scheduling Program\n\n";

  Scheduler officeSchedule( doctorArray );

  officeSchedule.ScheduleAllAppointments();

  officeSchedule.PrintAllAppointments( "appts.txt" );

  return 0;
}
```

Input/Output Files

doctors.txt:
Chong
Baker
Gonzalez
LightFoot
Williams

appts:txt:
Appointments for Dr. Chong
....

```
 8:00    Adams
10:45    Washington
17:45    Madison

Appointments for Dr. Baker
..................................
 9:00    Lincoln
12:00    Carter
12:15    Grant
16:00    Eisenhower

Appointments for Dr. Gonzalez
..................................
15:30    Cleveland
16:00    Reagan

Appointments for Dr. LightFoot
..................................
10:00    Hamilton
10:30    Roosevelt
13:00    Johnson
16:30    Kennedy

Appointments for Dr. Williams
..................................
16:15    Roosevelt
```

CHAPTER 7: DYNAMICALLY ALLOCATED ARRAY

LongArray Class Definition

```cpp
//**************************************
// LONG.H - LongArray Class Definition
//**************************************

#ifndef LONG_H
#define LONG_H

#include <assert.h>

class LongArray {
public:
  LongArray( unsigned sz = 0, long defval = 0 );
  // Construct an array of size sz, initialize all
  // elements with defval.
```

```
LongArray( const LongArray & L );
// copy constructor

~LongArray();
// destructor.

unsigned GetSize() const;
// Return the current allocation size.

void GrowBy( unsigned n );
// Increase the allocation size by n elements.

void Init( long defval = 0 );
// Initialize all elements to defval.

long Get( unsigned i ) const;
// Retrieve element at index position i.

void Put( unsigned i, long elt );
// Insert element at index position i.

private:
    long * data;    // ptr to array containing elements
    unsigned size;  // current allocation size
    long initv;     // initial value
};

#endif
```

Class Implementation

```
//*******************************************
// LONG.CPP - LongArray Class Implementation
//*******************************************

#include "long.h"

LongArray::LongArray( unsigned sz, long defval )
{
    size = sz;
    data = new long[size];
    Init( defval );
}

LongArray::LongArray( const LongArray & L )
{
    size = L.size;
```

```
  initv = L.initv;
  data = new long[size];
  for(unsigned i = 0; i < size; i++)
    data[i] = L.data[i];
}


LongArray::~LongArray()
{
  delete [] data;
}


long LongArray::Get( unsigned i ) const
{
  assert( i < size );
  return data[i];
}


unsigned LongArray::GetSize() const
{
  return size;
}


void LongArray::GrowBy( unsigned growBy )
{
  unsigned tsize = size + growBy;
  long * temp = new long[tsize];

  // Copy the existing data.
  unsigned i;
  for(i = 0; i < size; i++)
    temp[i] = data[i];

  // Set new positions to initial values.
  for(i = size; i < tsize; i++)
    temp[i] = initv;

  size = tsize;    // update the size value
  delete [] data; // delete the old array
  data = temp;     // save pointer to new data
}


void LongArray::Init( long defval )
{
  initv = defval;
  for(unsigned i = 0; i < size; i++)
    data[i] = defval;
}
```

```
void LongArray::Put( unsigned i, long elt )
{
  assert( i < size );
  data[i] = elt;
}
```

Test Program

```
//***********************************
// MAIN.CPP - LongArray Test Program
//***********************************

#include <stdlib.h>
#include <iostream.h>
#include <new.h>    // for set_new_handler()
#include "long.h"

void arraysize_error()
{
  cout << "Array too large. Aborting program.\n";
  exit(1);
}

int main()
{
  set_new_handler( arraysize_error );

  const unsigned ArraySize = 20;
  LongArray L(ArraySize, 0xFFFF );
  unsigned i;

  cout << "Initialized with default values:\n";
  for(i = 0; i < L.GetSize(); i++)
    cout << L.Get(i) << ',';
  cout << "\n--------------------------------\n";

  for(i = 0; i < L.GetSize(); i++)
    L.Put(i, rand());

  cout << "Initialized with random values:\n";
  for(i = 0; i < L.GetSize(); i++)
    cout << L.Get(i) << ',';
  cout << "\n--------------------------------\n";

  LongArray Z( L );  // copy constructor

  cout << "After copying the array:\n";
```

```
  for(i = 0; i < Z.GetSize(); i++)
    cout << Z.Get(i) << ',';
  cout << "\n---------------------------------\n";

  const unsigned GrowValue = 5;
  Z.GrowBy( GrowValue );
  Z.Put( 0, 9999 );

  cout << "After expanding by 5 and changing elt(0):\n";
  for(i = 0; i < Z.GetSize(); i++)
    cout << Z.Get(i) << ',';

  return 0;
}
```

CHAPTER 8: RANGE ERROR EXCEPTION CLASS

```
//***************************************
// RANGE.H - RangeError Exception Class
//***************************************

#ifndef RANGE_H
#define RANGE_H

#include <iostream.h>
#include <string.h>

const unsigned FileNameSize = 40;
// Make this >= longest file name on target system.

class RangeError {
public:
  RangeError( const char * fname,
              unsigned line,
              unsigned subscr )
  {
    strncpy(fileName, fname, FileNameSize);
    lineNumber = line;
    value = subscr;
  }

  friend ostream & operator <<( ostream & os,
        const RangeError & R )
  {
    os << "\nRangeError exception thrown: "
       << R.fileName
```

```
          << ", line " << R.lineNumber
          << " value = " << R.value
          << endl;
     return os;
  }

private:
  char fileName[FileNameSize+1];
  unsigned lineNumber;
  unsigned value;
};


#endif
```

CHAPTER 8: PACKAGE SHIPPING SERVICE

Class Definitions

```
//**********************************
// ITEM.H - Item Class Definition
//**********************************

// An Item is the abstract base class for all objects
// that are inserted in a Table (see table.h).

#ifndef ITEM_H
#define ITEM_H

#include <iostream.h>

class Item {
public:
  virtual ~Item() {   }

  virtual int Compare( const Item & I2 ) const = 0;
  // Compare this object to Item I2; return -1 if
  // this object is less than I2, 0 if equal, and
  // 1 if greater than I2.

  friend ostream & operator <<( ostream & os, const Item & I );
  friend istream & operator >>( istream & inp, Item & I );

private:
  virtual void printOn( ostream & os ) const = 0;
  virtual void readFrom( istream & inp ) = 0;
};
```

```
#endif


//*****************************************
// PACKAGE.H - Package Class Definition
//*****************************************

#ifndef PACKAGE_H
#define PACKAGE_H

#include <string.h>
#include <iostream.h>
#include <iomanip.h>
#include "item.h"

class Package :public Item {
public:
  Package();

  Package( long trackNumP, long originP,
           long destinP, long dateP,
           float costP, float weightP );

  long GetDestination() const;
  long GetTrackingNumber() const;
  float GetWeight() const;
  void PrintLong( ostream & os ) const;

  int Compare( const Item & I2 ) const;
    // Compare *this to Package I2,
    // return -1 if *this is less than I2,
    // return 0 if *this is equal to I2,
    // and return 1 if *this is greater than I2.

  // Functions that set data member values:

  void SetTrackNum( long trackNumP );
  void SetOrigin( long originP );
  void SetDestination( long destinP );
  void SetDate( long dateP );
  void SetCost( float costP );
  void SetWeight( float weightP );
  void Init();

private:
  long  trackNum;      // tracking number
  long  origin;        // originating zip code
```

```
    long   destin;      // destination zip code
    long   date;        // date sent (yymmdd)
    float  cost;        // shipping cost
    float  weight;      // weight in kilograms

    virtual void printOn( ostream & os ) const;
    virtual void readFrom( istream & is );
};

#endif



//**********************************
// TABLE.H - Table Class Definition
//**********************************

// This abstract class defines the public interface
// for the Table class. A Table contains objects whose
// classes are derived from Item.

#ifndef TABLE_H
#define TABLE_H

#include "item.h"
#include "limits.h"

class Table {
public:
    virtual ~Table() {   }

    virtual void AddItem( Item * ) = 0;
    // Add a new item to the table.

    virtual void Clear() = 0;
    // Empty the table.

    virtual unsigned GetCount() const = 0;
    // Return the number of entries in the table.

    virtual Item * GetItemPtr( unsigned i ) const = 0;
    // Retrieve pointer to item at position i.

    virtual unsigned IndexOf( const Item * P ) const = 0;
    // Search for a matching item in table;
    // if found, return its index position,
    // otherwise return UINT_MAX.
```

```
  virtual void Sort() = 0;
  // Sort the table in ascending order.
};

#endif


//*********************************************
// TABLEARR.H - TableAsArray Class Definition
//*********************************************

#ifndef TABLEARR_H
#define TABLEARR_H

#include <iostream.h>
#include <iomanip.h>
#include <assert.h>
#include "table.h"

class TableAsArray : public Table {
public:
  TableAsArray( unsigned tableSize );

  virtual ~TableAsArray();

  virtual void AddItem( Item * I );

  virtual void Clear();

  virtual unsigned GetCount() const;

  virtual Item * GetItemPtr( unsigned i ) const;

  virtual unsigned IndexOf( const Item * P ) const;

  virtual void Sort();

  friend ostream & operator <<( ostream &,
        const TableAsArray & );

private:
  Item ** data;   // array of pointers to Items
  unsigned size;  // allocation size
  unsigned count; // number of Items

private:
  void swap( Item * & p1, Item * & p2 );
```

```
};

inline TableAsArray::~TableAsArray()
{
  Clear();
}

inline unsigned TableAsArray::GetCount() const
{
  return count;
}

inline Item * TableAsArray::GetItemPtr( unsigned i ) const
{
  assert( i < count );
  return data[i];
}

#endif
```

Class Implementations

```
//**************************************
// ITEM.CPP - Item Class Implementation
//**************************************

#include "item.h"

ostream & operator <<( ostream & os, const Item & I )
{
  I.printOn( os );
  return os;
}

istream & operator >>( istream & inp, Item & I )
{
  I.readFrom( inp );
  return inp;
}


//*********************************************
// PACKAGE.CPP - Package Class Implementation
//*********************************************

#include "package.h"
```

```
Package::Package()
{
  Init();
}

Package::Package(
    long trackNumP,
    long originP,
    long destinP,
    long dateP,
    float costP,
    float weightP )
{
  SetTrackNum( trackNumP );
  SetOrigin( originP );
  SetDestination( destinP );
  SetDate( dateP );
  SetCost( costP );
  SetWeight( weightP );
}

void Package::Init()
{
  SetTrackNum( 0 );
  SetOrigin( 0 );
  SetDestination( 0 );
  SetDate( 0 );
  SetCost( 0.0f );
  SetWeight( 0.0f );
}

long Package::GetDestination() const
{
  return destin;
}

long Package::GetTrackingNumber() const
{
  return trackNum;
}

float Package::GetWeight() const
{
  return weight;
}

void Package::SetTrackNum( long trackNumP )
```

```
{
  trackNum = trackNumP;
}

void Package::SetOrigin( long originP )
{
  origin = originP;
}

void Package::SetDestination( long destinP )
{
  destin = destinP;
}

void Package::SetDate( long dateP )
{
  date = dateP;
}

void Package::SetCost( float costP )
{
  cost = costP;
}

void Package::SetWeight( float weightP )
{
  weight = weightP;
}

void Package::printOn( ostream & os ) const
{
  // Save the current flags and precision before modifying them.
  unsigned svflags = os.setf( ios::showpoint | ios::fixed );
  int svprecision = os.precision(2);

  os << '['
     << trackNum << ','
     << origin   << ','
     << destin << ','
     << date << ','
     << cost << ','
     << weight << "]" << endl;

  // Restore the previous flags and precision.
  os.precision( svprecision );
  os.flags( svflags );
}
```

```cpp
void Package::PrintLong( ostream & os ) const
{
  // Save the current flags and precision before modifying them.
  unsigned svflags = os.setf( ios::showpoint | ios::fixed );
  int svprecision = os.precision(2);

  os << ".........................\n"
     << "Tracking number: "
     << trackNum << '\n'
     << "Origination zip code: "
     << origin   << '\n'
     << "Destination zip code: "
     << destin << '\n'
     << "Date sent: "
     << date << '\n'
     << "Shipment cost: "
     << cost << '\n'
     << "Package weight "
     << weight << endl;

  // Restore the previous flags and precision.
  os.precision( svprecision );
  os.flags( svflags );
}

void Package::readFrom( istream & inp )
{
  Init();
  inp >> trackNum >> origin >> destin >> date >> cost >> weight;
  inp.ignore( 10, '\n' );
}

int Package::Compare( const Item & I2 ) const
{
  if( trackNum < ((Package &)I2).trackNum )
    return -1;
  else if( trackNum == ((Package &)I2).trackNum )
    return 0;
  else  // if( trackNum > ((Package &)I2).trackNum )
    return 1;
}


//****************************************************
// TABLEARR.CPP - TableAsArray Class Implementation
//****************************************************
```

```cpp
#include "tablearr.h"

// Create a table of size sz. Make sure that
// sz is less than UINT_MAX.

TableAsArray::TableAsArray( unsigned sz )
{
  size = sz;
  assert( size < UINT_MAX );
  count = 0;
  data = new Item *[size];
  for(unsigned j = 0; j < size; j++)
    data[j] = 0;
}

// Add an item to the table. P cannot be pointer to const
// because data[] does not contain pointers to constants.

void TableAsArray::AddItem( Item * P )
{
  if( count < size )
    data[count++] = P;
  else
    cout << "Error: Table full; item not added.\n";
}

// Empty the table. Delete all objects pointed to
// by the array and delete the array of pointers.

void TableAsArray::Clear()
{
  for(unsigned i = 0; i < count; i++)
    delete data[i];

  delete [] data;
  count = 0;
  size = 0;
}

ostream & operator <<( ostream & os, const TableAsArray & T )
{
  for(unsigned i = 0; i < T.count; i++)
    os << setw(3) << i << ": " << *T.data[i] << endl;

  return os;
}
```

```
// Attempt to locate item P in the table. If successful,
// return its index position; otherwise, return UINT_MAX,
// a standard constant defined in limits.h.

unsigned TableAsArray::IndexOf( const Item * P ) const
{
  for(unsigned i = 0; i < count; i++)
    if( P->Compare(*data[i]) == 0 ) return i;

  return UINT_MAX;
}


// Sort the table using a Selection sort.

void TableAsArray::Sort()
{
  for(unsigned curr = 0; curr < count-1; curr++)
  {
    unsigned minIndex = curr;

    for(unsigned k = curr+1; k < count; k++)
      if( data[k]->Compare(*data[minIndex]) < 0 )
        minIndex = k;

    if( minIndex != curr )
      swap( data[curr], data[minIndex] );
  }
}

void TableAsArray::swap( Item * & p1, Item * & p2 )
{
  Item * temp;
  temp = p1;
  p1 = p2;
  p2 = temp;
}
```

Main Program

```
//************************************************
// SHIPPING.CPP - Package Shipping Program
//************************************************

#include <iostream.h>
#include <fstream.h>
#include "package.h"
#include "tablearr.h"
```

```cpp
int main()
{
// Open input file, get number of Packages,
// open output file, create table.

ifstream input( "PACKAGES.TXT" );
if (!input) return 1;
ofstream outfile("outfile.txt");

unsigned numRecords;
input >> numRecords;
input.ignore( 1, '\n' );
if( numRecords < 1 )
{
  cout << "Package file is empty. Ending program.\n";
  return 0;
}

// Read all Packages from the input file,
// add them to the table, and display the table.

TableAsArray ptable( numRecords );
Package * pkg;
unsigned i;

for(i = 0; i < numRecords; i++)
{
  pkg = new Package;
  input >> *pkg;
  ptable.AddItem( pkg );
  if( input.eof() ) break;
}
outfile << ptable << endl;   // output the table

// Get each Package from the table, add its
// weight to a total, and display the total
// weight of all packages.

Package * z;
float sum = 0.0;

for(i = 0; i < ptable.GetCount(); i++)
{
  z = (Package *)ptable.GetItemPtr( i );
  sum += z->GetWeight();
}
```

```
outfile << "Total weight of packages = "
    << sum << "\n\n";


// Sort and display the table.

ptable.Sort();
outfile << "Packages sorted by tracking number......\n"
        << ptable << '\n';

// Search for a particular package by its tracking
// number. If found, retrieve and display the package.

pkg->Init();
pkg->SetTrackNum( 101400L );
unsigned n = ptable.IndexOf( pkg );

if( n != UINT_MAX )
{
  pkg = (Package *)ptable.GetItemPtr( n );
  outfile << "Package " << *pkg
    << " found at position " << n << '\n';
}
else
  outfile << "Package not found.\n";

return 0;
}
```

CHAPTER 9: FSTRING CLASS WITH OPERATORS

Class Definition

```
//*******************************************
// FSTRING.H - FString Class Definition
//*******************************************

// This version uses operator overloading.

#ifndef FSTRING_H
#define FSTRING_H

#include <iostream.h>
#include <strstream.h>
#include <iomanip.h>
#include <string.h>
```

```cpp
#include <stdlib.h>  // for strtol()


class FString    // fixed-length string class
{
public:
  // Constructors
  FString();
  FString( const char * s );
  FString( const FString & s );
  FString( const char ch );

  // Assignment operators
  FString & operator =( const char * s );
  FString & operator =( const FString & s );
  FString & operator =( char ch );

  // Append & Concatenate operators
  FString & Append( const FString & s );
  FString & operator +=( const FString & s );
  FString & operator +=( const char * s );
  FString & operator +=( char c );
  FString operator +( const FString & s2 );

  // Cast operators
  operator const char *() const; // cast to C-style string
  operator long() const;         // cast to long integer

  // Comparison operators and functions
  int operator ==( const FString & s ) const;
  int operator !=( const FString & s ) const;
  int operator < ( const FString & s ) const;
  int operator > ( const FString & s ) const;
  int operator <=( const FString & s ) const;
  int operator >=( const FString & s ) const;

  // Stream I/O operators and functions
  void GetLine( istream & inp );
  friend istream & operator >>( istream & inp, FString & s );
  friend ostream & operator <<( ostream & os, const FString & s );

private:
  enum { MaxSize = 255};
  char str[MaxSize+1];
};


inline void FString::GetLine( istream & inp )
```

```
{
  inp.getline( str, MaxSize+1 );
}

inline FString::operator const char *() const
{
  return str;
}

inline int FString::operator ==( const FString & s ) const
{
  return strcmp( str, s.str ) == 0;
}

inline int FString::operator !=( const FString & s ) const
{
  return strcmp( str, s.str ) != 0;
}

inline int FString::operator < ( const FString & s ) const
{
  return strcmp( str, s.str ) < 0;
}

inline int FString::operator > ( const FString & s ) const
{
  return strcmp( str, s.str ) > 0;
}

inline int FString::operator <=( const FString & s ) const
{
  return !(*this > s);
}

inline int FString::operator >=( const FString & s ) const
{
  return !(*this < s);
}

inline FString & FString::operator +=( const char * s )
{
  return *this += FString(s);
}

inline FString & FString::operator +=( char c )
{
  return *this += FString(c);
```

```
}

inline FString FString::operator +( const FString & s2 )
{
  FString temp( *this );
  return temp += s2;
}

#endif
```

Class Implementation

```
//**********************************************
// FSTRING.CPP - FString Class Implementation
//**********************************************

#include "fstring.h"
#include "range.h"

FString::FString()
{
  str[0] = '\0';
}


FString::FString( const char ch )
{
  str[0] = ch;
  str[1] = '\0';
}

FString::FString( const FString & s )
{
  *this = s;
}

FString::FString( const char * s )
{
  size_t n = strlen( s );
  if( n > MaxSize )
    throw RangeError( __FILE__, __LINE__, n );
  strcpy( str, s );
}

// Append FString s to this FString.

FString & FString::operator +=( const FString & s )
```

```
{
  size_t n = strlen( str ) + strlen( s.str );
  if( n >= MaxSize )
    throw RangeError( __FILE__, __LINE__, n );

  strcat( str, s.str );
  return *this;
}

FString & FString::operator =( const FString & s )
{
  size_t n = strlen( s.str );
  if( n > MaxSize )
    throw RangeError( __FILE__, __LINE__, n );
  strcpy( str, s.str );
  return *this;
}

FString & FString::operator =( const char * s )
{
  return *this = FString(s);
}

FString & FString::operator =( char ch )
{
  str[0] = ch;
  str[1] = '\0';
  return *this;
}

// Convert digit string to long integer.

FString::operator long() const
{
  return strtol( str, 0, 0 );
}

istream & operator >>( istream & inp, FString & s )
{
  inp >> setw(s.MaxSize+1) >> s.str;
  return inp;
}

ostream & operator <<( ostream & os, const FString & s )
{
  os << s.str;
  return os;
}
```

CHAPTER 9: BITARRAY CLASS

Class Definition

```
//*******************************************
// BITARRAY.H -  BitArray Class Definition
//*******************************************

// Each bit is mapped to an ordinal value between
// 0 and N-1, where N is the set size. N may be 1
// to UINT_MAX.

#ifndef BITARRAY_H
#define BITARRAY_H

#include <iostream.h>
#include "range.h"

// The type of a single component of the array holding
// the bits can be unsigned char, unsigned int,
// or unsigned long.

typedef unsigned int elttype;


class BitArray {
public:
  BitArray();
  // default constructor

  BitArray( size_t sz = 0 );
  // Construct a bit array of size sz.

  ~BitArray();
  // destructor

  size_t Count() const;
  // Return the number of '1' bits.

  BitArray & operator =( unsigned long n );
  // Construct a bit array from n. This is a
  // departure from the draft standard.

  BitArray & operator |=( const BitArray & S );
  // Form the union of bits in current array
  // with those in Bit array S.
```

```
  BitArray & operator &=( const BitArray & S );
  // Form the intersection of bits in current array
  // with those in Bit array S.

  friend ostream & operator <<( ostream &, const BitArray & );
  // stream output operator

  friend istream & operator >>( istream & inp, BitArray & BA );
  // stream input operator

  void Reset();
  // Clear all bits.

  void Reset( size_t n );
  // Clear bit n.

  void Set( size_t n );
  // Set bit n.

  int Test( size_t n ) const;
  // Return value of bit n.

  void Toggle( size_t n );
  // Toggle bit n.

private:
  enum { BitsPerByte = 8,
         NumBits = sizeof(elttype) * BitsPerByte };

  size_t size;         // maximum number of bits
  size_t numElements;  // size of bits[] array

  elttype * bits;      // array of bits
};

#endif
```

Class Implementation

```
//**************************************************
// BITARRAY.CPP - BitArray Class Implementation
//**************************************************

#include "bitarray.h"

size_t min( size_t t1, size_t t2 )
{
```

```
  if( t1 < t2 )
    return t1;
  return t2;
}


BitArray::BitArray()
{
  size = 0;
  numElements = 0;
  bits = 0;
}


BitArray::BitArray( size_t sz )
{
  size = sz;
  numElements = ((size -1) / NumBits) + 1;
  bits = new elttype[ numElements ];
  Reset();
}


BitArray::~BitArray()
{
  delete [] bits;
}


size_t BitArray::Count() const
{
  size_t tally = 0;
  for(size_t i = 0; i < size; i++)
  {
    if( Test(i) )
      tally++;
  }
  return tally;
}


BitArray & BitArray::operator |=( const BitArray & B2 )
{
  size_t count = min( numElements, B2.numElements );
  for(size_t i = 0; i < count; i++)
    bits[i] |= B2.bits[i];
  return *this;
}


BitArray & BitArray::operator &=( const BitArray & B2 )
{
  size_t count = min( numElements, B2.numElements );
```

```
  for(size_t i = 0; i < count; i++)
    bits[i] &= B2.bits[i];
  return *this;
}


BitArray & BitArray::operator =( unsigned long n )
{
  Reset();
  for(size_t i = 0; i < size, n != 0; i++, n >>= 1)
    if(n & 1)
      Set(i);
  return *this;
}

ostream & operator <<( ostream & os, const BitArray & BA )
{
  for(size_t i = BA.size; 0 < i;)
    os << (BA.Test(--i) ? '1':'0');
  return os;
}

istream & operator >>( istream & inp, BitArray & BA )
{
  BA.Reset();
  char ch;
  for(size_t i = BA.size; 0 < i;)
  {
    --i;
    inp >> ch;
    if( ch == '1' )
      BA.Set(i);
  }
  return inp;
}

void BitArray::Reset()
{
  for(size_t i = 0; i < numElements; i++)
    bits[i] = 0;
}

// Clear bit n.

void BitArray::Reset( size_t n )
{
  if( n >= size )
    throw RangeError(__FILE__,__LINE__,n);
```

```cpp
    bits[n / NumBits] &= ~((elttype)1 << n % NumBits);
}

void BitArray::Set( size_t n )
{
    if( n >= size )
        throw RangeError(__FILE__,__LINE__,n);

    bits[n / NumBits] |= ((elttype)1 << n % NumBits);
}

int BitArray::Test( size_t n ) const
{
    if( n >= size )
      throw RangeError(__FILE__,__LINE__,n);

    int z = bits[n / NumBits] & ((elttype)1 << n % NumBits);
    return z != 0;
}

void BitArray::Toggle( size_t n )
{
    if( n >= size )
      throw RangeError(__FILE__,__LINE__,n);

    bits[n / NumBits] ^= ((elttype)1 << n % NumBits);
}
```

Test Program

```cpp
//*********************************
// MAIN.CPP - BitArray Test Program
//*********************************

#include <iostream.h>
#include <iomanip.h>
#include <fstream.h>
#include <conio.h>
#include "bitarray.h"
#include "fstring.h"
#include "nofile.h"    // NoFileError exception class


void Test1()
{
    // Assign a long integer to a BitArray.
```

```
  BitArray X( 20 );
  X = (1 + 4 + 8 + 32 + 128 + 1024 );   // assign long integer
  cout << X << '\n';

  // Set and reset an individual bit.

  X.Set( 12 );
  cout << X << '\n';
  X.Reset( 12 );
  cout << X << '\n';
}

void Test2()
{
  // Read a string of bits from a file.

  FString fileName( "bits.txt" );

  cout << "Reading file: " << fileName << '\n';
  ifstream bfile( fileName );
  if( !bfile ) throw NoFileError( fileName );

  BitArray filebits(16);
  bfile >> filebits;
  cout << filebits << '\n';
}

void Test3()
{
  // Add several integers to a set.

  const size_t SetSize = 16;
  BitArray B( SetSize );
  B.Set(1);    // add several elements
  B.Set(5);
  B.Set(8);
  B.Set(15);

  cout << '\n'
       << "BitArray B:    " << B << '\n';

  // Test for set membership.

  for( int i = 0; i < SetSize; i++ )
    if( B.Test(i) )
      cout << setw(2) << i << " is a member" << '\n';
```

```
   // Perform union and intersection operations.

   BitArray A( SetSize );
   A.Set(3);
   A.Set(4);
   A.Set(9);
   cout << "\nBitArray B:     " << B
        << "\nBitArray A:     " << A;

   A |= B;
   cout << "\nA union B:      " << A;

   A.Toggle(4);
   cout << "\nToggled bit 4: " << A << '\n';
}

void Test4()
{
   // Create a room-scheduling application, and
   // determine which rooms are both requested
   // and available.

   enum { _101,_110,_112,_114,_120,_190,_192,_200,
          _201,_205,_208,_210,_220,_221,_225,_230 };

   const size_t RoomMax = 16;

   BitArray rooms( RoomMax );
   rooms.Set(_101 );
   rooms.Set(_110 );
   rooms.Set(_120 );
   rooms.Set(_220 );
   rooms.Set(_221 );
   rooms.Set(_225 );
   cout << "\nrooms:             " << rooms;

   BitArray requests( RoomMax );
   requests.Set(_101);
   requests.Set(_110);
   requests.Set(_120);
   requests.Set(_225);
   requests.Set(_230);
   cout << "\nrequests:          " << requests;

   BitArray approved( RoomMax );
   approved |= requests;          // union
   approved &= rooms;             // intersection
```

```
  cout << "\nrequests approved: " << approved << '\n';
}

int main()
{
  cout << "Examples using the BitArray class." << endl;

  try {
   Test1();
   Test2();
   Test3();
   Test4();
  }
  catch( const RangeError & re ) {
    cout << re;
  }
  catch( const NoFileError & nf ) {
    cout << nf;
  }
  return 0;
}
```

CHAPTER 10: FTSTRING CLASS TEMPLATE

Class Definition

```
//***************************************
// FTSTRING.H - FTString Class Template
//***************************************

#ifndef FTSTRING_H
#define FTSTRING_H

#include <iostream.h>
#include <iomanip.h>
#include <string.h>
#include "range.h"

template <size_t MaxSize>
class FTString {
public:
  FTString();

  FTString( const char * s );

  void GetLine( istream & inp );
```

```
   int Length() const;

   FTString & operator =( const char * s );

   operator char *();

   int operator ==( const FTString & s2 ) const;

   friend istream & operator >>( istream & inp,
         FTString<MaxSize> & s )
   {
     inp >> s.str;
     return inp;
   }
   friend ostream & operator <<( ostream & os,
         const FTString<MaxSize> & s )
   {
     os << s.str;
     return os;
   }
private:
  char str[MaxSize+1];
};
```

Class Implementation

```
// (also in FTSTRING.H)


template<size_t MaxSize>
int FTString<MaxSize>::Length() const
{
 return strlen(str);
}


template<size_t MaxSize>
FTString<MaxSize>::FTString()
{
  str[0] = '\0';
}

template<size_t MaxSize>
FTString<MaxSize>::FTString( const char * S )
{
  size_t n = strlen(S);
  if( n >= MaxSize )
```

```
      throw RangeError(__FILE__,__LINE__,n);
  strcpy( str, S );
}


template<size_t MaxSize>
void FTString<MaxSize>::GetLine( istream & inp )
{
  inp.getline( str, MaxSize+1 );
}


template<size_t MaxSize>
FTString<MaxSize> & FTString<MaxSize>::operator =
        ( const char * S )
{
  strcpy( str, S );
  return *this;
}


template<size_t MaxSize>
FTString<MaxSize>::operator char *()
{
  return str;
}


template<size_t MaxSize>
int FTString<MaxSize>::operator ==
    ( const FTString<MaxSize> & S2 ) const
{
  return strcmp(str,S2.str) == 0;
}


#endif
```

Demonstration Program

```
//**************************************
// TSTRING.CPP - FTString Test Program
//**************************************

#include "ftstring.h"

int main()
{
  FTString<30> name;
  FTString<40> street;
  FTString<15> city;
  FTString<2>  state;
```

```
    FTString<5>  zip;

    cout << "Enter a name: ";
    name.GetLine( cin );
    street = "222 North Orange Place";
    city = "Metropolis";
    state = "ND";
    zip = "60606";

    cout << name.Length() << endl;

    cout << name << ',' << street << ','
         << city << ',' << state << ','
         << zip << endl;

    return 0;
}
```

CHAPTER 10: ARRAY CLASS TEMPLATE

```
//*********************************
// ARRAY.H - Array Class Template
//*********************************

#include <iostream.h>
#include "range.h"

template <class T>
class Array {
public:
  Array( unsigned sz );
  ~Array();
  T & operator[]( unsigned i );

private:
  T * values;
  unsigned size;
};

template<class T>
T & Array<T>::Array( unsigned sz )
{
  values = new T[sz];
  size = sz;
}
```

```
template<class T>
T & Array<T>::operator[] ( unsigned i )
{
  if( i >= size )
    throw RangeError(__FILE__,__LINE__,i);
  return values[i];
}


template<class T>
Array<T>::~Array()
{
  delete [] values;
}
```

CHAPTER 10: DICTIONARY CLASS TEMPLATE

Class Definition and Implementation

```
//*************************************
// DICT.H - Dictionary Class Template
//*************************************

#include <iostream.h>
#include "range.h"

class DictionaryFull {
public:
  friend ostream & operator <<(ostream & os,
        const DictionaryFull & F)
  {
    os << "Dictionary is full.";
    return os;
  }
};

class DuplicateKey {
public:
  friend ostream & operator <<(ostream & os,
        const DuplicateKey & F)
  {
    os << "Attempt to add duplicate key.";
    return os;
  }
};
```

```
template<class TKey,class TVal>
int Dictionary<TKey,TVal>::Add( const TKey & tk,
                                const TVal & tv )
{
  if( !Find( tk ) ) // not already in dictionary?
  {
    if(IsFull())            // dictionary full?
      throw DictionaryFull();
    unsigned i = avail++;  // save position
    keys[i] = tk;          // add new key
    values[i] = tv;        // add associated value
    return 1;              // success!
  }
  throw DuplicateKey(); // attempt to add duplicate key
}

template<class TKey,class TVal>
int Dictionary<TKey,TVal>::Find( const TKey & tk )
{
  for(unsigned i = 0; i < avail; i++)
    if( tk == keys[i] )
    {
      current = i;    // save current position
      return 1;
    }
  return 0;
}

template<class TKey,class TVal>
int Dictionary<TKey,TVal>::IsFull() const
{
  return avail >= size;
}

template<class TKey,class TVal>
TVal Dictionary<TKey,TVal>::Get() const
{
  return values[current];
}

template<class TKey, class TVal>
ostream & operator <<( ostream & os,
        const Dictionary<TKey, TVal> & D )
{
  for(unsigned i = 0; i < D.avail; i++)
    cout << D.keys[i] << " -> "
         << D.values[i] << '\n';
```

```
    return os;
}
```

Test Program

```cpp
//*************************************************
// DICT.CPP - Dictionary Template Test Program
//*************************************************

#include <iostream.h>
#include <fstream.h>
#include <except.h>  // xalloc exception
#include "dict.h"    // Dictionary class
#include "fstring.h" // FString class
#include "nofile.h"  // NoFileError Exception class

// Create a Dictionary of customer account numbers
// (int) and file record numbers (long).

void create_customer_accounts()
{
  Dictionary<unsigned, long> accounts( 100 );
  cout << "Customer Accounts:\n";

  try {
    accounts.Add( 101, 287 );
    accounts.Add( 152, 368 );
    accounts.Add( 173, 401 );
    accounts.Add( 185, 368 ); // duplicate value is ok
    accounts.Add( 152, 399 ); // duplicate key forbidden
  }
  catch( const DuplicateKey & dk ) {
    cout << dk << endl;
  }
  cout << accounts << endl;  // display the list

  cout << "Account number to find? ";
  unsigned n;
  cin >> n;
  if( accounts.Find( n ))
    cout << "Account number " << n
         << " may be found at record "
         << accounts.Get() << '.' << endl;
  else
    cout << "Account not found." << endl;
  cout << endl;
}
```

```
// Create a dictionary of automobile part
// numbers (long) and part descriptions (String).

void create_parts_list()
{
  FString filename( "parts.txt" );
  ifstream infile( filename );
  if( !infile ) throw NoFileError( filename );

  // Add part numbers and descriptions to a dictionary.

  unsigned long partNum;
  FString descrip;


  cout << "Automobile parts list:\n";
  Dictionary<unsigned long, FString> pList( 200 );

  try {
    infile >> partNum;
    while( !infile.eof())
    {
      descrip.GetLine( infile );
      pList.Add( partNum, descrip );
      infile >> partNum;
    }
  }
  catch( const DuplicateKey & dk ) {
    cout << dk << endl;
  }
  cout << pList;

  cout << "Part number to find? ";
  cin >> partNum;

  if( pList.Find( partNum ))
    cout <<
      "Part " << partNum << " is a "
        << pList.Get() << '.' << endl;
  else
    cout << "Part number not found." << endl;
}

// Create two dictionaries and handle all
// uncaught exceptions.
```

```
int main()
{
  cout << "Dictionary Template Demo Program\n\n";
  try {
    create_customer_accounts();
    create_parts_list();
  }
  catch ( xalloc ) {
    cout << "Memory allocation error\n";
  }
  catch ( const DictionaryFull & df ) {
    cout << df;
  }
  catch ( const NoFileError & nf ) {
    cout << nf;
  }
  catch ( ... ) {
    cout << "Unknown exception caught.\n";
  }
  return 0;
}
```

CHAPTER 11: SINGLY LINKED LIST CLASS

Class Definition

```
//************************************************
// SLIST.H - Snode and Slist Class Definitions
//************************************************

// The Snode and slist classes implement a simple
// linked list class that could be further refined
// by deriving new classes.

#ifndef SLIST_H
#define SLIST_H

#include <iostream.h>
#include <assert.h>

typedef int NodeType;

class Snode
{
    friend class Slist;
```

```
public:
  Snode();
  // default constructor

  Snode * Next() const;
  // Return pointer to the next node.

  friend ostream & operator <<( ostream &, const Snode & );
  // stream output operator

protected:
  NodeType value;     // data stored in node
  Snode * next;       // points to next node

  Snode( const NodeType & val );
  // Construct a node from a value.
};

class Slist
{
public:
  Slist();
  // default constructor

  ~Slist();
  // destructor

  void Clear();
  // Empty the list.

  int Empty() const;
  // Return 1 if the list is empty.

  NodeType Get() const;
  // Get the node at the current position.

  void InsertAfter( const NodeType & nodeVal );
  // Insert new node after current one.

  void Replace( const NodeType & newVal );
  // Replace the data in the current node.

  int operator ++();
  // Prefix increment the current position. Return 0 if
  // at end of the list; otherwise, return 1.

  friend ostream & operator <<( ostream &, const Slist & );
```

```
  // Write the list to an output stream.

protected:
  Snode * head;       // dummy head node
  Snode * tail;       // dummy tail node
  Snode * current;    // current position
};

#endif
```

Class Implementations

```
//****************************************************
// SLIST.CPP - Snode and Slist Class Implementations
//****************************************************

#include "Slist.h"

//...........Snode Class ............

Snode::Snode() :next(0)
{ }

Snode::Snode( const NodeType & val )
      : value(val),next(0)
{ }

ostream & operator <<( ostream & os, const Snode & S )
{
  os << S.value << ',';
  return os;
}

Snode * Snode::Next() const
{ return next; }


//........... Slist Class ............


// Create head and tail nodes, and attach them,
// making a circular list.

Slist::Slist()
{
  head = new Snode;
  tail = new Snode;
```

```cpp
  head->next = tail;
  tail->next = head;
  current = head;
}

Slist::~Slist()
{
  Clear();
  delete head;
  delete tail;
}

void Slist::Clear()
{
  current = head->next;
  assert( current );

  while( current != tail )
  {
    Snode * P = current;
    current = current->next;
    delete P;
  }
  current = head;
  head->next = tail;
}

int Slist::Empty() const
{
  return head->next == tail;
}

NodeType Slist::Get() const
{
  assert( current );
  return current->value;
}

void Slist::InsertAfter( const NodeType & nodeVal )
{
  assert( current );
  Snode * p = new Snode( nodeVal );
  p->next = current->next;
  current->next = p;
  current = p;
}
```

```cpp
void Slist::Replace( const NodeType & newVal )
{
  assert( current );
  current->value = newVal;
}

int Slist::operator ++()
{
  assert( current );
  if( current->next != tail )
  {
    current = current->next;
    return 1;
  }
  return 0;
}

ostream & operator <<( ostream & os, const Slist & S )
{
  if( S.Empty()) return os;

  Snode * p = S.head->Next();
  while( p != S.tail )
  {
    os << *p;
    p = p->Next();
  }
  os << endl;
  return os;
}
```

Test Program

```cpp
//*******************************
// MAIN.CPP - Slist Test Program
//*******************************

#include <stdlib.h>
#include "slist.h"

int main()
{
  Slist scores;

  for(int i = 0; i < 10; i++)
  {
    int n = rand() % 100;
```

```
    scores.Append( n );
  }
  cout << scores << endl;

  scores.GoLast();
  cout << "Last item: " << scores.Get() << endl;

  scores.GoTop();
  ++scores;
  cout << "First item: " << scores.Get() << endl;

  scores.Replace( 101 );
  cout << "Replaced first node with value 101:"
       << endl << scores << endl;

  scores.Clear();
  if( scores.Empty())
    cout << "The list is empty." << endl;

  return 0;
}
```

CHAPTER 11: LIST CLASS TEMPLATE

```
//*********************************************
// TLIST.H - Tnode and Tlist Class Templates
//*********************************************

#include <iostream.h>

class NoCurrentNode {          // exception class
public:
  friend ostream & operator <<( ostream & os,
        const NoCurrentNode & nc )
  {
    os << "List exception: No current node.";
    return os;
  }
};

template <class T>
class Tnode {
  friend class Tlist<T>;
public:
  Tnode():next(0){ }
```

```cpp
   Tnode( const T & val );

   Tnode<T> * Next() const;

   friend ostream & operator <<(ostream & os,
          const Tnode<T> & N);

private:
   T value;           // data stored in node
   Tnode * next;      // points to next node
};

template <class T>
class Tlist {
public:
   Tlist();
   ~Tlist();

   int Advance();
   // Return 0 if current position is already at
   // the end of the list; otherwise, increment
   // current and return 1.

   void Append( const T & nodeVal );
   // Add a new node to the end of the list.

   void Clear();
   // Remove all nodes.

   T Get() const;
   // Get the data at the current position.

   void GoLast();
   // Set current to the last node in the list.

   void GoTop();
   // Set current to the header node.

   void InsertAfter( const T & nodeVal );
   // Insert new node after current one.

   int IsEmpty() const;
   // Return 1 if the list is empty; otherwise,
   // return 0.

   void Prepend( const T & nodeVal );
   // Insert a node at the beginning of the list.
```

```
   void Replace( const T & newVal );
   // Replace the data in the current node.

   friend ostream & operator <<(ostream &, const Tlist<T> &);

private:
   Tnode<T> * head;        // dummy head node
   Tnode<T> * tail;        // dummy tail node
   Tnode<T> * current;     // current position
};

//...........Tnode<T> Class ...........

template <class T>
Tnode<T>::Tnode( const T & val ): value(val)
{
   next = 0;
}

template <class T>
Tnode<T> * Tnode<T>::Next() const
{
   return next;
}

template <class T>
ostream & operator <<( ostream & os, const Tnode<T> & N )
{
   os << N.value << ',';
   return os;
}

//........... Tlist<T> Class ...........

template <class T>
Tlist<T>::Tlist()
{
   head = new Tnode<T>;
   tail = new Tnode<T>;
   head->next = tail;
   tail->next = head;
   current = head;
}

template <class T>
Tlist<T>::~Tlist()
{
```

```
    Clear();
    delete head;
    delete tail;
}

template <class T>
int Tlist<T>::Advance()
{
  if( !current ) throw NoCurrentNode();
  if( current->next != tail )
  {
    current = current->next;
    return 1;
  }
  return 0;
}

template <class T>
void Tlist<T>::Append( const T & nodeVal )
{
  GoLast();
  InsertAfter( nodeVal );
}

template <class T>
void Tlist<T>::Clear()
{
  current = head->next;
  while( current != tail )
  {
    head->next = current->next;
    delete current;
    current = head->next;
  }
  current = head;
  head->next = tail;
}

template <class T>
int Tlist<T>::IsEmpty() const
{
  return head->next == tail;
}

template <class T>
T Tlist<T>::Get() const
{
```

```
  if( !current ) throw NoCurrentNode();
  return current->value;
}

template <class T>
void Tlist<T>::GoLast()
{
  if( !current ) throw NoCurrentNode();
  while( current->next != tail )
    current = current->next;
}

template <class T>
void Tlist<T>::GoTop()
{
  current = head;
}

template <class T>
void Tlist<T>::InsertAfter( const T & nodeVal )
{
  if( !current ) throw NoCurrentNode();
  Tnode<T> * p = new Tnode<T>( nodeVal );
  p->next = current->next;
  current->next = p;
  current = p;
}

template <class T>
void Tlist<T>::Prepend( const T & nodeVal )
{
  GoTop();
  InsertAfter( nodeVal );
}

template <class T>
void Tlist<T>::Replace( const T & newVal )
{
  if( !current ) throw NoCurrentNode();
  current->value = newVal;
}

template <class T>
ostream & operator <<( ostream & os,
        const Tlist<T> & S )
{
  if( S.IsEmpty()) return os;
```

```
  Tnode<T> * p = S.head->Next();
  while( p != S.tail )
  {
    os << *p;
    p = p->Next();
  }
  os << endl;
  return os;
}
```

CHAPTER 11: SEARCHING A GRAPH

Graph Class Definition

```
//************************************
// GRAPH.H - Graph Class Definition
//************************************

// Defines a graph with nodes and arcs, represented
// as an adjacency matrix. Uses the Tlist class template.

#ifndef GRAPH_H
#define GRAPH_H

#include <iostream.h>
#include <iomanip.h>
#include "range.h"    // RangeError class
#include "tlist.h"    // Tlist class template

class Graph {
public:
  Graph( unsigned n );
  // Create a Graph capable of containing
  // as many as n nodes.

  ~Graph();
  // destructor

  void AddArc( unsigned v1, unsigned v2 );
  // Add an arc between nodes v1 and v2.

  int Search( unsigned v1, unsigned v2, Tlist<unsigned> & path );
  // If a path can be found from v1 to v2,
  // return 1 and display the path; otherwise, return 0.

  friend ostream & operator <<( ostream & os, const Graph & T);
```

```cpp
private:
  unsigned size;                  // number of nodes
  unsigned * visited;             // array of visited nodes
  Tlist<unsigned> * adjList;      // array of lists

  int searchDFS( unsigned v1, unsigned v2, Tlist<unsigned> & path );
  // internal DFS search
};


#endif
```

Class Implementation

```cpp
//*****************************************
// GRAPH.CPP - Graph Class Implementation
//*****************************************

#include "graph.h"

// Construct a graph by allocating an
// array of linked lists.

Graph::Graph( unsigned n )
{
  size = n;
  adjList = new Tlist<unsigned>[size];
  visited = new unsigned[size];
}

// Delete each of the adjacency lists
// by calling each of their destructors.

Graph::~Graph()
{
  delete [] adjList;
  delete [] visited;
}

// Node v1 has an arc leading to node v2, so
// add v2 to the list adjList[v1].

void Graph::AddArc( unsigned v1, unsigned v2 )
{
  if( v1 >= size )
    throw RangeError(__FILE__,__LINE__,v1);
  if( v2 >= size )
    throw RangeError(__FILE__,__LINE__,v2);
```

```
    adjList[v1].Append( v2 );
}


// Search for a path between v1 and v2. Returns
// 1 if a path is found; otherwise, returns 0.

int Graph::Search( unsigned v1, unsigned v2,
    Tlist<unsigned> & path )
{
  for(unsigned i = 0; i < size; i++)
    visited[i] = 0;

  if( searchDFS( v1, v2, path ))
  {
    path.Prepend( v1 );
    return 1;
  }
  return 0;
}


// Internal search, using DFS algorithm. Returns 1 if
// a path is found from v1 to v2; otherwise, returns 0.

int Graph::searchDFS( unsigned v1, unsigned v2,
         Tlist<unsigned> & path )
{
  if( v1 == v2 ) return 1;
  if( v1 >= size )
    throw RangeError(__FILE__,__LINE__,v1);
  if( v2 >= size )
    throw RangeError(__FILE__,__LINE__,v2);

  visited[v1] = 1;
  Tlist<unsigned> & L = adjList[v1];

  if( !L.IsEmpty() )
  {
    L.GoTop();
      L.Advance();
      do {
        unsigned n = L.Get();
        if( !visited[n] )          // If node not already visited,
        if( searchDFS( n, v2, path )) // search following nodes.
        {
          path.Prepend( n );   // Insert node on the path list.
          return 1;
        }
```

```
      } while( L.Advance() );
  }
  return 0;   // no path found
}

ostream & operator <<( ostream & os, const Graph & T )
{
  for(unsigned v = 0; v < T.size; v++)
  {
    Tlist<unsigned> & L = T.adjList[v];
    os << setw(2) << v << ": ";

    if( !L.IsEmpty() )
    {
      L.GoTop();
      L.Advance();
      do {
        os << L.Get() << ',';
      } while( L.Advance() );
    }
    os << endl;
  }
  return os;
}
```

Main Program

```
//*****************************************
// GRTEST.CPP - Graph Class Test Program
//*****************************************

// Short test program that reads vertices from a data
// file, displays the adjacency list, and performs
// a depth-first traversal.

#include <fstream.h>
#include "graph.h"

void GraphTest( ifstream & input )
{
  unsigned grsize;
  input >> grsize;
  Graph G( grsize );

  unsigned v1, v2;
  input >> v1 >> v2;
```

```
  try {
    while( !input.eof() )
    {
      G.AddArc( v1, v2 );
      input >> v1 >> v2;
    }
  }
  catch( const RangeError & R ) {
    cout << R;
  }

  cout << G; // display graph as adjacency list

  // Create an empty path list, and search for a
  // path; if found, display the path.

  cout << "Searching for a path. Enter first and\n"
       << "last nodes, separated by a space: ";

  unsigned first, last;
  cin >> first >> last;
  Tlist<unsigned> path;

  try {
    if( G.Search( first, last, path ))
      cout << "Path found: " << path << endl;
    else
      cout << "Path not found." << endl;
  }
  catch( const RangeError & R ) {
    cout << R;
  }
}

int main()
{
  ifstream input( "GRAPH.TXT" );
  if( !input )
    return 1;

  try {
    GraphTest( input );
  }
  catch( ... ) {
    cout << "Unknown exception thrown.\n";
  }
  return 0;
}
```

CHAPTER 11: DOUBLY LINKED LIST CLASS

DblNode Class Definition

```
//****************************************
// DBLNODE.H - DblNode Class Definition
//****************************************

// This is an abstract class.

#ifndef DBLNODE_H
#define DBLNODE_H

#include <iostream.h>

class DblNode {
  friend class DblList;
  friend class DblIterator;

public:
  DblNode();
  virtual ~DblNode() {   }

  DblNode * Next() const;
  // Return pointer to next node.

  DblNode * Prev() const;
  // Return pointer to previous node.

  DblNode * Detach();
  // Detach node from its neighbors.

  virtual int operator ==( const DblNode & N )
            const = 0;

  friend ostream & operator << (ostream & os,
         const DblNode & N );
  friend istream & operator >> (istream & inp,
         DblNode & N );

private:
  virtual void printOn( ostream & os ) const = 0;
  virtual void readFrom( istream & is ) = 0;

  DblNode * next;      // pointer to next node
  DblNode * prev;      // pointer to previous node
};
```

```
inline DblNode::DblNode()
{
  next = prev = 0;
}

inline DblNode * DblNode::Next() const
{
  return next;
}

inline DblNode * DblNode::Prev() const
{
  return prev;
}

#endif
```

DblList Class Definition

```
//****************************************
// DBLLIST.H - DblList Class Definition
//****************************************

#ifndef DBLLIST_H
#define DBLLIST_H

#include "dblnode.h"

class DblList {
  friend class DblIterator;

public:
  DblList();
  // Construct an empty list.

  ~DblList();
  // Destructor: delete all nodes.

  void Append( DblNode * N );
  // Add node to end of the list.

  void DeleteAll();
  // Delete all nodes in the list.

  DblNode * Find( const DblNode & N ) const;
  // Find a node in the list.
```

```
  DblNode * Remove( DblNode * N );
  // Remove a node from the list.

  int IsEmpty() const;
  // Return 1 if the list is empty.

  DblNode * First() const;
  // Return pointer to first node.

  DblNode * Last() const;
  // Return pointer to last node.

  long GetSize() const;
  // Return the number of nodes.

  friend ostream & operator << ( ostream & os,
        const DblList & L );

private:
  virtual void printOn( ostream & ) const;

  DblNode * first;  // first node in the list
  DblNode * last;   // last node in the list
  long size;        // number of elements
};

#endif
```

DblNode Class Implementation

```
//*********************************************
// DBLNODE.CPP - DblNode Class Implementation
//*********************************************

#include "dblnode.h"

DblNode * DblNode::Detach() // detach from surrounding nodes
{
  if ( next )            // any node in front?
    next->prev = prev;   // let it point to previous node

  if ( prev )            // any node in back?
    prev->next = next;   // let it point to next node

  prev = 0;              // detach current node
  next = 0;
  return this;
```

```
}

ostream & operator << ( ostream & os,
   const DblNode & N )
{
  N.printOn( os );
  return os;
}

istream & operator >> (istream & is, DblNode & N )
{
  N.readFrom( is );
  return is;
}
```

DblList Class Implementation

```
//**********************************************
// DBLLIST.CPP - DblList Class Implementation
//**********************************************

#include "dbllist.h"

DblList::DblList()
{
  first = 0;
  last = 0;
  size = 0;
}

DblList::~DblList()
{
  DeleteAll();
}

void DblList::Append( DblNode * P )
{
  if( !P ) return;

  if( last )        // is there a last node?
  {
    last->next = P;  // yes: attach new node to it
    P->prev = last;
  }
  else              // no: attach new node to first
    first = P;
```

```
  last = P;          // last points to appended node
  size++;            // increment size of list
}

void DblList::DeleteAll()
{
  while( first )
    delete Remove( first );
}

// Find a node. If successful, return a pointer to the
// list element that matches P; otherwise, return 0.
// Requires definition of operator ==().

DblNode * DblList::Find( const DblNode & N ) const
{
  DblNode * P = first;
  while( P )
  {
    if( N == *P )
      return P;
    P = P->next;
  }
  return 0;
}

DblNode * DblList::First() const
{
  return first;
}

long DblList::GetSize() const
{
  return size;
}

int DblList::IsEmpty() const
{
  return first == 0;
}

DblNode * DblList::Last() const
{
  return last;
}

// Private member function that outputs the
```

```
// list to a stream.

void DblList::printOn( ostream & os ) const
{
  DblNode * N = first;
  while( N )
  {
    os << (*N);
    N = N->next;
  }
}

DblNode * DblList::Remove( DblNode * P )
{
  if( !P ) return 0;

  if( P == first )      // removing the first node?
    first = first->next;
  if( P == last )       // removing the last node?
    last = last->prev;

  P->Detach();    // detach node from its neighbors
  size--;         // decrement list size
  return P;
}

ostream & operator << (ostream & os,
    const DblList & aList)
{
  aList.printOn( os );
  return os;
}
```

CHAPTER 11: DBLITERATOR CLASS

Class Definition

```
//*******************************************
// DBLITER.H - DblIterator Class Definition
//*******************************************

#ifndef DBLITER_H
#define DBLITER_H

#include "dblnode.h"
#include "dbllist.h"
```

```
typedef void (* IterFtype)( DblNode * );
// Function type used by Apply().

class DblIterator  {  // friend of DblNode, DblList classes
public:
  DblIterator( const DblList & L );

  DblNode * Advance();
  DblNode * BackUp();
  DblNode * GoFirst();
  DblNode * GoLast();

  DblNode * GetCurrPos() const;
  // Return pointer to node at current position.

  void Apply( IterFtype );
  // Pass each list member to a function.

private:
  const DblList * aList;  // the list being iterated
  DblNode * currPos;       // current position in list
};

#endif
```

Class Implementation

```
//***************************************************
// DBLITER.CPP - DblIterator Class Implementation
//***************************************************

#include "dbliter.h"

DblIterator::DblIterator( const DblList & L ):aList(&L)
{
  currPos = aList->first;
}

DblNode * DblIterator::GoFirst()
{
  return currPos = aList->first;
}

DblNode * DblIterator::GoLast()
{
 return currPos = aList->last;
}
```

```
DblNode * DblIterator::GetCurrPos() const
{
  return currPos;
}

DblNode * DblIterator::Advance()
{
  if( currPos->next )
    return currPos = currPos->next;

  return 0;
}

DblNode * DblIterator::BackUp()
{
  if( currPos->prev )
    return currPos = currPos->prev;

  return 0;
}

void DblIterator::Apply( IterFtype fp )
{
  GoFirst();
  do
    fp( currPos );   // call the function
  while( (*this).Advance() );
}
```

Book Class Definition

```
//********************************
// BOOK.H - Book Class Definition
//********************************

#ifndef BOOK_H
#define BOOK_H

#include <iostream.h>
#include "dblnode.h"
#include "ftstring.h"

class Book : public DblNode {
public:
  Book();
  Book( const FTString<20> & isbnV,
        const FTString<30> & authorV,
```

```
          const FTString<50> & titleV,
          int yearV, float costV);

  virtual ~Book();

  Book & operator =( const Book & B );

  float GetCost() const;

  // pure virtual function inherited from DblNode:
  virtual int operator == (const DblNode &) const;

private:
  virtual void printOn( ostream & os ) const;
  virtual void readFrom( istream & is );

  FTString<20> isbn;
  FTString<30> author;
  FTString<50> title;
  int year;
  float cost;
};

inline float Book::GetCost() const
{
  return cost;
}

#endif
```

Book Class Implementation

```
//***************************************
// BOOK.CPP - Book Class Implementation
//***************************************

#include "book.h"

Book::Book()
{
  year = 0;
  cost = 0.0;
}

Book::~Book()
{
}
```

```
Book::Book(const FTString<20> & isbnV,
      const FTString<30> & authorV,
      const FTString<50> & titleV,
      int yearV, float costV)
  {
    isbn = isbnV;
    author = authorV;
    title = titleV;
    year = yearV;
    cost = costV;
  }

void Book::readFrom( istream & is )
{
  isbn.GetLine( is );
  if( isbn.Length() == 0 ) return;

  title.GetLine( is );
  author.GetLine( is );
  is >> year;
  is >> cost;
  is.ignore( 255, '\n' );
}

// Write each field on a separate line.

void Book::printOn( ostream & os ) const
{
  os
  << title  << endl
  << author << endl
  << year   << endl
  << isbn   << endl
  << cost   << endl;
}

Book & Book::operator =( const Book & B )
{
  title = B.title;
  author = B.author;
  year = B.year;
  cost = B.cost;
  return *this;
}

// Case-sensitive comparison of book titles.
// Redefinition of virtual function in DblNode class.
```

```
int Book::operator ==( const DblNode & B ) const
{
  return title == ((Book &)B).title;
}
```

Test Program

```
//****************************************
// MAIN.CPP - DblIterator Test Program
//****************************************

#include <iostream.h>
#include <fstream.h>
#include <except.h>
#include "nofile.h"    // NoFileError exception class
#include "dbllist.h"   // DblList class
#include "dbliter.h"   // DblIterator class
#include "book.h"

const char inFileName[] = "books.txt";

ofstream log( "iter.txt" );


void CalcPrice( DblNode * np )
{
  float retailPrice = ((Book *)np)->GetCost() * 1.20;
  log << *np << "Retail Price = " << retailPrice
      << endl << endl;
}

void IteratorTest()
{
  DblList titles;
  ifstream input( inFileName );
  if( !input ) throw NoFileError( inFileName );

  Book * B = new Book;  // allocate a new book
  input >> (*B);        // input a book

  while( !input.eof() )
  {
    titles.Append( B ); // add it to the list
    B = new Book;       // create a book node
    input >> (*B);      // input a book
  }
```

```
    DblIterator I( titles );   // create an iterator

    cout << "\nCalculating Retail Prices:\n\n";
    I.Apply( CalcPrice );

    cout << "\n\nTitles in reverse order:\n\n";
    I.GoLast();

    do {
      Book * B = (Book *) I.GetCurrPos();
      cout << *B;
    } while( I.BackUp());
}

int main()
{
 try {
  IteratorTest();
 }
 catch( xalloc ) {
   cout << "Memory allocation exception caught.\n";
 }
 catch( const RangeError & R ) {
   cout << R << endl;
 }
 catch( const NoFileError & nf ) {
   cout << nf << endl;
 }

 return 0;
}
```

REFERENCES

[ANSI-95]   Accredited Standards Committee (X3J16/95-0087 and WG21/N0687). *Working Paper for Draft Proposed International Standard for Information Systems—Programming Language C++*, American National Standards Institute, April 1995.

[ARM]   Ellis, Margaret A., and Bjarne Stroustrup. *The Annotated C++ Reference Manual*. Addison-Wesley, 1990.

[Booch]   Booch, Grady. *Object-Oriented Analysis and Design with Applications, 2nd Ed*. Benjamin/Cummings, 1994.

[de Bruijn]   Bruijn, Michel de, "Keep Your Data Under Lock and Key," *Visual Basic Programmers Journal*, 9/95.

[Eckel]   Eckel, Bruce. *Thinking in C++*. Prentice Hall, 1995.

[Kamenz]   Kamenz, George J, "call me George K," [unpublished work] 1996, (excerpted from email exchanges with the author).

[Lippman]   Lippman, Stanley B. *C++ Primer, 2nd Ed*. Addison-Wesley, 1991.

[Martin/Odell] Martin, and Odell. *Object-Oriented Analysis and Design*. Prentice Hall, 1992.

[Plauger]   Plauger, P.J. *The Draft Standard C++ Library*. Prentice Hall, 1995.

[Stroustrup91] Stroustrup, Bjarne. *The C++ Programming Language, 2nd Ed*. Addison-Wesley, 1991.

[Stroustrup94] Stroustrup, Bjarne. *The Design and Evolution of C++*. Addison-Wesley, 1994.

[Stubbs/Webre] Stubbs, Daniel F. and Neil W. Webre. *Data Structures with Abstract Data Types and Pascal*. Brooks/Cole, 1984.

INDEX